T0192245

Communications
in Computer and Information Science   1894

Rationale
The CCIS series is devoted to the publication of proceedings of computer science conferences. Its aim is to efficiently disseminate original research results in informatics in printed and electronic form. While the focus is on publication of peer-reviewed full papers presenting mature work, inclusion of reviewed short papers reporting on work in progress is welcome, too. Besides globally relevant meetings with internationally representative program committees guaranteeing a strict peer-reviewing and paper selection process, conferences run by societies or of high regional or national relevance are also considered for publication.

Topics
The topical scope of CCIS spans the entire spectrum of informatics ranging from foundational topics in the theory of computing to information and communications science and technology and a broad variety of interdisciplinary application fields.

Information for Volume Editors and Authors
Publication in CCIS is free of charge. No royalties are paid, however, we offer registered conference participants temporary free access to the online version of the conference proceedings on SpringerLink (http://link.springer.com) by means of an http referrer from the conference website and/or a number of complimentary printed copies, as specified in the official acceptance email of the event.

CCIS proceedings can be published in time for distribution at conferences or as post-proceedings, and delivered in the form of printed books and/or electronically as USBs and/or e-content licenses for accessing proceedings at SpringerLink. Furthermore, CCIS proceedings are included in the CCIS electronic book series hosted in the SpringerLink digital library at http://link.springer.com/bookseries/7899. Conferences publishing in CCIS are allowed to use Online Conference Service (OCS) for managing the whole proceedings lifecycle (from submission and reviewing to preparing for publication) free of charge.

Publication process
The language of publication is exclusively English. Authors publishing in CCIS have to sign the Springer CCIS copyright transfer form, however, they are free to use their material published in CCIS for substantially changed, more elaborate subsequent publications elsewhere. For the preparation of the camera-ready papers/files, authors have to strictly adhere to the Springer CCIS Authors' Instructions and are strongly encouraged to use the CCIS LaTeX style files or templates.

Abstracting/Indexing
CCIS is abstracted/indexed in DBLP, Google Scholar, EI-Compendex, Mathematical Reviews, SCImago, Scopus. CCIS volumes are also submitted for the inclusion in ISI Proceedings.

How to start
To start the evaluation of your proposal for inclusion in the CCIS series, please send an e-mail to ccis@springer.com.

Ranjeet Singh Tomar · Shekhar Verma ·
Brijesh Kumar Chaurasia · Vrijendra Singh ·
Jemal H. Abawajy · Shyam Akashe ·
Pao-Ann Hsiung · Ramjee Prasad
Editors

Communication, Networks and Computing

Third International Conference, CNC 2022
Gwalior, India, December 8–10, 2022
Proceedings, Part II

 Springer

Editors
Ranjeet Singh Tomar (iD)
ITM University
Gwalior, India

Brijesh Kumar Chaurasia (iD)
IIIT Lucknow
Lucknow, India

Jemal H. Abawajy
Deakin University
Burwood, VIC, Australia

Pao-Ann Hsiung
National Chung Cheng University
Chiayi, Taiwan

Shekhar Verma (iD)
IIIT-Allahabad
Allahabad, Uttar Pradesh, India

Vrijendra Singh
IIIT-Allahabad
Allahabad, India

Shyam Akashe (iD)
ITM University
Gwalior, Madhya Pradesh, India

Ramjee Prasad
Aarhus University
Herning, Denmark

ISSN 1865-0929   ISSN 1865-0937 (electronic)
Communications in Computer and Information Science
ISBN 978-3-031-43144-9   ISBN 978-3-031-43145-6 (eBook)
https://doi.org/10.1007/978-3-031-43145-6

This Springer imprint is published by the registered company Springer Nature Switzerland AG
The registered company address is: Gewerbestrasse 11, 6330 Cham, Switzerland

Paper in this product is recyclable.

Preface

The book focuses on communication, networks, and computing to simplify the real-time problems occurring in different domains of communication, networks, and computing. Presently, research is entering a new era of convergence of these domains wherein the established models and techniques are being challenged. New ideas are being proposed and established ideas are being retested. Evaluating the performance of emerging smart technologies, however, poses a huge challenge.

The book includes high-quality papers presented at the 3rd International Conference on Communication, Networks and Computing (CNC 2022), organized by ITM University Gwalior, India. Offering significant insights into this domain for academics and industry alike, we hope the book will inspire more researchers to work in the field of next-generation networks for communication systems. The theme of the conference was "Next-Generation Digital Technology Innovations for Society". This theme covered the exciting new areas of wired and wireless communication systems, high-dimensional data representation and processing, networks and information security, computing techniques for efficient networks design, vehicular technology and applications and electronic circuits for communication systems that promise to make the world a better place to live in.

ITM University Gwalior, India, is a multidisciplinary university with an international reputation for the quality of its research and teaching across the academic spectrum. The university has received more than 40 awards and has been ranked in the top category by a number of governmental and other agencies. The university is ranked 32nd in management and 58th in engineering in 2016 by the National Institutional Ranking Framework, Ministry of HRD, Government of India. The university is approved by the regulatory bodies required to run courses in engineering, management, pharmacy, commerce, agriculture, architecture, computer applications, teacher education, art and design, physical education, sciences, law, India and South Asia studies, journalism, nursing etc. It is at the forefront of learning, teaching and research and the leader in different fields. It seeks to sustain and enhance its excellence as an institution of higher learning through outstanding teaching and the world-class societies it serves.

The ITM School of Engineering and Technology is one of the flagship and leading schools of central and north India. The school is unique in that it tries to assimilate cutting-edge ideas in engineering and technology through a variety of projects in association with industry. In addition, prominent industries directly contribute to the knowledge and skill sets of students through various augmentation programs customized for students of ITM University. A mix of lectures, tutorials, laboratory studies, seminars and projects are used to groom the conceptual and analytical abilities of students. For the first time in India, ITM University Gwalior has taken the initiative to introduce activity-based continuous assessment (ABCA) and project-based learning (PBL) in order to increase the employability of students.

This conference was successful in facilitating academics, researchers and industry professionals to deliberate upon the latest issues, challenges and advancements in communication, networks and computing. In total, 152 papers were submitted for six tracks. After a thorough review process, 52 papers were selected for oral presentation during the conference. All these selected papers were presented at the conference and only those best 52 papers are published in the book.

This conference proceedings volume will prove beneficial for academics, researchers and professionals from industry as it contains valuable information and knowledge on the recent developments.

June 2023

Ranjeet Singh Tomar
Shekhar Verma
Brijesh Kumar Chaurasia
Vrijendra Singh
Jemal H. Abawajy
Shyam Akashe
Pao-Ann Hsiung
Ramjee Prasad

Organization

Chief Patron

Ramashankar Singh (Founder Chancellor)	ITM University Gwalior, India
Ruchi Singh Chauhan (Chancellor)	ITM University Gwalior, India

Patrons

Kanupriya Singh Rathore (Chairperson)	ITM (SLS) Baroda University, India
Ravindra Singh Rathore (Managing Director)	ITM (SLS) Baroda University, India
Daulat Singh Chauhan (Pro Chancellor)	ITM University Gwalior, India
Sher Singh Bhakar (Vice-chancellor)	ITM University Gwalior, India
Santosh K. Narayankhedkar (Pro Vice-chancellor)	ITM University Gwalior, India
Omveer Singh (Registrar)	ITM University Gwalior, India

General Chairs

Shekhar Verma	IIIT Allahabad, India
Ranjeet Singh Tomar	ITM University Gwalior, India
Ramjee Prasad	Aarhus University, Denmark

Program Chairs

Pao Ann Hsiung	National Chung Cheng University, Taiwan
Vijay K. Bhargava	University of British Columbia, Canada
Brijesh Kumar Chaurasia	IIIT Lucknow, India

Technical Committee Chairs

Jemal Abawajy	Deakin University, Australia
Vrijendra Singh	IIIT Allahabad, India
Shyam Akashe	ITM University Gwalior, India

Publications Chairs

Sanjay Jain	ITM University Gwalior, India
Sadhana Mishra	ITM University Gwalior, India

Publicity Chairs

Pallavi Khatri	ITM University Gwalior, India
Shashikant Gupta	ITM University Gwalior, India

Workshop/Tutorial Chairs

Rishi Soni	ITM University Gwalior, India
Arun Kumar Yadav	ITM University Gwalior, India

Hospitality Chairs

Mukesh Kumar Pandey	ITM University Gwalior, India
Keshav Kansana	ITM University Gwalior, India
Manish Sharma	ITM University Gwalior, India

Local Organizing Committee

Geetanjali Surange	ITM University Gwalior, India
Shailendra Singh Ojha	ITM University Gwalior, India
Ashish Garg	ITM University Gwalior, India
Bhupendra Dhakad	ITM University Gwalior, India
Abhishek Saxena	ITM University Gwalior, India
Abhishek Tripathi	ITM University Gwalior, India
Upendra Bhushan	ITM University Gwalior, India

Organizing Secretariat

Mayank Sharma   ITM University Gwalior, India

Contents – Part II

Computing Techniques for Efficient Networks Design

Vehicular Technology and Applications

Contents – Part I

Electronics Circuits for Communication Systems

High Dimensional Data Representation and Processing

Brain Tumor Classification Using Feature Extraction and Non-linear SVM Hybrid Model

Lalita Mishra$^{(\boxtimes)}$, Shekhar Verma, and Shirshu Varma

Indian Institute of Information Technology Allahabad, Allahabad, Uttar Pradesh 211015, India
rsi2018502@iiita.ac.in

Abstract. Brain tumors must be correctly diagnosed using magnetic resonance imaging (MRI) for patients to obtain better and more efficient therapy. In this paper, we used VGG (all variants) and Nonlinear-SVM (Soft and Hard), to classify brain tumors into glioma & pituitary, and tumorous & non-tumorous categories, and created a hybrid model. The proposed model is trained on two different brain MRI datasets containing two classes and is used for binary classification of brain tumor types. To maximize the accuracy of tumor classification, all the variants of VGG are trained using Pytorch. The procedure is divided into three steps: scaling and normalizing the brain MR images; feature extraction using various iterations of the VGG model. In the last stage, non-linear SVM (hard and soft) was employed for brain tumor classification. For the first dataset and the second, we achieve an accuracy of 98.18% and 99.78%, respectively, using VGG19. With linear and RBF kernels, non-linear SVM classification accuracy is 95.50% and 97.98%, respectively. SVM with soft margins and RBF kernel with D1 and D2 classification accuracy is 97.95% and 96.75%, respectively. The results seem to show that the VGG-SVM hybrid model, and substantially for VGG 19 with SVM, outperforms the currently available comparable techniques and achieves good accuracy.

Keywords: VGG · Support Vector Machine · Magnetic Resonance Image · Brain Tumor Classification · Medical Image Processing · Soft SVM · Feature Extraction

1 Introduction

Brain tumor (BT) is one of the deadly deceases which spread into the human body because of the growth of abnormal cells in the brain. It is the cancerous or noncancerous mass that grows abnormally in the brain. Cancer starts forming in other body parts except for the brain; however, it can spread to the brain. Further, the tumors can start growing in the brain and can be cancerous or noncancerous. According to the national center for biotechnology information (NCBI) 5 to 10 people in every 100000 population were registered in 2016, showing an increasing trend in tumor detection [1]. Dasgupta et al. [1] categorized five different types of frequent tumors were medulloblastoma (11.4%), ependymal tumors (4.8%), craniopharyngioma (9.7%), astrocytoma (47.3%), and nerve

R. S. Tomar et al. (Eds.): CNC 2022, CCIS 1894, pp. 3–14, 2023.
https://doi.org/10.1007/978-3-031-43145-6_1

sheath tumors (4.1\%). Although, some of them are low incensed and can be treated if found in the initial stages. Thus, it is crucial to detect the tumor in its initial stages so one can take preventive measures for treatment. Nowadays, machine learning is one of the novel approaches to tumor detection. Moreover, we required to classify the tumor according to the international classification of diseases for ontology, which was defined by WHO [2]. Thus, classification has become an essential aspect of tumor detection. MRI image is one of the most accurate ways for tumor detection, and we can use machine learning techniques for image classification to detect the tumor. Most of the organization uses the grading-based method to categorize each tumor based upon its intensity or aggressiveness, as.

- **Grade 1** is generally a benign tumor, mostly found in children, and this type of tumor is mostly curable.
- **Grade 2** includes Astrocytomas, Oligodendrogliomas, and Oligoastrocytoma, commonly found in adults. It can progress slowly to high-grade tumors.
- **Grade 3** is generally the combination of Anaplastic Astrocytomas, Anaplastic Oligo-dendrogliomas or Anaplastic Oligoastrocytoma. These are quite aggressive and dangerous.
- **Grade 4** is generally glioma multiform tumor, the most aggressive tumor in the WHO category.

Machine learning can classify the image based on the characteristics of the MR image. So, we recognize three types of tissues for the tumor classification as: Tumor Core, the region of tumor tissues, which has the malignant cells that are actively proliferating. Necrosis identifies the region where tissues/cells are dying or dead. This characteristic is used to differentiate between low grades of gliomas and GBM and perifocal oedema occurs because of the glial cell distribution in the brain. Because of this, a swelled region forms around the brain, and fluid is filled around the tumor core.

Imaging methods such as MRI can be used for diagnosis. MRI image [3] helps us to identify the location where the tumor formed. MR images provide the physiology, anatomy of the lesion, and metabolic activity with its haemodynamic. Thus, MR images are used for primary diagnosis. However, errors in the manual detection with these methods can be threatening to life. The detection accuracy of the tumor is significant; manual processes are time-consuming and unreliable. Therefore we need appropriate precise detection and classification measures for BTs.

Non-Linear SVMs are utilized to classify non-linearly separable data that is, if, for any dataset, the classification cannot be performed using straight line, then it is non-linear data, and to classify such data, non-linear classifiers are used, such as non-linear SVM classifier. However, SVM either takes each image as a data points or requires handcrafted features. Both limit the utility and accuracy of SVM. CNN is able to extract features with manual intervention. However, accuracy of these methods needs to be improved.

Novelty and Contribution of the study:

We have proposed a two-stage model of BT classification using the VGG model with SVM, VGG-SVM, to acquire performance enhancement. In other studies, researchers have applied these models individually and obtained good results; however, the integration of various SVMs with VGG models results validate our approach. Our major contributions can be listed as:

- We have utilized untrained VGG models (VGG11, VGG13, VGG16, and VGG19)for feature extraction and trained the models with MRI images containing brain tumors.
- We have flattened the extracted features and passed these extracted features to non-linear SVMs (soft and hard) for classification brain tumor classification.

2 Related Works

In this section, we discuss the existing work and compare the existing classification results. We have covered several papers utilizing VGG models, variants of SVM and some integrated models for BT classification and compare their performance in Table 1, which combines the working model and the obtained results by each author.

Khan et al. [4] applied k-means and discrete cosine transform algorithm to partition the dataset, transfer learning for feature extraction, and ELM for tumor classification and achieved 97.90% classification accuracy for a BT. Sajjad et al. in [5] segmented the tumor using InputCascadeCNN, having two streams, one is 7×7 fields for local feature extraction, and the other is 13×13 field for global feature extraction. They used rotation, skewness, flipping, and shears for extensive data augmentation and transfer learning approach for pattern learning and VGG19 for tumor grade classification. Latif et al. in [6] utilized a 17-layer CNN for feature extraction and, after that, used several machine learning classifiers, like, SVM, MLP, NB, and RF, for tumor classification. They have obtained the best classification results using SVM. Whereas in [7] by Senan et al., minmax normalization was applied before feature extraction and then classified the tumor grade by AlexNet, Resnet18, AlexNet with SVM, and ResNet18 with SVM models. Vadhnani et al. in [8] utilized Otsu thresholding for tumor segmentation; discrete wavelet transforms algorithm for feature extraction, principal component analysis for reducing the extracted features, and SVM for tumor type classification.

Bodapati et al. in [9] first used k-means clustering for tumor segmentation from MR images and then applied a median filter on the segmented tumor data. They measured the distance from each cluster center using the Euclidean distance and classified the BT using improved SVM. Rajinikanth et al. customize the pre-trained VGG19 model by using serially fused deep features and handcrafted features and then classify the BT using several classifiers, including VGG19, linear SVM and kernel SVM in [10]. Tazin et al. in [11] used MobileNetV2 for image preprocessing, transfer learning to categorize data, and VGG19 for tumor classification. N. Nar et al. in [12] applied rotation and shifting operations together with scaling for data augmentation. After the augmentation, they applied transfer learning for feature extraction from MR images and VGG19 along with several DL models for tumor classification.

We have listed the obtained classification accuracy by each surveyed paper in Table 1 to provide a comparative view of the results. Although they have obtained good results, however, we have obtained better classification accuracy using a variety of VGG models in integration with non-linear SVM for BTs in VGG-SVM.

We have reviewed several recent approaches, as shown in Table 1, and compared them in terms of their model and classification accuracy. It is illustrated in Table 1 that these state-of-the-art works lack in providing better tumor classification. Thus, we propose an integrated model for tumor classification.

Table 1. Comparative Literature Survey

Paper	Model Used	Classification Accuracy
Khan et al. [4] 2020	VGG19 + ELM	97.90%
Sajjad et al. [5] 2019	VGG19	94.58%
Latif et al. [6] 2022	SVM	96.19% for HGG 95.46% for LGG
Senan et al. [7] 2022	AlexNet + SVM, ResNet18 + SVM	95.10% 91.20%
Vadhnani et al. [8] 2022	SVM(RBF), SVM(Linear)	97.6% 94%
Bodapati et al. [9] 2022	K-means + ISVM	95%
Rajnikanth et al. [10] 2020	VGG19, SVM(RBF), SVM(Linear)	95.90%, 95.30%, 95.60%
Tazin et al. [11] 2021	VGG19	88.22%
Nar et al. [12] 2022	VGG19	97.20%

3   VGG-SVM Model

In this section, we present VGG-SVM architectural and implementation details along with the description of the evaluation datasets. It describes the flow and working of the model. It consists of three parts, as follows:

3.1   Model Architecture

In this work, we integrate the VGG model with non-linear SVM.

In Fig. 1 the architecture of the VGG-SVM model is shown. Here, we have used VGG19 architecture only. Variation of VGG models is applied similarly, with several non-linear SVM variants.

Feature Extraction:

Variations of VGG models are used to extract the MRI features. Features are defined as important information about a particular task. For MRI image processing, features are the texture, intensity value, shape, and boundary of a particular image. Large datasets contain an enormous amount of variables, among which only some are important for that particular task. Feature extraction is the segregation of the most important information.

In our case, extracted features are the tumor characteristics, such as tumor area, circularity, tumor shape, etc. The features are extracted using the fully connected layer of VGG models. We have selected the VGG model for feature extraction because of its deep nature and usage of the most minor receptive field, that is, 3×3, and stride 1. Thus, they provide fewer parameters & the most relevant features at the fully connected layer compared to other DL models having 11×11 or 7×7 receptive fields with 4, 5, and higher stride values. Less number of parameters provides fast convergence of the model

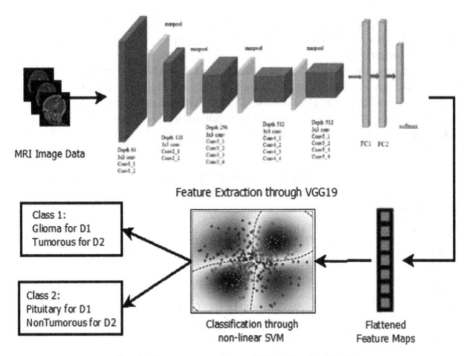

Feature Extraction through VGG19

MRI Image Data

Class 1:
Glioma for D1
Tumorous for D2

Class 2:
Pituitary for D1
NonTumorous for D2

Classification through
non-linear SVM

Flattened
Feature Maps

Fig. 1. Feature extraction and Classification Model

and reduces the overfitting problem. Among the variety of VGG models, VGG16 and VGG19 provide a significant change in performance.

Classification:

These extracted features are then fed to non-linear SVM for classifying the tumor type. We have used non-linear SVM because, in our case, we have non-linear data of BTs in the form of MR images. We have applied SVM with soft and hard margins to cover each possibility for improving the classification accuracy.

We have provided the extracted features from each VGG model to the non-linear SVM with RBF and linear kernel and non-linear SVM with soft margins to obtain the final tumor classification.

3.2 Implementation Details and Preprocessing

In this paper, we applied the binary classification of BTs among glioma & pituitary tumors and tumorous & non-tumorous images. Before classification, we have extracted the image features using VGG models.

Feature Extraction:

We resize the images as 224 × 224. Then, we have created *X train; y train; X test*, and *y test* using 7: 3 random split for training and validation sets for all VGG models. We have used the batch size of 32 at the time of training the VGG model, with a 0.001 learning rate. We have trained the VGG models for 200 epochs. After training the VGG model, we changed the batch size to 1 at a time, extracted the image features from the third last fully connected layer to obtain the maximum number of extracted features and minimize the loss, and stored these extracted features in the form of NumPy array.

Classification:

We then pass the extracted features through VGG models to non-linear SVM for binary classification of the BT MRI. We have used RBF and linear kernel functions with the hard SVM and RBF kernel with the soft SVM. VGG and non-linear SVM models are implemented using PyTorch, with a python script, both with Google Colab. The VGG and SVM hyperparameters are illustrated in Table 2.

Table 2. Model Hyperparameters

Hyperparameters	Value
Optimizer	Optim
Image Size	224 × 224
Weight	VGG19
Loss	Crossentropy
Matrices	Accuracy and Loss (VGG)
	Accuracy, Precision, Recall, f1-score, Hinge Loss (SVM)
Epochs	200
Batch Size	32 (VGG Training)
	1 (Feature Extraction)
Activation Function	ReLU
Learning Rate	0.001
Error Control Parameter(C)	0.001
Gamma (γ)	0.001

3.3 Dataset Description

We have used two different datasets for classification and better comparative results. We have obtained all the five datasets from Kaggle and all the datasets are publically available and containing MRI images. The first dataset (D1) [13] contains total of 1800 images (900 Glioma and 900 Pituitary). The second dataset (D2) consists of 3000 images (1500 Tumorous and 1500 Non-tumorous) downloaded from [14].

Table 3. Dataset Description

Dataset	Total No. of Images	Image Type
D1	1800	Glioma (900) and Pituitary (900)
D2	3000	1500 Tumorous and 1500 Non-tumorous

4 Experimental Results and Discussion

4.1 Results

We have used accuracy and loss evaluation metrics for VGG models and accuracy, precision, recall, f1-score, and hinge loss for non-linear SVMs. The mathematical formulation of these evaluation metrics is given using following equations:

$$Accuracy = \frac{(TP + TN)}{(TP + TN + FP + FN)}$$

$$Precision = \frac{TP}{(TP + FP)}$$

$$Senstivity = \frac{TP}{(TP + FN)}$$

$$F - score = \frac{2TP}{(2TP + FP + FN)}$$

$$HingeLoss = \max\{0, 1 - y_i\left(\omega^T x_i + b_i\right)\}$$

where, TP is true positive, TN is true negative, FP is false positive, and FN is false negative, ω and b are parameters of hyperplane and x_i is input variable.

We have shown the graphical representation of obtained accuracies in a comparative way in Fig. 2, using all VGG models during model training for D1. Figure 2 shows that the obtained accuracies are showing much difference in initial epochs, however, with each increasing epochs the difference converges. The final classification results obtained from non-linear SVMs are illustrated in Tables 3 and 4 for the first and second datasets, respectively. We have shown all the results, including VGG training and classification using non-Linear SVM with linear kernel, non-Linear SVM with RBF kernel, and non-Linear SVM with soft margins and RBF kernel in the Tables 3 and 4. Further, the confusion matrix for D1 and D2 is shown in Fig. 3 for non-linear SVM with RBF kernel.

Table 4. Our Experimental results for First Dataset

	VGG11	VGG13	VGG16	VGG19
VGG Training				
Accuracy	91.37%	95.76%	96.75%	**98.18%**
Loss	0.0076	0.0045	**0.0022**	0.0031
Non-Linear SVM with Linear Kernel				
Accuracy	92.56%	94.19%	**96.20%**	95.50%
Precision	0.8760	0.9332	0.9250	0.9440
Sensitivity	0.9751	0.9623	0.9250	0.9733
F - score	0.9223	0.9475	0.9250	0.9584
Hinge Loss	0.098	0.079	**0.0382**	0.0395
Non-linear SVM with RBF Kernel				
Accuracy	93.06%	94.89%	96.79%	**97.98%**
Precision	0.9702	0.9439	0.9650	0.9798
Sensitivity	0.9702	0.9439	0.9650	1
F - score	0.9702	0.9439	0.9650	0.9798
Hinge Loss	0.096	0.081	**0.0376**	0.0391
SVM with soft margin and RBF Kernel				
Accuracy	93.45%	94.19%	95.91%	**98.76%**
Precision	0.9345	0.9419	0.9591	0.9795
Sensitivity	0.9347	0.9474	0.9641	1
F - score	0.9345	0.9446	0.9615	0.9896
Hinge Loss	0.1192	0.0985	**0.0235**	0.0398

4.2 Discussion

We have obtained the best classification accuracy with non-Linear SVM with soft margins and RBF kernel after the hyperparameter tuning with the output of the VGG19 model; however, the loss values are minimum with the VGG16 model. By referring to Table 1 from Sect. 2, we obtain that the surveyed models did not achieve the classification accuracy as VGG-SVM. Thus, VGGSVM outperforms the state-of-the-art models using VGG19 and non-linear SVM with soft margins and RBF kernel and other respective variants. We have shown the best values of accuracy and loss for each model in bold letters to make it easy to compare, for each model, in Tables 3 and 4, and found that the best result for classification accuracy is obtained after training with VGG19 and classify using non-linear SVM with soft margins and for loss is obtained after training with VGG16 and non-linear SVM with soft margins, both for D2 (Table 5).

Table 5. Our Experimental results for Second Dataset

	VGG11	VGG13	VGG16	VGG19
VGG Training				
Accuracy	92.95%	95.91%	99.12%	**99.78%**
Loss	0.0079	0.0046	**0.0013**	0.0019
Non-linear SVM with Linear Kernel				
Accuracy	93.51%	95.23%	**96.83%**	96.75%
Precision	0.8910	0.9389	0.9625	0.9610
Sensitivity	0.8910	0.9389	0.9650	0.9610
F - score	0.8910	0.9389	0.9637	0.9610
Hinge Loss	0.0923	0.0721	**0.0265**	0.0299
Non-linear SVM with RBF Kernel				
Accuracy	94.70%	97.33%	98.06%	**98.60%**
Precision	0.9120	0.9733	0.9806	0.9841
Sensitivity	0.9020	1	1	0.9860
F - score	0.9069	0.9685	0.9792	0.9850
Hinge Loss	0.087	0.0532	**0.0387**	0.0391
SVM with soft margin and RBF Kernel				
Accuracy	94.35%	95.16%	96.37%	**99.85%**
Precision	0.9435	0.9516	0.9637	0.9838
Sensitivity	0.9564	0.9865	1	1
F - score	0.9499	0.9687	0.9815	0.9918
Hinge Loss	0.1129	0.0964	**0.0425**	0.0492

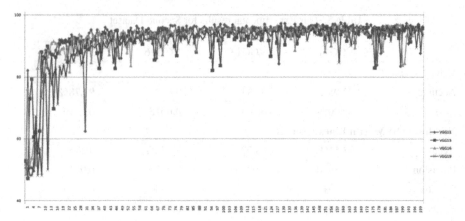

Fig. 2. Comparison of Accuracy using different VGG Models

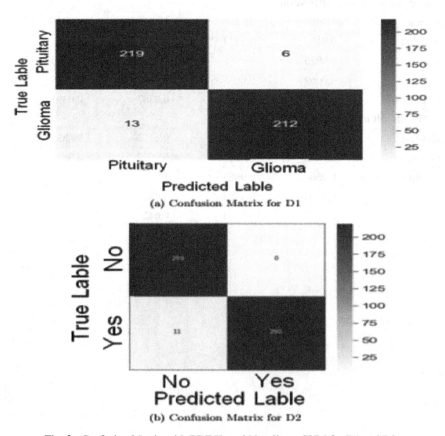

(a) Confusion Matrix for D1

(b) Confusion Matrix for D2

Fig. 3. Confusion Matrix with RBF Kernel Non-linear SVM for D1 and D2

5 Conclusion

This paper provides an automatic and hybrid classification model for MRI based BT classification by integrating non-linear SVM with VGG models. Various VGG models (VGG11, VGG13, VGG16, and VGG19) are trained with MRI images of BTs (two datasets, D1 and D2) for feature extraction, and a variety of non-linear SVMs for classification (with linear and RBF kernel, and SVM with soft margins and RBF kernel), with the soft SVM with RBF kernel achieving the best performance (best classification accuracy with VGG19 (99.85%) and minimum loss with VGG16 (0.0425) for the second dataset. The VGG-SVM produced better classification accuracy than the existing models using Table 1. The highest accuracy achieved by existing models, integrating VGG19 with an extreme learning machine (ELM), was 97.90%. We have obtained 98.18% accuracy with the VGG19 model during training, 97.98% classification accuracy using non-linear SVM with RBF kernel, and 98.76% classification accuracy using non-linear soft SVM with RBF kernel for D1, and 99.78% accuracy with VGG19 model during training, 98.60% classification accuracy using non-linear SVM with RBF kernel, and 99.85% classification accuracy using non-linear soft SVM with RBF kernel, for D2. We can conclude that feature extraction through VGG and classification through SVM obviates the need of manual feature extraction and also yields higher accuracy as compared to standalone classifiers. However, this is possible with higher number of layers in VGG that gives better features along with soft margin non-linear SVM.

References

1. Dasgupta, A., Gupta, T., Jalali, R.: Indian data on central nervous tumors: a summary of published work. South Asian J. Cancer **5**(03), 147–153 (2016)
2. Miller, K.D., et al.: Brain and other central nervous system tumor statistics, 2021. CA: Cancer J. Clin. **71**(5), 381–406 (2021)
3. Menze, B.H., et al.: The multimodal brain tumor image segmentation benchmark (brats). IEEE Trans. Med. Imag. **34**(10), 1993–2024 (2014)
4. Khan, M.A., et al.: Multimodal brain tumor classification using deep learning and robust feature selection: a machine learning application for radiologists. Diagnostics **10**(8), 565 (2020)
5. Sajjad, M., Khan, S., Muhammad, K., Wu, W., Ullah, A., Baik, S.W.: Multi-grade brain tumor classification using deep CNN with extensive data augmentation. J. Comput. Sci. **30**, 174–182 (2019)
6. Latif, G., Ben Brahim, G., Iskandar, D.N.F., Bashar, A., Alghazo, J.: Glioma tumor's classification using deep-neural-network-based features with SVM Classifier. Diagnostics **12**(4), 1018 (2022)
7. Senan, E.M., Jadhav, M.E., Rassem, T.H., Aljaloud, A.S., Mohammed, B.A., Al-Mekhlafi, Z.G.: Early diagnosis of brain tumour MRI images using hybrid techniques between deep and machine learning. Comput. Math. Methods Med. (2022)
8. Vadhnani, S., Singh, N.: Brain tumor segmentation and classification in MRI using SVM and its variants: a survey. Multimedia Tools Appl. 1–26 (2022)
9. Bodapati, N., Divya, A., Triveni, N., Indiradevi, N., Yamini K.: Brain tumor detection on MR images using improved support vector machine. In: 2022 International Conference on Electronics and Renewable Systems (ICEARS), pp. 1022–1029. IEEE (2022)

10. Rajinikanth, V., Joseph Raj, A.N., Thanaraj, K.P., Naik, G.R.: A customized VGG19 network with concatenation of deep and handcrafted features for brain tumor detection. Appl. Sci. **10**(10), 3429 (2020)
11. Tazin, T., et al.: A robust and novel approach for brain tumor classification using convolutional neural network. Comput. Intell. Neurosci. **2021** (2021)
12. Çınar, N., Kaya, B., Kaya, M.: Comparison of deep learning models for brain tumor classification using MRI images. In: 2022 International Conference on Decision Aid Sciences and Applications (DASA), pp. 1382–1385. IEEE (2022)
13. Dr. Saeed Mohsen, Brain MRI images dataset for brain tumor detection, Kaggle. https://www.kaggle.com/drsaeedmohsen/braintumordatasets
14. AHMED HAMADA, Br35H: Brain Tumor Detection 2020, Kaggle. https://www.kaggle.com/datasets/ahmedhamada0/brain-tumor-detection

Lightweight Django-Based Customer Relationship Management System

Riya Mehta[(⊠)], Tanya Soni, Vinayak Sharma, Zil Patel, and Prabhat Thakur

Symbiosis Institute of Technology, Symbiosis International (Deemed University), Pune,
Maharashtra 412115, India
{riya.mehta.btech2019,tanya.soni.btech2019,
vinayak.sharma.btech2019,zil.patel.btech2019,
prabhat.thakur}@sitpune.edu.in

Abstract. This paper's objective is to present a thorough conceptualization of a project that resembles an online customer query system which offers fundamental customer management services via a user-friendly Graphical User Interface (GUI). In this standalone project, we developed a system that offers existing customers a dashboard from which they add, update, preview, delete, and check their order-related history using technologies like Django and Bootstrap Framework. Added to that, we simplified and eased communication through various methods such as e-mails and WhatsApp. For the user interface of our web-based application, we are using HTML, CSS, and JavaScript.

Keywords: CRM · Website · HTML · CSS · customer satisfaction · customer needs · company-oriented framework · business instrument · Django framework

1 Introduction

Customer relationship management (CRM) has had several guises since its inception in the early 1990s [1]. The research there is no unified conceptual framework, and the research field is fragmented, the domain continuously works at diverse levels of analysis: theoretically, experimentally, and practically. Businesses are attempting to re- establish their operations following the recent COVID-19 outbreak, which caused an interruption in global economic activity [3]. Many organizations recognize that their focus must be geared toward their customers instead of cost-cutting tactics because competition is a real and ongoing threat to their existence and success. The formatter will create these mechanisms, incorporating the applicable standards that follow.

The firm is on its consumers. They are the major reason for the existence of organizations. CRM commenced to advantage traction as a separate look at an enterprise subject matter amongst lecturers and experts withinside the early 1990s. As a result of the increase in patron records, agencies confronted big hurdles in organizing these records for analysis. As a result, providers commenced offering business hardware and software program answers to higher control huge quantities of customer data [12, 13]. CRM operations in groups protected income pressure automation (SFA) and customer support and support. CRM steadily elevated to consist of more than simply the organization of client information. It has become a holistic method for controlling client interactions, and researchers started to emphasize contrasts among strategically and operationally centered approaches [13].

CRM is a project that maintains an organization's customer relations. It comprises utilizing technology to organize and simplify business developments and several new tactics and approaches to meet client expectations and increase the organization's income, profitability, and sales [8]. As a result, having a robust CRM system is crucial to the business plan of a firm. Employing a CRM significantly increases consumer trustworthiness to the organization. The CRM machine improves the company's capacity to serve clients via means of taking into consideration uninterrupted communication, non- interference in interaction, and the decision of complaints [9].

CRM is a topic that is extensively researched and being worked on. In this paper, we propose a CRM model with a novel idea of it being accessible to small-scale businesses that were previously not able to use it. The first part of working on an idea eccentrically is to conduct multiple types of research on that idea, getting to know about approaching the solution to the same problem in 'n' several ways, the problem each of them faces, and how they can tackle the problem. Similarly, our first step in the project is to read multiple research papers already dealing with the establishment and successful execution of CRM systems. The ease of use of CRM is also a major factor in consideration. Developing a user-friendly 'user interface and user experience' for the same purpose is a mandate.

With the use of tools like Django and Bootstrap Framework, we hope to create a system that gives current clients a dashboard from which they can add, update, preview, delete, and check the history of their orders. Additionally, we want to make communication smoother by using other means like WhatsApp and emails. Our web- based application will use HTML, CSS, and JavaScript for the development of its user interface (Fig. 1).

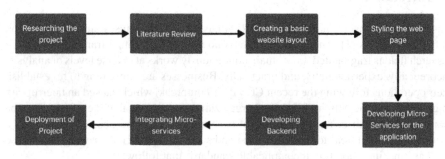

Fig. 1. Development of CRM

2 Literature Review

In this paper the author has done the following study and from their study we can conclude that In the last 10 years, the authors and three senior Bain consultants have examined both successful and ineffective customer-loyalty programmes at more than 200 businesses across a variety of sectors.

This article focuses on how executives' lack of knowledge of what they are installing, much alone how much it will cost or how long it would take, contributes to CRM failure. According to the authors' study, managers who try to implement CRM frequently run into four main obstacles. [8] Each stumbling block is the result of a single false assumption: CRM is a software programme that automatically manipulates client relationships. It's not. CRM, on the other hand, is the implementation of client approaches and tactics to build client loyalty, which is then supported by technology [8].

In this paper the author has done the following analysis and from their analysis we can conclude that The experiences of businesses expelled from CRM paradise are summarised in this analysis-based academic essay. The best course of action for those seeking a moral CRM implementation is to avoid committing these offences. In CRM implementation, we discovered the seven deadly sins and learnt how to avoid them for effective customer relationship management (CRM) projects. The best course of action for those seeking a moral CRM implementation is to avoid committing these offences [9].

In this paper the author has done the following study and from their study we can conclude that the truth of the connection between CRM and entrepreneurial marketing in company was examined in this report using a semi-systematic review. Using this strategy, it is possible to fully define the influence that CRM may have on the contemporary company environment by empowering entrepreneurial marketing. This white paper offers a systematic summary of various linked research on how CRM affects the creation of corporate marketing guidelines, with a focus on relationship marketing and customer-centric business models [11].

In this paper the author has done the following study and from their study we can conclude that The reason for this has a look at is to inspect consumer pride with a purchaser dating management (CRM) machine in Bahrain. The variables selected are perceived ease of use, perceived utility, consumer support, facilitating conditions, and social influence. The questionnaire changed into finished via way of means of a pattern of seventy personnel from a telecommunications company, however, only sixty questionnaires were returned. The approach also assists organizations in understanding why their customers favour them over their competitors, allowing the company's marketing staff to launch appropriate marketing promotions and counter the competitors' promotions [13].

In this paper the author has done the following study and from their study we can conclude that the reason for this has a look at is to inspect consumer pride with a purchaser dating management (CRM) machine in Bahrain. The variables selected are perceived ease of use, perceived utility, consumer support, facilitating conditions, and social influence. The questionnaire changed into finished via way of means of a pattern of seventy personnel from a telecommunications company, however, only sixty questionnaires were returned. The approach also assists organizations in understanding why their customers favor them over their competitors, allowing the company's marketing staff to launch appropriate marketing promotions and counter the competitors' promotions [13].

In this paper the author has done the following study and from their result we can conclude that, in this paper, the author Reconfigured the CRM framework's customer data function. As a result, this article starts with a short survey of CRM literature earlier than delving into the 3 CRM waves that characterize the converting importance of purchaser records in modern CRM systems. An empirical case observation is utilized to focus on the rising shift in purchaser records usage. After advocating new avenues for purchaser records exploitation, this text concludes with diverse ramifications, such as implications for the CRM framework [12].

3   Methodology

A CRM is a system that effectively manages customer data for an organization and renders the data for easy management and provides follow-up status that is clear briefly. In this project, we have used various technologies to create a web-based application. In this, the login and signup pages are created which will use Django crispy forms to create a user and check login credentials. DjangoCrispyforms is anapplication that helps to manage Djangoforms. It allows adjusting forms' properties to verify the user and control session. The token needs to be unique per user session. A CSRF secure application assigns an unique CSRFtoken for everyusersession (Fig. 2).

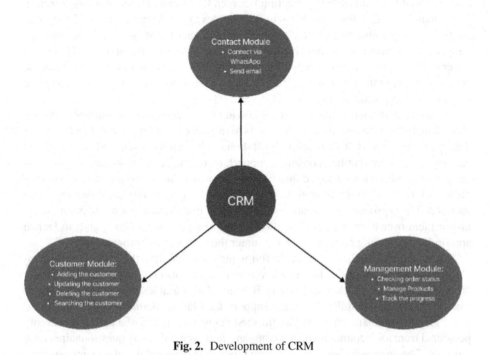

Fig. 2. Development of CRM

Next, a dashboard and other pages are created which will display different information to users. The frontend is created using Bootstrap, and CSS and pages incorporate this with HTML. To create and manage user data SQLite3 is used in the backend also various Django libraries such as user creation, login, views, and forms super-user among others are used.

3.1 System Feasibility and Requirement Analysis

From the perspective of technical viability, the open-source frameworks Django and Python are adequate choices, the database uses SQLite3 database, and these options are mature and have very wide community support thus providing low technical difficulty, and can entirely meet the requirement of small or medium-sized organizations. Regarding the system's functional requirements, a customer may be a private client of a certain salesperson or a public client of several sales during customer management. Additionally, some individuals who registered as customers will receive follow-up services from the sales staff. Due to the requirement for public, private, and customer follow-up records, the functional modules of the customer management system are each separated into several smaller functions such as Orders, Dashboard, and Contacts.

3.2 Design of the System

The system is divided into login, registration or signup, an overview of the system, and customer records. The database of the system is created using SQLite3 primarily for employee tables, department tables, customer tables, campus tables, class tables, follow-up record forms, application forms, and payment record forms which are used to store and manage data. Thus this data design complies with all requirements while maintaining the relational database's data independence and integrity.

3.3 Development Tools Used are Majorly Django, HTML, CSS, Bootstrap, and SQLite

Django is a web development framework that uses python underneath and is one of the most representative with a huge presence. The MVC pattern is a division of web applications into three parts: model (M), controller (C), and viewer (V), which are connected in an add in, lightly coupled manner. It is noted in the Web server development area. M stands for the model which we create, which oversees business object and database relationship mapping; T for the template, which determines how the page is displayed to the user; and V for the views, which handles business logic and makes calls to Model and Template. When necessary, the three layers call for a URL distributor to transmit URL page requests to various Views, which then call the relevant Model and Template.

The front-end pages are developed with HTML5, CSS, and JavaScript, and the register/signup login page uses the Django superuser model. SQLite3 is used to create an SQLite database file that can be managed, in these files tables can be defined, rows can be added to or removed, queries can be executed, and so on. It is used to create a customer database (Figs. 3, 4, 5, 6, 7, 8, 9, 10, 11, 12).

4   Experimental Results

Fig. 3. Home Page

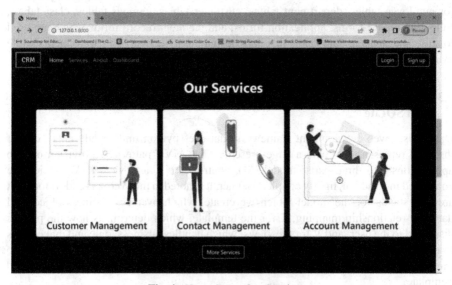

Fig. 4. Home Page: Our Services

Fig. 5. Home Page: About

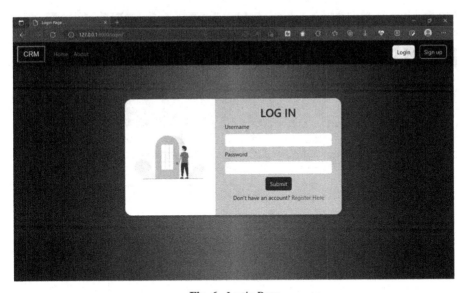

Fig. 6. Login Page

Fig. 7. Signup Page

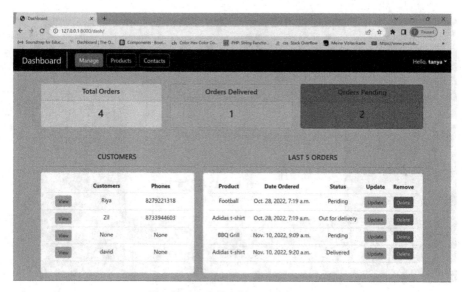

Fig. 8. Admin Dashboard: Manage

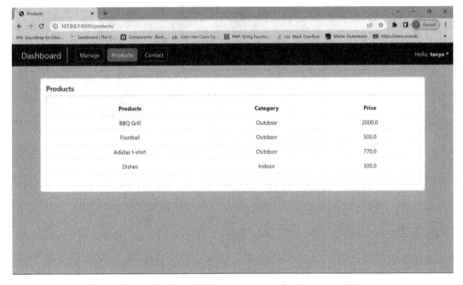

Fig. 9. Admin Dashboard: Products

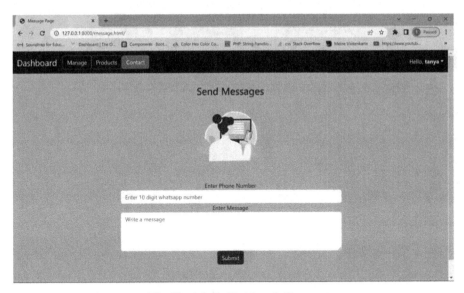

Fig. 10. Admin Dashboard: Contact

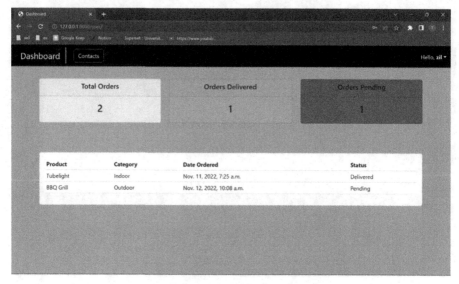

Fig.11. Customer Dashboard

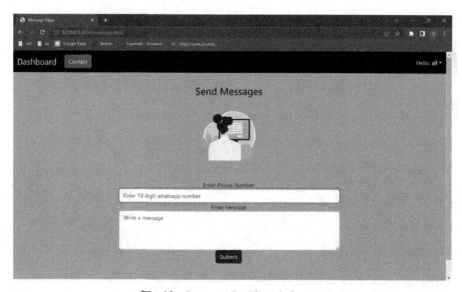

Fig. 12. Customer Dashboard: Contact

5 Conclusion and Future Scope

In this project, we developed a lightweight web-based CRM software that can be used by organizations to effectively manage their customers and track their sales as this is a web-based application it does not require much computation and can be easily rendered on the user's web browser the benefits of this approach are various small and medium size business owners can reap the benefits of CRM software without having much computation power directly to their web browser as the basic foundation of our project is based on JavaScript which is directly rendered on a web browser without any special software. The basic structures of the various CRM development stages are specified by the proposed CRM model. It might help academics focus their efforts on a particular research field while maintaining a broad perspective of the creation procedure.

On the other side, it can help businesses identify trouble spots in their current customer-based information system and inspire them to make improvements. Only approximately half of the firms, according to the survey's findings, use tools to systematically conduct customer satisfaction research and other customer-related examination, while the other half do not. Without embracing any CRM philosophies, relationships marketing. This recommends that Greek businesses should focus on creating an organizational culture that is positively geared toward employing and building customer-focused knowledge management tools. According to the technical indicators included in the earlier paper described model of CRM development, Greek businesses are also in the early phases of CRM maturity.

They can be classified as being in the mature CRM stage because only a very tiny percentage of them use integrated specialized CRM and SCM software. CRM, a new paradigm in marketing, will not be fully developed unless its essential components have been determined and put into practice. Gummesson (2002a) notes that CRM, as a developing subject, requires additional theoretical advancement. Therefore, it is crucial to identify the primary CRM dimensions. Advising practitioners or researchers that CRM is the key to effective marketing is no longer sufficient in the absence of details on the dimensions that truly construct relationships upon which CRM can be said to exist.

References

1. Study-gyaan, 'Django CRM Project - Contact Management Project' (2020)
2. Masood Momin, 'Teal CRM' (2020)
3. Qu, H.,Wang, H.: A Customer Relationship Management System Based on Django. School of Mechanical Engineering, Xijing University, Xi'an 710100, China (2020)
4. Dauzon, S., Bendoraitis, A., Ravindran, A.: Django Web Development with Python (2016)
5. Rupali, D.K., Dr. Meshram, B.B.: CSRF Vulnerabilities and Defensive Techniques. Veermata Jijabai Technological Institute, Matunga, Mumbai (2012)
6. Holovaty, H., Moss, J.M.: Web development done right (2009)
7. Spurlock, O.K.: Introduction to responsive Web-development Bootstrap (2013)
8. Rigby, D.K., Reichheld, F.F., Schefter, P.: (A Harvard BusinessReview), 'Perils of CRM' (2018)
9. Kale, S.: CRM failure and The Seven Deadly Sins. Bond University (2014)
10. Hassan, R.S., Nawaz, A., Lashari, M.N., Zafar, F.: Effect of customer relationship management on customer satisfaction (2015)

11. Guerola-Navarro, V., Gil-Gomez, H., Oltra-Badenes, R., Soto-Acosta, P.: Customer relationship management and its impact on entrepreneurial marketing, Published (2022)
12. Saarijarvi, H.: Customer relationship management: the evolving role of customer data (2012)
13. Al-Shammari, M.M., AlShowaikh, A.F.: Investigating user satisfaction of customer relationship management in a telecommunications company in the kingdom of Bahrain. University of Bahrain (2021)

Single Server Banking Management System

Rishab Dua, Priyanshi Shiwran$^{(\boxtimes)}$, Kartikey Pandey$^{(\boxtimes)}$, Rishit Kasliwal$^{(\boxtimes)}$, and Prabhat Thakur$^{(\boxtimes)}$

Department of Electronics and Telecommunication, Symbiosis Institute of Technology, Symbiosis International (Deemed University), Pune, Maharashtra 412115, India
{rishab.dua.btech2019,priyanshi.shiwran.btech2019, kartikey.pandey.btech2019,rishit.kasliwal.btech2019, prabhat.thakur}@sitpune.edu.in

Abstract. This paper presents a thorough conceptualization of a project that resembles an online banking system that offers fundamental financial services via a user-friendly GUI. In this standalone project, we have developed a system that offers existing customers a dashboard from which they may transfer, withdraw, and deposit money as well as check their transaction history. New users will be guided through a straightforward, step-by-step process to open an account, during which they will receive a special account number and be prompted with a few simple questions. The Single Server Banking Management System undertaken as a project is based on relevant technologies. This project serves the primary goal of creating software for a bank account management system. This project enables and enhances the process to complete tasks quickly and easily, which is not achievable with manual systems and is overcome by this program. This project is developed using Java, JavaFX, and MySQL to connect to the database.

Keywords: Banking · Java · Javafx · JDBC · EMI · SIP

1 Introduction

The "Single Server Banking Management System" project is a model Internet Banking Site. Customers can use a PC or laptop to complete simple banking operations while using this website from their offices or homes. Customers have access to the database so they may open accounts, initiate deposits and withdrawals, and look through information for all open accounts. Additionally, the project offers services including an email facility, SIP Calculator, EMI Calculator, and OTP Verification. Customers can examine their account information on the bank's website and conduct required transactions on their accounts. Traditional banking's brick-and-mortar setup is changed by internet banking into a click-and-portal paradigm. In the present day, banking is no longer just done in branches. Customers may conduct financial transactions around-the-clock and internationally thanks to e-banking.

1.1 Background and Overview

Banks today are more interested in customer management than in processing trans-actions [7]. To improve the corporate client experience that provides the bank with a strategic edge while also attracting more sincere, lucrative, and loyal customers, they are advancing much further than just managing customers as simple contact information to a whole new level of customer relationship management. [8] Internet Banking Systems are tools that enable bank customers to access their accounts and general information regarding the bank's products and services via a computer or other intelligent device. However, the majority of such system applications don't really concentrate on how to effectively manage and safeguard their customers' data.

The opportunities and threats that the internet indicates are no longer a big deal to the modern banking sector. Without an internet strategy, the non-traditional bank would be unwise to encounter investment analysts or new customers. The real aim of deploying electronic banking services is to provide customers with a more responsive and cost-effective alternative [10]. Customers have more authority than ever before, thanks to more secure options. Their expectations are regarding the security and confidentiality of their sensitive information [11]. They also expect personalized service and highly configurable products and services.

1.2 Problem Statement

At the moment, a huge percentage of the financial sector is still yet to address the continually rising cyberattacks on its sensitive information. Problems such as fraud can occur in a conventional setting. Furthermore, functionalities are still striving to comply with the established organizational structure, which is primarily structured for the traditional banking system and not for better management of their customers' data.

1.3 Objective

The purpose of this work is to build a Single Server Banking Management System to maximize customer satisfaction and revenue for financial institutions. The objectives are:

1. To design a user-friendly graphical user interface for the banking industry.
2. To improve banking efficiency, reducing the flow of people and long queues.
3. To perform financial transactions like deposits, withdrawals, and transfers.
4. To register an account, log in to an existing account.
5. To notify the account holder of every transaction made.
6. To develop a banking system with a multi-level security measure

1.4 Scope

The scope of this project is confined to some functions of a banking system's depart-ment, everything from opening an account, depositing cash, withdrawing cash, trans-ferring money from one account to another, and modifying personal information. This application does not concentrate on other internet-based- based services such as online shopping, payment services, loan applications, and so on.

1.5 Organization of the Paper

Section 1 covers the background, overview, objective, and organization of the report. Section 2 deals with the literature review which is based on the existing systems with a comparison and summary of those systems. Section 3 explains the characteristics and features of the system, the development of the project, and the system requirement analysis which comprises software requirements in which this system will be developed. Section 4 provides methodology, system analysis, results, and discussions. Section 5 summarizes the project and gives the concluding remarks, contribution, limitation of the system, and future scope of the project.

2 Paper Preparation

We examine the factors and features to be incorporated in E-banking for both users and non-users of internet banking and analyze and expose the banking channels and service preferences of most bank management systems. Despite the fact that the banking industry is growing, Customer management systems have yet to be fully utilized as a true value-added tool for improving customer relationships, providing better banking services, and achieving cost savings [12].

Meshram et al., in [1], proposed a management system for banks that enables customers of a bank to perform financial transactions without the need for a bank representative. In the proposed system, they deployed n-tier architecture in bank management systems to handle different tasks effectively and systematically. The n-tier architecture had a bottom-up approach with MVC architecture for the Presentation layer, SOA architecture for the Service layer, Design Pattern for the data access layer, and Entity framework for the Data access layer. This system includes capabilities like registration, login, financial transactions, and account validation, such as linking with the Aadhar Card. While the administrator has complete authority to manage user accounts and transactions in order to prevent unauthorized users. The user can also modify his credentials, such as his address and phone number, and migrate his account from one place to another.

Choudhary et al., in [2], proposed and analyzed a management system in a bank using Salesforce which is a popular cloud computing platform in the IT sector that is accessible via cloud computing techniques. This paper emphasizes customer relationship management (CRM) business strategy in banking management as Banks have led an aggressive effort to manage the quality of their interactions with customers in recent years. This paper claims that a bank's success is based on understanding data and serving customers, thus they propose a CRM system that gathers and processes client data. CRM's purpose is to guarantee that customer interactions are consistent and suitable across all delivery channels. ACRM has a unified profile repository that houses the bank's client sales and service plans. In [3] Felix, designed and implemented a Bank customer management system that offers a more secure method to handle the bank's customer information and enhances ties between banks and their customers by delivering the necessary solutions that rely on multi-level security to enhance customer satisfaction.

This project's bank customer management system was created with the aim to maximize bank profits while satisfying customers. The project's functions include account opening, depositing funds, withdrawing funds, transferring funds from one account to another, and updating personal information. The technology used in developing this project is ASP.NET, the programming language used is C#, and the IDE used in designing the front end is Microsoft Visual Studio 2013 professional, while the back end uses Microsoft SQL Server 2012.

Giridharan et al., [4], developed a project Bank Management System with the objective to create a more user-friendly interface for customers of a bank. The project included frontend GUI design of some basic web pages like the Main menu, admin, manager, account creation, amount withdrawal, update information, and deposits. The project was developed using the programming language C#, and the IDE used in designing the front end is Microsoft Visual Studio, while the back end uses SQL. In [5] Uddin and Nuruzzaman made a project named Bank Account Management System which keeps daily tally records. Moreover, it may be used to preserve data on account types, account opening forms, deposit and withdrawal funds, transaction searches, transaction reports, personal and corporate account opening forms, and transaction reports. The current aspect of this study shows transaction reports, interest information, and a statistical summary of account type. This project is deployed on the XAPM server and the front-end language used is PHP while the database in the back-end is managed using MySQL. In [6] Shubhara Jindal, discussed the E-Banking Scenario in India, as well as the evolution and modernization of the Indian banking sector. The study focused on e-banking services/functions provided by Indian banks, progress made by the Indian banking industry in the adoption of technology, and challenges faced. The paper also provides solutions and recommendations for the adoption of technology in the Banking sector of India. The paper also mentions the necessary features that E-banking applications should offer. These features are fund transfer, customer relationship management, view balance and transactions, bill payment mechanisms, mobile banking, and SMS services.

Customers in the aforementioned banking systems cannot conveniently change/reset their secured password without visiting the bank. When necessary, our system allows customers and administrators such as bank managers to update their personal information such as a home address, email, mobile number, and so on [9]. The surveyed banking systems lacked OTP verification and could not send an automatic email notification to the customer for every fund transfer. Our single-server banking management system will also make it much easier to transfer funds and manage customer information. It also protects them against attacks and unauthorized access (Table 1).

Table 1. Comparison with existing Banking Management Systems.

System	Features/Capabilities									
	Register	Login	E-mail	Fund Transfer	Account Information	Balance	Password	Reset Password	OTP Secured	Update Personal Info
Bank Management System	Yes	Yes	Yes	Yes	Yes	Yes	Yes	No	No	Yes
Salesforce Bank Management System	Yes	Yes	No	Yes	Yes	Yes	Yes	Yes	No	Yes
Bank Customer Management System	Yes	Yes	No	Yes	Yes	Yes	Yes	Yes	No	Yes
E-Bank Management System	Yes	Yes	No	Yes	Yes	Yes	Yes	No	No	No
Bank Account Management System	Yes	Yes	Yes	Yes	Yes	Yes	Yes	No	No	No
Single Server Banking Management System	Yes	Yes	Yes	Yes	Yes	Yes	Yes	Yes	Yes	Yes

3 Characteristics and Features

Characteristics of this project:

- This program may be used by any bank to enhance customer service.
- Customers may easily access all of their accounts across all of their bank's locations with just one click.
- Because clients may do transactions online, the workload of all staff can be reduced owing to this method (Fig. 1).

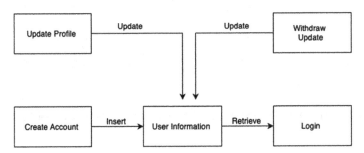

Fig. 1. User Information Data Flow Chart of Single Server Banking Management System

User Information is requested when a new user opens an account. Unique login credentials are produced for the same data. The user can change details if they want to make changes, to both new and existing users. (upgrading their profile, allowing them to modify, or remove previously entered data. The system also offers the option of withdrawing an update, giving them the ability to undo any incorrect details that may have been altered.

The major functions the product must perform:

- Any Login/Logout Process
- Creating New Account
- Update Dashboard Profile
- Funds' deposit/withdraw
- Change of password
- View transaction history
- Adding validation

3.1 SIP Calculator

This module allows the customer to calculate the estimate of the return on mutual fund Investments made through the SIP of their account. The stimulus for the module is a string of words/characters/numbers or a combination of them. The system will process and display the estimated amount with respect to the particular rate of annum.

3.2 EMI Calculator

This module allows the customer to determine their monthly payouts and balance their budget accordingly. The stimulus for the module is a string of words/characters/numbers or a combination of them. The system will process and display the estimated loan amount with respect to the particular rate of annum the customer is eligible for.

3.3 OTP Verification

This feature allows the customer to authenticate using OTP via mail. The stimulus for the module is a string of numbers. The feature helps in creating accounts as well as in changing pin (Fig. 2).

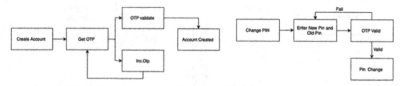

Fig. 2. OTP Verification Procedure. (a) For a New User, (b) For an Existing User

When a new user registers and creates an account, an OTP is generated and delivered to the email address, they provided while filling out the user information. If the OTP is entered correctly, it will be validated and the account will be created; however, if the OTP is entered incorrectly, the procedure of generating a new OTP must be repeated; after the proper OTP is registered and validated, the account will be created. The user will be required to enter both the old PIN and the new PIN that is to be updated if they choose to change their PIN, which is an option. An OTP will then be generated and sent to the user's email address.

3.4 Email Facility

This feature allows the customer to authenticate to create an account by generating OTP. The stimulus for the module is a string of numbers. The feature helps in creating an account as well as sends a message to the customer whenever he/she withdraws, transfers, or deposits money or changes the PIN of their account (Fig. 3).

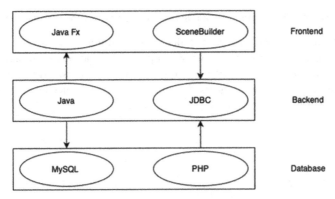

Fig. 3. Workflow and processes involved to develop the Single Server Banking Management System.

4 Methodology

The backend of this application is written in JAVA. There are various controllers defined for different functionalities of the application. The controllers are:

- Login screen Controller: This module allows valid users to log in to the application. The priority of this module is HIGH.
- SIP controller: This module allows the customer to calculate the estimate of the return on mutual fund Investments made through the SIP of their account. The priority is MEDIUM. The stimulus for the module is a string of words/ characters/ numbers or a combination of them. The system will process and display the estimated amount with respect to a particular rate of annum.
- EMI Controller: This module allows the customer to determine their monthly payouts and balance their budget accordingly. The priority is MEDIUM. The stimulus for the module is a string of words/ characters/ numbers or a combination of them. The system will process and display the estimated loan amount with respect to the particular rate of annum the customer is eligible for.

The frontend of our application is designed using scene builder:

With the aid of JavaFX Scene Builder, users may quickly and simply create user interfaces for JavaFX applications without the need for programming. The FXML code for the structure the user is designing is automatically written in the backdrop when they drag and drop UI components into a work area, modify their settings, and apply style sheets. By linking the UI to the application's logic, an FXML file is produced that can be merged with a Java project.

For our application to work we need 4 tables in our database.

- User Data: This database contains all the user data such as Name, Phone number, email id, etc.
- Withdrawal History: This database helps individuals to withdraw funds from their accounts.
- Deposit History: This database allows users to deposit money from their accounts.

- Transfer History: This database enables users to transfer funds from their accounts.

phpMyAdmin: Free PHP program called phpMyAdmin is used to control MySQL operations online. A wide range of MySQL operations is available in phpMyAdmin. The user interface may be utilized for frequently performed tasks (handling datasets, tables, columns, relations, indexes, users, permissions, and so on), but any SQL query can still be run directly (Fig. 4).

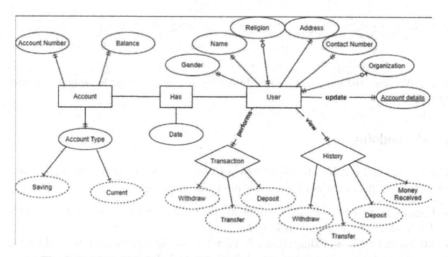

Fig. 4. Database E-R Diagram of Single Server Banking Management System

The Database E-R Diagram illustrates the functionality of our complete database. Starting with the user's account, there are two different sorts of accounts that may be opened in our dataset: a current account and a savings account. The account number and the current balance are the two most important details that are kept in the database for the account. The user is requested for a few personal details when creating an account on the system. These details include gender, name, religion, address, mobile number, organization, and account details. Users of this platform can do three operations withdraw, transfer, and deposit. Additionally, history is accessible, allowing the user to observe any money received as well as the history of transfers, deposits, and withdrawals (Fig. 5, 6, 7, 8, 9, 10, 11, 12).

4.1 Results

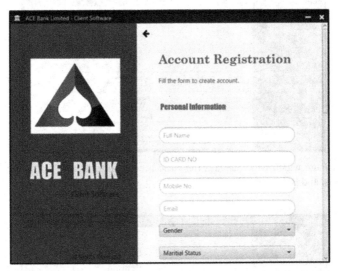

Fig. 5. Account Registration Page for new users to register and create an account after entering personal details and validating using the OTP.

Fig. 6. Login Page for existing users to log in into their accounts.

The project titled "Single Server Banking Management System" ensures basic banking operations with multi-level security to be performed at remote locations and without any bank's assistance. Customers have access to the system so they may open accounts, execute deposits and withdrawals, and look through reports for all open accounts.

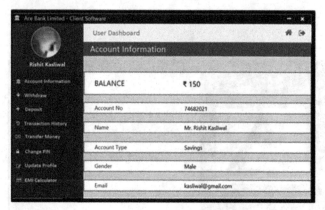

Fig. 7. Home Page which page displays the basic account information like Account Number, Personal details, and Balance.

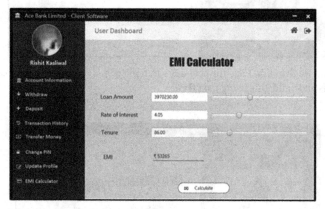

Fig. 8. EMI Calculator Page which page allows the user to calculate and estimate the EMI according to his/her time period and loan amount.

Additionally, the project provides services like Email notifications, SIP Calculator, EMI Calculator, and OTP Verification. Any bank may use our product, and consumers can manage all of their accounts across all of the bank's locations with a single click. By giving clients internet access to their transaction rights, this solution lessens the effort of all staff and makes banking a quick and simple operation.

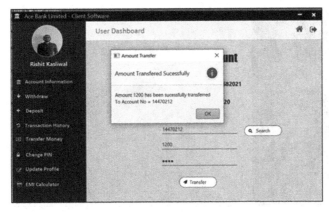

Fig. 9. Transfer Page with a pop-up that shows that the user has successfully transferred funds to the desired account.

Fig. 10. PIN Change Page with a pop-up of successfully changing a PIN.

Fig. 11. Profile Update Page that allows the user to modify his/her personal details after validating using the OTP.

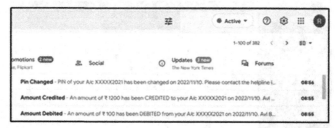

Fig. 12. Email Notifications that are sent to the registered E-mail Id for every transaction or change in details.

5   Conclusion

According to the study, a significant proportion of account holders are aware of all online banking services widely available because, in recent years, internet banking has received considerable attention due to various factors, including the advantages it brings to users, such as the opening of bank accounts, the deposit of funds, checking account balances and records, including year-to-date data, as well as the ability to transfer money from one account to another. And we can do all of these tasks from the convenience of our own homes.

Our Single Server Banking Management System is entirely data-oriented and only operates on a single server. By offering a distinct user id and password that prevent unauthorized users from logging in, this banking management system safeguards critical data against unauthorized access. Additionally, the system provides real-time email notifications and is end-to-end encrypted. The Single Server Banking Management System can be deployed at any bank which can utilize this application to give their customers better service.

5.1 Future Scope

The project can be further extended to be able to link to government databases and verify as well as check about the user's identity proofs. Online payment systems and UPI can be linked to this Single server Banking Management Application. New web pages can be created for commercial and internet dealings as well as trade-related transactions. The project can also be extended to the Bank's internal processes like analyzing a bank's profit day-to-day transactions as well as daily total deposits, withdrawals, and money left in the bank. It can also be extended to store information about the staff of the bank and their salary structures.

References

1. Meshram, M. K., Gaware, K., Bansod, S., Madwatkar, D., Anjankar, P.: Bank management system. Int. Res. J. Eng. Technol. **05**(03) (2018)
2. Choudhary, Y., Katare, T.V., Markandewar, A.L., Shyamkuwar, H.M., Kathikar, P.M., Ladke, P.G.: Bank management system using salesforce. Int. J. Res. Appl. Sci. Eng. Technol. **10**(2) (2022)
3. Felix, A.: Bank customers management system (2015)
4. Kumar, N., Kannan, M., Raghavan, S., Giridharan, K.: Bank management system. Int. J. Eng. Manag. Res. **7**(3) (2017)
5. Uddin, M.D., Nuruzzaman, M.D.: Bank account management system. Int. J. Eng. Manag. Res. (2015). https://doi.org/10.13140/RG.2.1.4335.9120
6. Jindal, S.: Abstract of study of E-banking scenario in India. Int. J. Sci. Res. (IJSR) (2015)
7. Sharma, G. Study of internet banking scenario in India. Int. J. Emerg. Res. Manag. Technol. **19**(10) (2017). ISSN: 2278-9359
8. Dagar, A.: Online banking: benefits and related issues. Int. J. Commerce Bus. Manag. (IJCBM) **3**(5) (2014). ISSN: 2319-2828
9. Md. Titu, A.S., Md. Rahman, A.: Online banking system-its application in some selected private commercial banks in Bangladesh. IOSR J. Bus. Manag. (IOSR-JBM) **9**(4) (2013). e-ISSN: 2278-487X
10. Saeidipour, B., Ranjbar, H., Ranjbar, S.: Adoption of internet banking. IOSR J. Bus. Manag. (IOSR-JBM) **11**(2) (2013). e-ISSN: 2278-487X
11. Amutha, D.: A study of consumer awareness towards eBanking. Int. J. Econ. Manag. Sci. **5**(4) (2016). ISSN: 2162-6359
12. Khan, F.: E-banking: benefits and issues. Am. Res. J. Bus. Manag.

Prioritization of MQTT Messages: A Novel Approach

Jiby J.Puthiyidam[(✉)] and Shelbi Joseph

School of Engineering, Cochin University of Science and Technology, Kochi, Kerala 682022,
India
{jibyjp,shelbi}@cusat.ac.in

Abstract. The past few decades have seen rapid development in the Internet of
Things (IoT) field. IoT makes everyday devices smart by enabling sensing, processing and transmission capabilities. Contradicting the standard internet applications that use HTTP for data transmission, IoT applications use devices with limited processing power, memory capacity and low resource consumption. Hence,
HTTP is insufficient and specialized communication protocols are required for
IoT applications. Message Queuing Telemetry Transport (MQTT) is a prominent
and widely used protocol in IoT environments. MQTT protocol does not prioritize incoming messages. MQTT broker forwards the incoming messages in the
same order as they arrive. In many applications, some messages or messages from
specific sources are more critical than others. This paper analyzes the methods
proposed in the literature to assign priority to MQTT messages and proposes
a novel approach for identifying and processing urgent messages in the MQTT
applications.

Keywords: Internet of Things · MQTT · message priority · network traffic

1 Introduction

The advancement in the computing and communication field exponentially increased the
number of devices connected to the internet. These connected devices and communication technologies form the revolutionary concept of Internet of Things (IoT). There is
no universal definition of what the IoT encompasses [1]. One of the definitions covering
most aspects of the Internet of Things is given in [2] as "An open and comprehensive network of intelligent objects that can auto-organize, share information, data and resources,
reacting and acting in the face of situations and changes in the environment". Generally, IoT environment consists of many physical devices connected to the internet and
communicating using a network and providing any service for users [3]. These physical
objects sense their surroundings, process information collected, share information with
other devices and make decisions. The main objective of IoT is to provide a system
for monitoring and controlling the physical world. The Internet of Things is a platform
where everyday devices become smarter, everyday processing becomes intelligent, and
everyday communication becomes informative [2, 4]. IoT makes the communication

© The Author(s), under exclusive license to Springer Nature Switzerland AG 2023
R. S. Tomar et al. (Eds.): CNC 2022, CCIS 1894, pp. 40–52, 2023.
https://doi.org/10.1007/978-3-031-43145-6_4

between human-to-human, human-to-things and things-to-things possible by providing a unique identity to each object [2, 5]. IoT is used for various applications such as health care, manufacturing, electricity meter reading, smart homes and agriculture, to name a few. The projected market share of each IoT application [6] is shown in Fig. 1.

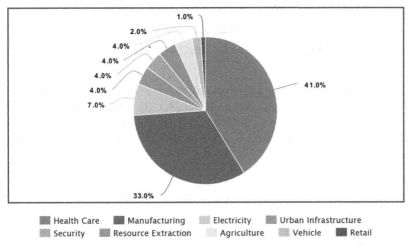

Fig. 1. Projected IoT Application share by 2025 [6]

For the IoT revolution to survive, there should be effective Machine-to-Machine (M2M) [7] communication over the internet. Hyper Text Transfer Protocol (HTTP) [8] is the prominent protocol for most Internet communications. However, when HTTP is applied to IoT applications, it causes serious problems, such as the consumption of network resources and performance degradation. IoT environments require specialized communication protocols as their applications use constrained devices with limited processing power, memory capacity, and bandwidth. Many application protocols such as CoAP, MQTT and AMQP are available for IoT environments.

1.1 Message Queuing Telemetry Transport (MQTT) Protocol

MQTT [9] is a widely used IoT messaging protocol. It is based on the TCP/IP stack and uses publish-subscribe pattern to transport data. MQTT has low overhead, meaning that it sends a very small amount of data as the message. The MQTT message header is incredibly small (only 2 bytes) in comparison with other protocols like HTTP or CoAP (Fig. 2).

Major components in the MQTT architecture include a central broker server and clients in the role of publisher and subscriber. Initially, the clients establish a connection with the broker. Subscribing clients report their topics of interest to the broker at the time of connection. The broker receives with message topic from publishers, filter these messages based on the message topic and then forward the message to the subscribers subscribed to this topic. The broker forward messages to the subscribers in a First Come,

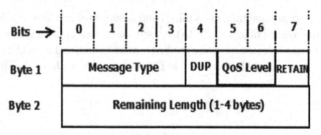

Fig. 2. MQTT message fixed header format [10]

First Serve basis. Figure 3 shows the basic architecture of an MQTT broker. Popular MQTT brokers include mosquitto broker, RabbitMQ, Hive MQ, VerneMQ, HBMQTT etc. Mosquitto [11] is a widely used broker in MQTT applications. It is open source and written in C language. HBMQTT [12] is another popular MQTT broker written in Python.

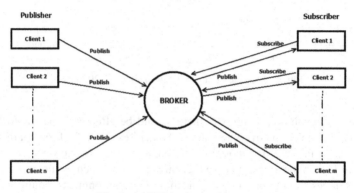

Fig. 3. MQTT broker architecture

Among different IoT protocols, the Quality of Service (QoS) features of MQTT make it unique. MQTT supports three Quality of Services for reliable of message delivery. QoS should be selected based on the application requirement. An important message should reach the destination in any case. Such a message is assigned with a QoS that may be slow, but the delivery is guaranteed (e.g.:- gas leak sensor data in an industrial environment). Whereas, if the speed of delivery is essential and can afford the loss of some data, the message may be assigned a QoS that does not support retransmission of data (e.g.:- atmospheric temperature data).

1.2 Problem Statement

In many real-life applications, hundreds and thousands of sensors are deployed. Big data from multiple applications may lead congestion problems in cloud networks and cause several disadvantages such as decreasing throughput, packet loss, and latency. It may also increase the risk of critical data not being processed on time or the possibility of getting lost in the network. In many IoT applications, messages from some publishers may be more important than messages from other sources and require immediate attention and treatment. Standard MQTT has no prioritization technique to distinguish and treat critical data separately. Forwarding messages based on their relevance is vital in many IoT applications. For example, an alarming value from a fire or gas leak sensor is more important in an industrial environment than an atmospheric temperature or pressure sensor message. If we follow the FIFO queue in the broker, these critical messages may lose some crucial time waiting in the queue and lead to unpredictable damage or loss. Since it is a very relevant research topic, in this paper, we study the proposals in the literature to prioritize MQTT messages and propose a framework to efficiently assign priority to MQTT messages.

This paper is organized as follows: Sect. 2 discusses related works on prioritizing MQTT messages. Section 3 presents the proposed method in detail, and the results are discussed in Sect. 4. Section 5 concludes our discussion.

2   Related Work

In [13], Geonwoo Kim et al., proposed a method that adds a priority field by modifying a part of a fixed header, i.e. expanding the size of the fixed header from two to three bytes. This method uses two bits of the third byte in the MQTT header packet for priority setting. With two bits, we can set four levels of priority. It is a multi-level queue-based structure and maintains four independent message queues for each priority level. Work [14] also follows a similar approach by adding the priority field in the third byte of the fixed header. Two bits of the third byte in the MQTT header are used for setting the priority flag. The higher the number of the priority flag, the higher the priority. Both approaches increase the size of the MQTT message fixed header size. The minimum header size increases from two to three bytes. In [15], the authors propose a method that utilises the reserved packet types (packet 0 and packet 15) of the MQTT standard packet types as priority packets and the remaining 14 packet types (packets 1–14) as normal packets. Message type 0 indicates urgent messages with the highest priority, and message type 15 denotes critical messages with the second-highest priority. This method maintains three separate queues for each priority level.

Works [13] and [15] use a plurality of queues as many as the number of priority types. Messages published by different publishers are stored in the corresponding priority queue by a classifier component which classifies incoming messages based on their priority. Messages in the high-priority queue are processed first, and then messages in the following high-priority queue and so on. Paper [13] uses a message scheduling method based on Weighted Round Robin (WRR) to prevent excessive processing delay of a queue having low priority. This method requires more CPU resources than a single queue method because a plurality of queues needs to be generated, managed and scheduled. Implementing a message processing priority approach with these methods may be incompatible with many other high-level application programs such as NodeRED or AWS because they modify the MQTT standard.

Authors in [16] proposed a different approach for prioritising incoming messages without modifying the message header. The message topic name is used to assign priority to messages. The first character of the message topic determines the message priority. For example, if the message topic begins with a predefined rarely used character such as '^', it is assumed to have higher priority than a message topic beginning with other characters. Hence the priority of a message is sent with the 'PUBLISH' message, and it does not affect the existing MQTT standard. Also, they claim that the MQTT protocol can run with relatively low CPU resources.

In their work [17], Hwan Jung and Dong-Hee Lee proposed a method to modify the mosquitto broker to handle urgent messages efficiently. The improved mosquitto broker, U-mosquitto, maintains an urgent message list in addition to the subscription list of normal messages and processes the urgent message list before the subscription list.

Marwa O.E. et al., in their research [18], use the concept of the Back-off algorithm to calculate the average frequency rate of messages published by each publisher. Based on this average frequency, they proposed a priority scheduling algorithm that assigns priority from the broker's side, not the client's. The publisher with the highest average frequent rate (maximum delay between successive messages) is assigned the highest priority. Messages from such publishers are placed in the front of the queue. The one with the lowest average frequent rate is given the lowest priority and placed at the end of the array. Other publishers are sorted based on their average frequency and placed in their correct position in the array. Hence, this method prioritises incoming messages without modifying the MQTT packet structure. This method assumes that a publisher sending messages less frequently is more important than a publisher publishing messages frequently.

Researchers of [19] propose a priority assignment scheme to decrease the number of packets sent to the resource-constrained network. Two threshold values are identified, and if a new message external to the threshold values arrives, it is assigned with the highest priority. Also, suppose the difference between the previously measured data (di) and the newly measured data (di + 1) is within a pre-specified tolerance range. In that case, the proposed scheme considers the newest data the same as the previously measured value and assigns the lowest priority to it. The keep-alive message notification scheme is applied to transmit the lowest priority packets.

In [20], Park et al. propose an efficient multiclass message scheduling algorithm for healthcare IoT environments. This method classifies messages into three groups based on their characteristics, namely Unconditional messages (UNC), Real-time (RT) messages and delay-tolerant (DT) messages. Each message class has its message queue. UNC messages should be forwarded immediately. Whenever an RT message is sent, the priority of the RT message queue is decreased by 10%, and the priority of the DT message queue is increased by 10%. Similarly, whenever a DT message is sent, the priority of the DT message queue is decreased by 30% and the priority of the RT message queue is increased by 30%. This algorithm ensures that the transmission of DT messages is not blocked indefinitely.

3   Proposed Algorithm

From the analysis of attempts in literature to handle the message priority issue in the MQTT protocol, it is found that most of the methods either assign the responsibility to identify the priority messages to the input client nodes or they modify the standard MQTT packet structure. Both approaches are not recommended as the input client nodes are constrained devices and they are not supposed to deal with message priorities. Similarly, modifying standard MQTT protocol message header format is also not desirable. In all the proposals discussed, messages from some of the publishers are pre assigned as priority messages. In other words, some publishers are designated to generate priority messages.

In the proposed algorithm, we assign equal preference to all publishers. Input clients are not pre assigned with any kind of priority. Input nodes sense surrounding data and publish the sensed information at fixed intervals to the broker. We assume that a publisher node sends two types of messages. Normal messages provide regular updates on the status of its sensing environment and alert messages indicate something went wrong. Broker is responsible for determining whether an incoming message is a normal message or an alert message. In the standard MQTT broker, all messages are processed in the First Come, First Serve order [21]. Hence, alert messages must wait until all status update messages (normal messages) in front of the queue are processed. Hence, alert messages may be received too late by subscribers. We can forward alert messages ahead of normal messages by assigning priority to such messages.

In the proposed work, we consider the situation where multiple publishers publish data, and a single subscriber receives the data. This environment is ideal for many IoT applications, such as patient monitoring and industrial automation.

This work is divided into three modules:

(1) Identify the normal range (*min-max* range) of each publisher data,

(2) Forward high-priority messages ahead of normal messages and.

(3) Identify the trivial range for each publisher to reduce network traffic and congestion in a message queue.

3.1 Identifying *min-max* Range

We need to identify each publisher's *min-max* range (normal range). It is required for distinguishing high-priority messages from normal messages. Our algorithm monitors the first n messages from each publisher. This can be considered as a training period. The minimum and maximum values of the first n messages generated by each publisher are identified. These values serve as a boundary point for the successive values published by the publisher. Figure 4 depicts the process of determining the minimum and maximum values of first n messages of a publisher p_j. The value n may vary from a few hundred messages to data of one or more days, depending on the application. The initial n messages from each publisher are selected to determine the minimum and maximum range assuming that there will be no abnormal or uncommon event during the initial stage (training period). A message value within the *min-max* range is considered as a normal message and is treated using the standard MQTT message forwarding procedure. A message value outside this range is considered as an alert message. The procedure for identifying the *min-max* range is shown in Fig. 5.

When each publisher p_j publishes a message to the broker, the broker updates the current minimum and maximum values of p_j using Eqs. (1) and (2)

$$\min(p_j) = \min[mp_{ji}, \, curr\_\min(p_j)] \qquad (1)$$

$$max(p_j) = max[mp_{ji}, \ curr\_min(p_j)] \tag{2}$$

where,

    $min(p_j)$ - new minimum value for publisher p_j.

    $max(p_j)$- new maximum value for publisher p_j.

    curr_min(p_j)- present minimum value for publisher p_j.

    curr_max(p_j)- present maximum value for publisher p_j.

    mp_{ji}- ith message of publisher p_j.

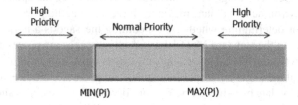

Fig. 4. Message priority setting

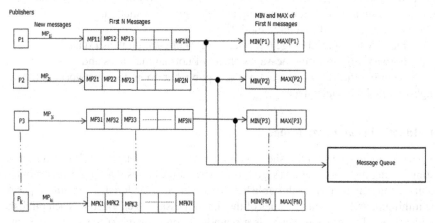

Fig. 5. Identifying *min-max* range of each publisher

The minimum and maximum value identified for each publisher from its first '*n*' initial message are stored in the corresponding position in the arrays min[] and max[]. The algorithm explaining the computation of min-max range of each publisher and its trivial interval is given in Fig. 6.

3.2 Forwarding High Priority Messages

After the minimum and maximum values of a publisher is computed and stored in the respective arrays, each subsequent message value sensed by the publishing sensor is compared with the stored *min* and *max* values. If the new value is outside this *min-max*

```
Input :    publishers p₁, p₂,....,pₖ
              number of initial messages, n
Output : array min[], array max[] and trivial interval t

Procedure
for each publisher pⱼ
      for each message mᵢ₌₁ to mᵢ₌ₙ
          read mᵢ
          add mᵢ to mq[]
      endfor
      compute pⱼ(min) = minimum(mpⱼᵢ₌₁ to mpⱼᵢ₌ₙ)
      compute pⱼ(max) = maximum(mpⱼᵢ₌₁ to mpⱼᵢ₌ₙ)
      save pⱼ(min) in Array min[pⱼ]
      save pⱼ(max) in Array min[pⱼ]

      compute trivial interval t = Σ (mᵢ −mᵢ₋₁)
                                   i=1    n-1

endfor
```

Fig. 6. Algorithm: Min-max range and trivial value calculation

range, it is an abnormal or critical message, and it should be treated urgently. Such a message is considered a high priority (*hpr*) message.

$$\text{hpr}(mp_{ji}) = mp_{ji} < \min(p_j) \text{ or } mp_{ji} > \max(p_j) \tag{3}$$

Such a high-priority message should be forwarded immediately to the subscriber for further action. In order to handle this message quickly, it should be placed at the first position in the message queue, bypassing all normal messages.

$$\text{mq}[0] = mp_{ji}$$

When the high priority abnormal message is placed at the front of the queue, it is immediately dispatched to the subscribers by the broker.

If the value of the new message is within the *min-max* range of the publisher, we assume no priority to the message, and it is treated like a normal message (*npr*).

$$\text{npr}(mp_{ji}) = \min(p_j) < mp_{ji} < \max(p_j) \tag{4}$$

Such normal messages are placed at the back of the queue in the next available position.

$$\text{mq}[N - 1] = mp_{ji}$$

where, N denote the number of elements present in the message queue currently. A schematic representation of this procedure is given in Fig. 7. The algorithm describing the processing of incoming messages based on their priority is presented in Fig. 8.

3.3 Identifying Trivial Range

Most of the messages from publishing clients carry information regarding the surroundings, such as temperature or humidity, which gradually changes in degree. So ignoring

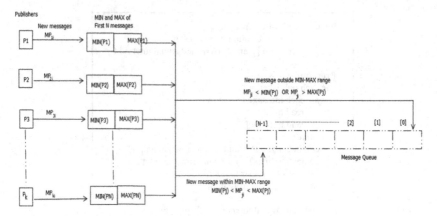

Fig. 7. Placing messages in message queue based on priority

```
Input : publishers p₁, p₂,....,pₖ
         trivial interval t
         arrays min[] and max[]
Output : message queue mq[] with priority messages at the front.

Procedure
 for each publisher pⱼ
     s = 0
     skip = 3
     for each message mᵢ
         if  mᵢ < min[pⱼ] or mᵢ > max[pⱼ]
                 set priority level of mᵢ = hpr // high priority message
                 set location of mᵢ = mq[0] //first location of mq[]
         elseif  min[pⱼ] <= mᵢ <= max[pⱼ]
                 if |mᵢ – mᵢ₋₁| <= t
                     ++s
                         if s < skip
                             skip mᵢ
                         else
                             set priority level of mᵢ = npr // normal message
                             set location of mᵢ = mq[n-1] //last item of mq[]
                             s = 0
                 else
                     set priority level of mᵢ = npr // normal priority
                     set location of mᵢ = mq[n-1] //last item of mq[]
         else
                 mᵢ is undecided
                 skip mᵢ
         endif
     endfor
 endfor
```

Fig. 8. Algorithm: To identify priority messages

some non-critical data may not result any severe consequence. Proper ignoring of some non-critical data reduces network traffic and long waiting in the message queue and thus improves the performance of message transmission. In order to reduce the network traffic and the number of messages in the message queue, our algorithm keeps track of a trivial interval within the *min-max* region. This interval region is computed using

$$t = \sum_{i=1}^{n} \frac{(m_i - m_{i-1})}{n-1} \tag{5}$$

Suppose the value of a normal message is within the trivial interval with its preceding message. In that case, both messages are considered to be identical, and the latter one need not be forwarded to the broker. However, this approach may skip a sequence of messages for some sensors, such as temperature sensors or atmospheric pressure sensors. It may cause an indefinite delay for a new message from such publishers to reach the subscriber. No message for a long time from a publisher may confuse the broker about the existence of a connected device. To avoid such a situation, we set a skip limit so that only the number of messages specified by the skip limit will be skipped off in a sequence.

An example describing the proposed algorithm for identifying and processing priority messages in MQTT communication protocol is explained next. Let the skip limit be 3. Two consecutive messages within this trivial interval will be skipped off, and the third one is forwarded to the broker. Let us consider 10 messages published by a temperature sensor as its initial set of messages to determine *min-max* range.

Temperature values: 29.8 29.5 29.6 29.8 29.6 29.9 29.5 29.8 29.6 29.9

From this set of initial reading, the following details are derived:

Minimum temperature $= 29.5\,^{0}C$

Maximum temperature $= 29.9\,^{0}C$

min-max range $= (29.5$ to $29.9)$

trivial interval (t) $= [(0.3 + 0.1 + 0.2 + 0.2 + 0.3 + 0.4 + 0.3 + 0.2 + 0.3)/9] = 0.255$.

Based on this *min, max and trivial* values, the behaviour of our new message priority algorithm with various message sequences is illustrated in Fig. 9.

Case 1 in Fig. 9 represents the situation where all messages are normal messages. Case 2 skips some messages within the trivial interval of previous message. Case 3 shows how the proposed algorithm treats high-priority messages and messages within trivial interval.

The configuration diagram of the proposed algorithm to assign priority to MQTT messages is given in Fig. 10. In the proposed algorithm, the priority is managed from the broker side. No modification or alteration of the MQTT packet structure or fixed header is required. Publisher clients sense data from the associated sensors/devices and transmit data packets to the broker using the standard MQTT packet forward procedure. Broker identifies the high-priority messages by using the algorithm explained. No additional overhead or computation is required at the constrained client nodes, and the additional computation or calculation is performed on the powerful server side. It saves the energy efficiency and memory capacity of the low-powered, lightweight nodes on the client side. It also increases the life of such client nodes.

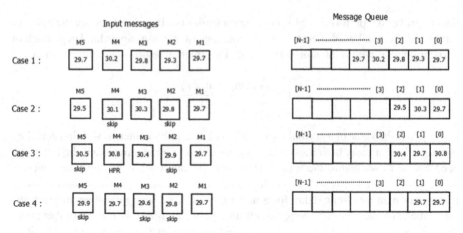

Fig. 9. Message transfer illustration

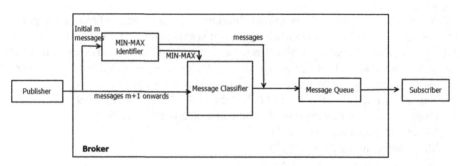

Fig. 10. System Architecture

4   Results and Discussion

Most of the existing research on prioritizing MQTT messages put the responsibility of assigning/identifying priority messages to the constrained publishing clients. In IoT applications, the input clients are devices with limited sensing, processing and memory capacity. Hence, adding the extra burden of prioritizing messages to such input devices is not desirable. Some proposed works in literature use reserved message types in the standard MQTT message format for assigning priority to messages. The four-bit message type field of the MQTT message header is used to specify the type of message, such as CONNECT, PUBLISH, SUBSCRIBE etc. It is unclear how the same four bits can also be used to denote the priority of messages. In all the proposals discussed, some modifications required in the broker. For example, in the technique that uses the first character of the topic name to determine the priority of messages, how the broker identifies the priority character is not mentioned. Some proposals indicate that a classification component classifies incoming messages into different priority queues. However, in many cases, the criteria used by the classification component to categorize messages are not clearly explained. The usage of multiple queues may increase the computational complexity of the broker server. A few other studies in literature need to increase the size of MQTT message fixed header size from two bytes to three bytes in order to set the priority field. Having small message header is one of the important advantage of MQTT protocol over other IoT communication protocols and increasing message header size is not acceptable. Some proposals need to set the input nodes that generate critical messages beforehand. Most of these shortcomings are addressed in the novel approach that is presented in this paper.

Our algorithm does not add any extra burden on the input sensing devices. The input sensors can sense the data and send it to the MQTT broker in the usual way. This method need not change the standard MQTT protocol specification. The four bits used for specifying message type can be used for the same purpose, and the reserved message types remain intact. In this work, any extra effort needed to determine the priority status of the incoming message rests on the powerful MQTT broker. The computational or processing complexity of the broker server is also not affected much as our new algorithm includes only comparison and simple mathematical computations. Each publisher's normal message range is determined during the initial training period. The training period may span from minutes to a couple of days, depending on the application. Once the normal message range is identified, our algorithm can find abnormal messages easily and treat them accordingly. Our approach can deal with many input clients and the massive quantity of data items these input devices generate. This algorithm assume that any input client can generate critical data at any point of time. All client nodes are treated equally and we need not locate priority nodes beforehand. In addition, with the help of trivial interval computed, our proposal reduces network traffic and congestion by avoiding the transmission of identical messages. This concept would be handy in many real-life situations like smart city and industrial automation.

5   Conclusion

MQTT is the most widely used protocol for IoT communications due to its lightweight nature, suitability for constrained applications, small message header etc. In many IoT applications, timely processing of critical messages from input sensors is crucial. Standard MQTT protocol cannot prioritize incoming messages. In this work, we have surveyed the attempts in the literature to assign priority to incoming messages in the MQTT protocol. Our analysis reveals that dealing with emergency messages in the internet of things scenario is a yet to explore research area. Most of the existing work in this field either overloads the constrained input clients or modifies the standard MQTT protocol specification for prioritizing input messages, which is not desirable. We have proposed a new algorithm that can prioritize the input messages irrespective of the number of client nodes and the quantity of data they produce. The client nodes and standard MQTT specifications are not affected in this approach. This procedure is able to identify the abnormal message generated by any input publisher node. The priority clients need not be located beforehand. The responsibility of determining the priority of data is with the powerful MQTT broker. This technique reduces network traffic by avoiding the transmission of identical messages. Hence our algorithm outperforms most of the existing approaches to prioritizing incoming messages. As a future work, this novel approach can be implemented with an MQTT broker and performance improvements can be monitored.

References

1. Wortmann, F., Flüchter, K.: Internet of Things. Bus. Inf. Syst. Eng. **57**(3), 221–224 (2015)
2. Somayya Madakam, R., Ramaswamy, S.T.: Internet of Things (IoT): a literature review. J. Comput. Commun. **03**, 164–173 (2015)
3. Lee, S.K., Bae, M., Kim, H.: Future of IoT networks: a survey. Appl. Sci. **7**(10), 1072 (2017)
4. Ray, P.P.: A survey on Internet of Things architectures. J. King Saud Univ.-Comput. Inf. Sci. **30**(3), 291–319 (2018)
5. Aggarwal, R., Das, M.L.: RFID security in the context of "internet of things". In: Proceedings of the First International Conference on Security of Internet of Things, pp. 51–56 (2012)
6. Al-Fuqaha, A., Guizani, M., Mohammadi, M., Aledhari, M., Ayyash, M.: Internet of things: a survey on enabling technologies, protocols, and applications. IEEE Commun. Surv. Tutorials **17**(4), 2347–2376 (2015)
7. Lawton, G.: Machine-to-machine technology gears up for growth. Computer **37**(9), 12–15 (2004)
8. Belshe, Mike, Roberto Peon, and Martin Thomson: Hypertext transfer protocol version 2 (HTTP/2). No. rfc7540. (2015)
9. Soni, D., Ashwin, M.: A survey on MQTT: a protocol of Internet of Things (IoT). In: International conference on telecommunication, power analysis and computing techniques, vol. 20, pp. 173–177 (2017)
10. Mishra, B.: TMCAS: an MQTT based collision avoidance system for railway networks. In: 2018 18th International Conference on Computational Science and Applications (ICCSA). IEEE (2018)
11. https://mosquitto.org. Accessed 26 June 2022
12. https://hbmqtt.readthedocs.io/en/latest/index.html. Accessed 05 July 2022
13. Kim, G., Park, J., Chung, K.: Priority-based multi-level MQTT system to provide differentiated IoT services. J. KIISE **45**(9), 969–974 (2018)
14. Kim, S.-J., Chang-heon, O.: Method for message processing according to priority in MQTT broker. J. Korea Inst. Inf. Commun. Eng. **21**(7), 1320–1326 (2017)
15. Kim, Y.-S., Lee, H.-H., Kwon, J.-H.: Message queue telemetry transport broker with priority support for emergency events in Internet of Things. Sens. Mater. **30**(8), 1715–1721 (2018)
16. Oh, S.-C., Kim, Y.-G.: A study on MQTT based on priority topic for IIoT. J. Inst. Internet Broadcast. Commun. **19**(5), 63–71 (2019)
17. Hwang, K., Lee, J.M., Jung, I.H., Lee, D.H.: Modification of mosquitto broker for delivery of urgent MQTT message.In: 2019 IEEE Eurasia Conference on IOT, Communication and Engineering (ECICE), pp. 166–167. IEEE (2019)
18. Al Enany, M.O., Harb, H.M., Attiya, G.: A new back-off algorithm with priority scheduling for MQTT protocol and IoT protocols. Int. J. Adv. Comput. Sci. Appl. **12**(11) (2021)
19. Jung, C.: Prioritized data transmission mechanism for IoT. KSII Trans. Internet Inf. Syst. (TIIS) **14**(6), 2333–2353 (2020)
20. Park, K., Kim, I., Park, J.: An efficient multi-class message scheduling scheme for healthcare IoT systems. Int. J. Grid Distrib. Comput. **11**(5), 67–77 (2018)
21. Abdul Ameer, H.R., Hasan, H.M.: Enhanced MQTT protocol by smart gateway. IRAQI J. Comput. Commun. Control Syst. Eng. **20**(1), 53–67 (2020)

Analysis of Crop Yield Prediction Using Machine Learning Algorithm

Chanchal Shrivastava[✉], Neha Garg, Sonali Garg, Asif Khan, and Akash Kumar

Department of CSA, ITM University, Gwalior (M.P.), India
chinkishrivastava222@gmail.com, nehagarg.cse@itmuniversity.ac.in

Abstract. We are all aware of how significant Indian agriculture is. In this study, yield estimates are provided for nearly all of the Indian crops. By using straightforward factors like temperature, humidity, season, weather, and location to produce a book, the user may predict the agricultural output in any given year. The yield is predicted by the article using sophisticated regression machine learning methods. A crucial role is played by machine learning (ML), which offers a tool for predicting crop yields. This study examines various machine learning (ML) algorithms used to estimate agricultural yields and offers a complete analysis of the approaches' accuracy.

Keywords: Agriculture · Machine Learning · Crop Prediction · supervised Algorithms

1 Introduction

In India, agriculture is both a common and low-paying profession. Design and development of artificial intelligence-based crop yield forecast that boosts output and, ultimately, profits from agricultural production Crop production forecasting demonstrates the accuracy of ML algorithms technology. The objective of the study is to provide a straightforward approach for yield forecasting by identifying several environmental factors. The future viability of agriculture is currently seriously threatened by changes in weather, climate, temperature, and other environmental issues. Crop yield prediction is a difficult process that involves a number of intricate stages. Although a higher yield prediction ability is still desired, crop yield prediction methods of today can fairly predict the actual yield.

A helpful technique that can more correctly predict yields is machine learning, a branch of artificial intelligence (AI) that focuses on learning. By identifying patterns, correlations, and patterns, machine learning (ML) may extract information from datasets. It is necessary to train the models with datasets that show the results based on prior knowledge. As various characteristics are used to create the prediction model, the parameters of the models are constructed using historical data during the training phase. Previously collected data from the training phase is used in part during the testing phase to assess performance. Farmers will be able to estimate their crop's yield using the research's findings before planting it in an agricultural field, enabling them to make educated decisions.

Need for Crop Yield Prediction

- The most significant role in national and international programming is played by crop forecasts, namely those for wheat, corn, and rice.
- Applications of ML algorithms to complicated systems with numerous inputs might result in models that are simpler and more accurate.
- It may be used to anticipate crops both long-term and short-term.

2 Literature Survey

In article [1] the authors concentrated on customer and expert evaluations for three distinct product categories: vendors, goods, and test products. Here, the majority of the cited studies attempted to ascertain how customer reviews would impact a product's price and chance of being purchased. The findings of this inquiry help to clarify the divergent conclusions of the individual research study.

In article [2], the authors compared linear regression, a more widely used statistical technique, to feed-forward neural networks. This study shows how neural networks and their statistical equivalents may be used to forecast agricultural productivity.

In article [3], the most profitable crop may be predicted using machine learning algorithms using the present weather, soil conditions, and environmental parameters, according to the authors' descriptions of an android-based application and a website. This method helps the former by giving them some control over the crops that will be cultivated, which will be advantageous to them over time.

Farmers' traditional agricultural methods are insufficient to meet the rising demand for foodstuffs. Farmers must embrace the most recent developments in agriculture, such as the utilization of cutting-edge equipment and tools and AI-based approaches, in order to meet this growing demand. It has been noted that the majority of farmers lack knowledge about pesticide applications, particularly regarding dosage and timing. These techniques have an escalating negative impact on soil fertility and yield output. Numerous academics have demonstrated how automation and AI may enhance crop growth. AI can benefit agriculture in a variety of ways. The authors explain why the following seven agricultural applications of AI.

Weather Forecasting

Weather forecasting is one of the key benefits of AI for agriculture. The most recent AI-based weather predicting technology has made it easier for farmers to make wise judgments while planning their crops, which was previously fairly difficult. Today, a variety of weather forecasting techniques are available to make forecasts about the weather. Sehgal et al. [4] presented a visual tool (ViSeed) based on long short-term memory (LSTM) [5] that may be used to predict weather and soil conditions. With the use of such farmer-friendly technology, one may properly organise their crop operations and crop kinds.

Smart Irrigation

We all know there is a water issue right now, thus we urgently need some clever irrigation methods that can irrigate more land with less water. Jha et al. have offered a comprehensive analysis of the various smart irrigation strategies. [6] However, there are a number of low-water-use irrigation options available, including sprinkler and drip watering systems. However, these choices require human intervention. By incorporating new characteristics into current irrigation systems, Intelligent irrigation systems are conceivable. The device constantly assesses the crop's water content and evaluates it against the average water need. This device may automatically start drips or sprinklers depending on the crop's need for water. For forecasting soil, Arif [7] et al. introduced ANN-based models.

Prediction of Plant Diseases and Health Monitoring

Traditional crop health monitoring methods take too long and are insufficient for large areas, such as thousands of acres. In order to overcome the problems with conventional agriculture, several researchers have developed a range of AI-based designs. Surveys of various architectural works are provided by Kamilaris and Prenafeta- Bold [8]. The use of AI-based methods that combine image processing, deep learning, and data analysis simplifies and improves disease prediction and health monitoring. The ability to continually evaluate a plant's health thanks to modern technology has enhanced methods for deciding when and how much pesticide to apply.

Weed Management

The management of weeds has traditionally included the use of herbicides, crop rotation, mechanical weed control, and other techniques. There are several alternatives for managing weeds using a mix of biochemicals; however, they all have the negative effect of lowering yield productivity [9]. The reason why agricultural productivity is dropping is because pesticides are being used more frequently and persistently in fields. AI offers an intelligent solution to this issue. AI-based weed management aims to automatically identify weeds using camera pictures gathered by autonomous robots, and then apply the necessary corrective actions (mechanical weed removal or pesticide spraying, for example). There are various AI-based techniques that are available, such as Blue River Technologies' [10] See and Spray, which uses AI to identify and spray specific plants in millisecond

Precision Agriculture

Precision farming strives to increase agricultural output and quality while reducing overall cost and environmental damage. Numerous elements, such as the soil, climate, irrigation, and others, affect a crop's production and quality. As a result, it's crucial to constantly assess each of these traits. Traditional monitoring methods fall short in order to precisely and successfully monitor these properties.

Crop Readiness Identification

An AI-based system that gathers and examines crop pictures determines if a crop is ready for harvest in a particular area. Depending on their level of preparation and other quality factors, the crops may be separated into numerous categories prior to being placed on the market. For categorization, many pattern clustering techniques are employed. Expectation maximization (EM), hierarchical clustering, fuzzy C-means (FCM), and K-means all play crucial roles.

Yield Prediction

For the past few decades, crop yield prediction has been of interest to researchers. Devices for yield mapping are needed for production prediction, however farmers [11] still do not have easy access to these tools. The issue of yield prediction may be easily and inexpensively solved using CNNs. Numerous researchers [11–13] have created crop yield prediction models utilizing AI-based techniques that make use of RGB/normalized difference vegetation index (NDVI) photos. Their experimental findings on publicly accessible datasets demonstrate the value of these models.

3   System Architecture

Crop yield prediction uses historical data, such as crop season, name, production, soil, and area parameters, to forecast a high crop yield. While deciding which characteristics are necessary for the goal feature, it constantly incorporates all the features essential for a good crop production. A yield may not be correctly represented by some. Using a linear regression technique with the response and the explanations as the two components is essential to the prediction process. The variables utilised for prediction are dependent variables in this scenario, whereas the input parameters operate independently. The most often used technique is a linear regression model, which extrapolates from current data to gauge the worth of outside domain expertise. The yield input variables are used in the range-based prediction method of the linear regression model. Additionally, farmers have made harvest projections in light of their knowledge of a certain land and crop. The entire puzzle is put together by the architectural system, which completes the specified task. A system that processes approaches to project examined agricultural statistics is suggested in this study. In our agricultural dataset, we have crop, seasons, crop year, area, and crop production (Fig. 1).

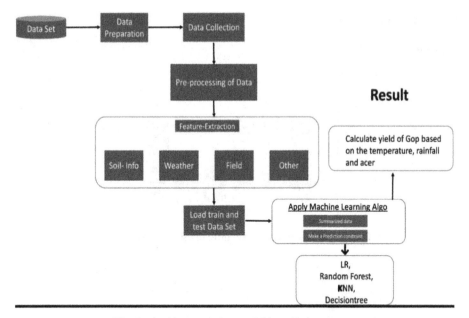

Fig. 1. Architecture of crop yield prediction system

4 Methodology

The suggested system's linear regression strategy for forecasting crop production is comprised of the subsequent steps, predicting the outcomes following analysis and the prediction entity is determined by the input entities.

The initial stage is to gather the experimental data set, which might include information on the crops and the soil as well as their results. Only the unprocessed data is difficult to obtain using the model, despite a few ways for gathering, formatting, and organizing the data.

The second phase is to gather the data, which is followed by preprocessing the dataset to remove noise and eliminate redundancy.

The third stage is splitting the data into training and testing datasets. The dataset's content has to be split into two pieces. Since the training dataset contains more information than the sample datasets do, it will teach them to deliver better results. After gathering the training samples, the testing dataset will make use of the remaining information to evaluate the system's performance.

The fourth phase is to implement machine learning algorithms, and on training datasets, linear regression yields the best results. Here, the system is reliant on both the structure and complexity of the data.

The fifth stage is using the For the test datasets, a linear regression model was trained. Calculating the R values, comparing the results to other linear regression models, and so on. One of the easy-to-use and reliable methods for predicting crop production is this one (Figs. 2, 3, 4, 5, 6).

5 Result Analysis

Coconut

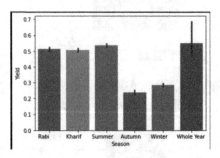

Fig. 2. Bar plot of coconut in different seasons and yield

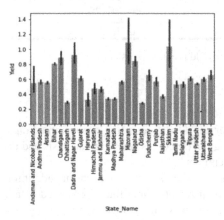

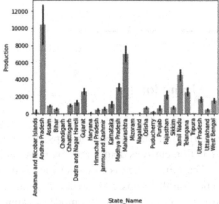

Fig. 3. Bar plot of coconut in between of coconut State name and yield

Fig. 4. Bar plot for production in different state name

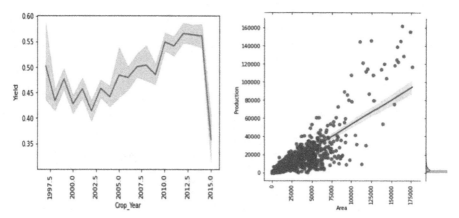

Fig. 5. Line plot in between crop between Area and year and yield

Fig. 6. Joint plot production of coconut

Result obtained:-

- Andhar Pradesh is the largest producing coconut states.
- Production per unit area in Mizoram and Sikkim.
- Coconut yield is decreasing in the year 2012 to 2015 (Figs. 7, 8, 9, 10).

Potato

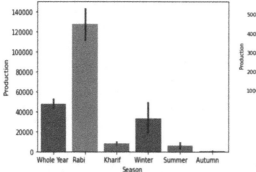

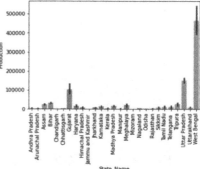

Fig. 7. Bar plot between Production of between Production potato in different seasons

Fig. 8. Bar plot in different state

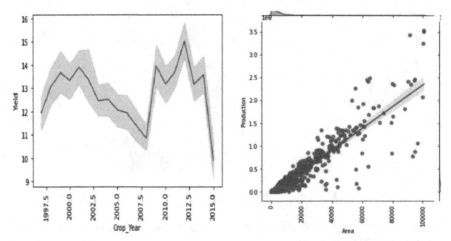

Fig. 9. Lineplot between crop year and yield

Fig. 10. Jointplot between Area and Production of Potato

Result obtained:-

- Potato is a rabi crop.
- West Bengal is the largest Producer of potato (Figs. 11, 12, 13, 14).

Onion:-

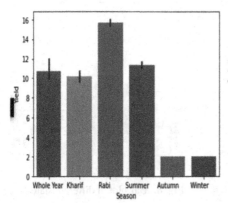

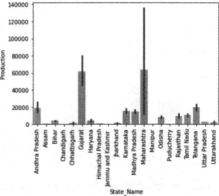

Fig. 11. Bar Plot between different production Seasons and yield

Fig. 12. Bar Plot between of onion in different states

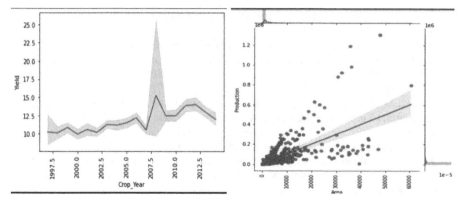

Fig. 13. Line Plot between crop year and yield

Fig. 14. Joint plot between Production of onion and area

Result obtained:-

- The Rabi crop is the onion.
- The two states that produce the most onions are Gujrat and Maharastra.

6 Conclusion

Agriculture has always been India's most vital industry for survival. Farmers encounter several challenges as a result of their ignorance. Because this document forecasts which crop to plant on which field, we must work with farmers. Making strategic judgments in crop prediction with a machine learning algorithm can help us get knowledge about the crop life, which is advantageous to farmers.

7 Future work

There will be an increasing demand for improved technology as smart agricultural techniques proliferate. The initiative, which is now a web-based programme, might be developed into an app that would allow farmers to learn more about their crop production. Once the forecast is made, we may enhance the automated procedure so that farmers can use a Smartphone app to remotely operate the field.

References

1. Ramesh, D., Vardhan, B.V.: Analysis of crop yield prediction using data mining techniques. Int. J. Res. Eng. Technol. (IJRET), **4** (2015)
2. Paswan, R.P., Begum, S.A.: Regression and neural networks models forprediction of crop production. Int. J. Sci. Eng. Res. **4**(9) (2013). ISSN 2229-5518
3. Zingade, D.S., Buchade, O., Mehta, N., Ghodekar, S., Mehta, C.: Machinelearning-based crop prediction system using multi-linear regression. Int. J. Emerg. Technol. Comput. Sci. (IJETCS) **3**(2) (2018)

4. Sehgal, S., et al.: Crop planning using stochastic visual optimization, 2017. IEEE Visual. Data Sci. VDS **2017**, 47–51 (2018)
5. Hochreiter, S., Schmidhuber, J.: Long short-term memory. Neural Comput. **9**(8), 1–32 (1997)
6. Jha, K., Doshi, A., Patel, P., Shah, M.: A comprehensive review on automation in agriculture using artificial intelligence. Artif. Intell. Agric. **2**, 1–12 (2019). https://linkinghub.elsevier.com/retrieve/pii/S2589721719300182
7. Arif, C., Mizoguchi, M., Mizoguchi, M., Doi, R.: Estimation of soil moisture in paddy field using artificial neural networks. Int. J. Adv. Res. Artif. Intell. **1**(1), 17–21 (2013)
8. Hinnell, A.C., et al.: Neuro-drip: estimation of subsurface wetting patterns for drip irrigationusing neural networks. Irrig. Sci. **28**(6), 535–544 (2010)
9. Kamilaris, A., Prenafeta-Boldú, F.X.: Deep learning in agriculture: a survey. Comput. Electron. Agric. **147**, 70–90 (2018) McAllister, W., Osipychev, D., Davis, A., Chowdhary, G.: Agbots: weeding a field with a teamof autonomous robots. Comput. Electron. Agric. **163**(September 2018), 104827 (2019). https://doi.org/10.1016/j.compag.2019.05.036
10. Chostner, B.: Smart machines for weed control and beyond (2017)
11. Nevavuori, P., Narra, N., Lipping, T.: Crop yield prediction with deep convolutional neural networks. Comput. Electron. Agric. **163**(April), 104859 (2019). https://linkinghub.elsevier.com/retrieve/pii/S0168169919306842
12. Crane-Droesch, A.: Machine learning methods for crop yield prediction and climate change impact assessment in agriculture. Environ. Res. Lett. **13**(11) (2018)
13. Pantazi, X.E., et al.: Wheat yield prediction using machine learning and advanced sensing techniques. Comput. Electron. Agric. **121**, 57–65 (2016). https://doi.org/10.1016/j.compag.2015.11.018

Big Data Analytics for Classification in Sentiment Analysis

Nikhil[✉], Mayank Singh Tomar[✉], Yogendra Singh Bhadouriya[✉],
Shalini Pandey[✉], and Harshita Chaurasiya[✉]

Department of CSA, ITM University, Gwalior, Madhya Pradesh, India
malhotra.nikhil011@gmail.com, tomarmayank101@gmail.com,
ysbhadouriya786@gmail.com, shalinipandey02135@gmail.com,
harshitachaurasiya.cse@itmuniversity.ac.in

Abstract. The term big data is for huge/immense data sets that have a very large, complex, and varied structure that the traditional methods can face trouble in storing, analyzing, and visualizing the data. Big data analytics is the utilization of advanced analytics approach on sundry data sets that include structured, semi-structured, and unstructured data of very large sizes and complexities. The suggestion/judgment that is given by someone by which their thoughts, emotion, and feelings can be shown is termed as sentiment. The type of analysis of data which are obtained from news articles, reviews, social media, or micro blogging sites is known as sentiment analysis. This paper is a review that surveys various approaches including hybrid, batch, and real-time big data and tools for the big data analytics.

Keywords: Big data · Sentiment Analysis · Classification techniques · Opinion Mining

1 Introduction

After looking over the past decade's trends we have seen that the data we are producing is not that can be measured in terra bytes or Peta bytes, rather there is a huge growth in the production of data, with which a new term emerges as big data. The market capital of big data is being increased rapidly, the term "big data" is expected to become more popular in the next years. The data that surrounds us can be broadly categorised into three types: structured, semi-structured, and unstructured data. The structured data are in low numbers compared to the unstructured data, studies tell that 80% of the worldwide data that will be generated by 2025 will be unstructured.

In year 2021, it was predicted that the total data created over the world would get to 79 zettabytes and is expected to get double by 2025. In today time the world data is nearly 90% copied, and only 10% is the real one, new data, The amount of data produced, utilised, copied, and kept is Predicted to achieve greater than 180 zettabytes by 2025. The development of big data business analytics has also been aided by the enormous usage of technology and the astonishing flow of data over time.

R. S. Tomar et al. (Eds.): CNC 2022, CCIS 1894, pp. 63–73, 2023.
https://doi.org/10.1007/978-3-031-43145-6_6

McKinsey Global Institute says that, "Big Data is a term used to describe datasets that are too large to be captured, stored, managed, and analysed by conventional database software tools. [12] With this rapid growth of data, they're growing a lot of other challenges, storing such huge data, processing big data, etc. our standard databases seem incapable of handling, storing, and processing such huge data sets. Text mining or the process of finding insights from data has always provided organizations the ability to take better decisions and to do a progressive evaluation of their own, this paper describes the various cognitive computing approaches to perform sentiment analysis/opinion mining with the help of big data analytics emerging techniques. The three main aspects that characterize big data were: volume, variety, and velocity, but with time it evolves to have two more essential properties known as veracity, and volume describes big data well.

1.1 The 5 V'S of Big Data

Volume: It is a significant characteristic of big data which helps to whether the data can be recognise as big data. The volume is the amount in with the data exist, that is the data when present in huge amount can be called as big data.

Velocity: It is also a vital characteristic of big data which refers as the rate at which the data is generated, in our everyday life the data is continuously generated in huge amount and also processed. Hence it is the speed at which data moves or generates.

Variety: This characteristic determines the different categories of big data and their source of generation, data is generating from different sources like mobiles, internet, media, IOT etc. and which is of different types such as structured, semi-structured or unstructured.

Veracity: the data which is generated is not perfect there is many uncertainty and errors, as data is in huge amount sometimes it become chaotic and its difficult to handle the quality of data.

Value: It is the most important characteristic of big data, as on considering rest characteristic the data, the data present has no importance, hence organizations processes the data so that the useful information can be add value in the growth of organization.

1.2 Big Data Generation

IoT (Internet of Things): The term Internet of Things that is also shortly called IoT is derived from the two words Internet and Things. Iot would also be called an open and comprehensive network of smart things that can automatically manage and perform tasks according to the information [9].

Social Media: At this time, social media (Meta, Tiktok, Youtube, etc.) are generating a large amount of data in the form of sentiments. Instagram has 2 billion active users, with more than 50 billion pictures and video shared in this platform.

1.3   Sentiment Analysis

Sentiment analysis is also termed as opinion mining is a way to recognise opinions from the data.[15] Opinion mining is the process that analyses the semantic orientation which can be of three types positive, negative and neutral. Human are more expressive so they give their reviews over different products, services and events etc., through social media or other platforms. The organisation uses the sentiments to make profits in their business and to provide better services to their customers.

1.3.1   Sentiment Analysis Approaches

- **Machine Learning:** We are able to apply a variety of techniques that can automatically recognise the current pattern in the data by using machine learning algorithms. It makes advantage of the underlying patterns to forecast future data or make appropriate decisions. Unsupervised and supervised machine learning are the two categories into which it can be divided. In a supervised learning environment, algorithms are first taught before being evaluated, whereas in an unsupervised learning environment, a model only has to predict under certain predetermined parameters. There exist different algorithms for supervised learning such as classification, naïve bayes, support vector machine etc. and unsupervised learning algorithm such as clustering and association [6]
- **Dictionary based:** The simplest approach to perform sentiment analysis is dictionary based approach. WordNet, SentiwordNet are openly available dictionary to perform sentiment analysis. They can be created by supplying set of sentiment word repetition of algo ends when there is no new word found in dictionary (Table 1).

Table 1. Sentiment analysis approaches

	Method	Positives	Negetives
Machine Learning	It uses various supervised and unsupervised learning algorithms	It can be customized to deal with different domains	Classification is only limited to two categories that is positive and negetives
Dictionary based	Uses wordnet, Sent wordnet are openly available dictionary to perform sentiment analysis	Computation overhead is lesser as there is not training of dataset	It is not suitable for domain specific classification
Ontology based	Uses concept of the domain which depicts the relation between the concepts	Mainly take care of semantic relationship between the features.	Updating ontology is a difficult task

2   Literature Review

In [17], In this paper to lessen the issues users have while executing big data analytics, the author develops a BBSO-FCM model and applies cognitive computing approaches to big data sentiment analysis. To handle big data, they used the Hadoop mapReduce tool. To find and filter out unusual data, they used the Term Frequency-Inverse Document Frequency (TF-IDF) technique. They also used the Binary Brain Storm Optimization (BBSO) algorithm for the Feature Selection (FS) to improve classification performance. Finally, they used a classifier to determine the positive, negative, and neutral sentiments. Uncertain Cognitive Maps (FCMs) and in this research they find that the BBSO-FCM model has the ability to perform sentiment analysis on standard data very fast and accurately.

In [18] This paper belongs to the research on Internet of vehicles it's architecture, anatomy and their open challenges and to check, how big data analytics techniques are helpful in predicting better outcome in the field of internet of vehicles (IoV). The procedure and techniques used in this paper are: first they collected data from sensory devices, information systems, electronics, and other physical objects then make ready data for transference and storage. Then they created a model which has six different levels of data transforming and analysis which are: Data accession, Data modification, Data Storage, pre-processing of data, Data analysis, Decision making. In this research they found that in future big data will have extreme bump on the future plans of IoV and it will also come up with better transportation systems, protection, trustability and provide help in developing economy.

In [19] In the following paper the study was conducted deep learning approaches in text classification by constructing a model combining the feature extraction with deep learning techniques. The data set consist of six different types in which the first three contains 43 tweets, for word embedding two different techniques word2vec and glove were carried out with previously trained word vectors and created a Feature N-model, and deep learning methods were suggested, as a result the proposed work turn out to be better as comparing with already existing techniques in text classification.

In [20] The main aim of this paper is to explore the new way of computing of big data known as BDCC- big data cloud computing this paper effectively focuses on the factor that are responsible for adoption of the big data cloud computing by the tech oriented environment in the organizations so that they can enhance their technical capabilities. The data used in this research work were taken from the organizations as research questionnaire to know much about how the organization used the big data and cloud computing whether this adoption is beneficial for them and the challenges faced by them. The results implicates that despite facing some minor challenges the organizations increased their performances and achieved customer satisfaction hence the integration of the two technologies was beneficial.

In [21] In the paper the author has explored a research on E-commerce industry by applying big data analytics techniques to understand the need of customers to increase their business and give better facilities to the customers and also for making better fruitful decisions in future in this research work they used k-means algorithm and RFM (Recency-Frequency–Monetary) algorithms on Online retail dataset to understand and increase their business by using Big data framework, and to get an exact classifying procedure for customer reviews based on online women clothing reviews.

In [22] The major focus of this work is on sentiment analysis and opinion mining, two text classification approaches that employ natural language processing (NLP) to gather views on a subject. They used machine learning; lexicon based method in the research and found that there is still unveil research area need to be improved of the Sentiment Classification algorithms or opinion mining. As well as Naive Bayes (NB) and Support Vector Machines (SVM) are the measuredly used supervised Machine learning techniques for Opinion mining or Sentiment classification. After all the observations the Author found that there is still lack of research and resources in other languages also no live procedure was found which was more appropriate to be language free.

In [23] This study combines Hadoop with Apache Flume and Hive to increase the working efficiency of the Hadoop framework. The main goal of the study is to investigate novel big data approaches for classification and sentiment analysis on Twitter data using a MapReduce application paradigm. In this study, researchers examined a number of algorithms, including Lexicon and basic NBC with uni-gram and bi-gram feature sets, and discovered that the N-gram NBC model gave 82% accuracy with a multi-cluster configuration, working more quickly than the others.

In [24] This paper is belonging to the field of automation established on Hadoop and MapReduce frameworks which are easily provided by the cloud to work on huge range of data mining and predictive analytics. In this paper they have applied different methodologies like Data Mining on MapReduce with Mahout, Text Categorization with Mahout's Naive Bayes, Build a recommended engine system with the help of cloud-based libraries, and databases like Apache Hive for data warehousing and Apache Mahout libraries for data mining in presaging analytics. Also, they have shown the results in conditions of text categorization, exhortation engine and resolution. After doing all this work they got that the Cloud is the technology which can serve you plenty of services or a platform just by paying as per the need of the user, they also engaged open-source application packages, like Hadoop, Hive and Mahout which can be easily used in big data analytics.

In [25] This paper reveals about the future opportunities of big data for sentiment analysis. This paper is divided into two parts in 1st part they analyse the features of sentiment analysis approaches with sentiment polarity recognition, sentiment classifying techniques and their applications where, in 2nd part they analyse that the sentiment analysis is suitable or not for big data frameworks, and also call attention to gaps comes in research and to investigate more on that. They used various machine learning methods in this paper like Support Vector Machine (SVM) for text classification, Naive Bayes (NB) it is a bayes theorem-based classifier used in random sampling, Maximum Entropy (ME) is a machine learning text classifier algorithm works effectively in natural language functions, by using all this method finally they got that the relationship of sentiment analysis approaches with the sentiment analysis in big data is still very strong.

In [26] In this paper the author discussed about an flexible sentiment analysis app-roach that classify social media posts and draw out useful view point from it.so they designed a dynamic dictionary of words' opposition which is lay on given set of hash-tags which looks similar to the subject, and then characterised the tweets in different classes by declaring new properties that are strongly fully tune-up the opposition of a post. They used 120000 tweets data of US president election held in 2016 and divided them into 30000 tweets for positive and negative reviews, In this paper the methods used are first they build a dictionary of sentiment words, then they use classification method where data collection, pre-processing, scoring balancing and classification is done and the last stage is of prediction, by using these methods they got that sentiment analysis or opinion mining is fruitful in analysing peoples opinion on social big data.

In [27] Sentiment analysis becomes an important part of our daily life. Sentiment analysis is a Natural Language Processing technique helps to determine whether the data is positive, negative, or neutral. As the data increasing rapidly every second it needed to be handled. The following paper included the study of Amazon's Food data that is growing exponentially. So the Big Data techniques was used to get rid from this problem. The used techniques were Linear SVC, Logistic Regression, and Naïve Bayes by using MLlib which is Apache Spark's library for ML, with the accuracy of more than 80%. The conclusion evolved at the end was that the efficiency of Linear SVC is more than Naïve Bayes and Logistic Regression.

In [28] In the era of internet most of the things is becoming easier to get. Here's the proposed work with the dataset of reviews from tourists about the hotels and the places where they stayed. These evaluations include a range of emotional undertones, therefore it requires sentiment analysis to determine if they are good, negative, or neutral more quickly. Techniques like the Multinomial Naive Bayes Classifier Method and model comparisons employing preprocessing, feature extraction, and feature selection were employed for this sort of categorization. The utilization of these processed reviews through internet to grow and evaluate their hotels and places for tourism according to the choice of tourists. From the used methods the best result is given by the processing and feature selection with 10 fold cross validation have an average F1-Score more than 91%

In [29] Twitter, a social networking service has a wide discussion over sports, health, music, technology. In there a bunch of information is available about these four and this research came about the development of a software and the categorization of this bunch using Logistic Regression. It involved fetching tweets, pre-processing, text feature extraction and machine learning. The pre-processing process included removal of URLs, punctuation, and stop words, tokenization, and stemming. In this 1800 labelled tweets for each topic were used as training dataset and than the classifier was evolved with 450 tweets for each topic. The accurate result with confusion matrix showed the classification of tweets was up to 92% in to the selected topics.

In [30] Here's the study of Surabaya restaurant customer satisfaction. This is the essential part for a business organization that requires more attention in the service to consumers. This study used the Naïve Bayes technique to get behaviour of customer through online media and WebHarvy tools for crawling of data sampling. Both the methods get customer responses but the results showed Naïve Bayes was more accurate and had a value of 72.06% which is better (about 2.94%) than TextBlob sentiment analysis.

In [31] This research work involved the study over sentiment classification task and how the online stored data can be mined as a valuable information and used for decision making. The decision that based on real time reviews was handled by various supervised machine learning classifier. Supervised machine learning classifier is the machine or software that are trained using well "labelled" training data. Real time reviews categorized into two: positive or negative. The researchers used the Naïve Bayes and

Logistic regression for the classification and the performance measured over accuracy, precision, and throughout.

In [32] Sentiment analysis in ML awards with the emotional tone from a massive amount of data but greatest assets to use Deep Learning is analysing big data. The research involves the study of the data of financial social networks such as StockTwits and Seeking Alpha. For StockTwits to execute sentiment analysis more effectively, the researcher looked into deep learning models. Convolutional neural networks (CNN), long short-term memory, and other neural network models are some of the neural network types that are utilised to analyse stock market comments published on StockTwits. The outcome of this study demonstrates that CNN, which forecasts authors' attitudes in the StockTwits dataset, is the best model for financial sentiment analysis. This study paves the way for someone to reasonably accurately forecast stock market movement via financial social networks.

In [33] The development of classifier ensemble for sentiment classification task was done in this research, using Naïve Bayes (NB), Support Vector Machine (SVM). The aim of the development was the production of more accurate classification through efficient integrated different feature sets and classification algorithm. The method used for making the classifier based on coupling classification methods using arcing classifier and the performance was analyzed in terms of accuracy. The proposed classifier ensemble showed to be superior to individual approaches for movie review data in terms of classification accuracy. The efficiency of ensemble in the areas of NLP, data mining, ML, and other had tested, presented and conclusions are drawn for sentiment analysis.

In [34] As the sentiment analysis is a helpful technique so it becomes the centre of interest among organizations with large amount of datasets with different sentiments. The Apache Spark framework, which is regarded as an open-source distributed data processing platform, was used by the author in the work that follows. Utilizing Apache Spark's MLlib is intended to handle more data effectively. It also suggests certain preprocessing and ML text feature extraction techniques for obtaining classification results from sentiment analysis. The answer analyses Apache Spark's performance in terms of its scalability and the efficacy of the suggested technique in achieving better classification results than Naive Bayes, Logistic Regression, and Decision Trees classification algorithms.

In [35] MapReduce is a programming representation which is used for efficient parallel processing of huge data sets within Hadoop clusters and widely used in the field data science, the researchers in this paper conducted study on usability, design and execution process of the Apache Hadoop and the two largely used data pre-processing frameworks of Hadoop and both supports distributed data processing. The experiment was done utilizing system usability scale (SUS) which is a tool to measure the utility, participant casted scores to the items in SUS. Participants votes shows that they preferred Apache Spark and Flink in comparison with MapReduce.

In [36] a Hybrid approach in Machine Learning Algorithms indeed is a way to experiment the better performance and accuracy. The authors in this paper performed sentiment analysis using the pipeline Spark architecture that follows some sequence at different stages, utilizing machine learning library of Spark. In the Multi-Node environment they performed text classification and used the combination of Convolutional

Table 2. Methodologies Used

Reference No.	Proposed Method	Dataset	Result	Future Scope
19.	Used deep learning method using word2vec and Ensemble of Features N-Model	6 datasets were used containing tweets	TextBlob used lexicon based approach proves to give better result over Word Sense Disambiguation	Following method can also be used for different languages and for emotion analysing
21,	used k-means algorithm and RFM (Recency-Frequency–Monetary) algorithms with big data architecture.	online retail company data, with 541909 transactions and 8 attributes	Using ML models gives a better understanding on CRM-customer relationship management	For analysing sales data similar model should ne used in future.
27.	Performed SA using Apache Spark's MLIB library algorithm used - Linear SVC, Logistic Regression, and Naïve Bayes	Amazon's food dataset consists of 568454 reviews,	Linear-SVC gives better results when used with TF-IDF vectorization.	NLP based model can be used with similar Big data frameworks.
30.	Used naïve bayes classifier and TextBlob sentiment analyser.	TripAdvisor dataset having food reviews	Accuracy of Naive Bayes classifier found to be 72.06% and that of Textblob is 69.12%	For large number of reviews the comparison can be done with implementing the similar model with big data frameworks.
32.	applied several neural network models such as long short-term memory, doc2vec, and convolutional neural networks	latest stock prices, price movement, stock exchange history StockTwits	CNN found to be most effective among the models used	Neural networks can also used to predict market analysis.
33.	Used Naive Bayes (NB), SVM, and hybrid NB-SVM Method for sentiment classification.	2000 movie reviews, 1000 labelled positive and 1000 labelled negative	Proposed hybrid NB-SVM methods shows the highest accuracy of 94.15%	Similar hybrid approaches should be used for larger data .
34.	Apache Spark's Machine learning library (MLIB) is used for getting better classification result on big data by using Naïve Bayes, Logistic Regression and Decision trees classification algorithms.	Twitter data having 1.578.627 classified tweets.	The results shows accuracy of Naive Bayes and Logistic Regression increases with increasing the volume of dataset having accuracy of 78 person both, but no such changes is seen in decision tree classification	Using deep learning models for similar dataset and comparative study can be done.
36.	Using Apache sparks MLIB TensorFlow to performed text classification using logistic regression, naïve bayes, SVM, random forest and proposed hybrid method using CNN-SVM	Amazon online product review of about 100,000 reviews	The hybrid CNN-SVM model showed accuracy of 96% tested on 8000 reviews, performs better than rest of classification algorithms.	More hybrid neural network based classification can be done on big dataset .

Neural Network- Support Vector Machine model. They provided a brief about spark's deep learning pipeline and about various ML algorithms such as random forest, logistic regression, SVM, CNN-SVM, Naïve Bayes, also they used Sparkflow for machine learning which helped to combine deep learning pipelines with tensorflow. The proposed hybrid model gives improved result as compared to additional classifiers.

In [37] This study has proposed a look over on the usage of multimodal feature learning approaches and used model based on neural network for example skip-gram, Denoising autodecoder to perform sentiment analysis on micro-blogging content. in the proposed model Continuous bag of words (CBOW) which is a architecture of word2vec word embedding model. In this work four datasets has been taken from twitter consisting of different number of tweets further they performed binary classification of the tweets, they used semi-supervised leaning method of CBOW-LR which is a elongated type of CBOW the comparison between accuracy stated that the CBOW-LR gives better results when applied on similar quantity of textual data. For acquiring better performance skip-grams and feature learning both requires large amount of datasets.

In [38] The aim of this paper was to evaluate the performance of different big data platforms, the authors in this paper has conducted comparison between apache sparks machine learning library Mlib and Sci-Kit learn and rapid miner using various text classification algorithms namely as Random forest classification, decision tree classification, logistic regression and the fourth and last gradient boosted tree regressor. The data for this experiment contains four different dataset named as, SUSY, Higgs, Hepmass and Bank marketing. The data is pre-processed and all the four algorithms both of supervised and unsupervised learning was implemented using stated different platforms and the result was evaluated. The results showed that in the case of bank data set the gradient booster tree classifier had max ROC score and proves to be top scorer attaining the accuracy of 92 percent (Table 2).

Conclusion and Future Scope

Big data is complex voluminous data set hard to manage by traditional data processing softwares, despite it is useful to address business problems that can't be tackle before. Big data analytics helps organizations to control and make use of their data to identify new opportunities. Voluminous data set is of different types and big data analytics use advance analytical techniques to process these types of data set. In the present scenario the word "big data" can be explained as Data which is generated in the areas including Internet searches, HealthCare's, Social media, Education, Geographic information systems, and Business informatics is too large in size and very difficult to process or store easily in a conventional machine that Data is can be defined as Big Data.

In the research we reviewed that in current scenario big data is performing a very important role in many fields like, education, weather forecasting healthcare, business development, big data analytics is widely used by organisations in their systems to improve their strength, deliver better customer services, make their own marketing strategies and take some actions that, eventually, can increase growth and revenue of the company by giving future prediction for better results. Using hybrid approaches of modelling the architecture proves to be better way getting good results also the processing using the cloud based computing platforms with the big data tools are the area needs to be explored more. Selection of tool according to the quantity of data present is a lacking point as sometimes it seems vague for the organization while choosing appropriate technology. In the healthcare field more work can be done on the real-time monitoring also the development of predictive and prescriptive modelling using big data analytics can be taken way further.

References

1. Kubick, W.R.: Big data, information and meaning. Appl. Clin. Trials **21**(2), 26 (2012)
2. Elgendy, N., Elragal, A.: Big data analytics: a literature review paper. In: Industrial Conference on Data Mining, pp. 214–227. Springer, Cham (2014). https://doi.org/10.1007/978-3-319-08976-8_16
3. Golchha, N.: Big data-the information revolution. Int. J. Adv. Res **1**(12), 791–794 (2015)
4. Mehta, J., Patil, J., Patil, R., Somani, M., Varma, S.: Sentiment analysis on product reviews using Hadoop. Int. J. Comput. Appl. **142**(11), 38–41 (2016)
5. Anees, A.F., Shaikh, A., Shaikh, A., Shaikh, S.: Survey paper on sentiment analysis: Techniques and challenges. EasyChair2516–2314 (2020)
6. Abirami, A.M., Gayathri, V.: A survey on sentiment analysis methods and approach. In: 2016 Eighth International Conference on Advanced Computing (ICoAC), pp. 72–76. IEEE (2017)
7. El Alaoui, I., Gahi, Y.: The impact of big data quality on sentiment analysis approaches. Procedia Comput. Sci. **160**, 803–810 (2019)
8. Court, D.: Getting big impact from big data. McKinsey Q. **1**(1), 52–60 (2015)
9. Madakam, S., Lake, V., Lake, V., Lake, V.: Internet of Things (IoT): A literature review. J. Comput. Commun. **3**(05), 164 (2015)
10. Agrahari, A., Rao, D.: A review paper on big data: technologies, tools and trends. Int. Res. J. Eng. Technol. **4**(10), 10 (2017)
11. + Big Data Statistics (2022) - Big Data Statistics 2022: How Much Data is in The World? https://firstsiteguide.com/big-data-stats/. Accessed on 25 Sept 2022
12. Shayaa, S., et al.: Sentiment analysis of big data: methods, applications, and open challenges. IEEE Access **6**, 37807–37827 (2018)
13. Chen, H., Chiang, R.H., Storey, V.C.: Business intelligence and analytics: From big data to big impact. MIS Q. **36**(4), 1165–1188 (2012)
14. Joshi, B.M., Patel, S.V.: Comparative study of analytic tools of BigData
15. Zainuddin, N., Selamat, A.: Sentiment analysis using support vector machine. In: 2014 International Conference on Computer, Communications, and Control Technology (I4CT), pp. 333–337. IEEE (2014)
16. Al-Barznji, K., Atanassov, A.: A framework for cloud based hybrid recommender system for big data mining. J. Sci. Eng. Educ. **2**, 58–65 (2017)
17. Jain, D.K., Boyapati, P., Venkatesh, J., Prakash, M.: An intelligent cognitive-inspired computing with big data analytics framework for sentiment analysis and classification. Inf. Process. Manage. **59**(1), 102758 (2022)
18. Arooj, A., Farooq, M.S., Akram, A., Iqbal, R., Sharma, A., Dhiman, G.: Big data processing and analysis in internet of vehicles: architecture, taxonomy, and open research challenges. Arch. Comput. Methods Eng. **29**, 1–37 (2021). https://doi.org/10.1007/s11831-021-09590-x
19. Pandian, A.P.: Performance evaluation and comparison using deep learning techniques in sentiment analysis. J. Soft Comput. Paradigm (JSCP) **3**(02), 123–134 (2021)
20. Na Abiodun, M. K., et al.: Cloud and big data: a mutual benefit for organization development. In: Journal of Physics: Conference Series, vol. 1767, no. 1, p. 012020. IOP Publishing (2021)

21. Zineb, E.F., Najat, R.A.F.A.L.I.A., Jaafar, A.B.O.U.C.H.A.B.A.K.A.: An intelligent approach for data analysis and decision making in big data: a case study on e-commerce industry. Int. J. Adv. Comput. Sci. Appl. **12**(7)
22. Saberi, B., Saad, S.: Sentiment analysis or opinion mining: a review. Int. J. Adv. Sci. Eng. Inf. Technol. **7**(5), 1660–1666 (2017)
23. Rodrigues, A.P., Chiplunkar, N.N.: A new big data approach for topic classification and sentiment analysis of Twitter data. Evol. Intell. **15**, 11–11 (2019). https://doi.org/10.1007/s12 065-019-00236-3
24. Hammond, K., Varde, A.S.: Cloud based predictive analytics: text classification, recommender systems and decision support. In: 2013 IEEE 13th International Conference on Data Mining Workshops, pp. 607–612. IEEE (2013)
25. Sharef, N.M., Zin, H.M., Nadali, S.: Overview and future opportunities of sentiment analysis approaches for big data. J. Comput. Sci. **12**(3), 153–168 (2016)
26. El Alaoui, I., Gahi, Y., Messoussi, R., Chaabi, Y., Todoskoff, A., Kobi, A.: A novel adaptable approach for sentiment analysis on big social data. J. Big Data **5**(1), 1–18 (2018). https://doi. org/10.1186/s40537-018-0120-0
27. Ahmed, H.M., Awan, J.M., Khan, N.S., Yasin, A., Shehzad, H. M.: Sentiment analysis of online food reviews using big data analytics Hafiz Muhammad Ahmed, MazharJaved Awan, Nabeel Sabir Khan, Awais Yasin, Hafiz Muhammad Faisal Shehzad (2021) Sentiment analysis of online food reviews using big data analytics. Elementary Educ. Online, **20**(2), 827–836 (2021)
28. Farisi, A.A., Sibaroni, Y., Al Faraby, S.: Sentiment analysis on hotel reviews using multinomial naïve bayes classifier. In: Journal of Physics: Conference Series, vol. 1192, no. 1, p. 012024. IOP Publishing (2019)
29. Indra, S.T., Wikarsa, L., Turang, R.: Using logistic regression method to classify tweets into the selected topics. In: 2016 international conference on advanced computer science and information systems (icacsis), pp. 385–390. IEEE (2016)
30. Laksono, R.A., Sungkono, K.R., Sarno, R., Wahyuni, C.S.: Sentiment analysis of restaurant customer reviews on TripAdvisor using Naïve Bayes. In: 2019 12th International Conference on Information & Communication Technology and System (ICTS), pp. 49–54. IEEE (2019)
31. Prabhat, A., Khullar, V.: Sentiment classification on big data using Naïve Bayes and logistic regression. In: 2017 International Conference on Computer Communication and Informatics (ICCCI), pp. 1–5. IEEE (2017)
32. Sohangir, S., Wang, D., Pomerants, A., Khoshgoftaar, T.M.: Big data: deep learning for financial sentiment analysis. J. Big Data **5**(1), 1–25 (2018)
33. Govindarajan, M.: Sentiment classification of movie reviews using hybrid method. Int. J. Adv. Sci. Eng. Technol. **1**(3), 73–77 (2014)
34. Elzayady, H., Badran, K.M., Salama, G.I.: Sentiment analysis on twitter data using apache spark framework. In: 2018 13th International Conference on Computer Engineering and Systems (ICCES), pp. 171–176. IEEE (2018)
35. Akil, B., Zhou, Y., Röhm, U.: Technical Report: On the Usability of Hadoop MapReduce, Apache Spark & Apache Flink for Data Science (2018). arXiv preprint arXiv:1803.10836
36. Raviya, K., Vennila, M.: An implementation of hybrid enhanced sentiment analysis system using spark ml pipeline: a big data analytics framework. Int. J. Adv. Comput. Sci. Appl. **12**(5) (2021)
37. Baecchi, C., Uricchio, T., Bertini, M., Del Bimbo, A.: A multimodal feature learning approach for sentiment analysis of social network multimedia. Multimedia Tools Appl. **75**(5), 2507–2525 (2016). https://doi.org/10.1007/s11042-015-2646-x
38. Junaid, M., et al.: Performance evaluation of data-driven intelligent algorithms for big data ecosystem. Wireless Pers. Commun. **126**(3), 2403–2423 (2022). https://doi.org/10.1007/s11 277-021-09362-7

Ensemble Classifiers for Classification of Imbalanced Dataset of Malicious and Benign Websites

Sanjay Jain[✉]

Department of CSA, ITM University Gwalior, Gwalior, India
sanjayjain@itmuniversity.ac.in

Abstract. Today, we have millions of websites on the internet and it is important for users to be able to distinguish between potentially hazardous websites and genuine websites in order to safeguard one's personal information. In this paper, the collected dataset is imbalanced because in real-life benign websites are more as compared to Malicious websites. Therefore, balancing has done using Synthetic Minority Oversampling Technique(SMOTE). A dataset is analyzed using various factors such as the URL of the website, IP address and other factors, and applied to Naive Bays, KNN, Logistic regression, Decision Tree and ensemble machine learning models. We performed experiments on both unbalanced and balanced data sets of malicious and benign websites. Experimental studies using a number of benign and malicious websites from real Internet resources have shown better prediction performance on balanced data-sets compared to unbalanced data-sets. We have achieved an accuracy of about 99.85% using ensemble based classifiers.

Keywords: Ensemble classifier · Malicious and Benign Websites · Machine Learning · Imbalanced dataset

1 Introduction

The size, scope, and amount of information on the Internet is constantly increasing. Billions of people contribute to the wonders of the Internet every day. According to the latest statistics available, the number of Internet users is about 4.66 billion. This represents about 59% of the total population of the planet! The exact number of websites changes every second, but the World Wide Web has well over a billion websites (against 1,167,715,133 in January 2022, according to Netcraft's March 2022 web server survey. And 1,169,621,187).

The advancement in technology has opened up a new world, where all of our day-to-day activities such as banking, shopping, socializing etc. happen in a virtual cyberspace. This also opens up an opportunity for more cybercrimes and hence it is imperative to have methods to protect an internet user from various threats like phishing, link spamming, redirection spamming and DNS spoofing. Even though there are security tools used today to detect malicious websites, attackers use different methods to avoid detection by these methods. The most popular method to detect malicious websites is to keep a

R. S. Tomar et al. (Eds.): CNC 2022, CCIS 1894, pp. 74–88, 2023.
https://doi.org/10.1007/978-3-031-43145-6_7

record of blacklisted URLs. But this method is useless when it comes to new websites being created because the list cannot keep up with the numerous number of websites being created every day. Another method that is used for identifying malicious websites is Page Content Analysis. This is a more detailed analysis approach compared to the blacklist method. A downside to this method is the considerable amount of data that is to be collected about a particular website. Researchers have evolved various methods to locate malicious websites using distinct learning algorithms, however this problem still desires more attention from the researchers due to the fact new malicious web sites are being deployed every day and Attackers are using unique techniques to release their attacks. As a result, maximum solutions to malicious assaults are primarily based on small experimental datasets, and it is not feasible to establish the accuracy and effectiveness of these algorithms for truly huge datasets.

Therefore, the number of malicious websites is growing rapidly, and we also need to consider ways to detect malicious websites in real time from a large number of legitimate websites. It is imperative to develop intelligent algorithms that can detect more and more malicious attacks. On the Internet, Malicious Webpage's are few compared to Benign Webpage's. Therefore, during any machine learning process, adequate measures will have to be undertaken to handle or compensate this imbalance in order to get accurate results. In our proposed work, Our aim is to do the data analysis, data balancing and create a Machine learning classifier to classify a website as Malignant or Benign based on the features present in the dataset.

The rest of this paper is organized as follows. In Sect. 2 related work is discussed. Section 3 discusses the proposed approach. Data used for the experiments, relevant features in predicting malicious websites, Data analysis and preprocessing, data sampling and balancing techniques and the various classifiers, used for classification of malicious and benign websites are discussed. In Sect. 4, we discuss the performance evaluation of the various machine learning techniques used. Finally, the conclusion is presented in Sect. 5.

2 Related Work

Author [1] has proposed a solution that compares the implementation of the identification procedure with various detection strategies. SVM isapplied as machine learning model for abuse detection. The recognition accuracy has improved to 98.9%. The author [2] proposed an approach based on URL dictionaries and page content properties. He has Achieved 97% accuracy. This indicates a high true positive rate for functional group combinations.

The author [3] used logistic regression, sparse random projection, and deep learning architecture. A stacking denoising auto encoder was used to split the main layer from the highlights. He used LR as a ML model to characterize as malicious. More than 27,000 samples have been marked, with 95% accuracy and a FPR of at most fewer than 4.2%. The author [4] has recommended to create a list of, IP addresses, blacklisted domains, and URLs. The dataset used was a human response/blacklisted IPA. As a result, harmful website recognition can now be performed in actual time based on a specific list of IP addresses, URLs, and domains.

Creator [5] combines diverse attribute sets and attribute values with dynamically created website execution snapshots, timely updated feature types and value sets, and a richer feature set. The most important findings of this study were functional scope and functional values.

The author' [6] uses SVM to recognize malicious URLs. Two multi-tag placement strategies are used to differentiate between attack types. The records used are harmless URLs, spam URLs, phishing URLs, and malware URLs. As a result, the accuracy of this method is 98.2%. The author [7] addressed a feature extraction solution and used an online learning method. As a result, we found that this solution was 97% accurate. The author of [8] has proposed a method that provides two types of elements for web phishing. They had the ability to achieve a TPR of about 90% and a FPR of 0.6%.

The author [9] has used different machine learning approaches. A PhishTank dataset consisting of 6157 real websites and 4898 phishing websites were used. The author's in [10] proposes to use machine learning such as Naive Bayes, SVM, and ANN algorithms to group malicious web code for multiple purposes and detect user input abuse. Models show an accuracy of 98.60, 98.88, 98.60 respectively.

The author [11] identified web phishing based on related image, frame, text highlighting, and related artificial calculations on real and non-real pages. This method showed an accuracy of about 98.3%. In the article [12], the author systematically analyzed the properties of malicious websites and introduced crucial attributes of machine learning. The algorithms used include decision trees,naive Bayes, boost decision trees, and SVMs with an accuracy of 58.28, 94.74, 93.52, and 96.14,,respectively.

In the article [13], the author discuss various classification approaches of machine learning The most powerful classifiers are used to detect dangerous websites from the OpenPhish domain. The author [14] has used the SCIKIT learnlibrary to implement a multi-layer perceptron, random forest classifier, logistic regression, and decision tree classifiers. Each has a tokenized dataset and training and testing dataset, and result shows a slight difference in the accuracy of the results obtained from different classifiers.

In article [15], the detection model includes several components, such as malicious URL detection engine, topic analyzer, web page analyzer, comprehensive analysis and labeling engine, attack classification engine, and output. The author's in [16] proposed the new capsule-based neural network consists of four branches and uses a convolution layer and a two-layer capsule to determine if the URL is a legitimate URL or a phishing URL. To improve the generalization of the approach, the output of all four layers is averaged.

The author [17] proposed a method using logistic regression. The records provided to the algorithm contain various characteristics of the URL that the algorithm uses to determine which URLs are legitimate and which are not. The result was 98.42%.

The author in [18] uses machine learning techniques to identify malicious websites. He has achieved a accuracy of around 93%. The analysis of these relevant existing methods showed that the majority of presented machine learning methods have several restrictions.

3   Proposed Methodology

Our proposedmethodologyis shownin Fig. 1. In the Data acquisition phase, the dataset has acquired from Kaggle and then data summarization has done to understand the dataset. In the next phase, we have done the data analysis and itspre-processing. We have done the sampling and balancing of data in the Data Balancing phase usingsampling and balancing methods. We have done the splittingofdatasetintotrainingandtesting dataset. After that, variousmachine learningalgorithms have applied on the dataset. Evaluation of various machine learning models has done in the Performance analysis phase.

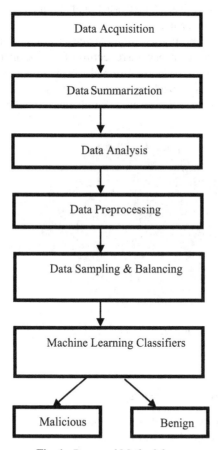

Fig. 1. Proposed Methodology.

3.1   Data Acquisition

The dataset for this work is taken from Kaggle. It consist of 11 attributes and over 0.364 million observations. The dataset contains extracted attributes from websites that can be used for Classification of webpage's as malicious or benign. The data has been collected by crawling the Internet using MalCrawler [19]. The labels have been verified using the Google Safe Browsing API [20]. Attributes have been selected based on their relevance [21]. The dataset comprises of 10 predictor features and one Class Label.

3.2 Data Summarization

On the Internet, Malicious Webpage's are few compared to Benign Webpage's. This inequality shows in our dataset as well, since it has been scraped from Internet. The class label attribute has two values- 'good' and 'bad' corresponding to Benign and Malicious Webpage's respectively. The Class Label and its inequality is visualized and analyzed in Fig. 2 using pie-chart.

Here we notice that the proportion of good websites in the dataset is larger as compared to bad websites. This imbalance is a reflection of the real internet where the number of good websites are more in proportion to bad websites and hence it can be used for effective analysis. During any machine learning process, adequate measures will have to be undertaken to handle or compensate this imbalance in order to get accurate.

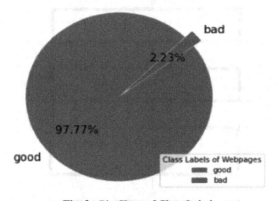

Fig. 2. Pie Chart of Class Label.

3.3 Data Analysis and Preprocessing

It is imperative to understand the relationship between the target variable and predictor variable to design a good machine learning models. Plots have been plotted to analyze the relationship of 'who_is' and 'https' variables with the target variable 'label'.

Figure 3 shows the proportion of good and bad websites with respect to the different classes in who_is and https columns. Https column implies whether the given website has a secure http or not. The who_is column refers to whether the who_is lookup returns the complete information regarding a website or not. The who_is lookup searches the who_is register for details regarding a website such as who or what entity owns or manages that domain name, including their contact information such as name, phone number and address. We see that the proportion of bad websites are more for cases where

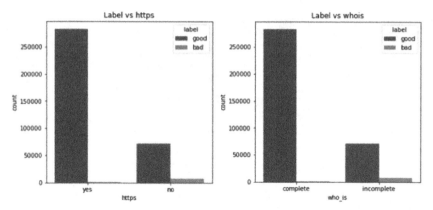

Fig. 3. Proportion of good and bad websites with respect to the different classes in who_is and https columns respectively.

the websites are not secured using https and also, in cases where the information of who owns a malicious website [who_is] is not readily available. Hence, a website is more likely to be safe if it uses https protocol as compared to those with http and if the who_is registration details are complete.

Another factor that may have an impact in the authenticity of a website is the geographical location where the site is registered. As it is not right to compare based on the number of benign or malicious websites alone, we come up with a relation that captures the relative proportion between the two types of websites in a particular country. A plot have been plotted in order to show the safety of websites from a country using the expression

$$ \mathrm{SWC} = \frac{\mathrm{NBW} - \mathrm{NMW}}{\mathrm{NBM} + \mathrm{NMW}} \tag{1}$$

where, SWC is Safety of websites in a country, NBW is Number of benign websites and NMW is Number of malicious websites. The safety factor for websites from each country is calculated and plotted. As the safety score for the websites from a country increase, it signifies that the country produces a better proportion of benign websites as compared to malicious ones. In the Fig. 4 graph, countries that are dark green are said to be producing the safest websites. The quality of websites decreases as the colour changes from darker shades of green to lighter shades to yellow to red. We see that Sri Lanka, Greenland, Guayana, Zimbabwe, Somalia, Ethiopia, South Sudan, Congo Republic, Guinea, Mali, Mauritiana, Niger, Chad, Libya, Uzbekistan, Tajikistan, Kazakhstan, Laos and New Guinea makes the safest websites according to the dataset with a safety score of 100%. Also it can be noted that Mongolia, Myanmar, Senegal, Afghanistan, Sierra Leone and Guinea are the countries that have comparatively lower safety scores.

A countplot for top-level-domain has shown in Fig. 5. It can be observed that different domains offer different probabilities for a site to be malicious. Out of the various observations, it can be noted that the '.gov' domain used for government websites are completely safe as per the given dataset. Also it can be noted that most of the.tw,.cn and.ie websites are authentic and can be trusted by the user.

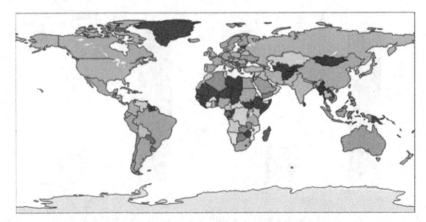

Fig. 4. Plot of safety factor for websites from each country.

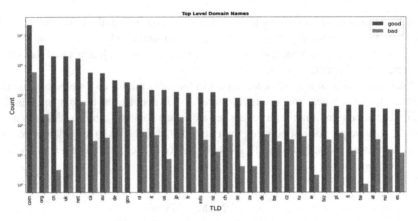

Fig. 5. Countplot for top-level-domain.

Our dataset contains various columns where the data is of type object. This is not suitable for prediction using machine learning algorithms. Therefore, we need to convert these into numerical values. The columns who_is, https, label, geo_loc and tld contain various categorical values of type object. We map each of these to numerical values using label encoder. After this operation, the dataset and its data types are shown in Fig. 6.

We have java script code length as well as obfuscated java script code length in our dataset. Obfuscated java script code is made from performing a series of transformations on the java script code and it is converted into a form that is hard to understand and reverse engineered. This is done in order to hide the logic of the code from the user as well as to reduce the size of the java script code. Since it is the java script code that is being obfuscated, we find that the columns that give the information regarding both of these parameters are correlated. This can be observed from the correlation plot as well as the scatter plot shown in Fig. 7.

```
<class 'pandas.core.frame.DataFrame'>
RangeIndex: 361934 entries, 0 to 361933
Data columns (total 11 columns):
 #   Column      Non-Null Count    Dtype
---  ------      --------------    -----
 0   url         361934 non-null   object
 1   url_len     361934 non-null   int64
 2   ip_add      361934 non-null   object
 3   geo_loc     361934 non-null   int64
 4   tld         361934 non-null   int64
 5   who_is      361934 non-null   int64
 6   https       361934 non-null   int64
 7   js_len      361934 non-null   float64
 8   js_obf_len  361934 non-null   float64
 9   content     361934 non-null   object
 10  label       361934 non-null   int64
dtypes: float64(2), int64(6), object(3)
memory usage: 30.4+ MB
```

Fig. 6. Attributes present in the dataset with their datatypes.

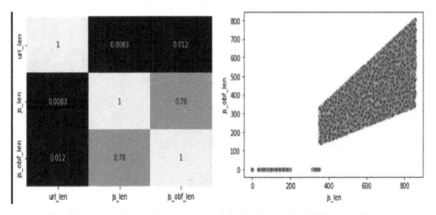

Fig. 7. Correlation and scatter plot of 'js_len' and 'js_obf_len' attributes.

We can observe from the plot that there is a positive correlation of 0.78 between 'js_len' and 'js_obf_len'. Also it can be seen from the scatter plot that the two parameters vary uniformly with each other. Hence for evaluation, it is necessary to use only one of these features. Hence the column js_obf_len is dropped. Now we also observe that the IP-address is also an object. We have IPv4 addresses. We can extract a lot of information from an IP-address, such as the class of the IP-address. We split the ip-address into 4 where each part is a byte of the IP address and these spitted values are converted to numeric data type and appended back into the data frame as separate columns for further analysis.

We now observe that we have two columns, namely url and content whose data type is object. It is imperative that we convert these to numerical values for prediction. For proper analysis of the content, we first remove the stopwords from the content. Stopwords are commonly used words in English such as "is", "and" etc. which do not contribute to the sentiment or validity of the content in a website and hence can be ignored. This was followed by stemming the data in the content column. Stemming is the process wherein we reduce words into their root form. In order for the content to be subjected to various classification algorithms, it is required to transform the text data into numerical data. For this, we apply the technique of count vectorization to the data.

Count vectorization is the process of transforming a text into a vector on the basis of the frequency of each word in the text. We have set the max_feature parameter during count vectorization as 500. This implies that we are taking the most significant/most occurring 500 words from the dataset for the purpose of analysis. After this operation, we will have 500 more columns or parameters for consideration while prediction.

Similarly, the above method of count vectorization has also been applied on URL. This was done after we split the url into individual words after removing the dots[.] and slashes [/] in the URL. Various parameters such as top-level domain [.com,.org etc.] as well as words like http, https and www are removed from the url. These are not necessary here as we already have separate columns for http and tld in the dataset. A box plot is plotted for url_len and it can be observed that there exists some outliers as shown in Fig. 8.

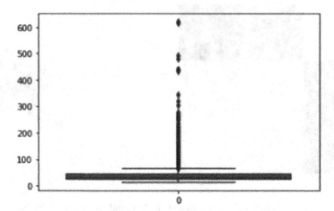

Fig. 8. Box plot of url_len attribute.

The IQR(Inter quartile range) is calculated and values less than minimum and greater than maximum are dropped, where

$$maximum = thirdquartile + 1.5 * IQR. \tag{2}$$

$$minimum = firstquartile - 1.5 * IQR. \tag{3}$$

3.4 Data Sampling and Balancing

There are two issues in our dataset one is the large number of observations in the dataset around .364 millions. It is very difficult to train the machine learning models using such a large dataset. Therefore, we have done the conditional random sampling and keep all the malicious observation from the original dataset and 10% random samples from the benign observations. Another issue is of unbalancing of data. Imbalanced data refers to the type of dataset in which the distribution of observed values in the target class is uneven. One class label has a very large number of observations and the other class label has a very small number of observations. In our dataset, the Label target class has a large number of observations of benign (97.77%) compared to malignant (2.23%). Here, the "benign" class is called the majority class, and the much smaller "malicious" class is called the minority class because of the large number of observations in the dataset.

The main question in predicting an imbalanced dataset is how accurately both the majority and minority classes are actually predicted. If there are far more records in one particular class than in another, the classifier can be biased towards prediction. In our case, it is important to identify the minority class. i.e., a malicious website to identify correctly. Resampling is used to up sample or down sample minority or majority classes. If you use an unbalanced dataset, you can oversample the minority class by replacing it. This technique is called oversampling. Similarly, you can randomly remove rows from the majority class to match a minority class called under sampling. After sampling the data, you can get a balanced dataset of both majority and minority classes.

However, simply adding duplicate minority class records often does not add new information to the model. Therefore, we used the Synthetic Minority Oversampling Technique (SMOTE) to oversample minority classes. SMOTE synthesizes a new instance from existing data. SMOTE examines the minority class instances, uses the k-nearest neighbors to select the random nearest neighbors, and randomly generates synthetic instances in the feature space. SMOTE has generate the balanced dataset. Now we have 67030 total observations in the dataset in which 33214 are benign and 33816 are malicious observations. We can Cleary see that both class label have equal representation in the target class.

3.5 Machine Learning Classifiers

In this phase our main task is to categorize the websites as malicious and benign using the preprocessed data created in the earlier step. We have used various supervised machine learning algorithms to determine which is the best algorithm that helps in classifying the website with maximum accuracy. The dataset has divided into training and testing part(80:20) ratio for building machine learning classifiers.

We have used numerous classifiers for training, testing and evaluating the performance. Naive Bayes (NB), Logistic Regression (LR), K-Nearest neighbours (KNN), Decision Tree (DT), Random Forest (RF), XGBoost, AdaBoost, Gradient Boost, DT Bagging and RF Bagging. Figure 9 shows the confusion matrix of different classifiers using balanced dataset of malicious and benign websites.

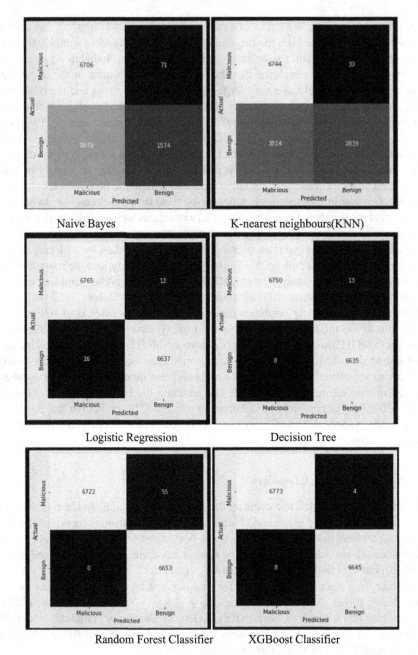

Fig. 9. Confusion Matrix of various Machine Learning Classifiers.

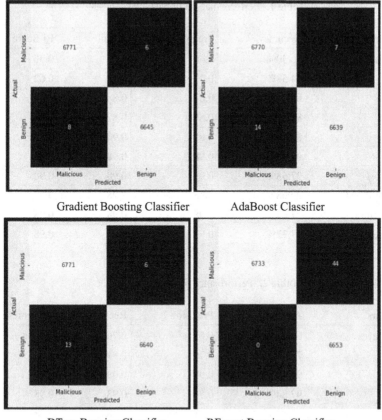

Gradient Boosting Classifier   AdaBoost Classifier

DTree Bagging Classifier   RForest Bagging Classifier

Fig. 9. (*continued*)

4   Performance Evaluation

Various performance indicators such as accuracy, precision, recall and F1 score were used to measure the effectiveness of the applied method.

Tables 1 and 2 summarizes the results (accuracy, precision, recall, F1-score) of all the classifiers: Naive Bayes, LR, KNN, Decision Tree, Random Forest, XGBoost, AdaBoost, Gradient Boost, DT Bagging and RF Bagging for balanced and imbalanced malicious and benign websites dataset, respectively. The accuracy and F1 score shows that the ensemble based models has higher accuracy on balanced dataset.

Table 1. Performance on Imbalanced data set.

Classifiers	Accuracy	Precision	Recall	F1 Score
Naive Bayes	36.30%	0.60	0.61	0.36
KNN	64.58%	0.72	0.78	0.62
LR	88.36%	0.87	0.88	0.87
DT	89.41%	0.89	0.89	0.89
RF	89.40%	0.88	0.90	0.89
XGBoost	97.67%	0.98	0.98	0.98
Ada Boost	97.63%	0.98	0.98	0.98
Gradient Boost	97.68.%	0.98	0.98	0.98
DT Bagging	97.64%	0.98	0.98	0.98
RF Bagging	97.37%	0.97	0.97	0.98

Table 2. Performance on balanced data set.

Classifiers	Accuracy	Precision	Recall	F1 Score
Naive Bayes	61.35%	0.61	0.76	0.55
KNN	70.52%	0.70	0.81	0.68
LR	97.78%	0.98	0.98	0.98
DT	97.84%	0.98	0.98	0.98
RF	97.54%	0.98	0.98	0.98
XGBoost	99.85%	1.00	1.00	1.00
Ada Boost	99.81%	1.00	1.00	1.00
Gradient Boost	99.83%	1.00	1.00	1.00
DT Bagging	99.85%	1.00	1.00	1.00

The accuracy obtained by using various algorithms are illustrated in the Fig. 10 for imbalanced and balanced dataset, respectively. We can clearly see from the accuracy tables and bar plots ensemble based classifier having high accuracy in comparison to other machine learning models on both imbalanced and balanced dataset. We have achieved a highest accuracy 99.85% from ensemble methods on balanced dataset.

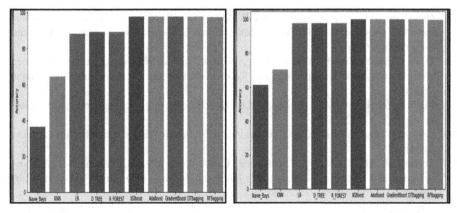

Fig. 10. Bar Plots of accuracy scores of imbalanced and balanced dataset.

5 Conclusion

We have analyzed the dependence of various features of a website and how it can be used to determine the authenticity of a website. Different machine learning algorithms were applied in order to come up with the algorithm that classifies the website as benign or malignant based on the factors under consideration. Based on the accuracy score observations, we can observe that ensemble based classifier having high accuracy. However, with technology developing day by day, thousands of websites are created on the internet day to day and hackers evolving with newer techniques, makes cyber security a serious threat for web users. Despite the advancement of artificial intelligence and machine learning, it is still a big challenge to ensure cyber security over the internet.

References

1. Yoo, S., Kim, S.: Two-phase malicious web page detection scheme using misuse and anomaly detection. Int. J. Reliable Inf. Assur. **2**(1), 1–9 (2014)
2. Sirageldin, A., Baharudin, B.B., Jung, L.T.: Malicious web page detection: A machine learning approach. In: Advances in Computer Science and its Applications: CSA 2013, pp. 217-224. Research Gate. Springer, Berlin Heidelberg (2014). https://doi.org/10.1007/978-3-642-41674-3_32
3. Wang, Yao, Cai, Wan-dong, Wei, Peng-cheng: A deep learning approach for detecting malicious JavaScript code. Secur. Commun. Net. **9**(11), 1520–1534 (2016). https://doi.org/10.1002/sec.1441
4. J Forensic Sci & Criminal Inves, Malicious Website Detection: A Review, Journal of forensic sciences and criminal investigation ISSN 2476–1311, 2018
5. Eshete, B., Villafiorita, A., Weldemariam, K.: Malicious website detection: Effectiveness and efficiency issues. In: Proceedings of the 2011 International Conference on Machine Learning and Cybernetics, Guilin, pp. 10–13 (2011)
6. Choi, H., Zhu, B.B., Lee, H.: Detecting malicious web links and identifying their attack types. Research Gate (2011)

7. Zhang, W., Ding, Y.X., Tang, Y., Zhao, B.: Malicious web page detection based on on-line learning algorithms. In: IEEE Xplore: International Conference on Machine Learning and Cybernetics (2011)
8. Yi, P., Guan, Y., Zou, F., Yao, Y., Wang, W., Zhu, T.: Web phishing detection using deep learning framework. Hindawi Wireless Communications and Mobile Computing Volume (2018)
9. Shahrivari, V., Darabi, M.M., Izadi, M.: Phishing detection using machine learning techniques, Research Gate (2020)
10. Komiya, R., Paik, I., Hisada, M.: Classification of Malicious Web Code by Machine Learning (2011)
11. Adebowale, M.A., Lwin, K.T., Sánchez, E., Hossain, M.A.: Intelligent Web-Phishing Detection and Protection Scheme using integrated Features of Images, Frames and Text (2018)
12. Hou, Y.T., Chang, Y., Chen, T., Laih, C.S., Chen, C. M.: Malicious web content detection by machine learning (2009)
13. Janet, S.B., Kumar, R.J.A.: Malicious URL Detection (2021)
14. Ganesh, J.S., Swarup. V.N., Kumar, R.M., Harinisree, A.: Machine Learning Based Malicious Website Detection (2020)
15. Zhao, S.Z., Yan, H.: Detecting Malicious Websites in Depth through Analyzing Topics and Web-page, Research Gate (2018)
16. Huang, Y., Qin, J., Wen, W.: Phishing URL Detection Via Capsule-Based Neural Network, IEEE 13th International Conference on Anti-counterfeiting, Security, and Identification(ASID) (2019)
17. Anandkumar, V.: Malicious-Url Detection Using Logistic Regression Technique, International Journal Of Engineering Business Management (2019)
18. James, J., Sandhya, L., Thomas, C.: Detection of Phishing URLs Using Machine Learning, International Conference on Control Communication and Computing (ICCC) (2013)
19. Singh, A.K., Goyal, Navneet: MalCrawler: A crawler for seeking and crawling malicious websites. In: Padmanabhan Krishnan, P., Krishna, Radha, Parida, Laxmi (eds.) Distributed Computing and Internet Technology, pp. 210–223. Springer International Publishing, Cham (2017). https://doi.org/10.1007/978-3-319-50472-8_17
20. https://developers.google.com/safe-browsing
21. Singh, A.K., Goyal, N.: A comparison of machine learning attributes for detecting malicious websites. In: 2019 11th International Conference on Communication Systems & Networks (COMSNETS), pp. 352–358. IEEE (2019)

Forecasting of Congestive Cardiac Failure Using Deep Learning Algorithms

H. Harish[1,2(✉)], Anita Patrot[1], A. Sreenivasa Murthy[2], M. V. Anushri[1], S. Meghana[1], and M. Vinutha[1]

[1] Maharani Lakshmi Ammanni College for Women Autonomous, Bangalore, India
hh.harish@gmail.com
[2] Electronics and Communication Department, UVCE, Bangalore University, Bangalore, Karnataka, India

Abstract. It is common knowledge that the heart is a veryimportant organ than the brain, despite the fact that both organs play crucial roles in the human body. It circulates blood, cleanses it, and distributes it to every part of the body. Nowadays, heart disorders are prevalent regardless of age. Heart cardiopathy is linked to fatality cases all around the world. Forecasting the incidence of heart cardiopathy is becoming necessary as instances rise and the condition does not strike suddenly. We must raise public knowledge of cardiac illnesses to bring awareness. Heart cardiopathy can be predicted using embedded intuitions in computer programs. A vast amount of patient information will be gathered and analyzed to forecast the growth of the disease. This study examines the predictive power of embedded intuitions in a computer program for heart disease. With the help of Cleveland dataset, Naive Bayes (NB), Artificial Neural Network (ANN), the Support Vector Machine (SVM), and Convolutional Neural Network (CNN) are utilized. Heart illness is implemented using the Jupyter notebook technology.

Keywords: Heart cardiopathy · Jupyter notebook · TensorFlow · Keras · Accuracy · Machine learning · Deep learning · Supervised · Unsupervised · ANN · CNN · SVM · NB

1 Introduction

By pumping blood, blood is distributed to every organs of the body, and purifying blood, the heart serves a vital role within the human structure. If the heart does not receive sufficient blood, it can lead to heart failure and even death. To increase the safety of life, it is essential to accurately and quickly identify cardiac cardiopathy. Rheumatic cardiopathy, controller cardiopathy, hypertensive heart disease, and cerebral vascular heart disease are all causes of heart failure.

Semeiotic– Chest pain or discomfort, shortness of breath, fainting, swelling of abdomen,limbs, or black spots around the eyes, and easily exhausting during activities and exercises.

© The Author(s), under exclusive license to Springer Nature Switzerland AG 2023
R. S. Tomar et al. (Eds.): CNC 2022, CCIS 1894, pp. 89–99, 2023.
https://doi.org/10.1007/978-3-031-43145-6_8

Machine learning algorithms enable us to predict and classify a wide range of heart conditions, assisting medical professionals in preventing sudden death in such circumstances. To Analyzethe growth of the disease, a significant amount of patient information will be gathered and analyzed. This study involves four different algorithms—Support Vector Machine, Naive Bayes, Artificial Neural Network, and Convolutional Neural Network—that have been applied.

The maingoal of this study is to find the accuracy of two deep learning and two machine learning algorithms and determine which is the more effective methodin predicting heart disease.

Even if heart disease symptoms are there and one of the typical facts is that not all of the symptoms will appear at once, it is terrible to recognize heart disease early or in its early stages. Therefore, it is crucial to recognize heart illnesses early in order to prevent death or lower the mortality rate. Since detecting heart illness is quite expensive, most people choose not to visit a doctor for advice for various reasons. The challenge in this paper is determining whether or not each individual will develop cardiac disease,from the information gathered about them.

The study employs DL and ML methods at utterly distinct levels of evaluation to accomplish the required goal. Despite the widespread use of DL and ML algorithms, the analysis of cardiac disease is anessential step in measuring the highest level of accuracy. As a result, several types of evaluation procedures are done to evaluate these algorithms. This will assist researchers and medical professionals in understanding the problem better and finding the most effective ways to forecast cardiac disease.

This study primarily contributes to Extracting categorized accuracy relevant for predicting heart illness, contrasting various ML and DL algorithms, and determining the optimal performance-based algorithm for predicting heart disease.

Artificial intelligence (AI) uses ML, which enables systems to automatically learn from their knowledge and get better over time without having to be explicitly programmed. ML is typically used when people train the computer then the work can be completed much more quickly.

Three categories of ML algorithms are recognized:

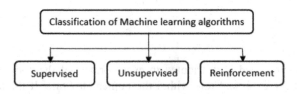

Fig. 1. ML classifications

Supervised Learning

Supervised learning has a supervisor as a teacher. In general, teaches or trains the machine using data that is well labeled. Supervised learning pacts with or studies with "categorized" data. This shows that some data is already tagged with the correct answer.

Classified into two types:

- Classification – employed when the result is categorical, such as "Yes" or "No."
    Algorithms used:
- Logistic Regression
- K Nearest Neighbour
- Random Forest
- Decision Tree
- Naïve Bayes
- Regression – employed when a value, such as stock prices, needs to be forecasted.

The algorithm used: Linear Regression (LR).

Unsupervised Learning
This is the procedure of teaching a computer or machine to use unlabelled, unclassified data and allowing the algorithm to function on the data without supervision. Since there is no teacher present in this, the machine won't receive any instruction. Categorized into two types:

- Clustering - When data needs to be arranged to uncover patterns, "product recommendation" clustering is used. The algorithm used: K means clustering
- Dimensionality Reduction

Reinforcement Learning
The actions and their outcomes, a computer learns how to operate in a given environment through the use of reinforcement learning, a feedback-based learning method. If the machine responds correctly, it receives positive feedback; if it responds incorrectly, the agent receives either negative feedback or a penalty. The machine learns automatically using feedback in reinforcement learning without any data labelled, unlike supervised learning.

Algorithms are not types of machine learning. In simple words, they are the methods of solving a problem.

The algorithms to be used depend on:

- The problem statements.
- The quantity, calibre, and kind of data.
- The complexity of the algorithm.

Deep Learning.
A chunk of ML is known as deep learning. DL is a field that is based on a computer algorithm that learns and develops on its own. It mimics how people function. When there are a vast amount of data, DL tech is applied.

When doing categorization tasks, a computer model directly learns from images, text, or sound.

One can categorize deep learning into two categories:

A. Supervised Learning
In scenarios like picture categorization or object identification, supervised learning is performed since the network is used to forecast a label or number.

Algorithms used:

- ANN
- CNN
- RNN

Unsupervised Learning

Unsupervised learning aims to build broad systems that can be learned using sparse amounts of input. Used in the situations such as web embedding, image encoding into lower or higher dimensional, etc.

Algorithms used:

- Self-Organizing map
- Boltzmann Machine
- Autoencoder

2 Literature Survey

The main reason researchers are working on this is that the heart is the most important key organ. It is needed for the body's blood circulation, which is as necessary as oxygen is; thereforeit has to be protected. As a result, several researchers are trying to changenew technologies. Heart-related issues are constantly analyzed for diagnosing, prognosis, or for prevention of any heart disease. The study was experimented by a number of factors, including AI, ML, and data mining.

Using a machine learning hybrid model, Dr. M. Kavitha, G. Gnaneshwar, R. Dinesh, Y. Rohit Sai, and R. Sai Suraj have worked on predicting heart disease. A hybrid model was created using Decision Tree and Random Forest and achieved an accuracy of 88% [1].

Utilizing neural networks, Tulay Karayilan and Ozkan Kilic had given try to predict cardiac disease. It utilizes the Clevland dataset. The neural network was trained using a backpropagation method to forecast the absence of cardiac disease with a 95% accuracy [2].

DNN have been studied by Minh Tuan Le et.al. Utilizing a multilayer perceptron neural network, heart failure is predicted (MLP). 88% of the time is right [3].

Using the UCI Machine Learning dataset, numerous research has taken place to predict cardiac disease.DNN technology has been used by P. Ramprakash et, al to predict cardiac disease [4]. The accuracy obtained by Mohammed Jawwad Ali Junaid and Dr. Rajeev Kumar using a hybrid of naive Bayes, Support Vector Machine, and Artificial Neural Network was 88% [5].

SVM, DT, linear regression, and K Nearest Neighbor have been used by Archana Singh and Rakesh Kumar. With an accuracy of 87%, K-Nearest Neighbor was the best among them [6].

On the embedded feature selection approach and deep neural network, Dengqing Zhang et al. have worked [7].Cardiac disease analysis using CNN was done by Awais Mehmood, Munwar Iqbal, Zahid Mehmood, Aun Irtaza, Marriam Mawaz, Tahir Nazir, and Momina Masood with an accuracy of 97% [8].

To forecast cardiac illness, Senthilkumar Mohan, Chandrasegar Tirumalai, and Gautam Srivatsava have built hybrid ML algorithms. KNN, Decision Tree, Genetic Algorithm, and Naive Bayes are the algorithms employed; they are merged to build a hybrid model with an accuracy of 88%. [9]. [10–15] are few research papers worked on the cardiac predication and detection. [16–19] uses various segmentation and classification techniques to detect the images. After reading the aforementioned publications, the fundamental goal behind the suggested system was to develop a cardiac disease forecasting system with the information indicated. To find the most accurate classification method that may be used to forecastcardiac disease, we compared the classification algorithms SVM, NB, ANN, and CNN.

3   Methodology

Even though heart disease signs are recognized, and the common characteristics is that not all of the symptoms will appear at once, it is highly challenging to detect heart diseases early on or in their early stages. Therefore, it is crucial to recognize heart illnesses early in order to prevent death or lower the mortality rate. The majority of them will not go to the doctor for a consultation because of numerous factors, including detecting cardiac disease is quite expensive. The challenge in this is to find whether each individual will get cardiac disease based on the data given about them.

3.1   System Architecture

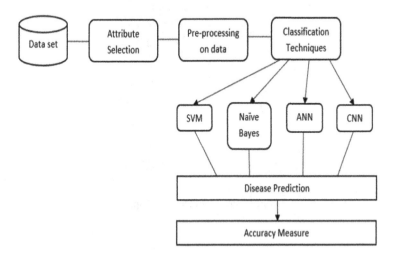

Fig. 2. System Architecture

Figure 1 demonstrates the overall architecture for classifying, identifyingand predicting the disease.

Data Collection

Data gathering and choosing the train and test datasets are the first steps in predicting accuracy. The dataset for Cleveland is taken from the Kaggle website. 30% of the dataset is used foranalyzing and 70% of dataset is assigned as a training dataset in the paper.

Attribute Selection

The attributes of the set of data are characteristics of the data-set that are needed for the system, and to the cardiac, many attributes are used, including predicted output specified in terms of 1 and 0. Other attributes needed for the heart include age, gender, heart bit rate, type of chest pain, and many more.

Table 1 gives the description of the features from the dataset:

Data Preprocessing

We should divide each categorical column into dummy columns with 1s and 0s to work with categorical variables. This is the most important steps that must be carried out to obtain correct results.

Data Balancing

We may make sure that both output classes are balanced to go to the next stage by using data balancing. "0" indicates that the individual is projected to have heart disease, while "1" indicates that the individual is forecasted to be cardiac disease-free (Table 2).

Figure 2 shows the graph (Figs. 3, 4, 5).

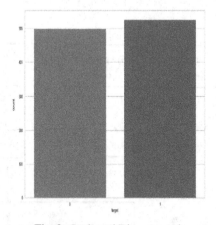

Fig. 3. Projected Disease graph

Table 1. Features description

SL No	Attribute	Description	Type
1	age	Years of age	Numeric
2	sex	Gender of the patient 0 = female; 1 = male	Nominal
3	cp	Type of chest discomfort 0 = Typical angina: reduction in the heart's blood flow 1 = Atypical angina: pain not related to heart 2 = Non-anginal pain: usually unrelated to heart 3 = Asymptomatic: no illness symptoms are present with the chest pain	Nominal
4	treetops	Blood pressure at rest	Numeric
5	chol	Mg/dl of serum cholestrol	Numeric
6	fbs	Glucose level at fasting > 120 mg/dl 0 = false; 1 = true	Nominal
7	restecg	Electrocardiographic readings while at rest 0 = Not applicable 1 = Denotes an aberrant ST-T wave 2 = Indicates whether there is left ventricular hypertrophy	Nominal
8	thalach	Reached maximum heart rate	Numeric
9	exang	Angina induced by exercise 0 = no; 1 = yes	Nominal
10	oldpeak	ST exercise-induced depression compared to rest	Numeric
11	slope	The exercise's peak's incline ST section 0 = Upsloping: denotes flat slope, little change (typical healthy heart) 1 = Denotes flat slope, little change(typical healthy heart) 2 = Downsloping: Heart disease warning indicators	Nominal
12	ca	Major vascular count (between 0 and 3), as colored by fluoroscopy	Numeric
13	thal	consequence of thallium stress 1,3 = regular 6 = indicates a flaw has been rectified, making it now ok 7 = reversible defect: indicates a correctable defect: improper blood flow during exercise	Nominal
14	target	Have a disease or not 1 = true; 0 = false(predicted attribute)	Nominal

Histogram of Attributes

The histogram aids in a clear comprehension of each attribute. The unique thing about this type of plot is how easy to draw and how much information it returns with only one command.

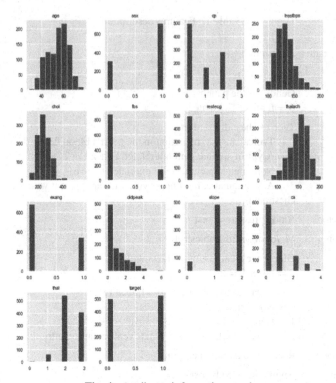

Fig. 4. Attributes information graph

3.2 Algorithms

Sector Vector Machine

A supervised study that splits data into two groups is called a support vector machine. SVM builds the model as it is primarily trained using a record that has been split into two groups. It is first to decide category where this new data point falls within. SVM considered as a non-binary linear classifier.

Naïve Bayes

The Bayes rule is the basis of the Naive Bayes algorithm. The principal presumption and most vital factor in classifying data and its properties. It is quick and simple to forecast and works best when the independence presumption is true.

Artificial Neural Network

An effective computing system called an artificial neural network take ups its key point from the analogy of biological brain networks. Because the weight typically excites or suppresses the signal being sent, this is done to answer a specific challenge for neurons. An activation signal refers to a neuron's intrinsic state. Output signals that can be transferred to other units are formed by connecting the input signals and the activation rule.

Convolutional Neural Network
An artificial neural network is implemented using a CNN or ConvNet. Many contemporary artificial intelligence techniques use CNN, particularly for processing.

4 Result

Jupyter Notebook
Jupyter notebook used as the simulation tool for projects in python programming. Figures, equations, links, and many more rich text components are included in Jupyter notebooks in addition to code. With these features Jupyter notebook can analysis description and its results, as well can execute in real time. It is an web-based interactive graphics, open-source and includes visualization.

Performance Evaluation
A proposed model's performance was calculated using various performance criteria, including precision, recall, and accuracy.

Precision: This metric provides precision in situations that are deemed to be favorable.

Precison $= TP / TP + FP$.

Recall: This metric provides the precision for classifying positive cases.

Recall $= TP / TP + FN$.

F-score: Recall and accuracy are combined to create the F-score.

F-score $=$ Recall x Precision / Recall + Precision.

Accuracy calculation.
Four values—true positive (TP), false positive (FP), true negative (TN), and false negative—determine how accurate the algorithms are (FN).

Accuracy $= (FN + TP) / (TP + FP + TN + FN)$.

The definition of TP, FP, TN, and FN's numerical value is:

- TP = Number of people with heart diseases
- TN = Number of individuals with and without heart disease
- FP = Number of people with no heart diseases

Table. 2. Performance of the Algorithms.

Algorithms	Accuracy	Precision	Recall	f1 - score
Support Vector Machine	0.85	0.84	0.85	0.85
Naïve Bayes	0.84	0.83	0.84	0.84
Artificial Neural Network	0.97	0.96	0.97	0.97
Convolutional Neural Network	0.98	0.98	0.97	0.98

• FN = Number of individuals with and without heart disease.

The accuracy of the CNN is more powerful than the other three algorithms employed in this paper, according to the testing and training outcome of the DL and ML techniques. With 98% accuracy, CNN is the best of the rest.

The Table 3 displays the comparison of various algorithm.

Table. 3. Comparison of Accuracy using various algorithm

Algorithm	Accuracy
Support Vector Machine (SVM)	85%
Naïve Bayes (NB)	84%
Artificial Neural Network (ANN)	96%
Convolutional Neural Network (CNN)	98%

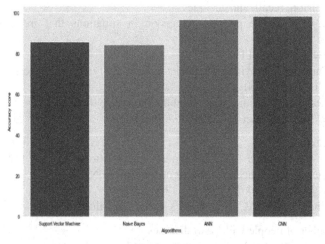

Fig. 5. Accuracy plot

5   Conclusion

This study gives an insight into ML and DL techniques for the grouping of cardiac diseases. The role of a classifier is important in the healthcare industry so that the outcome can be considered for forecasting the treatment that can be given to patients. It has become necessary to develop a system to anticipate heart diseases precisely and effectively due to the increase in the number of deaths brought on by cardiac diseases. The motive of this study was to identify a result-based algorithm for the identification of cardiac diseases. The probability of the algorithms is dependent upon the data set used for the purpose of testing and training to analysis the algorithms using the data set.

In the future, more machine learning and deep learning techniques will be used for the examining of cardiac diseases and can also use images to predict more accurately. In future algorithm can be combined to form a hybrid model to get more accuracy in the future.

References

1. Dataset - https://www.kaggle.com/rashikrahmanpritom/heart-attack-analysis-prediction-dat aset
2. Kavitha, M., Gnaneshwar, G., Dinesh, R., Sai Suraj, R., Rohit Sai, Y.: Prediction of Heart Disease using Random Forest, Decision Tree and Hybrid model (2019)
3. Karayilan, T., Kilic, O.: Prediction of heart disease using neural network (2020)
4. Le, M.T., Vo, M.T., Mai, L., Dao, S.V.: Predicting Heart failure using deep Neural Network (2020)
5. Ramprakash, P., Sarumathi, R, Nithyavishnupriya, S., Mowriya, R.: Heart Illness Prediction using Deep Neural Network (2020)
6. Kumar, R., Junaid, M.J.A.: Data Science and Its Application in Heart Disease Prediction ICIEM (2020)
7. Singh, A., Kumar, R.: Heart Disease Analysis Using ML Algorithms ICE3–2020. https://doi.org/10.1007/978-3-642-27443-5_25
8. Chen, Y., et al.: Heart Disease Prediction based on Embedded feature selection method and Deep Neural Network (2021)
9. Mehmood, A., et al.: Prediction of Cardiac Disease using Deep CNN (2020)
10. Mohan, S., Tirumalai, C., Srivatsava:, G.: Prediction of Cardiac Disease using Hybrid Model (2020)
11. Lutimath, N.M., et al.: Prediction of heart disease using ML. Int. J. Recent Technol. Eng. **8**(2S10), 474–477 (2019)
12. Ali, L., et al.: An Automated Diagnostic System for Heart Disease Prediction based on X2 Statistical model and optimally configured DNN (2019)
13. Fu, M., Pan, Y., Cheng, B., Tao, X., Guo, J.P.: Enhanced Deep learning assisted CNN for Cardiac Disease Prediction on the internet of medical things platform (2019)
14. Rana, M.D.R., Al-Musabbir, N.: Cardiac disease prediction using machine learning. International Journal of Recent Technology and Engineering (2021)
15. Fathim, K., Vimina, E.R.: Heart Disease Prediction Using Deep Neural Networks on the internet of medical things platform (2021)
16. Harish, H., Murthy, S.A.: Identification of lane lines using advanced machine learning. In: 2022 8th International Conference on Advanced Computing and Communication Systems (ICACCS), vol. 1. IEEE (2022)
17. Harish, H., Murthy, A.S.: Identification of lane line using PSO segmentation. In: 2022 IEEE International Conference on Distributed Computing and Electrical Circuits and Electronics (ICDCECE). IEEE (2022)
18. Harish, H., Murthy, A.S.: Lane line edge detection using machine learning. In: IJONS, vol 13, issue 75 (2022)
19. Harish, H., Murthy, A.S.: Edge Discerning Using Improved PSO and Canny Algorithm Communication, Network and Computing (CNC-2022) Part1, CCIS (1893)

Internet of Things-Based Smart Irrigation System for Moisture in the Soil and Weather Forecast

Dharmendra Pandey[✉], Aditya Vidyarthi, and Jitendra Singh Kushwah

Institute of Technology and Management, Gwalior, (MP), India
{dharmendra.pandey,aditya.vidyarthi,
jitendra.singhkushwah}@itmgoi.in

Abstract. The current world situation requires a satisfactory supply chain. Globally, it is becoming less resource (worldwide lack of access to safe water). The gulf that exists between both the digital and real worlds is filled by (IoT). They are based on gathering data and utilising smart technology from sensors in the smart farming environment that are specialised for each application. Smart irrigation systems powered by IOT can aid in achieving optimal water resource consumption. In this work, the advanced control method uses an OS. Methodology to generate monitoring land metrics. Like ground dryness, minerals, iron, level of fertility demand, (soil, atmospheric) temperature, and sun ray intensity, all the data are present in the online climate report. This technique is being used at present by a government pilot scale project. Unprocessed data is collected on the internet. This system informs us of small-2 details. We taking 3 weeks of data. The data got us the goods to some extent due to guesswork.

Keywords: IoT · Sensors · Prediction · Irrigation · Precision Agriculture

1 Introduction

India is farming land. Over history,the greatest and higher farming achievementsinthe agriculture field are updated from time to time by using modernization. There is an urgent need to modernise traditional agricultural practices in India, as 60–70% of the country's GDP is derived from agriculture. The groundwater level is lower because of unplanned water use [1]. The amount of water on earth is reducing day by day, and this is exacerbated by a lack of rain and a shortage of groundwater. One of the major issues in the world today is a lack of water. In every field, water is necessary. Water is necessary for daily living as well. One industry where a great deal of Agriculture demands water [2]. Water waste is the biggest problem in agriculture. Every time additional water is sprayed onto the fields. There are many methods for conserving water.

The system aims to protect water and energy resources. It measures the water level and manages the device both manually and automatically. Agriculture has not sufficiently produced in comparison to population growth because of climatic changes and a lack of cleanness [3]. Water is pumped into fields at regular intervals using canal systems and

R. S. Tomar et al. (Eds.): CNC 2022, CCIS 1894, pp. 100–109, 2023.
https://doi.org/10.1007/978-3-031-43145-6_9

ground well for irrigation, but there is no feedback about the water level in the ground. This type of irrigation is detrimental to crop wellness and development since some crops are much more dependent on the quantity of soil moisture.

The node has been developed software as a side server. Used decision support features and interactionhave given information representing view results [4]. Machine learning techniquesused as a sensor node these data also be noted by Novel algorithm process. Thesealgorithms give the best result less error result. It's a good approach to minimize water use and less water waste in the agriculture field.

Fig. 1. Smart Irrigation System

2 Related Work

Arduino technology is used to control water flow in the system. With the help of sensors devicesto collect the statistical analysis data(UV ray sensors, temperature sensors, moisture sensors, humidity sensors) decideto collect data and predict data similarity. Using Kalman filter and noisy intermediate scaled quantum devices (NISQs) use to suppress noise for sensor devices generate loud noise [5]. Agriculture system work to notify the humanity and temperature, PH value by the sensors.

Sensors informationto display on PC and LCD [2]. Introduced an easy outlook "Using an artificial neural network controller, automate irrigation control" ON/OFF controller system is given it [6]. But the ON/OFF control system is not Reliable giving the result is not satisfied and the system fails. However, It is now possible to adopt stronger and more efficient control thanks to ANN-based methods. ANN-based systems may save a substantial amount of resources (such as water and energy) and give optimal results consistently for all types of agricultural settings [7]. These controllers have the inherent capability to perform these tasks without the need for prior system knowledge. Created and put into use successfully together with a flow sensor. The DHT22 sensor, the rain sensor, and the soil moisture sensor [6].

The sector that still makes up the largest portion of India's GDP is agriculture. But when we look at the technology used in this subject, we find that the advancement is not significant [8]. Huge technical advances nowadays have an impact on a number of industry, such as agriculture, medicine, and others. In our nation, agriculture is the main industry. India's primary source of income is agriculture; hence the growth of agriculture is crucial. The majority of irrigation systems are still manually operated in modern times. Traditional irrigation methods like drip irrigation and sprinkler irrigation are readily available. To effectively exploit the water variety, these strategies must be paired with the Internet of Things. The Internet of Things facilitates information access and important decision-making [9]. The temperature and moisture contents of the soil is conveyed using a wireless sensor network that is linked to ZigBee [10]. GPRS is used to send data to a web server over a cellular network. Graphitic applications can be used to monitor data over the internet.

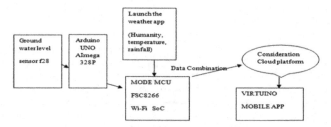

Fig. 2. Block Diagram: of the proposed system

As seen in Fig. 2, sensors, a microcontroller, a Wi-Fi module, and an Android application can all be used to automate irrigation. The field is regularly monitored by the in expensive groundwater level sensor. The Arduino board is connected to the sensors. The user can control irrigation by using the sensor data that has been acquiredand transmitted wirelessly [12].

The Smartphone application can be made to analyse the data it receives and compare it to the temperature, humidity, and moisture thresholds. Instead of automatically by the software without user interruption, a choice can be made manually through the software with user interruption. If the groundwater level is below the threshold value, the motor is turned ON, and if it is over the threshold value, the motor is turned OFF [12]. The sensors are wired to the Arduino. This gadget communicates using a wireless module, allowing the user to access the data using an Android app on his Smartphone, which can obtain sensor data from the Arduino through the wireless module [13]. Additionally, it offers a capability for scheduling watering. When the groundwater reaches a predetermined level, The user can plan when to water. The technology instructs users to maintain the threshold value based on data regarding the predicted pattern of precipitation and soil moisture. When the soil moisture reaches the set threshold value, the irrigation can be stopped automatically by the system. With this module, a water pump is connected by a relay switch controlled by a Wi-Fi node. The web service initiates node control for real-time monitoring through the adaptable web-based interface [14]. This web-based interface allows for manual and automatic remote control of the water pump.

Smart Irrigation System

Maximizing the use of water for crops is the main goal of an automated irrigation system using WSN and GPRS Module [9]. A wireless sensor network that is spread makes up this system. (WSN) that includes temperature and soil moisture sensors. Gateway units are used to manage sensor unit data, give commands to actuators for irrigation management, and transfer data from sensor units to base stations. An algorithm is proposed in the system to control the amount of water according to the needs and circumstances of the field. The actuator receives instructions from the microcontroller, which has been programmed, to control how much water flows through the valve unit. The entire system is powered by PV solar panels. The cellular network allows for two-way communication. A web application controls the irrigation through ongoing monitoring and irrigation scheduling programming. Web pages can be used to do this. The Bluetooth technology is described in the section that follows. A wireless sensor network crop monitoring program can be used by farmers to practice precision farming. The Micro controller, which is additionally integrated with the other electrical components mentioned above as shown in Fig. 1, as well as the water level sensor, which was previously included into the plant, is what makes this system work. The sensor collects data on the soil moisture and sends it along with other information to the microprocessor, which then activates the pump. Except that level. The microprocessor provides a signal to the relay module, which activates a pump and sends a specific volume of water to the plant, if the groundwater level drops below a predetermined level. The pump shuts off when there is enough supplied water. The role of the power supply is to provide power to the whole system, and the recommended voltage should fall between the microcontroller's incoming supply range of 7 V to 12 V.

3 Benefits of Smart Irrigation System

Smart irrigation has a number of advantages over traditional irrigation methods, some of which could be summed up as less crop loss, reduced energy usage, high cost-efficiency, and high performance efficiency. Fig. 3 illustrates the advantages of IoT use in irrigation systems. One of the main benefits of IoT systems for irrigation is that they use less water. In addition, the vast majority of irrigation-related chores are automated with this approach, only the necessary water is used for irrigation, and waste is reduced. Traditional irrigation methods that required human intervention lost a significant quantity of water because the majority of handling and operations were done manually. Little to no human contact occurs with smart irrigation, and water is only used when and where it is actually needed. High cost-efficiency is one of its extra benefits, as less water is utilized and the procedure is carried out with higher precision, which lowers costs and overall expenses. The strategy also considerably reduces energy use because less hours are spent running the machines, and controlled breaks are taken during the process to reduce overall energy usage. Additionally, because resources are few and companies must manage costs to some level, The need to cut costs and save resources cannot be overstated. Smart irrigation takes into account costs, allowing for successful completion of linked activities while using less money. Last but not least, one of the extra advantages is that plants and crops receive only the necessary amount of water with enhanced irrigation efficiency and groundwater management, which reduces crop loss from insufficient or excessive watering.

Fig. 3. Benefits of Smart irrigation System using IOT

4   Impect of Sustainability on Smart Irrigation System

It is possible to view sustainability as a crucial component of irrigation systems. Balance between the three sustainability pillars must be maintained for any system to remain sustainable. Economic, social, and environmental sustainability are the three pillars of sustainability. The potential effects of irrigation systems on the economy, ecology, and society are depicted in Fig. 3. The organisations engaged in the specific sector and related operations must take these factors into account because the components of sustainability could be evaluated in various contexts and media. Making sure that irrigation activities don't have a negative influence on the environment is one of the factors of sustainability. Irrigation is a vital part of the agricultural sector, but it is critical that the activities established for irrigation are developed in a way that does not endanger the health of people or wildlife. Additionally, water management may be included in sustainable irrigation systems. Water is used in agriculture, so it's important to effectively manage and control the resource to reduce water waste.There are therefore new requirements on how irrigation is established and managed as a result of the push for sustainable and better food systems. Every irrigation system, from local to national, has the ability to increase agricultural output, increase water security, promote inclusive growth, and promote progress toward the SDGs.

Pumping power is required to run drip irrigation systems. Different energy sources are used in the process to provide pumping power, which also has an adverse effect on the environment as a whole. When thinking about sustainable irrigation, it's important to make make ensuring that energy use and environmental effect are reduced by implementing environmentally friendly operational practices. Organizations engaged in irrigation activities must place a greater a focus on solutions that lower costs, sickness, pollution, and other issues. When irrigation doesn't deplete natural resources or human resources, It is possible to attain high irrigational sustainability. Sustainability in this sense may be largely related to financial and ecological considerations.

5 The Smart Irrigation Systems' Basic Architecture and Layout

Irrigation management and associated IoT solutions have been discovered to use multi-agent architectures pretty frequently and well. These distinct architecture categories aid in creating separation between the numerous constituent parts. In most cases, the layer of architectural elements determines how the architectural distinctiveness is established. For instance, a node that is currently at a higher position in the hierarchy may end up working as a broker for a node that is currently in a lower position. Many jobs and actions that must be carried out are assumed to be represented by functional blocks that make up the majority of designs. The administration, devices, communications, security, and services and applications are the main elements of these designs. The Internet of Things (IoT) systems are made up of many devices that can be used to control, monitor, detect, and take action on a variety of different tasks. Additionally, it is believed that these particular devices contain interfaces that allow connections to be made with other devices in order to convey the required data. In addition, it's common practice to interpret the data gathered from a variety of sensors and apply the conclusions reached to a range of actuators.It has long been accepted that the IoT architecture may be divided into three main tiers. These layers fall into three categories: application, network, and perception. A new layer called the service layer has been added in connection to the network and application levels. This specific layer is put into place to store and process the data using cloud computing and fog. Additionally, numerous researchers have created and presented a variety of new architecture proposals, with Ferrández-Pastor's four layered architectures being one of the most obvious.

IoT's architecture has traditionally been regarded as faulty. The four layers stated above are things, edge, communication, and cloud. The edge layer has been assigned in this concept to locate key applications and perform basic control actions. Regarding IoT irrigation systems, many tiered approaches have been used and put into practise, with varying degrees of success. The bottom layer often consists of actuators and sensor nodes, whereas the intermediate layer frequently consists of a gateway and allows data transport. Lastly, cloud services, apps, or databases make up the third tier of the architecture. Although these three are the most frequently used layers, they may also be distinct and vary with (Figs. 4, 5, 6 and 7).

6 Difficulties and Potential Outcome

Things, edge, communication, and cloud are the four levels that generally make up the IoT architecture. This proposal's edge layer has been located to facilitate criticism. This section covers the difficulties and potential of utilising machine learning. The creation of

Fig. 4. Environment impact, economical impact social impact

digital software programs and machine learning for smart irrigation systems to govern a variety of crops, notably to support sustainable agriculture, has a number of challenges. To address the food shortages, the overall food output must be raised. To meet industrial demands, Cotton and rubber need to be cultivated more as cash crops in particular when combined with sustainable materials to prevent soil pollution. Additionally, these issues pose a variety of challenges, such as the fall in agricultural labour, the shrinkage of arable land, the scarcity of water supplies, the consequences of climate change, etc. As urbanization takes hold worldwide, the Rural areas' populations are aging and shrinking quickly. There are several potential applications for IoT technologies in agriculture and food production. IoT's affordability, autonomy, portability, minimum maintenance requirements, effectiveness, sturdy construction, and dependability in smart irrigation are only a few of the many aspects that require more study. To ensure sustainable agriculture, these tools are highly valued. Agriculture and other stakeholder who use portable software solutions in conjunction with machine learning forecasting have a lot of opportunities (Table 1).

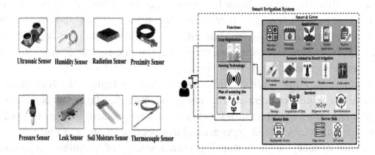

Fig. 5. Icons for intelligent irrigation systems were collected

The software uses the Internet of Things to remotely monitor the entire farm. Program uses two different types of terminals and a sensor network. In order to save energy, nodes apply energy-saving algorithms. Data collection from the node to the base station is done through a tree-based protocol. A system with two nodes, One of them gathers information on all environmental and soil variables, while the other features a camera for photographing and monitoring crops. With this system, sensor values are calculated

Table 1. Experiment case analyse

soil's current state	Moisture content	Publication status	Water pump content	Experiment case content
Dried	1000/500	Switch On	Switch On	True
dank	600/300	Switch Off	Switch On	True
humid	400	Switch Off	Switch Off	True

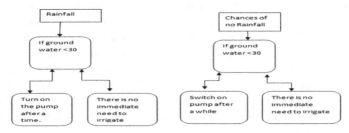

Fig. 6. System Algorithm

without taking climate into account. An application cannot be programmed by a system user. There is no system for controlling applications. [12].

Fig. 7. Instruments for detecting moisture levels

7 Conclusion

The level of soil water must be taken into account when designing an intelligent irrigation system. The soil water level is influenced by a variety of environmental conditions, including air temperature, air humidity, UV radiation, soil temperature, etc. Because of technological advancements, weather forecasting accuracy has substantially increased, and changes in soil moisture may now be predicted using weather forecast data.

This article presents a hybrid device learning-based smart irrigation architecture based on the Internet of Things to predict the soil water content. The created method uses sensor data from the most recent period plus information from weather forecasts to anticipate the soil water level for the upcoming days. The anticipated value for soil water level is more accurate and has a lower error rate.Furthermore, a standalone system prototype incorporates the forecasting approach. Since the system prototype is based on open standard technology, It is affordable. The auto mode allows a clever system to be further tuned for application-specific situations. We want to perform a feature analysis of water savings based on the proposed algorithm with many nodes and system cost reduction.

The irrigation system's effects on the environment should be considered.respect for and adherence to the Sustainable Development Goal sfulfil the three pillars' ultimate goals (ecological, social, and economiceconomic). It's important to prevent overuse of natural resources, which is possible with careful planning. Also, it must be assured that the cost of operation activities does no exceed the perceived outcomes in order to preserve sustainability. The costs associated with this continual automation and technological advancement are already quite effective and efficient, and they might be further decreased. The firm may be helped by a tendency toward green activities and functions to meet its objectives, and organisations may achieve great things if they place more of an emphasis on CSR.

References

1. Vidyarthi, A.: Comparative analysis of linear regression, random forest and support vector machine using dataset. Int. J. Innovative Eng. Manag. Res., **11**(01), 30- 35 (2022). https://doi.org/10.48047/IJIEMR/V11/I01/04
2. Rao, P., Yadav, V.K., Vidyarthi, A.: An Approach to find nearest location services through skyline query & amp; KNN. In: Conference SCI-2K19
3. Vidyarthi, A.: Wireless communications and mobile computing. Wiley-Hindawi, **2022**, 11, https://doi.org/10.1155/2022/1191492. 1191492
4. Kushwah, J.S., Vidyarthi, A.: Comparative analysis of linear regression,random forest and support vector machine using dataset, **11**(01) (2022). Jan 2022
5. Kushwah, J.S., et. al.: Comparative study of regressor and classifier with decision tree using modern tools. In: First International Conference on Design and Materials (ICDM)-2021 of "Materials Today: Proceedings" ISSN: 2214–7853, vol. 56, Part 6, pp. 3571–3576 (2022)
6. Kushwah, J.S., et al.: A comprehensive system for detecting profound tiredness for automobile drivers using a CNN, (LNEE, volume 914), Print ISBN: 978–981–19–2979–3, Online ISBN: 978–981–19–2980–9. Springer, Singapore https://doi.org/10.1007/978-981-19-2980-9_33. Accessed 31 Aug 2022
7. Obaideen, K., et al.: An overview of smart irrigation systems using IoT. Energy Nexus **7**, 100124 (2022)
8. Viani, F., Bertolli, M., Salucci, M., Polo, A.: Low-cost wireless monitoring and decision support for water saving in agriculture. IEEE Sens. J. **17**(13), 4299–4309 (2017). https://doi.org/10.1109/JSEN.2017.2705043
9. Suryotrisongko, H., Musashi, Y.: Evaluating hybrid quantum-classical deep learning for cybersecurity botnet DGA detection Hatma Suryotrisongko et al. Procedia Comput. Sci. **197,** 223–229 (2022)
10. Velmurugan, S., Balaji, V., Bharathi, T.M., Saravanan, K.: An IOT based smart irrigation system using soil moisture and weather prediction. In: International Journal of Engineering Research & Technology (IJERT) Conference Proceedings. ECLECTIC-2020 Conference Proceedings, vol 8, issue 07 (2020). ISSN: 2278–0181 ECLECTIC-2020. www.ijert.org

11. Badreldeen, M.M., Ragab, M.A., Sedhom, A., Mamdouh, W.M.: IoT based smart irrigation system. Int. J. Indus. Sustain. Dev. (IJISD), **3**(1), (2022). August 2022 Print ISSN 2682–3993 Online ISSN 2682–4000

12. Lage, A., Correa, J.C.: Weather station with cellular communication network. In: 2015 XVI Workshop on Information Processing and Control (RPIC), Oct 2015, pp.1–5 (2015)

13. Gheith, A., et al.: IBM bluemix mobile cloud services. IBM J. Res. Dev. **60**(2–3), 7:1-7:12 (2016)

14. Jaguey, J.G., Villa-Medina, J.F., Lopez-Guzman, A., Porta-Gandara, M.A.: Smartphone irrigation sensor. IEEE Sens. J. **15**, 5122–5127 (2015). https://doi.org/10.1109/JSEN.2015.2435516

Visual Cryptography: An Emerging Technology

Gauri Kothekar, Pallavi Khatri[✉], and Geetanjali Surange

ITM University, Gwalior, India
gkothekar.gk@gmail.com, {Pallavi.khatri.cse,
Geetanjali.surange}@itmuniversity.ac.in

Abstract. In the present era, the data has become the most important asset for an individual, community and organization. Data handling and protection from attacks has become a key concern for people. To protect the information from uninvited invasions and attacks, researchers are developing new security techniques. Numerous cryptography methods have been discovered, and many more are still hidden. The visual cryptography is one of them. In this paper, visual cryptography, a new technique, has been highlighted. Visual cryptography is a method of data hiding in which the data is encrypted and concealed using visuals. A secret image is split up into numerous share images in visual cryptography. Although these share images are noisy or damaged, they are nonetheless relevant. Combining these share photos can make the original secret photo visible.

Keywords: Information · cryptography · visual cryptography · image cryptography

1 Introduction

Cryptography is the process of transforming plain text into cipher text. Naor & Shamir first proposed the idea of visual cryptography in 1994 and this is another technique termed "visual cryptography". They contend that an image can be encrypted using n shares of an image and that n shares must be made available to decrypt the image for it to be unlocked. The benefit of this approach is that an image cannot be decrypted if it has n-1 shares. When all n shares are superposed, the original image would be seen. Binary, grayscale, and color images are among the different types of images that can be used for visual cryptography.

1.1 Visual Cryptography for Binary Image

The (k, n) threshold technique is proposed in [1] segments a given secret image into n shadow pictures (shares), as seen in Fig. 1. Any k or more of these shadow pictures, but any k-1 or less can help to physically decode the secret image system. By reading the secret message from numerous overlapping shares using the human visual system, it overcomes the limitation of conventional cryptography's requirement for complicated calculation. Applications for the core idea of visual cryptography, first introduced by Naor and Shamir, include information concealment, general access structures, visual authentication, and identification. Due to technical limitations, all of these programmes can only accept binary photographs as input.

R. S. Tomar et al. (Eds.): CNC 2022, CCIS 1894, pp. 110–120, 2023.
https://doi.org/10.1007/978-3-031-43145-6_10

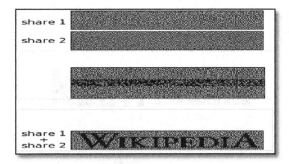

Fig. 1. Sample Binary Image

1.2 Visual Cryptography for Gray Image

Participants in [17] receive n bits of a concealed digital image using traditional visual cryptography techniques. The visual encryption for binary images that is suggested in this paper includes the ability to watermark and verify. The proposed method allows the generation of two shadows which serve as a check on the precision of the picture reconstruction by enclosing an n-image watermark in an n-image secret image. A participant cannot unwittingly or accidentally provide false information by analysing each shadow before using it to reconstruct the hidden image as can be seen in Fig. 2.

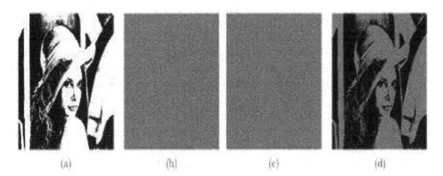

(a)   (b)   (c)   (d)

Fig. 2. Sample Gray Image

1.3 Visual Cryptography for Colored Images

Authors in [17] propose a novel visual cryptography-based cryptography system for safeguarding colored images, as seen in Fig. 3. Both the input data and the key used to encrypt and decrypt the colour picture that needs to be secured are binary images. A secret colour picture to be shared is split into three monochrome images using the YCbCr colour space system. Binary image data is created from these monochromatic photos, which is then shared-1 encrypted with a binary key image to generate binary cipher images. The three half-tones of the secret colour image and the binary key picture are separately encrypted using the exclusive OR operation. For the purpose of obtaining share-second, binary images are merged.

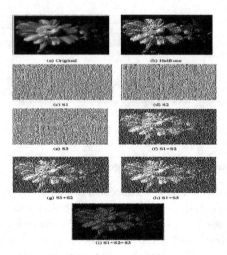

Fig. 3. Sample Color Image

2 Literature Survey

Several scientists have worked on the Naor and Shamir's suggested subject to enhance the performance. A fundamental idea behind Visual cryptography is being proposed by researchers in 1994 [1] where a secret image is split into two pieces as shown in Fig. 4. The number of shares generated is insignificant. Once the two shares are combined, the first secret picture is produced. Only black-and-white photographs are affected by this. In 1996, Ateniese, Blundo, and Stinson [2] suggested extending the use of visual encryption. Significant shares are involved in this scam. The (2,2) EVC motif that was projected throughout this called for the enlargement of 1 element every time to four subpixels, which could then be picked to create the necessary images for each share. Visual cryptography techniques were only used with black and white graphics until 1997. Verheul and Tilborg devised the first technique for coloured visual cryptography [3]. The shares produced by this plan had no value. Wu and Chen [4] develop visual cryptography techniques to send two secret images via two shares in 1998. Hsu et al. [5] in 2004 developed yet another approach that involved rotating two share images at random angles to conceal two hidden images. Verheul and Van Tilborg offered a further approach [3]. Authors suggested a method for sharing coloured hidden images. In this, a coloured visual cryptography was created using the arcs principle theme. S J Shyu et al. [11] were the ones who initially suggested that visual cryptography may share numerous secrets.

A set of n 2 secrets are encoded using this theme into 2 circular shares. The first share and second share that have been obtained typically allow for the acquisition of the

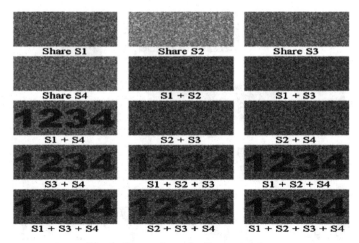

Fig. 4. Image shares for Reconstruction

n secrets one at a time rotated with n different rotation degrees. In [8], a novel method for halftone image processing was proposed that improves the clarity of recovered hidden images in a VC scheme. They later propose a hardware-efficient visual cryptography approach in 2016 [10]. It makes the best use of image transmission time. Shamir's equation was modified to shorten the calculation time [17].

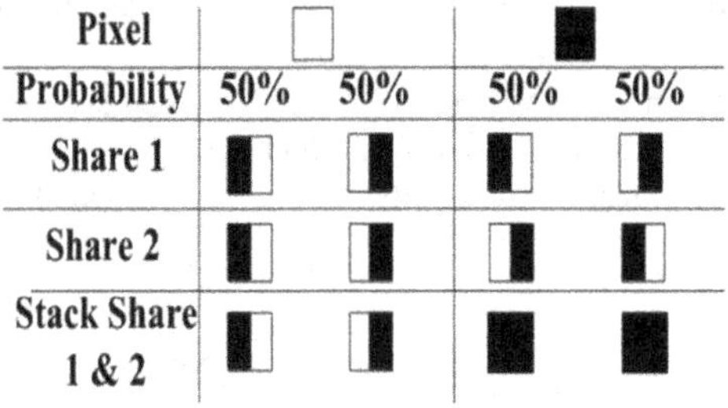

Pixel	□		■	
Probability	50%	50%	50%	50%
Share 1	▐	▌	▐	▌
Share 2	▐	▌	▌	▐
Stack Share 1 & 2	▐	▌	■	■

Fig. 5. Reconstruction technique

Comparative Study of all the techniques is summarized in Table 1 and Table 2 summarizes the comparative analysis of all the techniques of visual cryptography referred in the literature.

3 Applications of Visual Cryptography

The use of the visual cryptography approach has grown as a result of its demonstrated security and dependability. Here, we'll talk about a few applications.

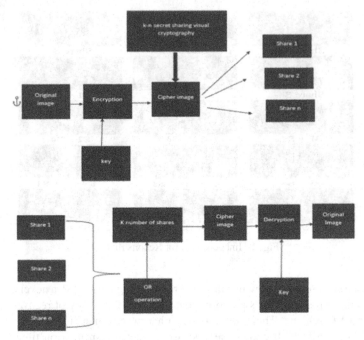

Fig. 6. Architecture of Visual Cryptography

Table 1. Comparative study of visual cryptography

Sr. no	Author	Year	number of hidden images	Image reconstruction quality	Complexity of construction	Image format	Kind of share produced
1	Naor and Shamir	1994	1	Low contrast	No	binary	random
2	Wu and Chen	1998	2	Average Contrast	No	binary	random
3	Hsu et al	2004	2	Average Contrast	No	binary	random
4	S. J. Shyu et al	2007	n(n > =)	Average Contrast	No	binary	random
5	S.J.Shyu	2006	1	Average Contrast	No	Color	random
6	C.N. Yang	2004	(k,n)	Average Contrast	No	binary	random
7	Kafri and keren	1987	2	Average light transmission	No	binary	random

Table 2. Performance Analysis of Existing Techniques

Techniques	Advantage	Disadvantage
Visual cryptography for binary images	Contains only two shares, making computation simple simply piling one on top of the other. It is impossible to decrypt data without the n-1 share	not suitable for text-based messaging
Visual cryptography for gray images	There are more than two shares in it. Image decryption is less difficult when the sharing is incomplete	Accuracy may be assessed and data can be recognized without all shares
Visual cryptography for color images	more secure than standard methods More shares, overall	Any two shares can be combined to determine the original image's intensity

3.1 Watermarking

The process of watermarking incorporates visual cryptography. There are two steps in the process. Watermark embedding is done in steps one and two. With the aid of a visual cryptography technique, the watermark is split into shares throughout the embedding process. Following this, one share is retained by the owner while the host image and another are embedded together according to the frequency domain of the host image [12]. Owner must take another share from the image in order to retain ownership of the original. Extracted share and owner's share are combined to create the original image.

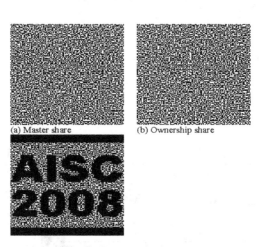

(a) Master share   (b) Ownership share

Fig. 7. Watermarked Images

3.2 Anti- Phishing Systems

Sensitive data like Security pins, card numbers, and passcodes are examples of vital information that intruders may steal. Additionally, phishing is frequently used to steal owners' secret credentials. It is possible to use cryptography to protect against phishing attempts. Visual cryptography gives users the assurance of security they need to utilise any website. The user can assure a website is free of phishing by enforcing the two shares—one obtained from the server and the second that is owned by the user [13].

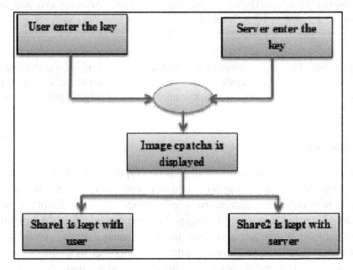

Fig. 8. Anti Phishing system

3.3 Human Machine Identification

The human/terminal machine identification method shown in Fig. 9 is presented by Kim et al. Following Katoh and Imai's [15] plan, Kim extended it in a more broad manner (Figs. 5, 6, 7, 8 and 13).

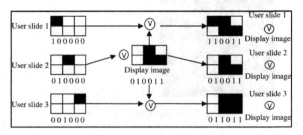

Fig. 9. Human Machine Identification system

3.4   Secure Banking Communication

There is a possibility of coming across a forged signature during a transaction in the core banking sector. Additionally, the client's password in the web banking system is compromised. A plan for protecting customer information and preventing possible password stealing is put forward in [16]. Visual cryptography uses image processing techniques for achieving the security as shown in Fig. 10.

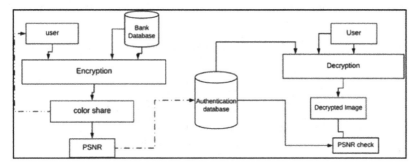

Fig. 10. Secure Banking system

3.5   Defense System

Technique of Visual cryptography is used to encrypt the written material using a combination of methods. When secret information, such as a code, needs to be transported from one location to another, it can be buried in a cover image, and the image's share needs to be converted into shares. The technique can be incredibly useful in defensive systems to protect private data. These numerous shares remain intact with numerous partners. To retrieve the data from the image all the shares are used. One single share will not be able to retrieve the complete data from the image. Information is therefore secure with multiple shares. Figure 11 shown one such image hiding.

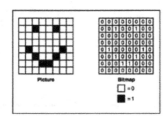

Fig. 11. Code Transmission system

3.6 Captcha

It was suggested that CAPTCHA be used as an authentication method that supported
Visual Cryptography in [8]. Flow depicted in Fig. 12 shows how visual cryptography
can be used to generate and verify captcha image ensuring security.

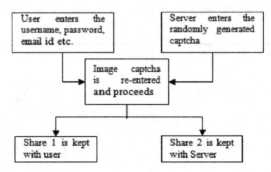

Fig. 12. Procedure for Captcha Verification

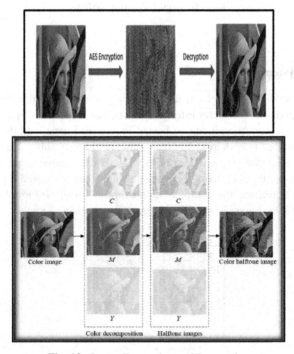

Fig. 13. Image Encryption and Decryption

4 Results

The schemes are secured but when it comes in the hands of intruder, using two shares of the image, intensity of the data image can easily be judged [Fig. 4] so that in order to make it secure some more techniques need to be implemented.

5 Conclusions

It's impossible to beat visual cryptography for coolness. When it comes to distributing data in the form of photos, it is much better. The importance of protecting data during communication is what spurs researchers to investigate various visual cryptography systems. An encryption method used to share confidential images is called visual cryptography (VC). The image is encoded into n shares. These shares are either encoded and saved digitally or printed on transparencies. To retrieve secret data, all shares are necessary. Numerous variables have an impact on these strategies' effectiveness. The quantity of shares, image format, size of encrypted shares, and the kind of share to be produced are a few of the variables. The paper lists the numerous qualities of each method examined in a table of comparisons. As discussed in numerous applications, the use of visual cryptography techniques can increase the security and dependability of systems. Each technology has its drawbacks, this article highlights a few benefits and drawbacks of visual cryptography.

References

1. Naor, M., Shamir, A.: Visual cryptography. In: Eurocrypt., A., Santis., D., (eds.) In Advances in Cryptology, vol. 950 of Lecture Notes in Computer Science. Springer-Verlag, Berlin, pp 1–12, (1995). https://doi.org/10.1007/BFb0053419
2. Ateniese, G., Blundo, C., Santis, A., Stinson, D.: Extended capabilities for visual cryptography. ACM Theory. Comput. Sci. **250**, 143–161 (2001)
3. Verheul, E., van Tilborg, H.: Construction & properties of k out of n visual secret sharing schemes, Designs, codes & cryptography. Int. J. Comput. Appl. **11**(2), 179–196 (1997). (0975 – 8887) volume 174 – no.5, September 43 2017. https://doi.org/10.1023/A:1008280705142
4. Wu, L., Chen, H.A.: Study On Visual Cryptography, Master Thesis, Institute of Computer and Information Science, National Chiao Tung University, Taiwan, R.O.C (1998)
5. Hsu, H., Chen, T., Lm, Y.: The ring shadow image technology of visual cryptography by applying diverse rotating angles to hide the secret sharing. In: Proceedings of the 2004 IEEE International Conference on Networking, Sensing & Control, Taipei, Taiwan, pp. 996–1001, March (2004)
6. Wang, D., Feng, Y., Xiaobo, L.: On general construction for extended visual cryptography schemes. Pattern Recogn. **42**(2009), 3071–3082 (2009)
7. Malik, S., Jaya, A.A.: Keyless approach to image encryption. In: 2012 International Conference on Communication systems and Network Technologies ©2012 IEEE
8. Kumar, H., Srivastava, A.: A secret sharing scheme for secure transmission of color images. In: International Conference on Issues and Challenges in Intelligent Computing Techniques (ICICT) (2014)

 9. Vaya, D., Khandelwal, S.: A fast and hardware efficient visual cryptography scheme for images. In: Advances in Intelligent Systems and Computing, vol. 379, pp. 133–142. Springer, New Delhi (2016). https://doi.org/10.1007/978-81-322-2517-1_14

10. Shyu, S., Huanga, S., Lee, Y., Wang, R., Chen, K.: Sharing multiple secrets in visual cryptography. Pattern Recognit. **40**(12), 3633–3651 (2007)

11. Warren, H., Akhawe, D., Jain, S., Shi, E., Song, D.: Shadowcrypt: Encrypted web applications for everyone. In: Proceedings of the 2014 ACM SIGSAC Conference on Computer and Communications Security, pp. 1028- 1039. ACM (2014)

12. Reddy, L.S., Prasad, M.V.N.K.: Extended visual cryptography scheme for multi-secret sharing. In: Nagar, A., Mohapatra, D.P., Chaki, N. (eds.) Proceedings of 3rd International Conference on Advanced Computing, Networking and Informatics. SIST, vol. 44, pp. 249–257. Springer, New Delhi (2016). https://doi.org/10.1007/978-81-322-2529-4_26

13. Kim, M., Park, J., Zheng, Y.: Human-machine identification using visual cryptography. In: Proceedings of the 6th IEEE International Workshop on Intelligent Signal Processing and Communication Systems, pp. 178- 182 (1998)

14. Katoh, T., Imai, H.: An application of visual secret sharing scheme concealing plural secret images to human identification scheme. In Proc. SITA **96**, 661–664 (1996)

15. Chandrasekhara, V.: Jagadisha, Secure Banking Application Using Visual Cryptography against Fake Website Authenticity Theft, International Journal of Advanced Computer Engineering and Communication Technology (IJACECT), ISSN (Print): 2278–5140, vol. 2, issue – 2 (2013)

16. Visual cryptography. Wikipedia, The Free Encyclopedia. https://en.wikipedia.org/w/index. php?title=Visual_cryptography&oldid=1112850520 . Accessed 28 Nov 2022

17. Shrivas, B., et al: (IJCSIT) International Journal of Computer Science and Information Technologies, **6**(2), 1076–1079 (2015)

Computing Techniques for Efficient Networks Design

Machine Learning Based Techniques for the Network Design of Advanced 5G Network, Beyond 5G (B5G) and Towards 6G: Challenges and Trends

Suman Paul[(✉)]

Department of ECE, School of Engineering, Haldia
Institute of Technology, Haldia, West Bengal, India
paulsuman999@gmail.com

Abstract. Rapid advancement of wireless communication and as well as telecommunication network play a crucial role in the diversified applications related to carrying of varying and heterogeneous traffic in multimedia communication and commercial applications. With the fastest pace of developments along with continuous up gradations in recent communications systems and networks related to the deployment of the advanced 5G, which is being rolled out, draws attention of several research challenges and exigent transition requirements from existing 4G to 5G, beyond (B5G) and towards the upcoming 6G. These network up gradations strongly demand for the requirements of run-time intelligent decisions with the incorporation Machine Learning (ML)-based techniques. In this paper, various research challenges associated with the rolling out related to the design of the advanced 5G network and beyond, the requirements of network intelligence in NGWN, the challenges and the trends involved related to the incorporation of ML have been investigated.

Keywords: Machine Learning (ML) · Beyond 5G Generation (B5G) · Sixth Generation (6G) · Next Generation Wireless Network (NGWN) · Network intelligence

1 Introduction

Wireless communication and network systems have greatly experienced considerable revolutionary progress in modern days. With the fastest developments of the standardization of 5G phase 2, the various applications are rigorously being developed and advanced 5G is rolling out commercially in several countries [1], with a strong focus of incorporation of intelligent learning and Machine learning (ML) based techniques and approaches in advanced 5G networks and beyond; for the continuous up gradations and the target network performance improvement. The three important key components play a vital role for the performance improvement of the 5G network are (i) the enhanced mobile broadband (eMBB), (ii) the ultra-reliable and low-latency communications (uRLLC) and (iii) the massive machine-to-machine communication (mMTC).

With the developments and as well the up gradations of 5G, several applications related to device-to device (D2D) communications, Internet of Things (IoT), Internet of Vehicles (IoV), machine-to-machine (M2M) communications, wearable technology, healthcare have been focused for potential research and developments. The typical use cases and as well as the applications of the advanced 5G are [2]: The cloud-based virtual and as well as augmented reality including the computer-based modelling and computer gaming (real-time); connected automotive including autonomous driving; smart manufacturing - for example, a cloud-based robot control; health sector (remote diagnosis); wireless home entertainment including the cloud-based gaming; connecting drones for security; social networking; smart cities including applicability of the video surveillance and personal AI assistant, etc. The following Fig. 1 depicts the up gradations of various services from 5G to 6G [3].

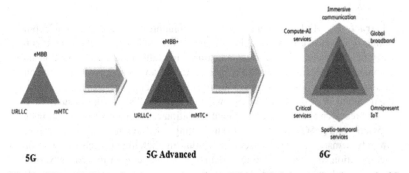

Fig. 1. Up gradations of various services from 5G, to 5G Advanced and towards 6G.

This rapid growth of 5G is endorsed by the Mobility Report of Ericsson [4], which forecasts and highlights that by the year 2027, sixty percent of the data traffic (global mobile network) likely to be over in the 5G network.

In 5G, the integration of Machine learning (ML) is acceptable due to the advantages of its applicability and as well as capabilities. The AI/ML, has the capability of training the systems to carry out the tasks independently depending on the data-driven required decisions. In spite of the diversified applications of AI and ML, the important common applications are [4]: the (i) prediction, (ii) classification, (iii) recommendation, (iv) categorization, (v) translation of the information and as well as in (vi) anomaly detection, etc. The primary aim of incorporation of the ML/intelligence in the network, is to estimate various driving network parameters and to support the required intelligent and interactive decisions at run-time. The processes of dynamic re-configurability at run-time are the important fields of research and development in advanced 5G, beyond (B5G) and towards the 6G network up gradations. Moreover, integration of AI/ML in telecom sector has a potential capability for the replacement of the conventional solutions (algorithmic/mathematical model-based) subject to the condition that the availability of sufficient data and as well as computational power [5].

The following Table 1 [6, 7] depicts a comparative illustrations of target key attributes and KPI for the requirements to be addressed for up gradations and rolling out from 5G advanced to 6G in near future, where adopting the target intelligence in the network will play a significant role for the telecom revolution towards the network speed along with the device mobility and for various diversified real-time applications.

Table 1. Comparative key attributes and KPI for 5G Advanced and 6G.

Attributes/ KPI	Advanced 5G	6G
Latency (ms)	1	<1
Peak data (rates)	100 Gbps	1 Tbps
Band (frequency)	Sub 6 GHz, mm Wave for fixed access	Sub 6G Hz mm Wave for mobile access, Terahertz-band, Non-RF (VLC)
Network type (implementation)	Network slicing, NFV, SDN	Incorporate extreme intelligence: AI/ML-based approaches, deep learning preferred for SDN, NFV, cloud, slicing (network)
Technology	Communication in D2D, in a network (ultra-dense), the NOMA (Non-Orthogonal Multiple Access), access of small cells, relaying	Communication: Quantum; Visible light; Haptic technology; hybrid access –based
Computing Techniques	Cloud computing, trends towards fog computing	AI-based computing (quantum), edge computing
Target Mobility	500 km h^{-1}	700 km h^{-1}
Architecture	Cells (small): Dense (sub)-6 GHz	Smart surfaces (cell-free), temporary applicable hotspots, drones applicable for the base stations
Frequency	3–300 GHz	1000 Ghz
Efficiency (Spectral)	30 bps/Hz	100 bps/Hz
Reliability (%)	99.9999	99.99999
Target Applications	(i)Reliable eMMB, (ii)URLLC, (iii) mMTC and (iv) hybrid	(i) MBRLLC, (ii) mURLLC, (iii) HCS and (iv)MPS

2 Motivation

The various crucial factors [8] driving the telecommunication industry next generation) for the adoption of ML/intelligent networking are: (i) for target business expansion and to address the growing demands of the present and future market requirements; (ii) the requirements of dynamic scheduling and as well as the flexibility in resource allocation due to the infrastructure and Network Functions Virtualization (NFV) along with the need of network slicing and technological advancements; and for (iii) the optimizing the operations management. The AI/ML based approaches play a critical role in the network operations and management including the intelligent RAN automation, various use cases of the power optimization, intelligent data-driven solution, etc.

However, integration of various ML based approaches cannot fully address the challenges associated with advanced 5G networks due to rapidly increase of traffic, requirements of carrying heterogeneous classes of traffic and for the complex criteria of time-constraint or real-time services. To address such challenges, researchers are continuously concentrating for the developments of the incorporation of ML in advancement of 5G, Beyond 5G (B5G) and for the near future sixth generation (6G) communication systems and networks. In spite of some progress related to the integration of ML in the network, still there are many challenges to be addressed to incorporate network intelligence applying ML. Overcoming such challenges along with the inherited issues involved with beyond 5G network is a process of rigorous and continuous monitoring, advanced analysis and challenging implementations for further technological up-gradations. The opportunities of incorporation of ML in NGWN the CSPs will further focus and investigations have been pointed out in the report of Ericsson [9]. It has been illustrated in the Fig. 2.

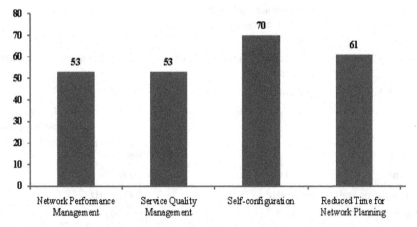

Fig. 2. The inclination of adopting network intelligence (AI/ML) by the CSPs in various sectors to be focused further [Data in percentage].

Accordingly, further rigorous investigations related to the recent state-of the-art developments, finding out of the future scope of work and focusing on the research trends for the deployment of network intelligence applying ML/AI in NGWN are the vital fields for further research and developments and relevant in the context of present and near future telecommunication industry.

2.1 Key Contributions

Recently, few survey based papers [10–15] related to the incorporation of ML-based approaches or intelligence in NGWN have been reported in the literature. However, in these surveys various critical issues related to the developments, associated challenges and furthermore, research trends of incorporating ML/ intelligence and applications of ML in the promising 6G network including the major thrust of edge intelligence, have not been specifically focused.

The key contributions of this paper are as follow:

- A comprehensive study of the characteristics of the NGWN, the background and the continuous up gradations, rolling out and as well as the deployments, the challenges involved from 5G to B5G and towards the 6G network considering the recent progress of the telecommunication industry have been pointed out.
- An extensive investigations on the strong requirements of intelligence in network and followed by the detailed survey on various state-of-the-art ML approaches, challenges involved of incorporating ML in the NGWN and as well as the target applications have been illustrated.
- A comprehensive study on the various open issues and research trends focusing on ML incorporation and network edge intelligence have been specifically investigated and highlighted.

3 Challenges Associated with NGWN

With the rapid progress of 5G, the key research areas which have a strong impact for the advancement of 5G are to deal with high speed data and as well as for the stringent requirements of the low latency traffic (real-traffic). These are the prerequisite of future 5G network and beyond. The research areas which have a significant impact are the deployment dense cells, millimeter-wave communications, implementation of massive MIMO (MMIMO) [16], D2D and as well as the M2M communication. The various inherited challenges [17] are associated with design and development of protocols, advanced coordinated multipoint (CoMP), multiple radio access technology (M-RAT), the carrier aggregation, the coding methods, implementation of network virtualization, integration with the cloud radio access networks (C-RAN), have a strong impact on rolling out towards advanced 5G and beyond (B5G) networks.

3.1 Deployment 5G (Denser) Cells

There exists a critical challenge for the identification of cell sites optimally and deployment of denser small cells in a small area to distribute the traffic and for the requirements of the enhancement of the signal power. Small cells may be deployed within a small area, subject to the constraint of frequency reuse. Moreover, deployment of such small cells will definitely invite the challenges associated with frequent handoff issues, resulting a very high probability of handoff failure or even significant rise call drops due to the fast as well as the frequent moving mobile devices or moving objects.

3.2 MIMO Along with Beam Forming

Massive Multiple Input Multiple Output (MMIMO) [16] and beam forming are the important enabling techniques for future advanced 5G network. The challenge is due to the pilot contamination, with the large number of antenna from the nearby cells. The issue is to optimize pilot orthogonality [17], in such a way that network resources should be least consumed. Furthermore, there is a challenge of channel estimation with the increasing count of antennas (TDD). More advanced algorithm is required for proper channel estimation (FDD) and to minimize the signaling overhead.

3.3 Challenges Associated with the System or Network Latency

5G needs a strong requirement of latency minimization with the advancement of emerging technologies like, cloud based applications in 5G network, real-time gaming and tactile Internet. The challenge is to provision the latency lower than 1 ms. This further will make a challenging concern for the design of other layers of the network.

3.4 Improvement of the Spectral Efficiency

To ensure ultra-fast speed data delivery, the Spectral efficiency should be increased. OFDM plays a vital role to combat with ISI. OFDM invites several challenges associated with high peak-to-average-power ratio (PAPR) which lowers the efficiency of the power amplifier deployed in the system.

4   The Requirements of Network Intelligence: ML in Advanced 5G

Incorporating artificial intelligence in the network is aimed to provide for the requirements of network adaptability; automatic network management (self-driven) and self –optimization (for example, Self-organizing Network: SON) [18]; auto-configuration and overall system performance improvement. The ITU-T steering committee [19], advocates for the solution related to the ML integrations in advanced 5G and beyond. The objective of integrating intelligence is to offer higher degree of throughputs, various categories of enterprise applications/ services, and for the connection requirements for a large number of devices/ user equipments (UE).

Moreover, there arises several challenges associated with network monitoring and management due to the rapid growth of network traffic. The advantage of deployment of network intelligence by incorporating ML is to address complicated network management and as well as for the network optimization problems (as of NP-hard). The advantages of the use of ML is that, it extracts systematically the required information from the incoming traffic-data. Moreover, ML discovers the patterns automatically for appropriate decisions. Moreover, integrating with the ML, traffic analysis including network slice-based, intelligent load balancing, network load forecasting can be executed at run-time. The intelligence in 5G is required to address the challenges involved due to the complexity of the network.

Accordingly, without the incorporation of ML and AI, it will be difficult for the telcos or the CSPs to deliver the services in a smarter way. In order to handle the a 5G network system and its various components there are categorically requirements arise for the computations of multiple parameters in a highly complex and as well as multi-varying system environment, the need of learning of various types of patterns requires different categories problem within the each component of the learning model. The incorporation and applications of various ML algorithms in 5G networks and systems are broadly categorized into: (i) the Supervised Learning (SL), (ii) the Unsupervised Learning (UL) and (iii) the Reinforcement Learning (RL). In addition, there are strong focus on other categories of machine learning algorithms, such as models based on Heuristics, Markovian models, for various 5G and Advanced 5G applications.

5 Application Areas of ML in 5G/B5G: Industry Perspective

The ML in the network can be applied for performance improvement and parameter estimation. It can be applied with financial metric, such as, (i) reliability, (ii) resource utilization, (iii) throughput, (iv) latency and (v) jitter for specific applications/ traffic in per slice, (vi) overall network system improvement, (vii) costs per bits and (viii) for the QoE improvement. The deployment of ML can be done at the edge of the network at run-time by applying lightweight ML/AI engines for real-time computation. This real-time computation is strongly recommended for IoT integrated 5G network, where low-latency applications run. A centralized deployment of ML in the network-system is generally used for high computation. In contrary, ML at the edge devices in the network are used for the requirements of prompt decisions and moreover, it has the advantage of having lower computational complexity. The following Fig. 3 depicts the typical challenging application scenarios of network intelligence applying ML in 5G, considering industry perspective.

Furthermore, the incorporating of AI/ ML in advanced 5G can enhance system performance, will support for accurate network planning, forecasting the expansion of the (i) network capacity, (ii) smart MIMO implementation, (iii) auto-optimizing the network coverage area (dynamically), (iv) dynamic resource scheduling, (v) integration with cloud network (dynamic), (vi) smart slicing, (vii) enhancement in O&M efficiency resulting cost reduction and (viii) overall optimization of the investment of the communication service providers (CSPs).

6 State-of-the-Art ML Approached in Advanced 5G, B5G and Towards 6G

The Machine Learning (ML) is a type of subset of Artificial Intelligence (AI), in which machines can able to learn, can perform and optimize their operations by utilizing the knowledge (operational) and the experience acquired in the form of the data [20]. More the investment in machine learning integrated network i.e. incorporation of network intelligence implies the better network performance. The Machine learning models are applied to learn the patterns. These models are applied in the tasks, for example, regression, classification and for interactions of an agent in an environment. Depending on the type of available data and the explicitness of the objectives of learning, in general, ML

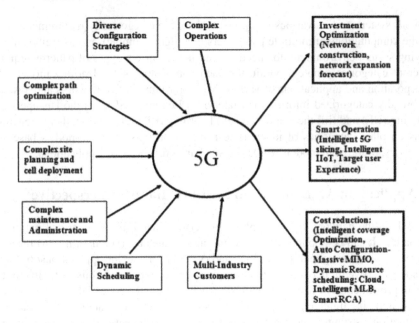

Fig. 3. Typical Application scenarios of Intelligence: Industry Perspective

can be categorized into three major variants. They are, categorically: (i) supervised, (ii) unsupervised, and (iii) reinforcement learning. Recently, diverse approaches of ML are being applied for continuous up gradations of performance improvement of the NGWN.

6.1 The Architecture of Radio Learning

The various methods of ML are being incorporated for the modelling and as well as for the addressing of the various technical and key challenges and issues involved in advanced 5G, B5G and towards the 6G. The target implementation of the network intelligence are in large scale MIMO, D2D networks and in heterogeneous networks having a large number of smaller (femto) cells. The following Fig. 4 depicts the various ML (radio learning) techniques and their potential target applications in the network.

6.1.1 Supervised Learning (SL)

The training of Supervised learning (SL) algorithms are performed applying labelled data-set. In these approaches, the system knows the input and as well as the desired output data to be predicted. In these types of approaches, it is important to have adequate data, to apply effectively in target applications. These models can be applied for the estimation of the network parameters. The typical application area as reported are, the channel estimation in MIMO, sensing the spectrum [21], detection of data, detection of the white space (cognitive radio), filtering (adaptive) in 5G communications, etc.

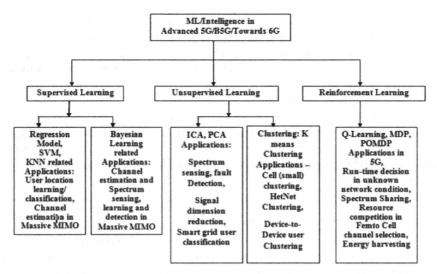

Fig. 4. Radio learning Architecture: Incorporation of ML/Intelligence in network.

6.1.2 Unsupervised Learning (USL)

The various applications of unsupervised learning (USL) in the network is based on the input data (for example, the incoming traffic pattern) itself heuristically. The application areas include the clustering of base station (heterogeneous) in the HetNets including load balancing, clustering of cells in small-cell networks (ultra-dense) in a cooperative manner, association of the access points in WiFi (ubiquitous) networks, the behaviour categorization of the end users, for detecting network fault and as well as the intrusion detection, etc.

6.1.3 Reinforcement Learning (RL)

Reinforcement learning (RL) is executed depending on an indicator (feedback-performance) or the reward learnt from the environment. This learning is performed after computing a precise output for a definite observation by converging (adaptively) to the desired best performance through the increment of the reward. RL is a method of negotiation form of the supervised and unsupervised learning. The reinforcement learning, an ML approach is a dynamic learning (iterative) and as well as decision making process which can be applied in advanced 5G networks and beyond. These types of learning approaches are applied to deal with the problems of sequential decisions making, which are dependent on Markov decision processes.

6.1.4 Deep Learning (DL)

Deep learning (DL), a type of neural network (having 3 or more layers) is a subset of machine learning [7]. These neural network try to simulate the actions of a brain (human), and apply learning from the data (large amount). Recently, it has been observed that there are potential growth of application related to the Deep learning, methods based on the artificial neural networks (ANNs) to solve many learning problems in telecom sectors. Deep Learning (DL) considers a rigorous system structure for the required representing and as wells as for learning structures (correlation) in the available data by executing in a supervised, unsupervised, reinforcement, or applying in a hybrid fashion/mode. The various approaches include the Multilayer perceptrons (MLPs), the Convolutional neural networks (CNN), for learning sequential models, the Recurrent Neural Networks (RNN), etc. However, the challenges involved are due to the issues associated with the dimensionality as these types of learning require large volume of dataset (training) in order to attain considerable performance improvement. Furthermore, the heterogeneity of the network is a challenging concern of applying DL due to the coexistence of various network operators [6].

6.1.5   Deep Reinforcement Learning (DRL)

The Deep Reinforcement Learning, a combination of RL with the Deep neural networks (DNN) is considered as an excellent performer in telecommunication networks. DRL is an alternate and potential solution to statistical models applied to address the network slicing challenges involved. In this type of learning, the interactions are performed in a trial and error method [22] and the learning from the actions in order to improve the rewards. In DRL there are certain pitfalls of poor performance related to the dimensionality in a very bulky state-action spaces. Applying RL, in combining with the DNN may be the possible solutions to resolve the challenges.

7   Challenges Associated with Applying ML in NGWN

Applying or deployment of appropriate learning process for optimizing the performance of the network is challenging task compared to the existing state-of-the-art deterministic models. As the learning is a continuous process (incremental type) of non-linear progress, there is high possibility to strike down the local minima. Accordingly, the performance of the network may get affected locally and then the network resumes improving related to its performance. The prediction may be inaccurate for the black-box perception of ML/AI, while processing large volume of data. Moreover, as predictions/ learning may be of higher variation of results compared to deterministic network (model), there is a challenge to apply appropriate ML techniques. In general, there is a trend that the network operators prefer to apply restricted approach of supervised learning model/ approach followed by other ML to avoid any undesirable deviation or failure from the expected results and to ensure a greater degree of accuracy of the desired outcome.

7.1   Challenges of Implementing the Process of Desired Learning

With the rapid progress of 5G standards, pre-commercial tests [23] and the rolling out of the advanced 5G networks in several countries along with diversified applications, the telco and service provides have to address various challenges due to complexity of the network, varied no of services and managing of the heterogeneous traffic classes and for the requirements of the end user's experience (QoE).

Complexity of the Network: As 5G network are densely distributed, the complexity of the network arises due to various factors including the complex site planning and installation.

Antenna Array: The complexity due to the configuration of densely deployed antenna arrays in a large-scale.

Scheduling: There is a requirement of complex scheduling algorithm for resource utilization.

7.2 Challenges of Implementing the Network Edge Intelligence

With the rapid up gradation and a large number of devices gets connected in 5G, there is a major need of distributed intelligence in network. The telcos are focusing to addressing various research challenges associated with the rapid transformation from a centrally cloud based learning to partially distributed as well as power efficient intelligence or learning at the network edge (edge cloud). Theses research trends will further accelerate to adoption of AI/ML a fully distributed way in 5G, where learning will take place at the edge devices.

7.3 The Trends for Addressing Challenges in Advanced 5G

To address various challenges in wireless communication and networks the Telcos, are focusing on design and development of data-driven solution controlled by AI/ML. Moreover there is trend of by the Telco applying ML, learning in the CORE and in the RAN. Furthermore, there are research trends to develop intelligent beam-forming and efficient power management. As spectrum utilization and the minimization of interference are of design issues of prime importance, the Telcos are working on to develop such dynamic-spectrum utilization, interference minimizations. The ML is applied also for network system protection to avoid the malicious attack.

8   ML Incorporation: Open Issues Offer Research Directions

Incorporation of ML in the NGWN draws significant attention for several open issues and as well as it attracts multi-dimensional research challenges to combat.

  i. **Time Convergence:** Incorporating ML, the convergence time for appropriate run-time decisions, estimation of the network parameters and the network driving factors have a strong impact and these are the potential areas for further research [14] and developments. It is a critical issue to optimize the time convergence, considering the constraint that the convergence due to the ML time convergence must not degrade the performance of the heavily dynamic 5G network having varying network environment.

ii. **CSI Acquisition in IRS:** In MISO-IRS enabled networks and in IRS-enhanced wireless communication, it is crucially important that the acquisition of CSI is in a accurate form and its captured in a timely manner. In such networks, finding out the CSI is a challenging task due to overhead during the process of training. Furthermore, in NOMA networks (IRS-guided), in general, the CSI of the users in a cluster is being shared with other users in the same cluster. In such cases, the processes of acquisition of CSI and as well as the exchange of information of CSI, are significantly challenging task. In such cases, there are research trends that ML and in particular, various DL-based approaches are being utilized to combat such issues.

iii. **Resource allocation:** Applying AI/ ML can be incorporated for various applications related to e-health. In case wearable sensor are used for remote medical treatments, there is a research challenge to balance the resource allocation for several technologies. The ML can be used to address for such balancing and it is a promising research area for further developments.

iv. **QoS and QoE:** Due to the characteristics of heterogeneity of a network having a large number of users, there are different requirements of the QoS and QoE. As for example, in video streaming applications, the users expect least delay but higher throughput, where the security is not the utmost concern, although it matters.

v. **UaaIS:** UAVs as an Intelligent Service (UaaIS) utilizes the technology of UAV to offer services related to 5G integrated edge computing [24] and caching, wireless communication, etc., where ML techniques can be applied for performance improvement.

8.1 Trends Towards ML-Powered 6G Network: Edge Intelligence

Researchers are strongly focusing for further research and developments, that the 6G will apply massive intelligence integrating with the target ML based approaches and particularly the deployment of edge intelligent computing [24] i.e. adopting ML, at the edge of the network which is a challenging task for implementation and draws major key attention. The integrating of ML in the 6G network will provide an optimized network and as well as its performance improvement.

9 Conclusion

This paper has portrayed a comprehensive illustrative study on incorporating of machine learning for the requirements of intelligence in the network of advanced 5G, beyond (B5G) and towards the forthcoming developing 6G network. The author has made an comprehensive detailed review of various state-of-the-art ML approaches, techniques integrating ML for NGWN and potential target applications. In this survey, several challenges arising out due to the deployment of the NGWN and ML incorporation in the advanced network have been specifically focused. The paper has outlined various open issues which offer potential future research directions.

References

1. Turtelboom, A., et al.: Special report: 5G roll-out in the EU: delays in deployment of networks with security issues remaining unresolved. European Court of Auditors, pp. 1–69 (2022). Available: https://www.eca.europa.eu/Lists/ECADocuments/SR22_03/SR_Security-5G-networks_EN.pdf
2. 5G Unlocks A World of Opportunities – Top Ten 5G Use Cases, whitepaper of Huawei, pp. 1–30 (2017). https://www.huawei.com/en/technology-insights/industry-insights/outlook/mobile-broadband/insights-reports/5g-unlocks-a-world-of-opportunities
3. Wikstgrom, G., et al.: 6G connecting a cyber physical world: a Research outlook toward 2030, Ericsson white paper, pp. 3–6 (2022). https://www.ericsson.com/4927de/assets/local/reports-papers/white-papers/6g---connecting-a-cyber-physical-world.pdf
4. Ericsson Mobility Report, pp. 1–40 (2022). https://www.ericsson.com/49d3a0/assets/local/reports-papers/mobility-report/documents/2022/ericsson-mobility-report-june-2022.pdf
5. Nawaz, S.J., Sharma, S.K., Wyne, S., Patwary, M.N., Asaduzzaman, M.: Quantum machine learning for 6G communication networks: state-of-the-art and vision for the future. IEEE Access **7**, 46317–46350 (2019). https://doi.org/10.1109/ACCESS.2019.2909490
6. A vision of artificial intelligence for 6G communications, a thought leadership white paper, Comarch, pp. 1–13 (2022). https://www.comarch.com
7. 5G Evolution and 6G, Whitepaper of NTT DOCOMO, INC. (Ver. 4), pp. 1–60 (2022). https://www.docomo.ne.jp/english/binary/pdf/corporate/technology/whitepaper_6g/DOCOMO_6G_White_PaperEN_v4.0.pdf
8. Deng, L., Liu, K., Zhang, Y., Banzi, M., Casey, S., Cohen, B.: White paper: intelligent networking, AI and machine learning - a telecommunications operator's perspective, LF Networking, pp. 1–26 (2022). https://lfnetworking.org/wp-content/uploads/sites/7/2022/06/LFN_IntelligentNetworking_Whitepaper_110421.pdf
9. Employing AI techniques to enhance returns on 5G network investments, Ericsson Report, (Ericsson AI and Automation), pp. 1–12, BNEW-19:007926 Uen. https://www.ericsson.com/49b63f/assets/local/ai-and-automation/docs/machine-learning-and-aiaw-screen.pdf
10. Ssengonzi, C., Kogeda, O.P., Olwal, T.O.: A survey of deep reinforcement learning application in 5G and beyond network slicing and virtualization. Array **14**(2022), 1–27 (2022). https://doi.org/10.1016/j.array.2022.100142
11. Jiang, C., Zhang, H., Ren, Y., Han, Z., Chen, K.-C., Hanzo, L.: Machine learning paradigms for next-generation wireless networks. IEEE Wirel. Commun. **24**(2), 98–105 (2017). https://doi.org/10.1109/MWC.2016.1500356WC
12. Salameh, A.I., Tarhuni, M.E.: From 5G to 6G - challenges technologies, and applications. Future Internet **14**(117), 1–35 (2022). https://doi.org/10.3390/fi14040117
13. Akhtar, M.W., Hassan, S.A., Ghaffar, R., Jung, H., Garg, S., Hossain, M.S.: The shift to 6G communications: vision and requirements. Human-Centric Comput. Inf. Sci. **10**, 1–27 (2020). https://doi.org/10.1186/s13673-020-00258-2
14. Ly, A., Yao, Y.-D.: A review of deep learning in 5g research: channel coding, massive MIMO, multiple access, resource allocation, and network security. IEEE Open Journal of the Commun. Soc. **2**, 396–408 (2021). https://doi.org/10.1109/OJCOMS.2021.3058353
15. Iliadis, L.A., Zaharis, Z.D., Sotiroudis, S., Sarigiannidis, P., Karagiannidis, G.K., Goudos, S.K.: The road to 6G: a comprehensive survey of deep learning applications in cell free massive MIMO communications systems. EURASIP J. Wirel. Commun. Netw. **68**(2022), 1–16 (2022). https://doi.org/10.1186/s13638-022-02153-z
16. de Figueiredo, F.A.P.: An overview of massive MIMO for 5G and 6G. IEEE Latin America Trans. **20**(6), 931–940 (2022). https://doi.org/10.1109/TLA.2022.9757375

17. Falahy, N.A., Alani, O.Y.: Technologies for 5G networks: challenges and opportunities. IT Prof. **19**, 12–20 (2017). https://doi.org/10.1109/MITP.2017.9

18. Papidas, A.G., Polyzos, G.C.: Self-organizing networks for 5G and beyond: a view from the top. Future Internet **14**(3), 1–30 (2022). https://doi.org/10.3390/fi14030095

19. ITU-FG ML 5G focus group. https://www.itu.int/en/ITU-T/focusgroups/ml5g/Pages/default.aspx

20. Michalski, R.S., Carbonell, J.G., Mitchell, T.M.: Machine Learning: An Artificial Intelligence Approach. Springer, Heidelberg (2013)

21. Sutton, R.S., Barto, A.G.: Reinforcement Learning: An Introduction. MIT Press (2018). ISBN: 9780262039246. https://mitpress.mit.edu/9780262039246/reinforcement-learning/

22. Kalogiros, C., Muschamp, P., Caruso, G., Hallingby, H.K., Darzanos, G., Gavras, A.: Capabilities of business and operational support systems for pre-commercial 5G test beds. IEEE Commun. Mag. **59**(12), 58–64 (2021). https://doi.org/10.1109/MCOM.003.2001059

23. Elsayed, M., Erol-Kantarci, M.: AI-enabled future wireless networks: challenges, opportunities, and open issues. IEEE Veh. Technol. Mag. **14**(3), 70–77 (2019). https://doi.org/10.1109/MVT.2019.2919236

24. Hu, Y.C., Patel, M., Sabella, D., Sprecher, N., Young, V.: Mobile edge computing - a key technology towards 5G, whitepaper of European Telecommunications Standards Institute (ETSI), France, ISBN No. 979-10-92620-08-5, pp. 4–14 (2015). https://www.etsi.org/images/files/etsiwhitepapers/etsi_wp11_mec_a_key_technology_towards_5g.pdf

Recognition of Speech Emotion Using Machine Learning Techniques

Akash Chaurasiya, Govind Garg, Rahul Gaud, Bodhi Chakraborty$^{(\boxtimes)}$, and Shashi Kant Gupta

ITM University Gwalior, Gwalior, MP, India
{bodhi.cse,shashikantgupta}@itmuniversity.ac.in

Abstract. Speech emotion recognition (SER) is a crucial portion of interaction between computers and machines. In this venture, we aim to classify speech that is taken as fair, joyful, sorrowful, amazed, panic, dislike, fume. Speech emotion recognition frameworks recognize feelings from the human voice in the areas of hospitality, the automobile industry, telecom centers, programmed interpretation frameworks, and human-machine interaction like robots. The **Audio** dataset was created by combining sound recordings from the Ryerson Audiovisual Database of Emotional Speech and Song (RAVDESS) and the Toronto Speech Set Data (TEES).The relevance of these highlighted feeling classifications is contrasted using methodologies such as Long Short Term Memory (LSTM), Decision Tree, MLP Classifier and K-Nearest Neighbour (KNN). In this classification 7 feelings are present. The LSTM training model achieved 92.5% accuracy; the Decision Tree training model achieved 100% accuracy.

Keywords: Audio · MFCC · LSTM · KNN

1 Introduction

Speech Emotion Recognition (SER) is discourse analysis to predict the speaker's emotional state [1, 2]. SER is an important study field for a variety of applications, such as healthcare, where the current passionate state of a person is identified by sound and appropriate administrations are provided. SER is also useful when driving a vehicle equipped with an SER framework [3–5]. A report from the United Nations predicts that, rather than being their accomplices, a growing number of people will be associated with the voice collaborator machine within the next five years. With the rise of Virtual Individual Colleagues (VPAs) such as Siri, Alexa, and Google Collaborator in our everyday lives, they take on the task of quickly and securely addressing our enquiries and providing our expectations. Despite the fact that these colleagues get our orders, they are not talented enough to recognize our temperaments and respond appropriately [6, 7]. In this manner, it is important to create a successful feeling acknowledgment framework that can upgrade the abilities of these associates and transform the whole sector. Speech is a rich and powerful method of expressing our views that can properly communicate information [8, 19, 25].There are two types of data: phonetic and paralinguistic. The

R. S. Tomar et al. (Eds.): CNC 2022, CCIS 1894, pp. 137–147, 2023.
https://doi.org/10.1007/978-3-031-43145-6_12

primary alludes to verbal substance and the fundamental dialect code, and the moment alludes to body dialect, motions, facial expressions, tone of voice, pitch, feelings, etc. [9–12]. It means that indirect data such as paralinguistic highlights can offer assistance in obtaining a person's mental state (feelings), sex, states of mind, lingo, and more. The recorded discourse has key highlights that can be used to methodically extricate data such as feelings. Gathering such data will be priceless in encouraging more characteristic discussions between the virtual right hand and the client due to the enthusiastic nature of regular human interaction [13, 14, 20]. Feeling persistent and distinct can be expressed in two ways: In continuous representation, talked-about feelings can be communicated as persistent values over different mental measurements [17, 18]. According to one report, feelings can be portrayed from two angles: enactment and esteem. Actuation is defined as "the sum of vitality required to specify a certain feeling," and it has been discovered that joy, panic, and fume are associated with high vitality and pitch [15, 16, 21], whereas sorrow and dislike are associated with moderate vitality and moderate speech. Valence brings more subtlety and makes a difference between feelings such as being amazed and being fair, where expanded actuation can speak to both [22–24]. In discrete expressions, feelings are fair, joyful, fume, and so on, and are independently expressed as certain categories while several attempts have been made in the past for various languages to differentiate sentiments from words [26, 27].

2 Proposed Methodology

Since the information are nearly equitably disseminated, exactness may be a substantial metric for comparing the execution of models. Each model was prepared for 100 epochs at diverse bunch size.

In this research, we are working with on dataset, which is named Audio. We are extracting features with MFCCs and implementing multiple algorithms for the best result. This LSTM algorithm was used with multiple dense features. Splitting data with the Sklearn library and displaying audio with visualisation tools like Seaborn, Matplotlib, and Librosa.

We are extracting MFCC highlights in lesson have 7 expectations found that the arrange may not get it records from the "Stunned" class. We thought this may well be due to the need of the "surprise" lesson with in the information. In this manner, the "Astounded" course was evacuated from the information set and assist examination was performed utilizing as it were 7 Classes: fume, joyful, sorrowful, amazed, panic and dislike. Expanding the number of MFCCs for LSTM (Fig. 1).

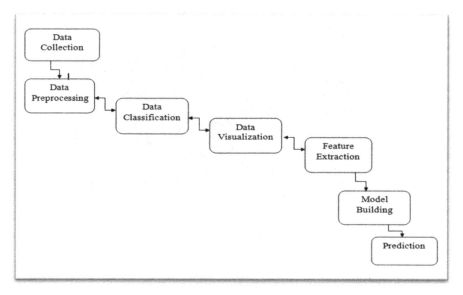

Fig. 1. There are few steps of Speech Emotions Analysis

2.1 Data Collection

The Ryerson Audiovisual Dataset of Emotional Speech and Song (RAVDESS) and Toronto Speech Set Data (TEES) were combined to analyze and form the dataset which is named is "Audio". In this dataset, many voices are present, each containing joyful, sorrowful, fume, amazed, panic, dislike, and fair emotions. There are a total of 4240 expressions in the Audio dataset. The Audio dataset is inherently very rich considering that it is not gender-biased, encompasses a broad spectrum of emotions with varying degrees of emotional intensity. Furthermore, we note that the Audio dataset is evenly distributed across all emotion classes. The distribution of data according to emotion classes is shown in the Figure. The distribution of data by emotion classes are shown in Fig. 2.

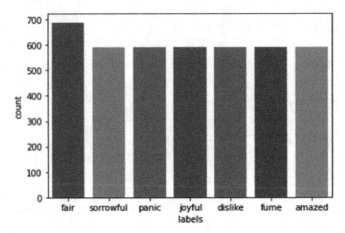

Fig. 2. Distribution of audio by emotion

2.2 Data Preparation

In all sound records contains multiple speech emotions identify, each speaking to methodology, feeling, passionate concentrated, expression, redundancy, and performing artist, individually. The naming tradition taken after a design where person performing artists or indeed performing artists spoken to male and female sexes, individually. The target variable is the feeling by which sound recording is identified. In cleaning the dataset we remove fields and rename some of emotions. The starting and the nonstop quiets. In spite of the fact that the sounds were professionally recorded, there were exceptionally little commotion designs within the information (Fig. 3).

For Merging Two Datasets

Audio=pd.concat([RAVD_df,TEES],axis=0,ignore_index=True)

For Changing Labels

```
Audio['labels']=Audio['labels'].replace({'neutral':'fair'})
Audio['labels']=Audio['labels'].replace({'sad':'sorrowful'})
Audio['labels']=Audio['labels'].replace({'fear':'panic'})
Audio['labels']=Audio['labels'].replace({'happy':'joyful'})
Audio['labels']=Audio['labels'].replace({'disgust':'dislike'})
Audio['labels']=Audio['labels'].replace({'angry':'fume'})
Audio['labels']=Audio['labels'].replace({'surprise':'amazed'})
```

Fig. 3. Dataset Merged and labels changed

2.3   Data Visualization

In this method, we have to visualise the waveplot and spectogram of all emotions by using the Seaborn and Librosa libraries. Data visualisation improves knowledge of the problem and the sort of solution to be produced. Python and R both include statistical tools for visualising data, as well as a number of other tools available for visualizing data such as Power BI, Weka, Excel and many more (Figs. 4, 5 and 6).

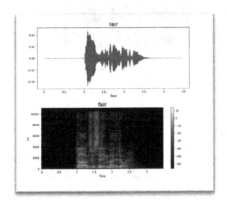
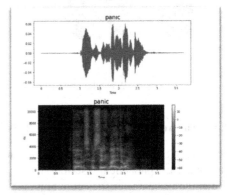

Fig. 4. Waveplot and Spectogram of fair and panic Emotion.

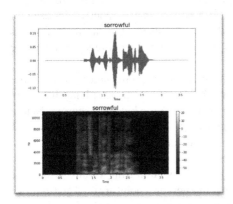
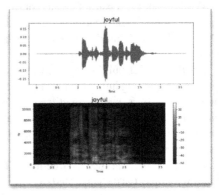

Fig. 5. Waveplot and Spectogram of Sorrowful and joyful Emotion.

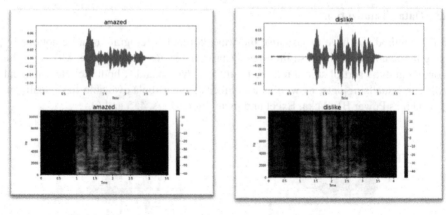

Fig. 6. Waveplot and Spectogram of Amazed and Dislike Emotion.

2.4 Feature Extraction and Model Building

Speech is a constantly changing sound signal. Humans may change the sound signal to pronounce the phonetic transcription using their auditory canal, tongue, and teeth. The extraction of characteristics common among speech signals provides a more accurate representation of the voice signals in order to extract as much information as possible from the language. Avoid features that are distinctive and particular to specific data samples. In the feature extraction we are extract the feature using Librosa library which name is Mel-Frequency Cepstral Coefficient (MFCCs).A collection of characteristics used for speech emotion identification is classified as the Mel Frequency Cepstrum Coefficients (MFCC).The scale used in Frequency versus Pitch measurement is represented by the term Mel.

In this model building step multiple algorithms are implemented to achieve our goal of recognizing human voice emotion. LSTM is an abbreviation for long short-term memory networks, which are utilized in Deep Learning. It is a kind of Recurrent Neural Network (RNN) that can learn long-term dependencies. The LSTM features feedback connections, which means it can process the whole data sequence. The Decision tree technique visualizes the full dataset as a tree. Each characteristic in the dataset is viewed as a decision node at the sub-tree level. The first tree is built using variables from the training sample. On the generated tree, the values of a new data point are tracked from root to leaf. The simplest categorization algorithm is K-Nearest Neighbor (KNN). When the optimum value of k is used, it requires no training and requires the shortest computation time. Make a decision based on the majority vote of the k closest locations in space to any new sample. The audio files are sent into the Speech Emotion Recognition System (SER). The data is transformed into the appropriate format, and characteristics such as framing, hamming, windowing, and so on are extracted. This aids in segmenting the files into the numerous parameters that indicate the frequency, time, amplitude, or other similar factors. The model is trained once the relevant features have been extracted.

3   Results and Discussions

We performed a thorough examination of several feature engineering and modelling strategies for emotion identification. We get considerably better results with manufactured characteristics like MFCCs and Log-mel spectrograms than using raw audio input, which is most likely due to a lack of data. Although MFCCs are the most often used features for speech-based emotion recognition, we find that Log-Mel spectrogram features perform much better. Adding tempo and velocity information to the MFCCs enhanced model performance as well, indicating that the MFCC features are lacking in tempo and velocity data, which is essential in sentiment forecasting. After implementing all the algorithms, we find some loss in training but get some accuracy, which is shown in Figs. 1.9 and 2.0. We make one confusion matrix and also make a table in which we describe training and testing the accuracy of multiple algorithms (Figs. 7, 8, 9, 10 and Table 1).

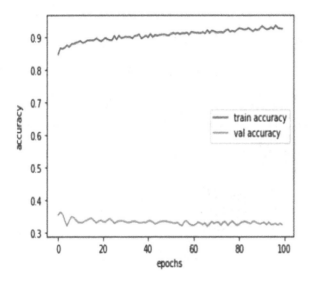

Fig. 7. Training Accuracy Graph

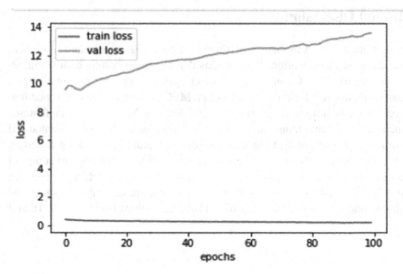

Fig. 8. Training Loss Graph

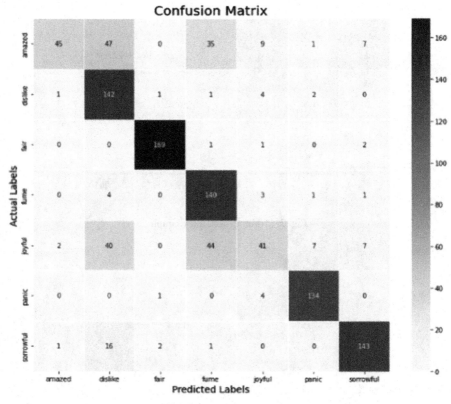

Fig. 9. Confusion Matrix

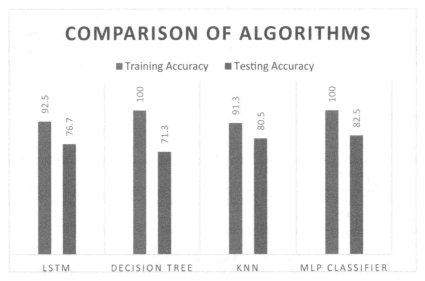

Fig. 10. Bar Graph of Algorithm Comparison

Table 1. Comparison Table

Algorithm Name	Training Accuracy(%)	Testing Accuracy(%)
LSTM	92.5	76.7
Decision Tree	100	71.3
KNN	91.3	80.5
MLP Classifier	100	82.5

4 Conclusion

The rise of artificial intelligence (AI) has ushered in a new era of automated gadgets that respond to human voice instructions. Many benefits may be created over present systems if, in addition to identifying words, robots also accommodate the speaker's emotion. A voice emotion detection system can be utilized in computer-based teaching applications, automated contact centre discussions, and diagnostic tools for mental diagnosis.

It has been found that an integrated feature space would result in a higher recognition rate than a single feature. A number of tests were conducted to understand fully the effects of each phase in the process of creating a speech emotion detecting system. The results of the experiment indicate that combining several characteristics into a single model results in a higher overall success rate.

Further modeling of the proposed project's effectiveness, precision, and usefulness is possible. Therapists can keep an eye on their patients' mood fluctuations by using such systems. Since it can be difficult to discern sarcasm from other emotions using simply the speaker's words or tone, sarcasm identification is a more challenging problem of emotion detection.

References

1. Ayadi, M.E., Kamel, M.S., Karray, F.: Survey on speech emotion recognition: Features, classification schemes, and databases. Pattern Recognit. **44**(3), 572–587 (2011). https://doi.org/10.1016/j.patcog.2010.09.020
2. Bottou, L., Bousquet, O.: The tradeoffs of large scale learning. In: Sra, S., Nowozin, S., Wright, S.J. (eds.) Optimization for Machine Learning, pp. 351–368. MIT Press, Cambridge (2012) 978-0-262-01646-9
3. Chen, C.H.: Signal Processing Handbook. Dekker, New York (1988)
4. Chenchah, F., Lachiri, Z.: Acoustic emotion recognition using linear and nonlinear cepstral coefficients. Int. J. Adv. Comput. Sci. Appl. **6**(11), 135–138 (2015)
5. Kingma, D.P., Ba, J.: Adam: a method for stochastic optimization arXiv:1412.6980 (2014)
6. Dupuis, K., Pichora-Fuller, M.K.: Toronto emotional speech set (TESS), University of Toronto, Psychology Department (2010)
7. Fux, T., Jouvet, D.: Evaluation of PNCC and extended spectral subtraction methods for robust speech recognition. In: 2015 23rd European Signal Processing Conference (EUSIPCO), Nice, pp. 1416–1420 (2015). https://doi.org/10.1109/EUSIPCO.2015.7362617
8. Donahue, J., et al.: Long-term recurrent convolutional networks for visual recognition and description, CoRR, volume = abs/1411.4389 (2014)
9. Haq, S., Jackson, P.J.B.: Speaker-dependent audio-visual emotion recognition. In: Proceedings International Conference on Auditory-Visual Speech Processing, pp. 53–58 (2009)
10. Hochreiter, S., Schmidhuber, J.: Long short-term memory. Neural Computation. MIT Press, Cambridge, MA, USA (1997)
11. Ji, S., Xu, W., Yang, M., Yu, K.: 3D convolutional neural networks for human action recognition. IEEE Trans. Pattern Anal. Mach. Intell. **35**, 221–231 (2010)
12. Krizhevsky, A., Sutskever, I., Hinton, G.: ImageNet classification with deep convolutional neural networks. In: Neural Information Processing Systems, vol. 25 (2012). https://doi.org/10.1145/3065386
13. Livingstone, S.R., Russo, F.A.: The Ryerson audio-visual database of emotional speech and song (RAVDESS): a dynamic, multimodal set of facial and vocal expressions in north American English. PLoS ONE **13**(5), e0196391 (2018). https://doi.org/10.1371/journal.pone.0196391
14. Lyons, J.: Mel Frequency Cepstral Coefficient (MFCC) tutorial
15. Müller, M.: Fundamentals of Music Processing. Springer, Heidelberg (2015). https://doi.org/10.1007/978-3-319-21945-5. ISBN 978-3-319-21944-8
16. Rabiner, L.R., Juang, B.H.: An introduction to hidden Markov models. IEEE ASSP Mag. **3**, 4–16 (1986)
17. Schuller, B., Rigoll, G., Lang, M.: Hidden Markov model-based speech emotion recognition. In: 2003 International Conference on Multimedia and Expo. ICME '03. Proceedings (Cat. No.03TH8698), Baltimore, MD, USA, pp. I-401 (2003). https://doi.org/10.1109/ICME.2003.1220939
18. Shaw, A., Kumar, R., Saxena, S.: Emotion recognition and classification in speech using artificial neural networks. Int. J. Comput. Appl. **145**(8), 5–9 (2016). https://doi.org/10.5120/ijca2016910710

19. Parthasarathy, S., Tashev, I.: Convolutional neural network techniques for speech emotion recognition. Microsoft Research (2018)
20. Stevens, S.S., Volkmann, J., Newman, E.B.: A scale for the measurement of the psychological magnitude pitch. J. Acoust. Soc. America **8**(3), 185–190 (1937). https://doi.org/10.1121/1. 1915893
21. Tomas, G.S.: Speech emotion recognition using convolutional neural networks. Technical University of Berlin (2019). https://www2.ak.tu-berlin.de/~akgroup/ak_pub/abschlussarb eiten/2019/Tomas_MasA.pdf
22. United Nations Educational, Scientific, and Cultural Organization. I'd blush if I could: closing gender divides in digital skills through education (Programme Document GEN/2019/EQUALS/1 REV 2) (2019). http://unesdoc.unesco.org/images/0021/002170/217 073e.pdf
23. Wiener, N.: Extrapolation, Interpolation, and Smoothing of Stationary Time Series. Wiley, New York (1949). ISBN 978-0-262-73005-1
24. Yamashita, Y.: A review of paralinguistic information processing for natural speech communication. Acoust. Sci. Technol. **34**(2), 73–79 (2013). https://doi.org/10.1250/ast.34.73
25. Chen, L.-C., Papandreou, G., Schroff, F., Adam, H.: Rethinking atrous convolution for semantic image segmentation, CoRR, abs/1706.05587 (2017). http://arxiv.org/abs/1706. 05587
26. Hossain, M.S., Sultana, Z., Nahar, L., Andersson, K.: An intelligent system to diagnose chikungunya under uncertainty. J. Wirel. Mobile Netw. Ubiquitous Comput. Dependable Appl. **10**(2), 37–54 (2019)
27. Iqbal, A., Barua, K.: A real-time emotion recognition from speech using gradient boosting. In: 2019 International Conference on Electrical, Computer and Communication Engineering (ECCE), pp. 1–5. IEEE (2019)

Convolution Neural Network Based Model for Classification and Identification of Fake Profile on Social Network

Taukeer Ahemad and Manoj Lipton[✉]

Department of Computer Science and Engineering, Radharaman Institute of Technology and Science, Bhopal, M.P, India
manojlipton6@gmail.com

Abstract. The use of social media for business and politics has led to more bad behaviour. Like personal, corporate, and political propaganda, social media engagement has encouraged people to do things that aren't good for them. The intruder gets a full platform to spread criticism after they hide behind a hacked profile. This study takes important parts from social media data that show a complicated connection in order to find out if there are any problems. The system is good at figuring out what's wrong with people's behaviour by looking for malicious or fake social network accounts. Influence, Homophily, and Balance Theory are used in a theory-based social framework to improve user space accuracy in classifying dangerous users. In this case, it uses the Jaccard coefficient to figure out how similar two things are. Use graphical and linguistic clues to classify end-users in User-space. The built-in framework is tested with standard parameters, like a confusion matrix, to see how well it works. It's better for social atom anomaly detection to use the friend connection identification framework that was suggested.

Keywords: Social Media · Social Media Mining · Fake user · Influence · Homophily · Balance Theory

1 Introduction

Social networking is a significant and worthwhile endeavour. Using user profiles and user-generated data, the traditional method in the literature is to label end users as malicious. However, the diversity and correctness are in danger due to the linguistic and graphical features' reduced engagement. The standard method for identifying end-user ideology and perspective on any product, politics, national and local issues, and other topics overlooks languages and opinion features. An efficient anomaly classification model for social media platforms is created using a social theory-based connection identification framework that includes user graphical and linguistic elements for creating user space. User space has an impact on the flow of destructive activity on social media, which leads to a solution, namely scalability in a large network.

There are some very influential issues on social networks. In this role, the primary goal is to find a social worker to replace the employer. As it is known that power users increase the growth of workers in a group that has the same problem of public access it is scalability i.e. large networks.

2 Social Media

Social media is viewed from the standpoint of online electronic communication as a tool that enables people to connect with one another and create online groups to share information, novel ideas, messages, and other private and public content [3]. Social media are any websites (such as Facebook, Twitter, YouTube, and others) that let users interact with one another, share information, and subscribe to news feeds [2].

Through social networking sites, people may publish and share their thoughts, images, and videos with their friends and other users. Social media services are used by the vast majority of internet users because they make it simple for people to post content on social media.

In the social media era, end-user involvement in business marketing, political propaganda, educational activities, and entertainment has increased significantly. Social media is now widely used for marketing, brand recognition, and other promotional activities in addition to education. The drawback of this promotion is that it draws intruders who act abnormally, such as making bogus profiles to spread poor publicity for malicious businesses.

Graph topologies that represent persons and edges that represent connections between them can be used to simulate the nodes of social networks. Networks are viewed as graphs in topology-based community detection techniques. However, the key components in the issue of classifying the charts into different groups vary depending on the methodologies used. For this reason, it is important to specify the structure of the Groups that will be established and belong to the graph first. Making ensuring that the community's connection density is higher than the connection density outside the community is the most basic strategy. Another technique for grouping similar nodes is to compute the distance between adjacent nodes using a set of similarity criteria.

Some traditional data clustering algorithms are utilised as a result. However, many data clustering issues are, regrettably, NP-hard issues. Due to this, numerous low complexity approach algorithms are used to design ways that attempt to approach the ideal solution.

Grouping techniques including graph segmentation, spectral clustering, divisive algorithms like Girvan Newman, modularity-based optimization algorithms, and statistics-based techniques are applied to the ensemble detection problem.

Through malicious community information, malicious activity identification captures both user and social characteristics. The results of this research could be useful in identifying spam reviews, false information, and rumours that circulate on social media. Additionally, in order to predict crime, identify criminal user groups, and analyse the influence of political ideologies during an election campaign, this work offers the user-space for manipulating harmful passive users by their ideology.

3   Social Media Mining

Criminal and suspicious activities can be uncovered through mining social media data. Mining large quantities of social media data is a new field, and social media mining has established the core ideas and algorithms for doing so. There includes discussion of a wide range of topics in computing, including data mining, machine learning, social network analysis, network science, ethnography, statistics, optimization, and mathematics. Formalizing, measuring, modelling, and mining huge volumes of social media data are all part of this framework [4].

Discovering novel and practical insights inside social network data is the ultimate objective of social media mining. As the data may contain personally identifiable information about social media users, it must be anonymized before publication or before being handed to data mining specialists.

4   Social Media Spam

Over the past few years, spam has become a problem for every online communication channel. Spammers have taken advantage of the explosion in popularity of social media sites like Facebook, Twitter, YouTube, etc. Since users may openly disclose any number of details about their social lives and relationships, spammers are only too happy to exploit this feature for their own ends. Spammers' attacks on e-mail and online search engines in the early days of the digital revolution piqued the interest of information scientists. As can be seen in Fig. 1 [5], in recent years researchers have focused heavily on developing methods to detect and block spam on social media platforms like Twitter and Facebook.

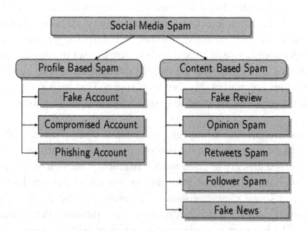

Fig. 1. Social Media User Features

Researches in the United States have concentrated on finding social network spammers because of their ubiquity and potential risks. Spammers in social networks may be identified using a combination of supervised, unsupervised, and graph algorithms. We employed the support vector machine's parameter J to describe the prior distribution of Spammer's percentage, adjusted J to strike a compromise between accuracy and recall, and made use of gain to maximise the former. The chi-squared test is useful for identifying differences [6]. Using MD5 text similarity and URL clustering, we created groups with similar characteristics, and then assigned Spammer scores to each group based on their share of the total distribution and the pace at which they sent out messages [7]. The spectral decomposition solution to the optimal weight was used to discover the Twitter spammer [8]. To function, supervised algorithms need signs of differentiating features, while unsupervised algorithms only need adequate similarity indicators. The spammer uses visible characteristics to evade detection, despite the method's effectiveness. Graph data is notoriously difficult to process due to its massive size and sparseness.

5 Related Work

Social media platforms like Facebook, Twitter, Google, Sina Weibo, and others have quickly become important parts of people's lives because of how easy they are to use, how flexible they are, and how full of content they are. Right now, the number of people who use online social networks is growing at a very fast rate. Because social networks have so much private information about their users and are worth so much money, they have become a target for criminals who want to avoid the law. Criminals send a lot of spam SMS as one of the most common ways to attack social media. In this article, "spam text" refers to the text of many product promotion texts, fake review texts, and rumours about hot events that are sent to spread false information about products and put network security at risk. From January to June 2013, spam messages on social networks went up by 35.5%, and one out of every 200 social texts was spam, according to a report on 2013 social network spam statistics. They changed 5% of the apps for social media. Spam text in social networks hurts the environment, ruins the user experience, and puts user information at risk, but it also has some effect on how well social networks work and how safe they are [1].

Malicious things like spamming, making fake accounts, phishing, and spreading viruses have grown along with the incredible growth of social media around the world. Magnetic anomalies point to social media in profile, insider, eclipse, and outside spam. Profile spammers use a user's login information to make spam, phishing, and hacked accounts. Both inside and outside of the site, these accounts can be used to send spam. User-generated data spam includes things like retweets, opinions, fake trends, and follower spam. Aside from spam operations like downloads, funding, product spam, etc.

One of the first graph segmentation methods is the Kernighan-Lin algorithm [5]. By randomly dividing the network into two equal halves and altering the node pairs in each half in a specific order, it locates the community. One of the most popular techniques [6], based on the boundaries of the Fiedler vector coordinates, is spectral bisection. The Girvan-Newman [4] approach, one of the differentiating algorithms, separates based on the value of the middle link (edge betweenness). Numerous heuristic optimization strategies have been proposed to address the NP-hard ensemble detection problem in complicated networks. To ensure that the network is divided into communities in the most effective manner, these solutions use the modularity function as the aim function. For instance, a backgammon simulation approach for global optimization has been developed, in which communities are divided or reunited when modularity increases [13]. The community finding problem is solved by a variety of heuristic techniques, including the tabu search algorithm [14–16]. An additional approach that is frequently employed in investigations and is based on modularity is the modularity optimization algorithm. The concept of modularity [7] is employed in a greedy hierarchical clustering algorithm to determine when to stop.

6 Proposed framework for Identifying Malicious Profile over Social Media

This study proposes an analytical and methodological framework for harmful user identification that substantially ties implicit and explicit link connections over the end-graphical user's viewpoint, as well as a malicious user identification framework, as shown in Fig. 2. Classify end-users as malevolent or legitimate users, extract their communal information, and create a sockpuppet node from their information.

Aiming at the problem that the text content contains a lot of noise in the filter layer, the DCNN model is based on the idea of a keyword-based detection method. For example, the design is based on Naive Bayes for the word sequence [y1, y2, ..., yn] contained in specific social network information. The attention mechanism of the weighting technique.

Attention mechanism based on naive Bayes weight technology: calculate the inexperienced Bayes weight of each word according to formula (1), and then select a certain number of keywords according to the conditions to filter noise.

$$s_i = \frac{(q_t^{y_i} + \alpha)/||q_t||1}{(q_{\sim y}^{y_i} + \alpha)/||q_{s\sim}||1} \tag{1}$$

(A) **Filter Layer**

Among them, $q_t^{y_i}$ represents the number of texts that contain the word y_i in the text of the spam category y, $q_{\sim y}^{y_i}$ represents the number of texts that contain the phrase y in the text of the non-spam category s, and 1 ‖ ‖sp represents the spam category The number of texts in means the number of texts in the non-spam category $||q_{s\sim}||1$ and α is the smoothing parameter. In the text, select words with i r more significant than 1 to enter the embedding layer.

(B) **Embedded layer**

After extracting keywords through the attention mechanism of the filtering layer, suppose that a piece of social network information is filtered from n words to k words and input the embedding layer, namely [y1, y2, ..., yn]. The embedding matrix is constructed according to different representation methods in the embedding layer, and each word yt is mapped into a real number domain eigenvector $h_t \in S^{f*1}$. The specific process consists of two steps.

(1) Construct the embedding matrix $Z_{wrd} \in Sf \times |K|$, where K is a fixed-size dictionary set, f is the dimension of the embedding word, and the embedding

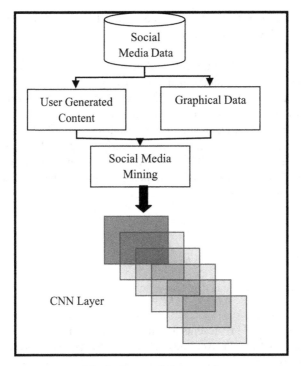

Fig. 2. Proposed Framework

matrix Zwrd needs to be learned by using different representations methods. Random embedding is used in the article., SkipGram [15], CBOW [15] and Glove [16] and other 4 feature representation methods. The SkipGram method and the CBOW method belong to the Word2vec model. They belong to the word vector model based on prediction. Still, there are specific differences: the SkipGram method uses the target word to predict the context word to obtain the feature vector representation of each term. The CBOW method accepts the feature vector representation of each word by predicting the target word by the context word. The disadvantage of this kind of prediction-based word vector model is that it does not fully utilize statistical information, and the training time is closely related to the size of the corpus. The advantage is the linear relationship between words can be extracted. The Glove method not only improves the training speed by constructing conditions similar to linear relations on the co-occurrence matrix but also utilizes the global statistical information of the corpus.

(2) For each word yt, the word yt is transformed into an embedded representation ht by matrix multiplication, and the expression is shown in formula (2).

$$h_t = Z^{wrd} k^t \tag{2}$$

Among them, $k^t \in S\ |k| \times 1$, the index position of h_t is 1, and the remaining parts are 0.

Finally, the feature vector of a piece of social network information formed by the embedding layer is expressed as [h1, h2, h3, ..., ht].

(C) **Pooling layer**

Aiming at the problem that the CNN pooling strategy is single and cannot be dynamically updated, the DCNN model abandons the original maximum pooling strategy in the pooling layer, and proposes a pooling strategy based on the attention mechanism according to the idea of the attention mechanism.

Pooling strategy based on attention mechanism: According to all the outputs of i convolution kernel structure, the output matrix of i convolution kernel structure can be obtained $D_i = \{\overrightarrow{D_{i,1}}, \overrightarrow{D_{i,2}}, \ldots, \overrightarrow{c_{i,M}}\}$. According to the idea of the attention mechanism, the MA-CNN model dynamically re-updates the weight of the attention mechanism pooling strategy, and the processing process is shown in Eq. (3), (4), (5)

$$z_i = \tanh(X^{(z)} D_i{}^R) \tag{3}$$

$$b_i = \text{softmax}(Z_i v_e) \tag{4}$$

$$k_i = D_i{}^R b_i z^i \tag{5}$$

Among them, $X^{(Z)}$ represents the attention mechanism pooling strategy matrix, and Z_i represents the updated output of i convolution kernel v_e represents the environment vector, where the processing method is the randomized selection and dynamically updated during the learning process b_i means the weight of the attention mechanism pooling strategy of i convolution kernel structure, and k_i represents the output of i convolution kernel structure of the pooling layer. $X^{(Z)} \in S^{(K-h_i+1)*M}$, $Z^I \in S^{(K-0_i+1)}$, $V_e \in S^{(K-0_i+1)*1}$, $b_i \in S^{(K-0_i+1)*1}$, $k_i \in S^{M*1}$. Since MA-CNN adopts m types of convolution kernel structure, the characteristic of specific social network information is expressed as $k = k_1 \oplus k_2 \oplus \oplus k_m, k \in S^{mM*1}$.

7 Result Analysis

To evaluate the performance of Proposed DNN-RIF classifier, Accuracy (Acc) has been calculated over the confusion matrix parameter shown in Table 1.

$$Accuracy(A) = \frac{\text{Positive}_{\text{Hit}} + \text{Negative}_{\text{Hit}}}{\text{Positive}_{\text{Hit}} + \text{Positive}_{miss} + \text{Negative}_{\text{Hit}} + \text{Negative}_{\text{Miss}}}$$

- **Positive-Hit** is the total number of genuine account that are truly labeled as genuine.
- **Negative-Hit** is the total number of malicious account that are truly labeled as malicious.
- **Positive-miss** is the total number of genuine account that are falsely labeled as genuine.
- **Negative-miss** is the total number of malicious account that are falsely labeled as malicious

Table 1. Confusion Metrics

Actual	Predicted		
		Genuine Account	Malicious Account
	Genuine Account	Positive Hit	Negative Miss
	Malicious Account	Positive Miss	Negative Hit

Table 2. Accuracy over Social Media Data Set

Approach	Data Set	
	Crude	CCSD
Random Forest	93.45	96.2
Bagging	93.14	95.98
J48	94.12	94.64
Random Tree	92.47	95.58
Logistic Regression	94.2	85.98
Proposed Work	95.89	98.54

Comparative analysis is presented performance evaluation of classifiers (RF, Bagging, J48, RT, and LR) and proposed DNN-RIF framework with feature fusion vector. Over Accuracy, the proposed DNN-RIF classifier gain approximately 95.89% and 98.54% Accuracy over Crude and CCSD data set respectively.

As seen in Fig. 3 and Table 2, Random Forest, Bagging, J48, Random Tree, and Logistic Regression each obtain 93.45%, 93.14%, 92.14%, 92.47%, and 96.2%, 95.98%, 94.64%, 95.58%, and 85.98% Accuracy over the Crude and CCSD data sets, respectively. Regarding Accuracy, DNN-RIF outperforms Random Forest, Bagging, J48, random tree, and logistic Regression by approximately 2.54–2.37%, 2.95–2.67%, 3.91–3.96%, 3.57–3.0%, and 4.61–12.7%, respectively.

The proposed technique achieves accuracy over the Crude and CCDS data sets of 95.89% and 98.54%, respectively. However, as demonstrated in Fig. 4–5, it gained and improved in accuracy over the crude and CCDS data set by 2.61%–4.83% and 2.43–14.61%, respectively. Whereas there is a 1.01% training to evaluation ratio decrease.

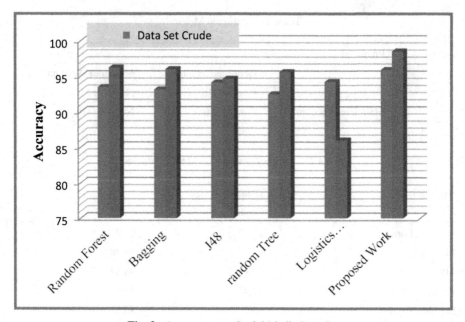

Fig. 3. Accuracy over Social Media Data Set

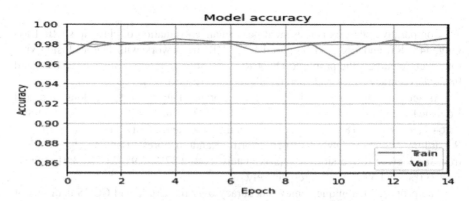

Fig. 4. Accuracy of Proposed DCNN model

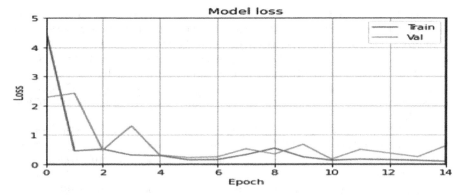

Fig. 5. Training Loss of Proposed DCNN model

8 Conclusion

End users are far more likely to utilise social media for commercial promotion, political propaganda, educational purposes, and amusement in the modern era of social media. More and more people are utilising social media for marketing, increasing brand aware-ness, and other promotional activities in addition to information sharing. The problem with this approach is that it appeals to lawbreakers. Using fictitious accounts to spread misinformation and sway social media users in order to do unlawful activities. Through the use of malicious community information, this piece demonstrates both user and society characteristics. The findings of this study may be used to identify spam reviews, false information, and rumours that circulate on social media platforms. Additionally included are the user spaces where the military can affect military users by their ideology, the election campaign can research the effects of political ideologies, and criminology prediction can identify criminal user groups.

References

1. Zolkepli, I.: Changing consumer culture in the wake of web 3.0: mobilizing online crowd competency and expertise through crowdsourcing engagement (2016)
2. Hurlburt, G.F.: Web 2.0 social media: a commercialization conundrum. IT Prof. **14**(6), 6–8 (2012)
3. Dekker, R., van den Brink, P., Meijer, A.: Social media adoption in the police: barriers and strategies. Gov. Inf. Q. **37**(2), 101441 (2020). http://www.sciencedirect.com/science/article/pii/S0740624X19300346
4. Zubiaga, A.: Mining social media for newsgathering: a review. Online Soc. Netw. Media **13**, 100049 (2019). http://www.sciencedirect.com/science/article/pii/S2468696419300047
5. Al-Qurishi, M., Alrubaian, M., Rahman, S.M.M., Alamri, A., Hassan, M.M.: A prediction system of sybil attack in social network using deep-regression model. Future Gener. Comput. Syst. **87**, 743–753 (2018). http://www.sciencedirect.com/science/article/pii/S0167739X17300821
6. Zhang, L., Yuan, Y., Wu, Z., Cao, J.: Semi-SGD: semi-supervised learning based spammer group detection in product reviews. In: 2017 Fifth International Conference on Advanced Cloud and Big Data (CBD), pp. 368–373 (2017)

7. Zhang, L., He, G., Cao, J., Zhu, H., Xu, B.: Spotting review spammer groups: a cosine pattern and network based method. Concurr. Comput. Pract. Exp. **30**(20), e4686 (2018). e4686 cpe.4686. https://onlinelibrary.wiley.com/doi/abs/10.1002/cpe.4686

8. Wang, Z., Gu, S., Zhao, X., Xu, X.: Graph-based review spammer group detection. Knowl. Inf. Syst. **55**(3), 571–597 (2018). https://doi.org/10.1007/s10115-017-1068-7

9. Hunt, K.M.: Gaming the system: malicious online reviews vs. consumer law. Comput. Law Secur. Rev. **31**(1), 3–25 (2015). http://www.sciencedirect.com/science/article/pii/S02673649 14001824

10. Sigala, M.: How "bad" are you? justification and normalisation of online deviant customer behaviour. In: Schegg, R., Stangl, B. (eds.) Information and Communication Technologies in Tourism 2017, pp. 607–622. Springer, Cham (2017). https://doi.org/10.1007/978-3-319-51168-9_44

11. Li, L., Lee, K.Y., Lee, M., Yang, S.-B.: Unveiling the cloak of deviance: linguistic cues for psychological processes in malicious online reviews. Int. J. Hosp. Manag. **87**, 102468 (2020). http://www.sciencedirect.com/science/article/pii/S0278431920300207

12. Latah, M.: Detection of malicious social bots: a survey and a refined taxonomy. Expert Syst. Appl. 113383 (2020). http://www.sciencedirect.com/science/article/pii/S0957417420302074

13. Cresci, S., Lillo, F., Regoli, D., Tardelli, S., Tesconi, M.: Cashtag piggybacking: uncovering spam and bot activity in stock microblogs on twitter. ACM Trans. Web **13**(2), 1–27 (2019). https://doi.org/10.1145/3313184

14. Zheng, X., Lai, Y.M., Chow, K.P., Hui, L.C.K., Yiu, S.M.: Sockpuppet detection in online discussion forums. In: 2011 Seventh International Conference on Intelligent Information Hiding and Multimedia Signal Processing, pp. 374–377 (2011)

15. Riquelme, F., Gonzalez-Cantergiani, P.: Measuring user influence on twitter: a survey. Inf. Process. Manag. **52**(5), 949–975 (2016). http://www.sciencedirect.com/science/article/pii/S0306457316300589

16. Wu, Y., Ngai, E.W., Wu, P., Wu, C.: Malicious online reviews: literature review, synthesis, and directions for future research. Decis. Supp. Syst. 113280 (2020). http://www.sciencedi rect.com/science/article/pii/S016792362030035X

17. Liu, Y., Pang, B.: A unified framework for detecting author spamicity by modeling review deviation. Expert Syst. Appl. **112**, 148–155 (2018). http://www.sciencedirect.com/science/article/pii/S0957417418303749

18. Barbado, R., Araque, O., Iglesias, C.A.: A framework for malicious review detection in online consumer electronics retailers. Inf. Process. Manag. **56**(4), 1234–1244 (2019). http://www.sciencedirect.com/science/article/pii/S030645731730657X

19. Liu, Y., Pang, B., Wang, X.: Opinion spam detection by incorporating multimodal embedded representation into a probabilistic review graph. Neurocomputing, **366**, 276–283 (2019). http://www.sciencedirect.com/science/article/pii/S0925231219311324

20. Rout, J.K., Dash, A.K., Ray, N.K.: A framework for malicious review detection: issues and challenges. In: 2018 International Conference on Information Technology (ICIT), pp. 7–10 (2018)

Social Distance Monitoring and Infection Risk Assessment in COVID-19 Pandemic

Shikha Gupta[1], Anu Rathee[1], Mohit Agarwal[2(✉)], and Nishi Gupta[3]

[1] Maharaja Agrasen Institute of Technology, GGSIPU, Sector-22, Rohini, Delhi, India
[2] Department of Computer and Communication Engineering, Manipal University Jaipur, Jaipur, Rajasthan, India
rs.mohitag@gmail.com
[3] The NorthCap University, Gurugram Sector 23A, Gurugram, Haryana, India

Abstract. Amidst the global pandemic of COVID-19, authorities tried a myriad of social distancing practices, including limiting travel, exercising control over borders, closing bars and clubs, and reminding people to make sure a safe distance of about 1.6 to 2 m amongst them. But on the other hand, determining the extent of virus dissemination and the effectiveness of the limits is a problematic issue. People would go out for basic needs such as food, medical supplies, and other vital items, activities, and jobs. This led to various novel technology-based results being refined to support health and medical organizations deal with the pandemic issues and suggesting effective social distancing strategies. Patient tracking and placement via GPS, as well as public monitoring and classification, are all part of these programs. In this paper, we will build a general model for automatically detecting objects (here a class of people) based on deep neural networks in complex places using existing CCTV cameras and for tracking and measuring distances between objects. It also performs real-time dynamic threat assessment based on statistical analysis of data on human movement in the field. This allows us to track people's movements and behaviors, assess the rate of social distancing violations for the entire population that currently exists, and identify areas of high risk in the short and long term.

Keywords: COVID-19 · Social Distancing · Risk Assessment · Infection Risk · Deep Neural Network

1 Introduction

The origin of the coronavirus can be traced back to Wuhan, China, in December 2019. In a few months later, in 2020, this infection spread globally. In May 2020, the World Health Organization (WHO) declared this situation a global pandemic and it had spread to 187 countries [1]. According to WHO statistics, as of 26 August 2020 this virus has affected 23.78 million people in 198 countries and the infectious disease death rate is also terribly high at 8,15,000. Besides the fact that patients tend to develop or rather recur, there is still no treatment available for this infection. Despite the reality that experts, medical groups, and analysts are persistently attempting to find suitable treatment or

R. S. Tomar et al. (Eds.): CNC 2022, CCIS 1894, pp. 159–170, 2023.
https://doi.org/10.1007/978-3-031-43145-6_14

remedies for the deadly disease, no remarkable improvement has been documented from now to the time of careful reading [2]. There are currently no proven medications or techniques for eliminating or battling this new virus. As a result, people all around the world have taken precautions to prevent the contamination from spreading. These grave circumstances have compelled global networks to look for alternative methods of reducing pathogen spread.

WHO strictly advised everyone to stay atleast 1.8 m or 6 feet away from each other to curb the spread of the virus gradually [3]. On-going research have affirmed that individuals with negligible or no indications may likewise hold the tendency of becoming the transporters of the Coronavirus infection. From now on, it is important that everyone follows controlled practices and adheres to social distancing norms. Many previous reports and research projects have shown that maintaining the social distance is a practical non-drug alternative [4] and has significant deterrent powers in preventing the spread of diseases such as SARS and COVID-19 [5] (Fig. 1).

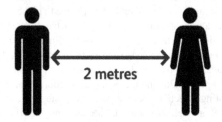

Fig. 1. Minimum Social Distance

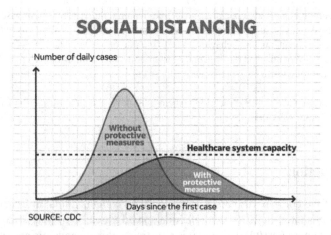

Fig. 2. Distribution of virus transmission rate, with and without social distancing.

Figure 2 shows the impact of adhering the suggested social separation norms on decreasing the virus transmission rates amongst the population [6]. A dynamic and broad curve with a smaller jump inside the scope of the healthcare service management constraints makes it quite simpler for the patients to combat infections by getting adequate and easy assistance from primary healthcare organizations. Any unanticipated dramatic increase in the pace of disease spread (as shown in Fig. 2) will leave the administration disappointed. The number of fatalities increased dramatically as the number of active cases increased and people died because of healthcare shortages and unavailability. Accordingly, social distancing currently preaches to be more crucial than imagined before and apparently a right approach to stop the outspread of the infection, despite wearing face masks [7]. Practically, all countries have understood its necessity and adopted it as a need of the hour or a required practice. Since the onset of the Covid, governments have tried to keep up social distancing at public places. The actions taken by the governments include restricting unnecessary travel, shutting down restaurants and bars, spreading awareness amongst the masses about taking mandatory precautions, and maintaining social distancing. Machine Learning and Artificial Intelligence may be crucial in supporting authorities in such a circumstance. This study proposes a novel method for monitoring social distance that requires minimal human intervention. It also recommends the use of video surveillance and drones to track human activity in public places [8]. We can identify each person in the photo and determine the corresponding distance between them. Anyone who breaks social distancing rules can be punished. As a result, the number of public gatherings and crowds in public places will decrease. Gathering of religious people at a place of worship may steeply increase the confirmed cases of COVID-19. In the past two years, most countries have introduced quarantine measures and citizens have been forced to stay at home for their wellbeing. Following that, remainder of the paper is organized as follows: Sect. 2 presents the related work. The methods for defining a measurement system to verify for human detection and social distance is proposed in Sect. 3. Test results are displayed in Sect. 4 and the paper concludes in Sect. 5.

2 Related Work

Syed Amir Abbas et al., in 2017 [9], proposed a Raspberry Pi and Open-CV system for people tracking, mafia control and jurisdiction. In this paper they define a Step wise classification which is performed through OpenCV for input-based head recognition using the properties of the Haar cascade classifier [10]. The goal was to capture compressed clips and key-frame video using a quad-core ARMv8 main processor and a Raspberry Pi 3 with a camera. The collection is regulated by counting the number of livestock and differentiating the collection amount according to the regulatory limit, and if the set limit is exceeded, necessary measures can be taken. Joel Joseph Joy et al., proposed a method for image retrieval for crowd density sensing systems. They used feed images to estimate latency and traffic volume [11]. Fuzzy logic is used on the input source image to address the concept of partial truth which may be wholly true or factually false. At a time when the coronavirus begins to spread to people and society, scientists have begun to find the optimal solution to curb its spread [12]. Jennifer Berglund proposed a technique using GPS and applications built into smartphones to track people infected with COVID-19. However, the technology is limited in tracking people without Wi-Fi or cellular coverage. Meanwhile, some authorities are using drones equipped with video cameras to monitor crowds outdoors [13]. This method is suitable for tracking COVID-19, which might be present during an outbreak of a coronavirus. With the advancement of deep learning, especially computer vision, the issue of classifying and recognizing objects in images has been resolved. The growth of computer vision has concentrated on a variety of topics, including neural style transmission, segmentation, tracking, and object identification [9]. Neil Bhave et al., published an add-on version and a model supporting object detection methods [14]. The model used the YOLO (You Only Look Once) real-time object detection that has fewer limitations, generates faster and more accurate results, and can be developed for over 200 classes. It uses a machine learning technique known as reinforcement learning which estimates the duration of a green phase based on an existing traffic problem and utilizes the actions taken. Adrian R.in 2020, published an article on monitors for social distancing using OpenCV and Computer Vision [15]. This paper focuses on tracking social distance with roadside surveillance cameras in the Corona era and provides insight into social distancing during Covid-19. A video camera monitors the pixel distance between people as a social distance detector and compares it to an average. The logic for a social distance analyzer programme is contained in the file.py script, which works with both web streams and webcams and loops through webcam frames to force people to maintain a standard distance from one another [16].

3   Methodology

This paper proposes a technique which includes human detection, location tracking, and inter distance estimation for social distance monitoring. The model is fully adaptable to all surveillance cameras from VGA to Full-HD. Time-lapse video from any CCTV system can also be analyzed to determine the metrics needed to ensure everyone adheres to social distancing guidelines [17].

3.1   Human Detection

The YOLO model is used to detect objects in frames. In this study, it is used to identify people in video frames. Prior to the advent of the YOLO model, different parts of the same image were processed multiple times with different sizes and purposes which was time consuming and reduced the efficiency. To alleviate this problem, we have used the YOLO object detection technique [18]. It scans the image only once and returns the detected object. It is now widely used in current models because of its speed and efficiency. YOLOv4 was trained on the COCO data set.

3.2   Location Tracking

The location tracking algorithm is used to find the Euclidean distance between the old and two new objects in successive video frames. Evaluate social distance by tracking the center of an object and measuring the distance between the centers. For each detected object, the algorithm uses bounding box coordinates (x,y) which trace the center on the frame. There are several ways to get the coordinates of these bounding boxes for video frames such as Haar Cascade, faster R-CNN, and HOG + Linear Support Vector Machine (LSVM). The center of the object can be easily calculated using the coordinates of the bounding box by using detection and centroid finding of the bounding box. This is the default set of boundary block coordinates. So, each is assigned a new identifier. For each subsequent frame of the video stream, this algorithm is applied again [19].

However, a new unique identifier is not assigned to each object as it does not optimize object tracking. First, we need to make sure we can find a new centroid (blue) from the existing centroid (green). For this, the Euclidean distance (highlighted in blue and purple) between the old and new centroids of the object is calculated [20]. Figure 4 shows that the center of the upper half is the old feature, and the center of the lower half is the new feature. Centroid tracking works under the assumption that a particular object will move in successive frames, but the distance between the old position at time (t) and the new position at time (t + 1) is much smaller than all other distances. The algorithm tries to find all object mappings from the previous frame to the next. If such an object can be found in a location close to the old object, it updates the old object's location without generating a new ID. So, tracking the same object in successive frames helps the model to keep track of the object.

We have used a tracking system called the Simple Online and Real-time Tracking (SORT) to track people which forms the basis for Kalman (K) filter as well as for the Hungarian optimization method [21]. The K-filter, an effective technique for constantly locating the person, predicts the person's location at (t + 1) depending upon the estimation time (t) and a mathematical description of human mobility. The Hungarian method uses a co-optimization algorithm to identify an object in a series of photographic frames by determining whether an object in the given frame is the same person who has been in earlier frames [22]. We need to make sure we can find a new centroid (blue) from the existing centroid (green). For this, the Euclidean distance (highlighted in blue and purple) between the old and new centroids of the object is calculated [20] (Fig. 3)

Fig. 3. Human Detection

Figure 5 shows that if an identified individual is spotted in a new place, the bounding box for that person is changed. Velocity and acceleration components are the basis of these mathematical derivations which are given by K framework. After that a matrix L_t, is defined which incorporates the location of (n) that recognizes the human's image in

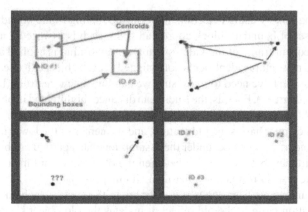

Fig. 4. Location Tracking (Color figure online)

Fig. 5. Identification, tracking, and depiction of movement trajectories for Humans

the carrier grid, for every input frame |w × h| at (t):

$$L_t = P^t_{(x_n, y_n)} | x_n \in w, y_n \in h) \tag{1}$$

3.3 Inter Distance Estimation

The pinhole camera has been used in this paper to capture the video as shown in Fig. 6. Using the principle of rectilinear motion of light, a relationship can be established between the known variables and unknown variables. The unknown variable, (d), is the distance between the object and the camera. The known variables are (f), camera's focal length, (r), the height of the object and R, the height of the image.

In our paper, we're looking for a cost-effective system that can be combined with a basic CCTV camera in public settings. Using a single camera projects a 3D world onto a 2D image plane, resulting in perspective effect, that is, unrealistic pixel lengths between the objects. It occurs when humans are unable to detect a uniform distribution of distances throughout an image. Every point in a 3D plane contains three parameters (x, y, z), but the image in a camera contains only (x, y), with the (z) value unknown [5].

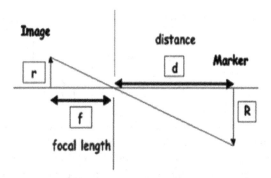

Fig. 6. Inter Distance Estimation

To use our approach, we first need to remove the parallax effect by setting the camera's calibration to z = 0. We also need other information such as camera position, height, and angle of view. We will use IMP technique shown in Eq. 2 to map the 2D pixel points (u, v) to the appropriate world coordinates (X_w, Y_w, Z_w). Equation 3 and Eq. 4 represent the rotation matrix, R and the translation matrix, T.

$$[uv1]^T = KRT[X_w, Y_w, Z_w, 1]^T \tag{2}$$

$$R = \begin{bmatrix} 1 & 0 & 0 & 0 \\ 0 & \cos\theta & \sin\theta & 0 \\ 0 & \sin\theta & \cos\theta & 0 \\ 0 & 0 & 0 & 1 \end{bmatrix} \tag{3}$$

$$T = \begin{bmatrix} 1 & 0 & 0 & 0 \\ 0 & 1 & 0 & 0 \\ 0 & 0 & 1 & \frac{-h}{\sin\theta} \\ 0 & 0 & 0 & 1 \end{bmatrix} \tag{4}$$

The following matrix depicts the camera's fundamental parameters and Camera Intrinsic Matrix, K:

$$K = \begin{bmatrix} f*ku & s & d_x & 0 \\ 0 & f*kv & d_y & 0 \\ 0 & 0 & 1 & 0 \end{bmatrix} \tag{5}$$

where (h) is the height of camera, (f) is its focal length, and ku and kv respectively specify the derived horizontal and vertical pixel coefficient values. The principal point shifts that correct the optical axis of the image plane are defined by (dx, dy). By projecting 3D coordinates in the global coordinate onto a retina plane, the camera creates a picture. Equation 6 defines the relationship between 3D coordinates and projected 2D image locations using homogeneous locations.

$$
\begin{bmatrix} u \\ (v) \\ 1 \end{bmatrix} = \begin{bmatrix} a_{11} \ a_{12} \ a_{13} \ a_{14} \\ a_{21} \ a_{22} \ a_{23} \ a_{24} \\ a_{31} \ a_{32} \ a_{33} \ a_{34} \end{bmatrix} \begin{bmatrix} X_w \\ Y_w \\ Z_w \\ 1 \end{bmatrix} \tag{6}
$$

K, R and T identify the camera location and frame of reference, and these are transferred to image points using the transformation matrix $A \in R3 \times 4$ with an element a_{ij}. The dimensions of the aforementioned equation can be simplified using the Eq. 7 to the form given if the picture plane of the camera is perpendicular to the z-axis in the world coordinate system where $z = 0$.

$$
\begin{bmatrix} u \\ (v) \\ 1 \end{bmatrix} = \begin{bmatrix} a_{11} \ a_{12} \ a_{13} \\ a_{21} \ a_{22} \ a_{23} \\ a_{31} \ a_{32} \ a_{33} \end{bmatrix} \begin{bmatrix} X_w \\ (Y_w) \\ 1 \end{bmatrix} \tag{7}
$$

and finally, the scalar is defined in Eq. 8 after shifting from viewpoint space to inverted perspective space (BEV).

$$
(u, v) = \left(\frac{a_{11} \times x_w + a_{12} \times y_w + a_{13}}{a_{31} \times x_w + a_{32} \times y_w + a_{33}}, \frac{a_{21} \times x_w + a_{22} \times y_w + a_{23}}{a_{31} \times x_w + a_{32} \times y_w + a_{33}} \right) \tag{8}
$$

3.4 Inter Distance Estimation

COVID-19 outbreak preventive measures must be emphasized to minimize the adverse implications of the pandemic on healthcare system and the worldwide trade and economy [22]. In the truancy of adequate antiviral medications and insufficient medical services, WHO recommends a variety of measures to control rates of infection spread and prevent draining the limited healthcare supplies. One of the non-drug strategies to lower the major component of SARS-CoV2 droplets ejected by an infected patient is to wear a face mask [23]. Irrespective of the arguments over healthcare facilities and types of masks, all nations demand the usage of masks that cover the mouth and nose to serve health protection of the masses. This work aims to construct a highly precise and real-world scenario for recognizing non-mask individuals publicly and mandating wearing masks in order to benefit public health. The method of recognizing whether a person is wearing a mask is called face mask detection [24]. In fact, the problem of identifying human faces using various machine learning methods for security, authentication, and surveillance is the reverse engineering of face recognition. A huge amount of research has led to the development of efficient face recognition algorithms in the past. In our research, when a person is detected, we extract the face coordinates and classify the face as masked or unmasked using a pre-trained face mask detection model. Masked or unmasked predictions are also displayed in the video output [25] (Fig. 7).

(a)   **(b)**

Fig. 7. Face Mask Detection- (a) input image; (b) output image

3.5 Inter Distance Estimation

The proposed approach is tested in terms of predicting human behavior in the long run. This information can help policymakers and managers in the healthcare industry make timely, life-saving decisions and save money. Our experiments have yielded some interesting results that may be important in controlling infection levels before they go out of control. By monitoring and recording people's motion trajectories, total number of persons, size distribution of every zone, individuals who breached the social-distance metrics, total duration of infringements for every human and as a complete, recognizing high-risk zones, and eventually developing an insightful risk heat-map, we investigated a long term spatio-temporal region quantitative model. To carry out the study, a 2D grid matrix (L_t) (initially supplied with zero) was made to track of the most recent position of people using the source frames. The width and height of the picture inserted is represented by (w) and (h) correspondingly. (G_t) reflects state of the matrix at time (t). Every new frame, the grid matrix (L) is refreshed, accumulating the most recent information on the observed people. Instead, it was much more beneficial to analyse both raw movement and tracking data as well as the number and location of the people who particularly violated the social distancing guidelines. After developing a long-term heat-map of detection, movement, and total social-distance violations, we can evaluate risk zones and put restrictions in place or adjust the location's structure to make it safe [26].

Each participant is classified into one of the following categories using the social distancing violation criteria:

- Everyone who followed the social distancing (green circles) was considered safe.
- Everyone who disobeyed the social distancing rule (red circles) was considered in high-risk zone.
- Those who entered together (yellow circles) and were assessed as paired; fell into the potentially risk zone (Fig. 8).

Fig. 8. A crowd heat map which is long term (Color figure online)

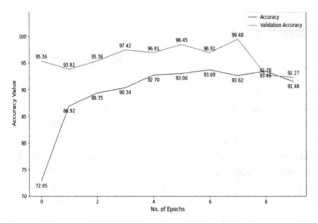

Fig. 9. Accuracy/Validation Accuracy vs Epoch Count

4 Results

Whether or not a person is wearing a mask has been trained and predicted using neural networks. The neural network is trained across ten epochs, and the best-performing epoch is used to select the model. At each epoch, the loss is calculated by comparing the predicted value to the original value. This loss acts as feedback for the next epoch, so the next epoch is expected to perform better than the previous epoch. We discover the accuracy and loss (calculated from the training data), as well as the validation accuracy and loss, for each epoch (computed from the test data).

In Fig. 9 we have demonstrated how the accuracy and validation accuracy changes with the number of epochs. It has been observed that there is a gradual increase in accuracy and a gradual decrease in loss over the epochs. After all epochs are complete, the epoch that provides the maximum validation accuracy is chosen.

5 Conclusion

We can clearly see the necessity for self-responsibility as we assess the world after the COVID-19 epidemic. The World Health Organization's (WHO) prescriptions would be the main emphasis of the scenario. COVID-19 spreads by close contact with infected people, social distancing would surely be the most prominent cutting solution for the same. An effective strategy for monitoring huge crowds is vital and this study focuses on that. With installed Cameras and drones, authorities can keep a close watch on people's movements and manage large gatherings, allowing people to assemble and follow the rules. This study can address the problem before it gets out of hand because managing a big crowd is tough. Thus, implementing this notion can reduce the police's on-the-ground efforts and, based on the zone-based risk assessment, they can solely focus on overseeing circumstances in those regions where conditions are adverse, allowing them to use resources productively and also save energy for appropriate scenarios. Also, this approach can work regardless of camera orientation because it is view-point neutral. It can be used in a variety of other industrial settings, such as driver assistance systems, surveillance systems, crowd management in public spaces, and sports action identification, among others.

References

1. Franchi, T.: The impact of the covid-19 pandemic on current anatomy education and future careers: a student's perspective. Anat. Sci. Educ. **13**(3), 312 (2020)
2. Hamidi, S., Sabouri, S., Ewing, R.: Does density aggravate the covid-19 pandemic? Early findings and lessons for planners. J. Am. Plan. Assoc. **86**(4), 495–509 (2020)
3. Olsen, S.J., et al.: Transmission of the severe acute respiratory syndrome on aircraft. New Engl. J. Med. **349**(25), 2416–2422 (2003)
4. Ferguson, N.M., Cummings, D.A., Fraser, C., Cajka, J.C., Cooley, P.C., Burke, D.S.: Strategies for mitigating an influenza pandemic. Nature **442**, 448–452 (2006)
5. Wu, C., et al.: Analysis of therapeutic targets for SARS-CoV-2 and discovery of potential drugs by computational methods. Acta Pharmaceutica Sinica B **10**(5), 766–788 (2020)
6. Fong, M.W., et al.: Nonpharmaceutical measures for pandemic influenza in nonhealthcare settings—Social distancing measures. Emerg. Infect. Dis. **26**(5), 976 (2020)
7. Yagna Sai Surya, K., Geetha Rani, T., Tripathy, B.K.: Social distance monitoring and face mask detection using deep learning. In: Nayak, J., Behera, H., Naik, B., Vimal, S., Pelusi, D. (eds.) Computational Intelligence in Data Mining. SIST, vol. 281, pp. 461–476. Springer, Singapore (2022). https://doi.org/10.1007/978-981-16-9447-9_36
8. Yadav, S., Gulia, P., Gill, N.S., Chatterjee, J.M.: A real-time crowd monitoring and management system for social distance classification and healthcare using deep learning. J. Healthc. Eng. **2022** (2022)
9. Abbas, S.S.A., Jayaprakash, P.O., Anitha, M., Jaini, X.V.: Crowd detection and management using cascade classifier on ARMv8 and Open CV-Python. In: 2017 International Conference on Innovations in Information, Embedded and Communication Systems (ICIIECS), pp. 1–6. IEEE (2017)
10. Li, C., Qi, Z., Jia, N., Wu, J.: Human face detection algorithm via Haar cascade classifier combined with three additional classifiers. In: 2017 13th IEEE International Conference on Electronic Measurement & Instruments (ICEMI), pp. 483–487. IEEE (2017)

11. Balamurugan, S.S., Santhanam, S., Billa, A., Aggarwal, R., Alluri, N.V.: Model proposal for a yolo objection detection algorithm based social distancing detection system. In: 2021 International Conference on Computational Intelligence and Computation Applications (ICCICA), pp. 1–4. IEEE (2021)

12. Sonbhadra, S.K., Agarwal, S., Nagabhushan, P.: Target specific mining of covid-19 scholarly articles using one-class approach. Chaos Solitons Fractals **140**, 110155 (2020)

13. Punn, N.S., Agarwal, S.: Automated diagnosis of covid-19 with limited posteroanterior chest x-ray images using fine-tuned deep neural networks. Appl. Intell. **51**(5), 2689–2702 (2021)

14. Bhave, N., Dhagavkar, A., Dhande, K., Bana, M., Joshi, J.: Smart signal–adaptive traffic signal control using reinforcement learning and object detection. In: 2019 Third International Conference on I-SMAC (IoT in Social, Mobile, Analytics and Cloud) (I-SMAC), pp. 624–628. IEEE (2019)

15. Rosebrock, A.: OpenCV social distancing detector (2020). Accessed 6 Feb 2020

16. Ahmed, I., Ahmad, M., Rodrigues, J.J.P.C., Jeon, G., Din, S.: A deep learning-based social distance monitoring framework for covid-19. Sustain. Cities Soc. **65**, 102571 (2021)

17. Ahmad, T., Ma, Y., Yahya, M., Ahmad, B., Nazir, S., et al.: Object detection through modified YOLO neural network. Sci. Program. **2020** (2020)

18. Balaji, S.R., Karthikeyan, S.: A survey on moving object tracking using image processing. In: 2017 11th International Conference on Intelligent Systems and Control (ISCO), pp. 469–474. IEEE (2017)

19. Faisal, M.M., et al.: Object detection and distance measurement using AI. In: 2021 14th International Conference on Developments in e Systems Engineering (DeSE), pp. 559–565. IEEE (2021)

20. Khataee, H., Scheuring, I., Czirok, A., Neufeld, Z.: Effects of social distancing on the spreading of COVID-19 inferred from mobile phone data. Sci. Rep. **11**(1), 1–9 (2021)

21. Matrajt, L., Leung, T.: Evaluating the effectiveness of social distancing interventions to delay or flatten the epidemic curve of coronavirus disease. Emerg. Infect. Dis. **26**(8), 1740 (2020)

22. Saponara, S., Elhanashi, A., Gagliardi, A.: Implementing a real-time, AI-based, people detection and social distancing measuring system for Covid-19. J. Real-Time Image Proc. **18**(6), 1937–1947 (2021)

23. Akepitaktam, P., Hnoohom, N.: Object distance estimation with machine learning algorithms for stereo vision. In: 2019 14th International Joint Symposium on Artificial Intelligence and Natural Language Processing (iSAI-NLP), pp. 1–6. IEEE (2019)

24. Parzych, M., Chmielewska, A., Marciniak, T., Dabrowski, A., Chrostowska, A., Klincewicz, M.: Automatic people density maps generation with use of movement detection analysis. In: 2013 6th International Conference on Human System Interactions (HSI), pp. 26–31. IEEE (2013)

25. Li, C., Wang, R., Li, J., Fei, L.: Face detection based on YOLOv3. In: Jain, V., Patnaik, S., Popenţiu Vlǎdicescu, F., Sethi, I.K. (eds.) Recent Trends in Intelligent Computing, Communication and Devices. AISC, vol. 1006, pp. 277–284. Springer, Singapore (2020). https://doi.org/10.1007/978-981-13-9406-5_34

26. Ghosh, G., Swarnalatha, K.S.: A detail analysis and implementation of Haar cascade classifier. In: Shetty D., P., Shetty, S. (eds.) Recent Advances in Artificial Intelligence and Data Engineering. AISC, vol. 1386, pp. 341–359. Springer, Singapore (2022). https://doi.org/10.1007/978-981-16-3342-3_28

Vibrations Signal Analysis of Cantilever Beam Using Machine Learning

Lali Sharma, Jai Kumar Sharma, and Pallavi Khatri[✉]

ITM University, Gwalior, India
lalisharma1605@gmail.com, {jaikumar.me,
Pallavi.khatri.cse}@itmuniversity.ac.in

Abstract. Vibrations are common phenomena seen in mechanical structures that can be detrimental to many systems. If not monitored, they can cause damage to structures, Vibrometer is sensor used for measuring vibrations of mechanical structures, machines, as well as sound level in an area and will collect lot of data that is to be analyzed to determine the strength of the structures. Machine learning is the basic working technology for prediction and determining the work proposes system aims to predict the health of a structure, converting the cantilever beam vibration reading to graph which is able to give the correct state or health of the structure. This work will cover all the major challenges faced due to natural down fall of quality of structure. The aims to able to check the Structural Health and able predict the condition of the structure.

Keywords: Vibrometer · Machine learning · Frequency · Structure strength

1 Introduction

Vibration is a phenomenon where the oscillation takes place at the equilibrium point. The term vibration stands for Shaking, brandishing. The Vibration are the singles consisting of number of frequencies, the reading of data set are pure reading in the time domain, which are required to be converted into frequency domain. Cantilever Beam is a type of beam with one end projecting ahead the point of support, this beam is free to move in a vertical plane under the influence of loads placed the free end and the support. This beam is generally small and is restricted to 2 m to 3 m. Vibrometer [1] is a two-beam laser measuring device used for measuring frequency difference between the internal reference beam and a test beam. The use of this device is to measure vibration amplitude. Automation System [2], is the demand and requirement of the future.

The system is the graphical representation of the vibrometer, the beam is the combination of two, infrared LDV and He-Ne SLDV from the target. The reading of the vibrometer is in continuous numerical and in the time domain the domain required is frequency.

The drawback of the vibrometer:
The signal are vibrations and it requires a converter to convert the signal into binary which are understood by the computer system. Machine Learning is a sub category of

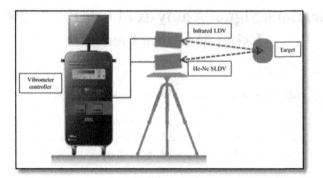

Fig. 1. [1] Vibrometer

Artificial Intelligence that generally used for training the data and finding insights and accuracies, the type of machine learning depending upon the dataset and available output are Supervised, Unsupervised, Reinforcement Learning, Vibration data is accompanied with output is under the Supervised Learning and the data is non-linear thus SVM Support Vector Machine will produce the most relevant result.

2 Literature Survey

The study in [3] covered that the Laser Vibrometer through which beam reading are obtained even the shapes too boundary, the nature of beam is free, the nature of reading is in the time domain the domain to which it should or required to be converted is frequency. The software used for analysis of FFT Fast Fourier Transform [4] is FEM Finite Element Model.

The experimental and numerical model also covered the accurate boundary conditions and the determined results have certain errors with the real result. The outcomes from this article covered are Nature of Beam, Nature of frequency, software used for analysis of FFT, FEM. The drawback or the area to be included in these the changing methods or how the conversion took place and it is difficult to convert one domain to other domain without proper knowledge,

The conversion of the beam reading, Shape boundary reading should also be done so the analysis and unit reading will become more understandable and the outcome will become more efficient after we convert these readings. The approach in [5] has the properties of the PSV-3D Scanning Vibrometer with robotics and makes it viable to utilize CAE Computer Aided Engineering data for defining the test. The main advantage for the model updating process is the potential to work with imported Finite Element geometries and coordinate systems and to automatically gather data at all nodal points. Use of robotics is after the successful steps and after the model is working virtually then connecting IOT and robotics come into picture. The work that needed to be done is the data that is being gather from the nodal point of the beam should be observed carefully and made it very sure the reading should in the domain frequency format automatically before the modelling into 3D Scanning as the frequency domain have for accurate results in 3D modelling.

The graphene NEMS [6] is working in a resonate mode which can be used for high performance of vibration sensors, the device is not able to predict the vibration value as expected but it does provide some fundamental effect with greater impact on device with high quality and have a very low stress. The idea or thing to overcome is the prediction value should be correct for the model to work according it, the values or reading must be accurate according to the resonant. Microelectromechanical systems (MEMS) proposed by authors of is a Structural Health Monitoring system, the lightweight construction build of material on which the Structural Monitoring System, this based on certain frequency to check the health, the frequency of 100 kHz at a certain distance of 0.2 m. The issue here is certain material which are not lightweight does not pass the ultra sound wave so no result check can be done. The Non-Linear data under the Supervised learning where the data does not follow any particular trend thus the use of classification algorithm of Supervised learning i.e. is SVM, Support Vector Machine is best suitable with the data set used, the SVM will able to predict the accurate result of the dataset. If the dataset belong to the category, like images, the deep learning and neural networks combined with Open cv and image processing methods of AI to include for performance measurement and predicting the result, CNN is the best suitable for image data, CNN is Convolution Neural Networks [7].

3 Proposed System

From the literature survey it is found that there are challenges in data collection using vibrometer and furthermore it is more difficult to predict the strength of the structures due to non-automated system of detection. Domain of automating vibrometer is very naïve and very less or no work is being found in the literature. This work hence proposes a system based on Machine learning techniques that will take the input from the vibrometer reading as shown in Fig. 1.

The working flow and the step by step assumed system is represented in this flowchart in Fig. 2.

The exact reading in seconds and volts, these reading are obtained through the cantilever Beam, through Vibrometer acting as a sensor.

This work proposes a machine learning model that will be trained and tested for the captured data. The goal here is to make the system real time by converting the reading of the vibrometer into visual wave to be able to predict the value to keep a check on the strength. Once the model is built on the dataset then the aim is to use the real or random values and check that the outcome is accurately fits or is able to provide the solution. The machine learning algorithms like Linear regression, SVM that have worked on the similar kind of vibration data is been taken in consideration.

The objective of the work is designing an automatic vibration detection system that is capable of doing

1. the data set analysis
2. machine learning model check
3. transformation of the data values into amplitude and frequency.
4. the method of FFT fast Fourier Transform for discrete data.

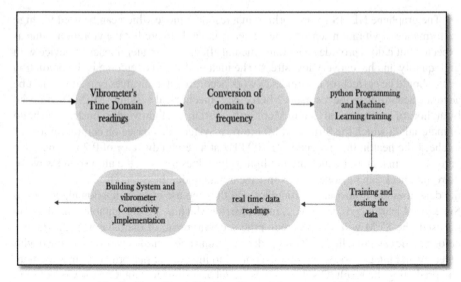

Fig. 2. Flow-Chart: Working Flow of the proposed System

Source	CH1
Second	Volt
-0.8192	-9.8
-0.81912	-9.8
-0.81904	-9.8
-0.81896	-9.8
-0.81888	-9.8
-0.8188	-9.8
-0.81872	-9.8
-0.81864	-9.8
-0.81856	-9.8
-0.81848	-9.8
-0.8184	-9.8
-0.81832	-9.8
-0.81824	-9.8
-0.81816	-9.8
-0.81808	-9.8
-0.818	-9.8
-0.81792	-9.8
-0.81784	-9.8
-0.81776	-9.8

Fig. 3. Original Dataset in Time Domain

The initial phase of the model is implemented and can be verified by visiting the Kaggle https://www.kaggle.com/datasets/lalisharma/vibrometerdataset?select=data+ml.csv [8].

The goal here is to make the system real time by converting the reading of the vibrometer into visual wave to able to predict the value or to keep a check. Once the model is build on the dataset then the aim is to use the real or random values and check that the outcome is accurately fits or is able to provide the solution. This work proposes a real time implementation of Structure strength prediction using machine learning techniques.

The methods are very much simple it the use of machine learning algorithms, time data, multi dimension linear regression algorithms.

4 Results

The original dataset is converted and the pre-processing has been applied the information is also attached here [8]. The python version here used is python 3.9 [9], the practical or model building is done on the Vibrometer dataset project on Kaggle form account [8]. It is a Notebook platform where all the performance and working and progress is available real time, and contribution is also appreciable.

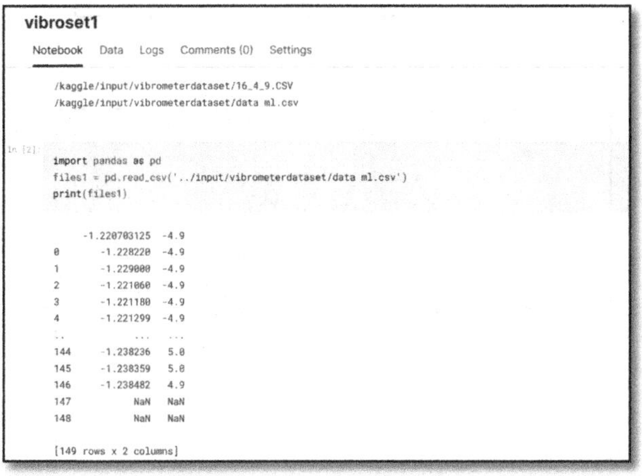

Fig. 4. Conversion of time domain to frequency domain [8]

The time domain dataset from Fig. 3 is converted into frequency domain as can be seen from Fig. 4 where the seconds in time to frequency in hertz. This was the first step where the domain conversion is the task and the outcome is in frequency domain.

The dataset is divided into two parts where major is the training part and the remaining is the testing as shown in Fig. 5(a) this figure is the algorithm and to find the discrete values in data also the spread or normalization of the data is represented.

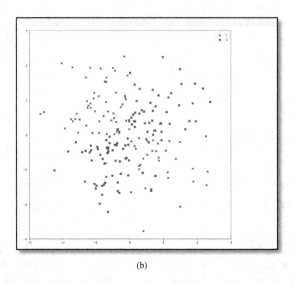

```
# Import packages to visualize the classifier
from matplotlib.colors import ListedColormap
import matplotlib.pyplot as plt
import warnings

# Import packages to do the classifying
import numpy as np
from sklearn.svm import SVC

# Create Dataset
np.random.seed(0)
X_xor = np.random.randn(200, 2)
y_xor = np.logical_xor(X_xor[:, 0] > 0,
                       X_xor[:, 1] > 0)
y_xor = np.where(y_xor, 1, -1)

fig = plt.figure(figsize=(10,10))
plt.scatter(X_xor[y_xor == 1, 0],
            X_xor[y_xor == 1, 1],
            c='b', marker='x',
            label='1')
plt.scatter(X_xor[y_xor == -1, 0],
            X_xor[y_xor == -1, 1],
            c='r',
            marker='s',
            label='-1')

plt.xlim([-3, 3])
plt.ylim([-3, 3])
plt.legend(loc='best')
plt.tight_layout()
plt.show()
```

(a)

(b)

Fig. 5. (a) Algorithm for identifying discrete values (b) Discrete Value Dataset representation [8]

The data is divided into training and testing as seen in Fig. 6(a) and 6(b) so as to work on it individually the training and testing important because the machine learning is self learner once trained correctly, to find the accurate results, testing is to check the working on new data values (Fig. 7).

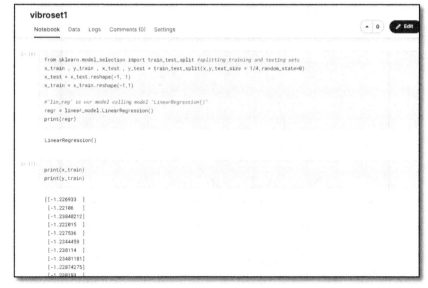

(a)

(b)

Fig. 6. (a) Training and Testing representation [8] (b) Training and Testing representation [8]

This algorithm works on the principle of divide and conquer where it divides the problem to find the optimal and accurate solution (Fig. 8).

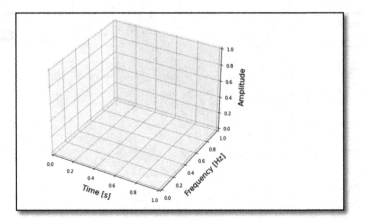

Fig. 7. FFT algorithm implementation [4]

```
[24]:  model = SVC(kernel = 'nonlinear', C = 1)


[21]:  x_train, x_test, y_train, y_test = train_test_split(x, y, test_size= 0.2)
       print(x_train)

[-1.23701138        nan -1.23408    -1.225129   -1.2359106  -1.2367665
 -1.227898   -1.22549    -1.22825    -1.226211   -1.23262    -1.22593
 -1.227174   -1.233228   -1.229568   -1.226018   -1.22822    -1.227536
 -1.221896   -1.221657   -1.2328996  -1.22106    -1.222135   -1.2311632
 -1.238114   -1.232134   -1.22357    -1.224409   -1.225249   -1.22118
 -1.230557   -1.2318911  -1.2368889  -1.22838    -1.22657    -1.234567
 -1.23092    -1.232741   -1.22585    -1.22464    -1.2357884  -1.236399
 -1.2373787  -1.238236   -1.2248889  -1.229709   -1.235177   -1.221538
 -1.236155   -1.22537    -1.233349   -1.2228526  -1.226452   -1.2287427S
 -1.22573    -1.23627782 -1.234324   -1.233498   -1.231527   -1.226692
 -1.2286219  -1.23401181 -1.221299   -1.23542202 -1.224289   -1.230072
 -1.22983    -1.231284   -1.234933   -1.232984   -1.231769   -1.226091
 -1.22741    -1.234089   -1.223211   -1.237991   -1.230193   -1.222972
 -1.222374   -1.229951   -1.2344459  -1.2277772  -1.235299   -1.231405
 -1.22405    -1.229211   -1.22417    -1.2350558  -1.2371338  -1.22345
 -1.2276566  -1.23554413 -1.230678   -1.233714   -1.232377   -1.226813
       nan -1.237623   -1.2366442  -1.223331   -1.229226   -1.230436
 -1.2334714  -1.222015   -1.226933   -1.2226134  -1.237866   -1.23031
 -1.224529   -1.228501   -1.228984   -1.230799   -1.23359    -1.22946
 -1.2256103  -1.23848212 -1.22476    -1.222733   -1.229    ]


[26]:  x_train = x_train.reshape(-1,1)
       model.fit(x_train, y_train)
```

Fig. 8. SVM model implementation [8]

SVM The supervised Classification algorithm used for the non linear kind of data, generally provides the support boundary depending on the type of data set its deals with. Though this algorithm the discrete Fourier in the dataset is being identified this is the first algorithm to be worked on. It will return the coefficients A, B etc. corresponding to some fixed frequencies. The methods fits the model and the real time data also fits the model we will able to see the working hardware called vibri (vibrometer laser system) converting and detecting the age, quality, vibration of the object or surface through the device which has the machine learning training and the real time data as the testing part.

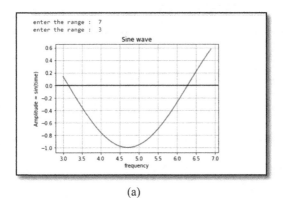

(a)

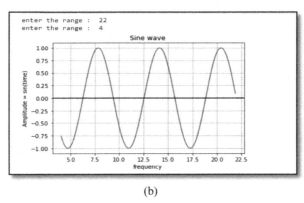

(b)

Fig. 9. (a) Sine Wave plot from the frequency and amplitude (b) Range of frequency – 22..00, Amplitude – 4.00 (b) Frequency – 2.6, Amplitude – 3.3 (b) Frequency – 9.8 Amplitude – 6.0 (b) Frequency – 32, Amplitude – 5

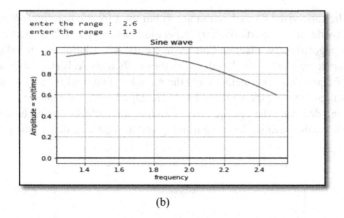

(b)

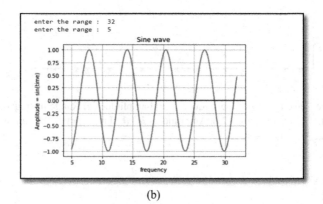

(b)

Fig. 9. (*continued*)

```
import numpy as np

import matplotlib.pyplot as plot

a = int(input('enter the range : '))
b = float(input('enter the range : '))
# Get x values of the sine wave

#time        = np.arange(0, 10, 0.1);
frequency = np.arange(b,a,0.1)


# Amplitude of the sine wave is sine of a variable like time

amplitude   = np.sin(frequency)


# Plot a sine wave using time and amplitude obtained for the sine wave

plot.plot(frequency, amplitude )



# Give a title for the sine wave plot

plot.title('Sine wave')



# Give x axis label for the sine wave plot

#plot.xlabel('Time')
plot.xlabel('frequency')


# Give y axis label for the sine wave plot

plot.ylabel('Amplitude = sin(time)')



plot.grid(True, which='both')


plot.axhline(y=0, color='k')


plot.show()


# Display the sine wave

plot.show()
```

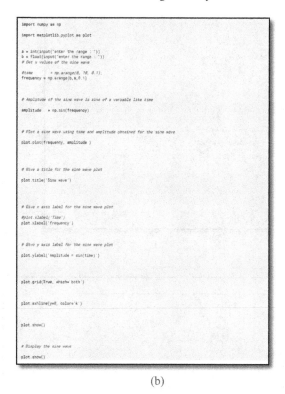

(b)

Fig. 9. (*continued*)

The plot in Fig. 9(a) is between the x and y axis with x label as frequency and y label as Amplitude

$$\textbf{\textit{Amplitude}} = \textbf{\textit{np.sin}}(\textbf{\textit{frequency}})$$

where np is numpy library of python and sin is the angle. The values of frequency and Amplitude are taken in a real time input as variable a, b.

Also included in Fig. 9(b).

The implementation for forming the sine function graph for analysis of the oscillations with respect to frequency and amplitude is given in Fig. 10(a).

The real time oscillation dumping though input ranges from the dataset reading, the matlplotlib is a visualization library, which is able to produce the frequency and time Amplitude.

Figure 10(b) The plotting result is able to produce the dumping between the frequency and Amplitude. As can be verified from 10(c) oscillations vary for different set of inputs. The values of frequency and Amplitude are to be taken as input.

```
# [X - t(time)], [V(velocity) - t(time)], [a(acceleration) - t(time)]
#[X - t(time)]

import numpy as np

from matplotlib import pyplot as plt

# ax'' = - bx' - kx

x_0 = -1.2

v_0 = -9.8

y_0 = np.array([x_0,v_0])          # first array

def Euler_Method(f,a,b,y0,step):

    t = np.linspace(a,b,step)

    h = t[1] - t[0]

    Y = [y0]

    N = len(t)

    n = 0

    y = y0

    for n in range(0,N-1) :
```

(a)

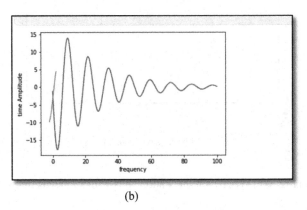

(b)

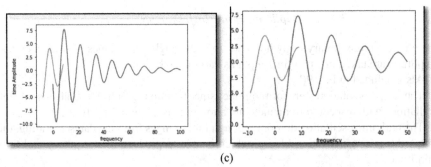

(c)

Fig. 10. (a). Code for oscillations w.r.t. Frequency and Amplitude (b) the oscillation from −5, 5 (the reading of frequency and Amplitude) 10 (c) the input reading differs the plot output

```
import numpy as np

import matplotlib.pyplot as plot

#a = float(input("enter value of a :"  ))
#b = float(input("enter the value of b :" ))

# Get x values of the sine wave
frequency        = np.arange(0,1.288 , 0.001);
amplitude   = np.sin(frequency)
print(amplitude)
plot.plot(frequency, amplitude)

plot.title('Vibration plot')

plot.xlabel('frequency')

plot.ylabel('amplitude')

plot.ylabel('Amplitude')


[0.       0.001     0.002      ... 0.95943746 0.9597189  0.95999938]
Text(0, 0.5, 'Amplitude')
```

(a)

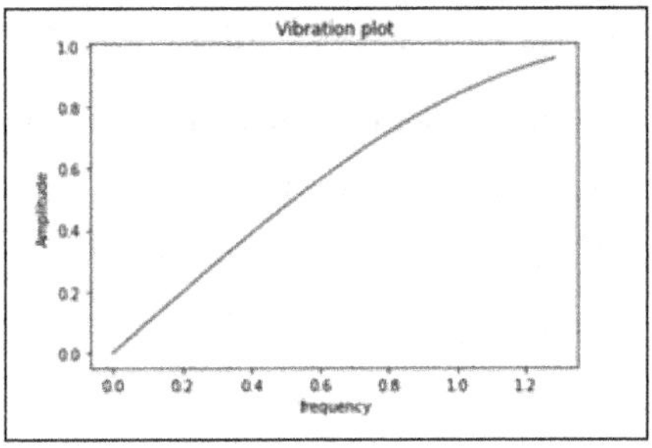

(b)

Fig. 11. (a) The range of vibration plot for frequency of 1.288. (b) Vibration plot for the input frequency range of -1.288

5 Future Scope of the Work

The future scope of the proposed model can be used for detecting earthquake, the age or quality check of dams, bridges, railway lines etc. This will check and also inform about the natural disasters which will be a helpful and reduce of losses of life and property. It can also be used in medical field for finding the for human bone strength. It will also be helpful in various other fields yet to discovered. If in future the dataset is in form image, the image processing including the concept of deep learning and CNN can be used and implemented to get the results, the CNN will directly able to identify the strength of structure through images.

References

1. Wikipedia contributors: Laser Doppler Vibrometer. In Wikipedia, The Free Encyclopedia, 23 October 2022. 05:55. https://en.wikipedia.org/w/index.php?title=Laser_Doppler_vibrometer&oldid=1117772843. Accessed 28 Nov 2022
2. Rubino, E., Ioppolo, T.: A vibrometer based on magnetorheological optical resonators. Vibration 1(2), 239–249 (2018)
3. Sharma, J.K.: Theoretical and experimental modal analysis of beam. In: Ray, K., Sharan, S.N., Rawat, S., Jain, S.K., Srivastava, S., Bandyopadhyay, A. (eds.) Engineering Vibration, Communication and Information Processing. LNEE, vol. 478, pp. 177–186. Springer, Singapore (2019). https://doi.org/10.1007/978-981-13-1642-5_16
4. Nussbaumer, H.J.: The fast Fourier transform. In: Nussbaumer, H.J. (eds.) Fast Fourier Transform and Convolution Algorithms. SSINF, vol. 2, pp. 80–111. Springer, Heidelberg (1981). https://doi.org/10.1007/978-3-662-00551-4_4
5. Sels, S., Ribbens, B., Bogaerts, B., Peeters, J., Vanlanduit, S.: 3D model assisted fully automated scanning laser Doppler vibrometer measurements. Opt. Lasers Eng. **99**, 23–30 (2017)
6. Haus, J.N., et al.: MEMS Vibrometer for structural health monitoring using guided ultrasonic waves. Sensors **22**(14), 5368 (2022)
7. Vibration Feature Extraction using signal processing techniques for structural health monitoring
8. Kaggle.com. https://www.kaggle.com/datasets/lalisharma/vibrometerdataset?select=data+ml.csv. Accessed 6 Nov 2022
9. Python.org. https://www.python.org/downloads/release/python-390/. Accessed 27 Oct 2022

Pneumonia Detection Using Deep Learning: A Bibliometric Study

Rekha Jatwani[✉] and Pharindra Kumar Sharma

Nirwan University, Jaipur, India
rekha.jatwani@nirwanuniversity.ac.in

Abstract. Purpose: The study's aim is to examine the most frequently referenced literature on Pneumonia disease.

Background: Owing to the unavailability of bibliographic studies that have been conducted of pneumonia lung disease, the objective of this study is to provide access, advancement and present state of development in the domain for the span 2000–2020. Pulmonary disease is one of the major cause of death all over the globe. Pneumonia, Cancer and POCD are the main participants in this category. A substantial number of studies have been published and contrition of researchers is acting like a key pillar for pulmonary disease diagnosis.

Method: To find all published articles from 2000 till 2020, Web of Science, Science Direct, IEEE Conference papers and various Citation Index reports were exploited and articles with noble citation on pneumonia disease or related to pneumonia disease were listed for total citation number, first author, published journal and geographic origin.

Keywords: Citations · Most-cited papers · Pneumonia · Pulmonary Disease · Bibliometric

1 Introduction

Bronchitis, asthma, chronic obstructive pulmonary (COPD) disease, measles, influenza, lung cancer, pneumonia, COVID19 and other respiratory disorders are lung diseases that affect humans. Although clinical symptoms of these diseases differ slightly, however, common signs are trouble in breathing, asphyxia like feeling, decreased ability to exercise, a stubborn unhealing cough, coughing up blood or colored mucus, pain during expiration/inspiration (Fig. 1).

Pneumonia is a life-threatening illness caused by either bacterial or viral infections that arise in the lungs. Early detection of this life-threatening disease is necessary. Study shows that it affects humans in all ages and is reported as single major cause of children's infectious death in children all over the globe.

It is a kind of lung infection and a major causes the death of millions of people every year [1]. Pneumonia is a major health concern for many people, particularly in developing countries where billions of people live in energy poverty and rely on polluting energy sources. Every year about 150 million individuals get afflicted with disease [2].

R. S. Tomar et al. (Eds.): CNC 2022, CCIS 1894, pp. 185–198, 2023.
https://doi.org/10.1007/978-3-031-43145-6_16

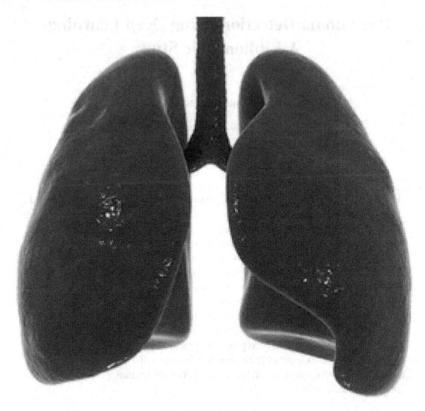

Fig. 1. Healthy Lung

It has the ability to be lethal for infants, people with various illnesses, people with weak immune systems, the elderly, people in hospitals and on ventilators, and people with chronic diseases like asthma and the ones who consume tobacco [3]. Pneumonia can be viral or bacterial in nature. Antibodies are used to cure bacterial pneumonia, but the virus may be treated on its own. These pathogens are transmitted through close contact with contaminated persons [4]. The disease can be diagnosed through analysis of Chest radiographs or chest x-ray is used for the diagnosis of several diseases like pneumonia, Tuberculosis (TB), lung cancer, and bronchitis etc. [5].

Physicians also use pulmonary radiography to diagnose diseases associated with the region more quickly at a lower cost than other imaging modalities such as Computed Tomography (CT) or Magnetic Resonance Imaging (MRI) [6]. Being affordable, Chest x-rays find a special place in the diagnosis of pneumonia. Chest X-ray (CXR) analysis has proven itself to be the most useful radiographic examination in identification of different types of pneumonia [7] (Fig. 2)

The radiographic examination is done using image processing which later on requires extracting important features from images and utilize them for classification. Texture based characterization of pneumonia pattern is an example of this approach. Detecting edges and segmentation of region under study are also associated with image processing

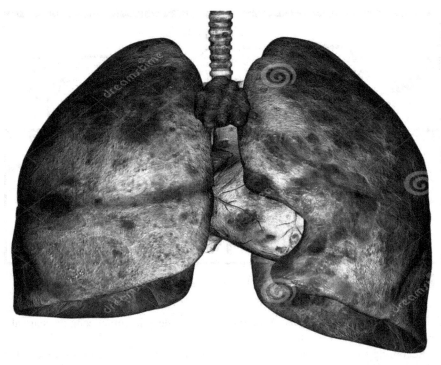

Fig. 2. Unhealthy Lung

[8]. Factors such as patient's position and the depth of inspiration, however, complicate the Image-based CXR investigations as these may alter the CXR's appearance. These conditions significantly increase the difficulties for clinicians in interpreting and evaluating CXR pictures [9]. Figure 3, demonstrate the classification model of training and testing modules to classify the input as normal or pneumonia infected image.

Deep learning has shown its remarkable performance for rapid and tremendous improvement on a variety of computer vision issues. The Deep learning algorithms have significantly improved the quantitative efficiency of target identification, recognition, and segmentation [10]. Deep learning is an excellent way to glean useful knowledge from medical information that is often complicated [11]. Use of data-driven deep learning (DL) methods helps in the automatic extraction and classification of feature sets [12]. Deep learning has been used profoundly for analysis of images in digital pathology [13]. In recent times, Convolutional Neural Networks (CNNs) have become the ideal choice for medical image classification which is mainly used in computer-aided diagnosis [2]. The growth of CNNs has resulted in significant developments in their ability to recognize patterns and artifacts within them [14]. CNN's remarkable performances are followed by the availability of vast volumes of annotated data [15]. These large collections of labelled data are not often available in clinical practice. Transfer learning is a feasible solution to CNN's full-fledged preparation. Transfer learning has become integral to many applications [16]. The process of using a well-formed network on a related task by copying its parameters and weights into work that is tailored to the current task is

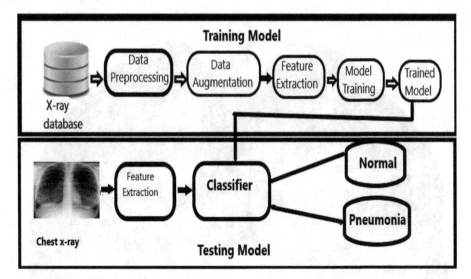

Fig. 3. Pneumonia classification using pulmonary CXR images

known as transfer learning [17]. Also in recent days, deep learning techniques are also applied to the diagnosis of pneumonia.

According to WHO reports the disease accounts for 15% of death in the children under the age of 5 years. CXR is an imaging technique used for pulmonary disease diagnosis and deep learning is imparting an important role in diagnosing the disease by classifying the medical images in infected and non-infected CXR. Researchers have contributed a lot for medical imaging classification and with development of computer vision imaging methods over recent decades, pulmonary imaging classification has shown a rapid growth. JAMA in 1987 defined a tool to check the excellence and acceptability of the article by other researchers and the tool is known as bibliometric analysis.

It has gained wide recognition as a unique quantitative measure, which has complemented the qualitative measure for published research to find the impact of one researcher on other. In literature pool we find plethora of articles that leverage deep learning algorithms to enhance the prediction accuracy, but we find no articles projecting bibliometric analysis of the prediction of disease using deep learning methods so this study will be the first one in this area and help other researchers to find good quality papers for literature review. Bibliometric analysis is a historical study to dig and find quality research and development in medical imaging. Accurate prediction of disease using deep learning is now a days gaining focus by different researchers and significant numbers of articles published by different researchers in peer reviewed journals is the evidence to support the fact. The recognition awarded by one researcher to other by referring their work in own article is known as citation and it is the only indicator to indicate the quality of article, it also contributes as a basis for IF of a journal (Impact factor). Also it helps the research community in providing the clear directions of research developments and makes recommendations to move forward. Various bibliometric studies have been reported in medical science.

Since there is a lack of bibliometric research studies in this area, the objective of the study is to access the evolution, development and current status of the research during 2000–2020 by analyzing research articles indexed in Springer, WOS databases, Science direct etc.

2 Materials and Methods

2.1 Selection of Articles

For identifying pneumonia disease highly-cited research papers, Author has used "Radiology, Medical Imaging and Computer Vision" subject categories. These terms were included for participation of high-impact multidisciplinary journals with no duplication between them and to involve wide spectrum of research communities' contributions. During search we found that pneumonia disease classification is not confined to only general or healthcare journals but also various other journals and conferences have published high cited articles in this category. Various multidisciplinary journals are the prime contributor in this area. Since it is a first study of this kind and the disease is attracting focus of various researchers, this study will give a platform and help researches to know about the present research status in this field. Here the articles with citation $>= 50$ are recorded and complied into a single table and is ranked according citation number. To ensure that the selected article is relevant to our search, to assure about the selection is mainly contributing papers towards pneumonia prediction using deep learning methods, author has taken into consideration the title and abstract of the articles. Author has excluded review research and book chapters for this study.

2.1.1 Analysis of Selected Research PAper's Characteristics

Author obtained abstracts or full texts of selected articles through online search for various journals and recorded the information. For all selected papers, following key attributes were extracted: journal of publishing with publication year, number of citations, first author's country, article type (original article, review article, guideline, case studies report or technical note), type of imaging technique used (conventional radiography, CT(computed tomography), MRI (magnetic resonance imaging) or combined technique). To analysis the collected information author has not used any specific statistical tools, rather descriptive statistics are used for data representation.

3 Results

After the emergence of COVID-19 disease the pulmonary diseases like pneumonia has attracted the focus of researchers and practitioners and now researchers are trying to automate medical diagnosis so that in case of emergency no patient is losses its life only because of non-availability of proper diagnosis. To help researchers author performed an extensive search and based on the search performed till March 2021 for pneumonia pulmonary imaging articles with citation count greater than 50, are listed in the Table 1. Since limited work is done focusing specially on this disease, citation count of articles

Table 1. Top Cited Articles with Their Citation

S. No	Article	Citation
1	[18]	9156
2	[19]	1965
3	[20]	1481
4	[21]	934
5	[22]	875
6	[23]	850
7	[24]	398
8	[25]	432
9	[26]	275
10	[27]	268
11	[28]	204
12	[29]	399
13	[30]	497
14	[31]	123
15	[2]	232
16	[3]	240
17	[32]	159
18	[33]	171
19	[34]	107
20	[35]	226
21	[36]	92
22	[37]	90
23	[38]	192
24	[39]	158
25	[7]	133
26	[40]	91
27	[41]	131
28	[42]	75
29	[43]	105
30	[44]	99
31	[45]	195
32	[46]	58

(*continued*)

Table 1. (*continued*)

S. No	Article	Citation
33	[47]	69
34	[48]	144
35	[49]	65
36	[50]	112
37	[51]	91
38	[36]	58
39	[1]	87
40	[52]	115
41	[53]	61
42	[54]	54

varies from 50 to 8758 (mean citation = 355.7872 and median citation = 79). Approximate 50% of frequently cited research were mainly published in year 2018–2020 (2020 (12 articles), 2019 & 2018 (5 articles in every year)). The highest citation article was published by [18] in 2016 with citation count of 9156 citations followed by paper published in 2017 by [19] with 1965 citations describing benchmark on localization of common pulmonary diseases.

Selected articles were published in various journals and conferences, led by International Journal of Medical Information (4), Applied Science (4), RSNA Technology (3), Journal of American Medical Informatics Association (3) and in IEEE Transection (3). Other journals and conferences contributed two or one papers only.

Twenty-Seven authors have contributed towards more than 2 articles in this research area (Table 2). United States is the top contributor in research for this disease followed by China and Europe (Table 3). Table 4 summarizes the imaging technique used in top cited journals and from Table 4 it can be seen the CXR images is the most commonly used techniques for disease diagnosis. One of the reasons behind it may be, the cost incurred. As CXR imaging is a cost-effective technique as compared to CT and MRI and it is in the reach of economic weaker section also, so majority of the research is focused on X-ray images only.

Table 2. Authors Who Contributed >= 2 Top-Cited Articles in Pneumonia Disease Classification

S. no	Author Name	Number of Articles Contributed	Position on Author List
1	L.L.G oliveira	2	First(2)
2	L. H. V. Ribeiro	3	First(1), third(1), Eight(1)

(*continued*)

Table 2. (*continued*)

S. no	Author Name	Number of Articles Contributed	Position on Author List
3	Renato Maurıcio de Oliveira	3	Forth(2), Fifth(1)
4	Ronald M. Summers	2	Third(1), Fifth(1)
5	Lin li	2	First(2)
6	lixin Qin	2	Second(2)
7	Zeguo X	2	Third(2)
8	Youbing	2	Four(2)
9	Xin Wang	2	Five(2)
10	bin Kong	2	Six(2)
11	Junjie Bai	2	Seven(2)
12	Yi Lu	2	Eight(2)
13	Zhenghan Fang	2	Nine(2)
14	Qi Song	2	Ten(2)
15	Kunlin Cao	2	Eleven(2)
16	Daliang Liu	2	Twelve(2)
17	Guisheng Wang	2	Thirteen(2)
18	Shiqin Zhang	2	Fourteen(2)
19	Juan Xia	2	Fifteen(2)
20	Jun Xia	2	Sixteen(2)
21	Sema Candemir	2	Second(2)
22	Sameer Antani	2	Third(1), Fifth(1)
23	George Thoma	3	Four(1), Seven(2)
24	Marcelo Fiszman	3	First(2), Second(1)
25	Wendy W. Chapman	2	First(1), Second()
26	S Rajaraman	2	First(2)
27	Mark I. Neuman	2	First(2)

Table 3. List of Countries with Number of Articles Submitted

S. No	Country	Number of Articles Submitted
1	USA	15
2	Turkey	5
3	India	3
4	China	3
5	U.K	4
6	Brazil	2
7	Spain	1
8	Canada	2
9	New Zealand	1
10	Italy	1
11	Iraq	1
12	Switzerland	1
13	South Africa	1
14	Morocco	1
15	Egypt	1

Table 4. Imaging Technique Used in Top Cited Articles

S. No	Imaging Technique	Number of Articles
1	X-Ray/Radiograph	31
2	CT Scans	4
3	MRI	2
4	Mixed	5

4 Discussion

Author has prepared a list of the articles in thotic imaging primarily focusing on Pneumonia prediction that were cited more than 50 while excluding articles about the heart and thoracic aorta as pulmonary imaging and cardiovascular imaging are clinical two different entities. This paper mainly focus on top-cited articles in pneumonia disease classification using deep learning and its related techniques. In present discussion, author analyzed the number of citations, publication year, Origin country and imaging technique used as it is the first article on bibliometric analysis in this area, in future work could be extended to include a metric that would track the number of citations over a particular time period, such as a 5-years or as required. Another metric can be defined to measure the quality and popularity of article as, how many times the article is down-loaded from a journal's website. All this will give a clear picture of current topic search and about the researchers' interest areas. It we look at the publication trends, highly cited 85% research for the topic in consideration were published in 2015–2020, reflecting radiology, including pulmonary imaging and clinical pulmonology recent evolutions and developments.

Sixty six percent of research considered here are based on CXR imaging, which is the most important modality in pulmonary imaging.

Earlier to 2000, the published research were mainly focusing on conventional radiography techniques along with limited research published using CT or combined imaging techniques. Although in other radiologic subspecialties such as neuroradiology CT and MRI has recently been used, but in the pulmonary studies CXR images are contributing as primary source of disease information.

Another observation that can be deduced from our study are:

- United States is the top contributor and has contributed 35% top-cited research articles
- Turkey is second among the top contributor and India, China and U.K are following Turkey.

Figure 4 visualize the contribution of various countries worldwide along with number of research articles submitted by researchers.

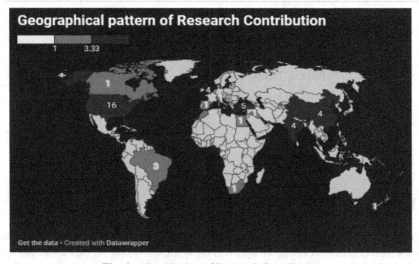

Fig. 4. Visualization of Research Contribution

The United States' domination can be traced to the country's strong science population, ample financial capital, and Country's researchers' proclivity to not only print in their own country journals but also to cite local articles, For this reason only the research published from US have also contributed towards high citations.

Eighty five percent of the top research were published in healthcare journals and conferences. Limited contribution is also recorded for IEEE transections. This indicates that pneumonia disease classification and diagnosis has become one of the prime research area with the emergence of COVID-19 pneumonia. Another surprising fact that author has deducted is that 60% of top cited papers are published in 2019–2020. This reflects the evolution, developments and focus of research towards pulmonary diseases and their classification.

The Radiography imaging is the most commonly and economic way to diagnose the disease, another methodology includes CT scans, which is also very effective but expensive technique as compared to CXR images. From this study it is very clear that primary imaging modality of pulmonary imaging is still CXR images.

Seventy percent top-cited pneumonia classification articles were published in health-care journals and healthcare international conferences, including International journals of Medical Information and JAMIA(Journal of American Medical Informatics Association) and rest were published in non-healthcare Journals. This indicates that this disease has attracted focus of many researchers from deep learning background and they have published articles in science and technology related journals also. Cross discipline publication is in trend now a days, in scientific publication, and a recent study reported that during 2018–2020, articles with medical background were also published in non-radiology journals. 35% of the first authors in this study were allied with Health Sectors, rest are either from Computer Science, Information Technology or from Electronics Departments. In short this field of research has attracted researcher from various departments and their contribution is commendable.

5 Conclusion

Our study focuses on frequently cited research related to pneumonia prediction and gives an insight into historical development in this field. This study is very helpful for the researchers to know the growth and recognize the future scope of improvement.

References

1. Sirazitdinov, I., Kholiavchenko, M., Mustafaev, T., Yixuan, Y., Kuleev, R., Ibragimov, B.: Deep neural network ensemble for pneumonia localization from a large-scale chest x-ray database. Comput. Electr. Eng. **78**, 388–399 (2019). https://doi.org/10.1016/j.compeleceng. 2019.08.004
2. Stephen, O., Sain, M., Maduh, U.J., Jeong, D.U.: An efficient deep learning approach to pneumonia classification in healthcare. J. Healthc. Eng. **2019** (2019). https://doi.org/10.1155/ 2019/4180949
3. Chouhan, V., Singh, S.K., Khamparia, A., et al.: A novel transfer learning based approach for pneumonia detection in chest X-ray images. Appl Sci. **10**(2) (2020). https://doi.org/10.3390/ app10020559
4. Naskinova, I.: On convolutional neural networks for chest X-ray classification. IOP Conf. Ser. Mater. Sci. Eng. **1031**(1), 012075 (2021). https://doi.org/10.1088/1757-899x/1031/1/012075
5. Automatic detection of major lung diseases using chest radiographs and classification by feed-forward artificial neural network, pp. 1–5 (2016)
6. Antin, B., Kravitz, J., Martayan, E.: Detecting pneumonia in chest X-rays with supervised learning, pp. 1–5 (2017)

7. Rajaraman, S., Candemir, S., Kim, I., Thoma, G., Antani, S.: Visualization and interpretation of convolutional neural network predictions in detecting pneumonia in pediatric chest radiographs. Appl. Sci. **8**(10) (2018). https://doi.org/10.3390/app8101715

8. Guillermo, M., De Jesus, L.C., Sybingco, E., Mital, M.E.: Android application for chest X-ray health classification from a CNN deep learning TensorFlow model. In: (LifeTech), pp. 255–259 (2020)

9. Li, B., Kang, G., Cheng, K., Zhang, N.: Attention-guided convolutional neural network for detecting pneumonia on chest X-rays. In: 2019 41st Annual International Conference of the IEEE Engineering in Medicine and Biology Society, pp. 4851–4854 (2019)

10. Tsai, M.J., Tao, Y.H.: Machine learning based common radiologist-level pneumonia detection on chest X-rays. In: 13th International Conference on Signal Processing and Communication Systems, p. 13 (2019)

11. Jakhar, K., Hooda, N.: Big data deep learning framework using Keras: a case study of pneumonia prediction. In: 2018 4th International Conference on Computing Communication and Automation ICCCA 2018, pp. 1-5 (2018). https://doi.org/10.1109/CCAA.2018.8777571

12. Khan, W., Zaki, N., Ali, L.: Intelligent pneumonia identification from chest X-rays: a systematic literature review, pp. 1–13. medRxiv (2020). https://doi.org/10.1101/2020.07.09.201 50342

13. Mahajan, S., Shah, U., Tambe, R., Agrawal, M., Garware, B.: Towards evaluating performance of domain specific transfer learning for pneumonia detection from X-ray images. In: 2019 IEEE 5th International Conference for Convergence in Technology, I2CT 2019, pp. 1–6 (2019). https://doi.org/10.1109/I2CT45611.2019.9033555

14. Kermany, D.S., Goldbaum, M., Cai, W., Lewis, M.A.: Identifying medical diagnoses and treatable diseases by image-based deep learning resource identifying medical diagnoses and treatable diseases by image-based deep learning. Cell **172**(5), 1122-1131.e9 (2018). https://doi.org/10.1016/j.cell.2018.02.010

15. Foxlin, E., Calloway, T., Zhang, H.: Design and error analysis of a vehicular AR system with auto-harmonization. IEEE Trans. Vis. Comput. Graph. **21**(12), 1323–1335 (2015). https://doi.org/10.1109/TVCG.2015.2481385

16. Morid, M.A., Borjali, A., Del Fiol, G.: A scoping review of transfer learning research on medical image analysis using ImageNet. Comput. Biol. Med. **128**, 104115 (2021). https://doi.org/10.1016/j.compbiomed.2020.104115

17. Vianna, V.P.: Study and development of a computer-aided diagnosis system for classification of chest X-ray images using convolutional neural networks pre-trained for ImageNet and data augmentation (2018). https://pytorch.org/docs/master/torchvision/

18. Radford, A., Metz, L., Chintala, S.: Unsupervised representation learning with deep convolutional generative adversarial networks. In: 4th International Conference on Learning Representations ICLR 2016 - Conference Track Proceedings, pp. 1–16 (2016)

19. Wang, X., Peng, Y., Lu, L., Lu, Z., Bagheri, M., Summers, R.M.: ChestX-ray8: hospital-scale chest X-ray database and benchmarks on weakly-supervised classification and localization of common thorax diseases. In: Proceedings of the IEEE Conference on Computer Vision and Pattern Recognition, CVPR 2017, 2017-January, pp. 3462–3471 (2017). https://doi.org/10.1109/CVPR.2017.369

20. Rajpurkar, P., Irvin, J., Zhu, K., et al.: CheXNet: radiologist-level pneumonia detection on chest X-rays with deep learning, pp. 3–9. arXiv (2017)

21. Anthimopoulos, M., Christodoulidis, S., Ebner, L., Christe, A., Mougiakakou, S.: Lung pattern classification for interstitial lung diseases using a deep convolutional neural network. IEEE Trans. Med. Imaging **35**(5), 1207–1216 (2016). https://doi.org/10.1109/TMI.2016.2535865

22. Xu, X., Jiang, X., Ma, C., et al.: A deep learning system to screen novel coronavirus disease 2019 pneumonia. Engineering **6**(10), 1122–1129 (2020). https://doi.org/10.1016/j.eng.2020.04.010

23. Li, L., Qin, L., Xu, Z., et al.: Artificial intelligence distinguishes COVID-19 from community acquired pneumonia on chest CT. Radiology **296**(2), E65–E71 (2020). https://doi.org/10.1148/radiol.2020200905

24. Li, L., Qin, L., Xu, Z., et al.: Using artificial intelligence to detect COVID-19 and community-acquired pneumonia based on pulmonary CT: evaluation of the diagnostic accuracy. Radiology **296**(2), E65–E71 (2020). https://doi.org/10.1148/radiol.2020200905

25. Jaeger, S., Candemir, S., Antani, S., Wáng, Y.X.J., Lu, P.X., Thoma, G.: Two public chest X-ray datasets for computer-aided screening of pulmonary diseases. Quant. Imaging Med. Surg. **4**(6), 475–477 (2014). https://doi.org/10.3978/j.issn.2223-4292.2014.11.20

26. Fiszman, M., Chapman, W.W., Aronsky, D., Scott Evans, R., Haug, P.J.: Automatic detection of acute bacterial pneumonia from chest X-ray reports. J. Am. Med. Inform. Assoc. **7**(6), 593–604 (2000). https://doi.org/10.1136/jamia.2000.0070593

27. Hoeper, M., Dinh-Xuan, A., Warwick, G., Thomas, P., Yates, D.: Imaging of pneumonia: trends and algorithms **32**(2), 503–512 (2008). www.erj.ersjournals.com/misc/

28. Er, O., Yumusak, N., Temurtas, F.: Chest diseases diagnosis using artificial neural networks. Expert Syst. Appl. **37**(12), 7648–7655 (2010). https://doi.org/10.1016/j.eswa.2010.04.078

29. Zhou, Z., Siddiquee, M.M.R., Tajbakhsh, N., Liang, J.: UNet++: redesigning skip connections to exploit multiscale features in image segmentation. IEEE Trans. Med. Imaging **39**(6), 1856–1867 (2020). https://doi.org/10.1109/TMI.2019.2959609

30. Wang, L., Lin, Z.Q., Wong, A.: COVID-Net: a tailored deep convolutional neural network design for detection of COVID-19 cases from chest X-ray images. Sci. Rep. **10**(1), 1–12 (2020). https://doi.org/10.1038/s41598-020-76550-z

31. Neuman, M.I., Monuteaux, M.C., Scully, K.J., Bachur, R.G.: Prediction of pneumonia in a pediatric emergency department. Pediatrics **128**(2), 246–253 (2011). https://doi.org/10.1542/peds.2010-3367

32. Walsh, S.L.F., Calandriello, L., Silva, M., Sverzellati, N.: Deep learning for classifying fibrotic lung disease on high-resolution computed tomography: a case-cohort study. Lancet Respir. Med. **6**(11), 837–845 (2018). https://doi.org/10.1016/S2213-2600(18)30286-8

33. Abiyev, R.H., Ma'aitah, M.K.S.: Deep convolutional neural networks for chest diseases detection. J. Healthc. Eng. **2018**, 1–12 (2018). https://doi.org/10.1155/2018/4168538

34. Chapman, W.W., Fizman, M., Chapman, B.E., Haug, P.J.: A comparison of classification algorithms to automatically identify chest X-ray reports that support pneumonia. J. Biomed. Inform. **34**(1), 4–14 (2001). https://doi.org/10.1006/jbin.2001.1000

35. Yadav, S.S., Jadhav, S.M.: Deep convolutional neural network based medical image classification for disease diagnosis. J. Big Data **6**(1) (2019). https://doi.org/10.1186/s40537-019-0276-2

36. Morillo, D.S., Jiménez, A.L., Moreno, S.A.: Computer-aided diagnosis of pneumonia in patients with chronic obstructive pulmonary disease. J. Am. Med. Inform. Assoc. **20**(E1) (2013). https://doi.org/10.1136/amiajnl-2012-001171

37. de Andrade, A.L.S.S., de Andrade, J.G., Martelli, C.M.T., et al.: Effectiveness of Haemophilus influenzae b conjugate vaccine on childhood pneumonia: a case-control study in Brazil. Int. J. Epidemiol. **33**(1), 173–181 (2004). https://doi.org/10.1093/ije/dyh025

38. Maghdid, H.S., Asaad, A.T., Ghafoor, K.Z., Sadiq, A.S., Khan, M.K.: Diagnosing COVID-19 pneumonia from X-ray and CT images using deep learning and transfer learning algorithms, pp. 1–8. arXiv (2020)

39. Liang, G., Zheng, L.: A transfer learning method with deep residual network for pediatric pneumonia diagnosis. Comput. Methods Programs Biomed. **187** (2020). https://doi.org/10.1016/j.cmpb.2019.06.023

40. Mortazi, A., Karim, R., Rhode, K., Burt, J., Bagci, U.: CardiacNET: segmentation of left atrium and proximal pulmonary veins from MRI using multi-view CNN. In: Descoteaux,

M., Maier-Hein, L., Franz, A., Jannin, P., Collins, D.L., Duchesne, S. (eds.) MICCAI 2017. LNCS, vol. 10434, pp. 377–385. Springer, Cham (2017). https://doi.org/10.1007/978-3-319-66185-8_43

41. Neuman, M.I., Lee, E.Y., Bixby, S., et al.: Variability in the interpretation of chest radiographs for the diagnosis of pneumonia in children. J. Hosp. Med. **7**(4), 294–298 (2012). https://doi.org/10.1002/jhm.955

42. Oliveira, L.L.G., e Silva, S.A., Ribeiro, L.H.V., de Oliveira, R.M., Coelho, C.J., Andrade, A.L.S.: Computer-aided diagnosis in chest radiography for detection of childhood pneumonia. Int. J. Med. Inform. **77**(8), 555–564 (2008). https://doi.org/10.1016/j.ijmedinf.2007.10.010

43. Mandell, L.A.: Community-acquired pneumonia: an overview. Postgrad. Med. **127**(6), 607–615 (2015). https://doi.org/10.1080/00325481.2015.1074030

44. Mackenzie, G.: The definition and classification of pneumonia. Pneumonia **8**(1), 1–5 (2016). https://doi.org/10.1186/s41479-016-0012-z

45. Jamshidi, M., Lalbakhsh, A., Talla, J., et al.: Artificial intelligence and COVID-19: deep learning approaches for diagnosis and treatment. IEEE Access **2020**(8), 109581–109595 (2019). https://doi.org/10.1109/ACCESS.2020.3001973

46. Rothrock, S.G., Green, S.M., Fanelli, J.M., Cruzen, E., Costanzo, K.A., Pagane, J.: Do published guidelines predict pneumonia in children presenting to an urban ED? Pediatr. Emerg. Care **17**(4), 240–243 (2001). https://doi.org/10.1097/00006565-200108000-00003

47. Elemraid, M.A., Muller, M., Spencer, D.A., et al.: Accuracy of the interpretation of chest radiographs for the diagnosis of paediatric pneumonia. PLoS ONE **9**(8), 6–10 (2014). https://doi.org/10.1371/journal.pone.0106051

48. El Asnaoui, K., Chawki, Y.: Using X-ray images and deep learning for automated detection of coronavirus disease. J. Biomol. Struct. Dyn. 1–12 (2020). https://doi.org/10.1080/07391102.2020.1767212

49. Aydoğdu, M., Özyilmaz, E., Aksoy, H., Gürsel, G., Ekim, N.: Mortality prediction in community-acquired pneumonia requiring mechanical ventilation; values of pneumonia and intensive care unit severity scores. Tuberk Toraks **58**(1), 25–34 (2010)

50. Khalifa, N.E.M., Taha, M.H.N., Hassanien, A.E., Elghamrawy, S.: Detection of coronavirus (COVID-19) associated pneumonia based on generative adversarial networks and a fine-tuned deep transfer learning model using chest x-ray dataset, pp. 1–15. arXiv (2020)

51. Toğaçar, M., Ergen, B., Cömert, Z., Özyurt, F.: A deep feature learning model for pneumonia detection applying a combination of mRMR feature selection and machine learning models. IRBM **41**(4), 212–222 (2020). https://doi.org/10.1016/j.irbm.2019.10.006

52. Ayan, E., Ünver, H.M.: Diagnosis of pneumonia from chest X-ray images using deep learning. In: 2019 Scientific Meeting on Electrical-Electronics & Biomedical Engineering and Computer Science, EBBT 2019, p. 4 (2019). https://doi.org/10.1109/EBBT.2019.8741582

53. Sharma, A., Raju, D., Ranjan, S.: Detection of pneumonia clouds in chest X-ray using image processing approach. In: 2017 Nirma University International Conference on Engineering NUiCONE 2017, 2018-January, pp. 1–4 (2018). https://doi.org/10.1109/NUICONE.2017.8325607

54. Xu, S., Wu, H., Bie, R.: CXNet-m1: anomaly detection on chest X-rays with image-based deep learning. IEEE Access **7**, 4466–4477 (2019). https://doi.org/10.1109/ACCESS.2018.2885997

Numerical Simulation Design of Multiple Users Offloading Using Improved Optimization Approach for Edge Computing

Harsh Vardhan Singh[✉] and Dushyant Singh

Department of Computer Science and Engineering, VGU, Jaipur, Rajasthan, India
araj64329@gmail.com

Abstract. It's no secret that the IoT (Internet of Things) has exploded in popularity over the past decade. IoT devices with limited resources have a lot of trouble keeping up with the growing number of latency-sensitive and computationally intensive IoT applications. By allowing devices with constrained resources to outsource their work to edge servers, edge computing looks to be a viable technique for expanding the computational capacity of IoT systems. Most of the existing literature on task offloading overlooks the interdependencies between tasks and subtasks, despite the fact that they provide a significant difficulty and may have a considerable influence on offloading decisions. Furthermore, the current research commonly considers offloading activities to specific edge servers, which may result in under-utilization of edge resources in very busy edge networks. In this research, we look at the problem of offloading tasks in dense edge networks while keeping dependencies in mind. To achieve full parallelism between edge servers and IoT devices, we measure task dependency using directed acyclic graphs (DAGs). In order to reduce both task delay and energy consumption, task offloading is frequently given as a joint optimization issue. We prove that this is an NP-hard issue and present a heuristic approach to guaranteeing subtask dependency while improving task efficiency. The suggested strategy is shown to be effective in reducing task latency in simulations of highly dense edge networks.

Keywords: Cloud Computing · Edge Computing · Resource Allocation · Genetic Algorithm · Optimization · Heuristic Optimization

1 Introduction

Improvements in the price, performance, and energy efficiency of IoT devices, network technologies (such as 5G), and distributed computing architectures have enabled the development of a wide range of new types of automated vehicles, augmented reality, cloud robotics, smart homes and cities, video surveillance, and streamed content. The transportation, medical, mining, entertainment, and safety sectors all make use of these programs. Because of the exponential increase of data, latency and regulation are becoming more vital factors in data processing and management. Bandwidth-intensive (video

© The Author(s), under exclusive license to Springer Nature Switzerland AG 2023
R. S. Tomar et al. (Eds.): CNC 2022, CCIS 1894, pp. 199–212, 2023.
https://doi.org/10.1007/978-3-031-43145-6_17

surveillance, video conferencing, traffic monitoring), latency-critical (autonomous vehicles, robotic surgery, safety), and peak-load-generating are all possible characteristics of the emerging breed of distributed applications (sporting events). High availability, low jitter, and data encryption may also be necessary for some applications.

It is expected that the broad use of IoTs and IIoTs would have a significant effect on the progress of smart cities. The cumulative cellular data from all of these gadgets might easily overload the system. In order to mimic a human driver's mental processes hundreds of times each second, these cars will need powerful computer engines. It would be impractical and expensive for on-board systems to do all of these tasks. Moving these responsibilities to a DC, however, will necessitate minimal latency in order to maintain operational security at a rate acceptable to the AVs. As smartphones with high-definition video cameras become more commonplace, users are increasingly drawn to live-streaming apps such as SnapChat, Facebook Live, and YouTube Live. Upstream cellular networks are under significant strain as a result of the data output by these applications. In a similar vein, video surveillance applications will need access to powerful computing resources to power artificial intelligence (AI) and machine learning (ML) systems that can quickly notify humans of suspicious activity. The data produced by these algorithms may be many gigabytes or even terabytes every second. All things considered, we need some sort of computer infrastructure to start dealing with the problems that these cutting-edge programs inevitably cause. High-capacity computing and storage capabilities are now provided by CDCs or cloud DCs. They save money through economies of scale and statistical multiplexing of the applications' compute resource needs [3], but they can't provide the Quality of Service (QoS) needed by many emerging ICT applications because of their long-distance network connections. Fee-for-service as a business concept. Traditional cloud service models may be broken down into three categories: service infrastructure (IaaS), platform (PaaS), and software (SaaS) (Fig. 1).

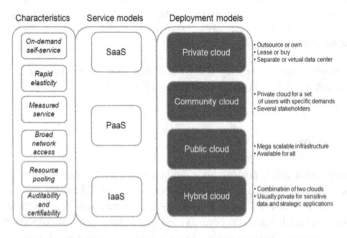

Fig. 1. Cloud: Characteristics, Service and Deployment Models

2   Mobile Edge/Fog Computing

Set-top boxes and access points are examples of services that are located at the network's edge in fog computing. Customers may satisfy their computing demands closer to the sources thanks to the built-in infrastructure for fog computing. The Fog Computing Framework is referred to as an intelligent device user who uses automobiles, cameras, and cell phones. Instead of sending requests to the cloud, users are served in the fog layer. Cloud computing services are nevertheless always accessible for computing jobs requiring more potent processors.

(a) Edge computing, commonly referred to as "Edge," carries out processing near the data source instead of sending it to the distant Cloud or other unified frameworks. Reduced transmission time increases data transmission speed and efficiency. Less time is spent traveling to the source. Figure 2 depicts edge computing from a fundamental standpoint.

(b) Edge processing should follow the fog computing standard. Additionally, it encourages the duty of calculating, stockpiling, and system administration benefits across end-to-end devices where data values are recognized in the Cloud. There are several uses for fog off-loading the Cloud for edge processing. Figure 3 shows the functional aspect of edge computing. Set-top boxes and access points are examples of services that are located at the network's edge in fog computing. Customers may satisfy their computing demands closer to the sources thanks to the built-in infrastructure for fog computing. The Fog Computing Framework is referred to as an intelligent device user who uses automobiles, cameras, and cell phones. Instead of sending requests to the cloud, users are served in the fog layer. Cloud computing is always accessible for computational jobs requiring more potent processing capabilities.

The administration of processing resources, applications, and the connectivity between the data source and the cloud are all made possible by a decentralized computing architecture known as "Edge computing." In other words, where data is gathered or where the client performs certain actions, computational demands may be met there.

The research work reported in this thesis has achieved the following objectives which are outlined below:

- To simulate the environment of fog computing and mobile edge computing.
- To design algorithm for energy harvesting in mobile edge computing environment.
- To formulate the improved soft computing based energy optimization for battery lifetime enhancement.
- To model the problem of minimum execution cost optimization using evolutionary computing based optimization.
- To analyze and compare the figure of merits for result analysis and comparative assessment through the optimization techniques.

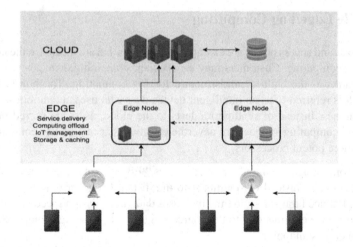

Fig. 2. Mobile Edge Computing

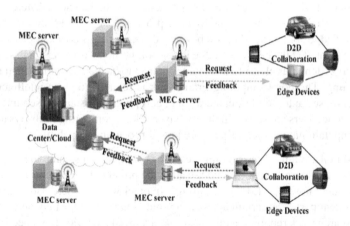

Fig. 3. Functional View of Mobile Edge computing

3   Related Works

Numerous To improve resource usage and service providing, Xu et al. [1] investigated CP method with various switching mechanisms. The CP-based LB paradigm allows for the use of many methods, including IDLE, NORMAL, and OVERLOADED. Actually, they are the partition's statuses, which are utilised to guide judgments. A partition is considered to be in IDLE condition if it is not processing any jobs. Similar to this, a partition is said to be in a NORMAL condition when it is processing data yet has a normal load. In contrast, a partition that is operating at full capacity and using all of its resources is said to be in an OVERLOADED condition. These conditions specifically aid in load balancing. The refresh time, however, has not yet been estimated using the best methods for refreshing and future improvement. This thesis truly closes this gap.

The cloud partitioning strategy for load balancing was examined by Tiwari et al. [2]. The cloud resources are divided up into divisions according to their model, and load balancers are set up in each partition. The performance of cloud computing is optimised as a consequence of the load balancers' strategic work scheduling decisions based on analyses of the load on each partition.

On the other side, Mesbahi and Rahmani [3] investigated several load balancing strategies. They divided load balancing strategies into static and dynamic categories. Distributed and non-distributed dynamic LB algorithms are further divided into several categories. There are two types of static algorithms: deterministic and probabilistic. They also investigated various load balancing techniques. Information strategy, triggering strategy, transfer strategy, and positioning strategy are some of them. The trust management-based LB, stochastic hill climbing (SHC), two-phase LB, and cloud-friendly LB were also discussed.

Randomized load balancing techniques were used by Ying et al. [4] to optimise performance. A potential technique for load balancing was determined to be the random selection of servers and traffic routeing to them. To have a load balancing technique known as batch-filling, sampling of randomised subset of queuing is used. The idea of the power of two options has been shown to improve cloud performance.

In addition to enhancing cloud computing performance, K. Shyamala et al. [5] developed effective resource allocation strategies in the cloud that are studied to have dynamic resource allocations. Investigated are several resource allocation algorithms. They include resource allocation based on user priority, multi-dimensional resource allocation, green cloud computing, and optimum joint multiple resource allocation.

ACO-based LB method was created by Pacini et al. [6] to enhance the performance of scientific applications on public clouds. They estimated the effectiveness of the ACO approach for LB using Parameter Sweep Experiments (PSE). In the trials, they made use of variables such as processor speed, RAM, storage, bandwidth, and others. However, this study does not cover prevalent online systems because they have already been studied.

A scheduling method for virtual machines (VMs) based on genetic coding (GC) was presented by Minxian Xu et al. [7]. One of the performance indicators used to assess the work is gain. As a possible remedy for LB, a survey on VM placement-based scheduling is discovered. They found that meta-heuristics outperform traditional heuristics in terms of outcomes.

On the other hand, Nishanth et al. [8]'s usage of ACO for node load balancing. In actuality, they expanded ACO to get other effects. In contrast to classical ACO, where each ant delivers a unique result set, ants' method continually updates a single result. Even at times when cloud systems are used to their full capacity, their system performed better. The course of the ants is changed when a barrier is met to improve load balance. Ants are permitted to move around in two ways. Both forwards and backwards motions are involved. This technique's main purpose is to redistribute workloads in order to achieve better load balancing.

As the cloud operates in distributed contexts, Randles et al. [9] investigated distributed load balancing techniques. They looked at the active clustering, biased random sampling, and honey-bee foraging behaviour distributed load balancing methods. The system's throughput is investigated in a variety of experimental resources.

The ACO algorithm and its modifications are investigated with examples for various applications in more detail by Marco Dorigoa et al. [10]. They looked at a number of recent attempts to formulate an ACO theory, highlighted linkages between In model-based search, ACO processes are utilized along with the stochastic gradient ascent and cross-entropy techniques. Finally, the effect of search bias on the effectiveness of ACO algorithms was investigated.

Tawfeek et al. [11] devised Modified Ant Colony Optimization (MACO) for load balancing by using a meta-heuristic technique. They changed the core ACO algorithm to emphasize task execution optimisation approach more strongly. They used the CloudSim toolkit to simulate their strategy. While MACO minimizes turnaround time and starts the optimum resource allocation for task groups in the cloud, it is limited in its capacity to determine the load balancing factor.

Falco et al.'s [12] discussion on external optimization attracted their interest. (EO). An EO-based method is used in cloud computing to balance the load. A two-step stochastic selection process is used in this technique. It outperformed both its (Genetic Algorithm) GA equivalent and the greedy totally deterministic technique.

Selvakumar and Gunasekaran [13] proposed an ACO-based solution for LB and found it to be adequate. They suggested that the optimum resource utilization is achieved with an ACO-based load balancing strategy. They tried to raise the quality of their services and provide the results they had promised on time. Therefore, it is still required to create a load balancing approach that can maximize resource consumption while enhancing cloud computing efficiency.

Zuo et al. [14] created a method based on ACO to improve scheduling in cloud computing. They proposed an improved ACO that would shorten makespan, utilize fewer resources, have a lower dead violation rate, and cost in order to keep the ACO from degrading into a local optimal solution.

Kim et al. presented a biogeography-based optimization (BBO) approach for LB. It is a technique for planning tasks that uses cloud load balancing. It was an adaptive method that, in comparison to the Genetic Algorithm (GA), was deemed to be better.

The Hybrid Job Scheduling (HJS) approach was developed by Javanmardi et al. [16] to improve LB in cloud computing. It considered the size of the workloads and the processing power of the VMs while scheduling. It is analyzed using metrics like Degree of Imbalance (DI), execution cost, and execution time. By maximizing CPU consumption, it gave load balancing more of a focus. A fuzzy inference engine was also incorporated into the solution for better optimization.

Shojafar et al. [17] have suggested a heuristic strategy for work allocation. The in question meta-heuristic handles cloud task scheduling. It employs a hybrid methodology that blends the genetic method with fuzzy theories. They enhanced the Standard Genetic Algorithm to achieve this. (SGA). For load balancing, they provided a scheduling-based CloudSim foundation simulation system. They considered task length, VM frequency, and RAM use while making their decisions. This work may be further developed to provide an efficient, reliable power-saving method by considering energy utilization and VM mobility.

Map Reduce programming in cloud computing for efficient task processing was attested by Zhang et al. [18]. They concentrated on the examination of the trade-offs between performance and optimization expenses. In order to conduct experiments with varied inputs and results, several benchmarks are utilized. Using Amazon Elastic Cloud Compute (EC2), Elastic Block Storage (EBS), and Elastic Map Reduce, they assessed it. (EMR). The dynamics of work size are examined together with job completion times.

Using Dynamic Programming, Wang and Shi [19] presented task-level scheduling methods and created a budget-driven scheduling system. (DP). Global Optimal Scheduling (GOS) and Global Greedy Budget were their methods. (GGB). GGB was created to optimize scheduling and load balancing within predetermined financial limits. The funding is allocated for sharing and storage of resources. Global budget distribution combined with predetermined limitations makes an algorithm greedy and leads to the best scheduling outcomes. The leftover budget and scheduling time are two crucial measures that are utilized to assess it.

Described by Sheikhalishahi et al. [20] was a technique. When scheduling jobs, Multi Capacity Aware Resource Scheduling (MCARS) makes advantage of multiple capacity, queuing, host selection, and multiple resource scheduling. Two elements that were included in the algorithm's evaluation were wait time and slowness. In order to accomplish load balancing and schedule optimization, it has a host selection strategy and a multi-capacity queuing system.

4 Modelling of the System

Cisco's groundbreaking idea of "fog computing" [1] in the cloud might turn the periphery of a network into a dispersed computing infrastructure suitable for Internet of Things (IoT) applications. Fog computing is an approach that tries to bring processing and storage capabilities closer to consumers by extending cloud computing to IoT devices that produce and consume data. Fog computing, also known as fog servers or fog nodes, is an alternative to cloud computing that tries to process some of the workloads generated by applications on devices located nearby to the network and close to the end users. These devices may be utilized everywhere there is an available network, which includes offices, shopping centers, power poles, railroad crossings, vehicles, etc. (Fig. 4).

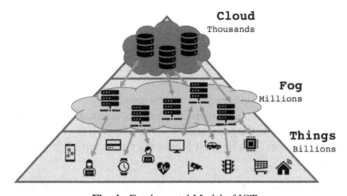

Fig. 4. Fundamental Model of IOT

Eventually, Cloud-Fog computing emerges as a complementary technology to Fog computing. The Cloud-Fog computing architecture offers several benefits, such as decreased latency, less network traffic, and better energy efficiency, but it also has certain drawbacks. Resource allocation and task scheduling are two of them.

The TCaS algorithm, which is deployed on the Fog broker and tries to discover the best job execution schedule by attaining time and cost efficiency, was developed to ensure system performance. Figure 5 breaks down our system model's operation step by step.

In the first stage (stage 1), a mobile user makes a request, which is then handled by the associated Fog node. This request (or job) is immediately communicated to the Fog broker. (Step 2). In Step 3, we divide each job into smaller jobs that can be handled by the distributed system. Based on these tasks, we can estimate the total number of instructions and the amount of resources we'll need. (Step 4). In Step 5, a scheduling algorithm is run by the Fog broker to establish a fair distribution of tasks among available nodes. After the results are tallied, the relevant Cloud and Fog nodes are notified and given their assignments. (Step 6). In Step 7, the individual nodes are responsible for accomplishing their assigned duties and reporting their status to the Fog broker. (Step 8). When all tasks have been completed, the Fog broker merges the results (Step 9). The reply is sent back to the mobile user through the linked Fog node. (Step 10).

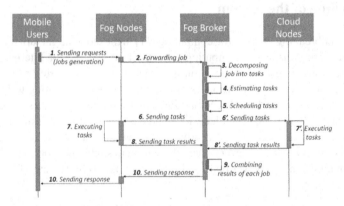

Fig. 5. Fundamental Mechanism of Simple Genetic Algorithm

The main mechanism involves the following phases mentioned in Fig. 6 as well.

(i) Generate the first population randomly.
(ii) Choose the right fitness qualities for chromosomes.
(iii) Using crossover and mutation operators to recombine selected chromosomes.
(iv) Include descendants in the population.
(v) Delete chromosomes with the best fitness if a stop criterion is met. Go to stage 2 otherwise.

In GA, the population is specified as the group of persons. A people are a generation experiencing new generation shifts. Like nature, GAs does have many members to boost the health of the community. A human population refers to a chromosome that is a gene set. A potential solution to the optimization problem is given by each human chromosome. The GA dimension relates to the search area dimension which is equal to the number of genes in every chromosome.

The chromosomal representation in GAs has a deep effect on GA-based results. Chromosomes such as binary encoding, value encoding, permutation encoding, tree encoding etc. are expressed with different method. Binary encoding suggested by Holland is the most widely used encoding. The individual value is coded as a bit string in this process, consisting of binary values of either 0 or 1. The same length of the binary string is used for each population chromosome. Suppose a program has two X and Y inputs with values of 8 and 6 and a binary string length of 5. You can then display X and Y as follows (Table 1).

Table 1. Binary Encoding

Chromosome	Value	ValueBinary Encoding
X	8	01000
Y	6	00110

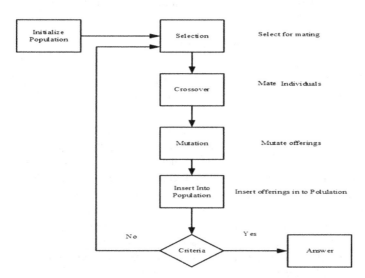

Fig. 6. Flow Chart of Genetic Algorithm

Every optimization problem is based on the fitness function. If fitness is not healthy, there are no optimisation methods to find the solution. The choice of fitness function is therefore a critical problem. The fitness function provides the GA with a way to evaluate each chromosome's success in the population. The GA assesses their quality solutions based on the information that this unit provides, and does not use direct structural data. In the case of a specific chromosome, the fitness function provides one value that is the value of the suitable solution. Depending on the optimization issue, fitness assessment functions can be complex or simple.

Selection
The selection operator chooses the present generation of chromosomes to be parents for the next generation. The dilemma is how to pick the chromosomes/persons. The best live to produce new offspring according to Darwin's theory of evolution. In pairs, parents are chosen. Selection strategies are used for choosing chromosomes of different kind.

Crossover
Simple crossover can be carried out in two phases after reproduction. The newly replicated string members in the mattress pool are randomly paired. The second is the crossing of each chromosome pair.

Mutation
Global searches are mutations. A likelihood of mutation is predetermined again before the algorithm starts, which is used to determine if it is inverted for each single bit of each offspring chromosome. Each character mutated with a certain probability Pm is created as new individuals. Mutation implies in plain GA 1 to 0 and vice versa with probability of mutation. The phases before and after mutation are shown in Table 2.

Table 2. Mutation Operator

Before Mutation	010100010010
After Mutation	011100000010

One of the best intelligent optimization strategies is the genetic algorithm (GA). It is a cross-sectional, probabilistic, random search method. It has a complex calculation model imitating biological theories of evolution. It can be used for complicated optimization problems due to its extremely parallel search capabilities. To achieve the final optimal solution, GA needs several steps. First there is a formulation of an initial approach and an assessment function. The assessment feature is the way to determine each person's fitness (possible solution). The selection process is then used to select the best reproductive individuals. Finally, two key jobs are being used for the development of new people and the final solution for the genetic model.

5 Simulation and Results

The method has been simulated to discover the optimal schedule for various numbers of jobs and CPUs in order to assess the algorithm's performance. Both a number of tasks with various attributes and a number of processing units with various attributes are produced at random. The previous GA strategy demonstrated that employing partly mapped crossover and swap mutations will still produce positive results. As a result, we will use these kinds of criteria to compare the performance of GA and IGA. For instance, N various occupations with various attributes are distributed at random. In a similar manner, N process units create attributes with random properties. We created the Mapping algorithm to examine the efficacy of the suggested IGA in comparison to other based techniques. We map job I to process unit I in the mapping procedure, after which we compute the cost (Table 3).

Table 3. Parametric Value Analysis

Parameters	Value
Cost Function	0.0821
Total Cost	128.8957
Make Span	0.9832
Total Distance	545.9389
Best Nodes For Task 1	1 3 3 1 1 3 3 3 1 1 3 1 3 1 1 1 1 1 1 3

Our algorithm's execution and job dropping for each mobile device can asymptotically produce the best outcomes for the entire system. The algorithm not only inherits the entire genetic algorithm, but it also seamlessly adjusts to the increasingly complicated environment. Results from simulations show that the technique can increase the percentage of offloading compute jobs by at least 10% whereas the QoE is certain (Figs. 7, 8 and 9).

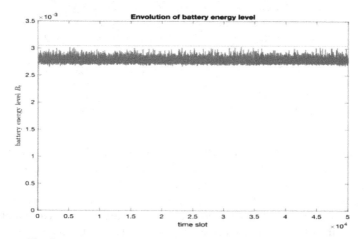

Fig. 7. Battery Energy Level Analysis Using Proposed Algorithm

In this research, we investigate an energy-harvesting multi-user, multi-server mobile edge computing system. Then, in order to achieve the lowest execution, we suggest one algorithm. Based on the cost and the greatest number of offloading computation tasks

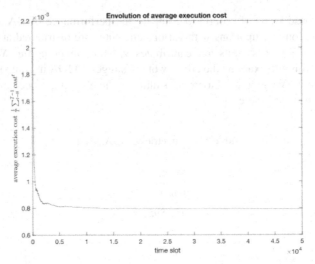

Fig. 8. Average Execution Cost Analysis Using Proposed Algorithm

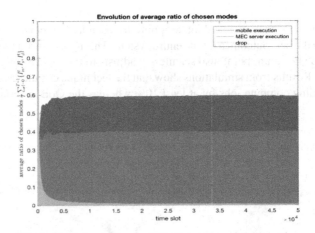

Fig. 9. Evolution Ratio Analysis Using Proposed Algorithm

LODCO-Based Genetic Algorithm on the proposed algorithm An online algorithm called Algorithm with Greedy Policy with minimal complexity Most importantly, it doesn't require anything. a lot of prior knowledge. After performance and simulation analysis, it is evident that the suggested algorithm inherits each of the proposed Algorithm's advantages and adjusts to the more perfectly in a complex environment and provides a ratio of more than 10% of delegating computation-related work. The suggested method can select the offloading mode as much as you can, as it can bring the advantages of MEC servers over resource-constrained ones. In summary, our research offers a practical method for creating a complicated mechanism that is considerably more realistic.

6   Conclusion

This article argues that Mobile Edge Computing (MEC) and Ultra Dense Computing (UDC) will play an increasingly important role in the 5G future as the demands on computing resources and vast data flows from the Internet of Things (IoT) continue to rise. Recent developments in the IoT have put stress on the cloud computing infrastructure due to the massive amounts of data they generate. Fog computing is envisioned as the next generation of cloud computing to meet the needs of the Internet of Things device network. One of the difficulties of fog computing is the allocation of computing resources to decrease completion times and running costs. This study introduces a new method for optimizing the scheduling of Bag-of-Tasks applications in a cloud-fog setting, which significantly reduces operational costs. In order to meet the need for the Internet of Things to consume less network bandwidth and to have faster reaction times, a novel computational paradigm known as fog computing was created. (IoT). One metaphor for the overlap between IoT and cloud computing is fog. Network users who grant access to their devices for the purposes of running applications or storing and analyzing data. This article explores recent advances in using evolutionary algorithms to improve fog architecture's resource management. In this paper, we investigate a distributed energy-harvesting mobile edge computing system with several users and servers. In this research, we examine a distributed energy-harvesting edge computing system with several users and servers. We then suggest one algorithm for the fastest possible runtime. Considering the least expensive and most abundant offloading computation workloads, better Algorithm built on top of another algorithm With the use of a straightforward web algorithm known as Algorithm with Greedy Policy In the final analysis, it really doesn't matter. The results of performance and simulation studies show that the suggested approach keeps all the advantages of the LODCO method while also being more flexible in the face of novel circumstances and providing a ratio of more than 10% when allocating computational tasks. The suggested method may provide the advantages of MEC servers over underpowered servers, so you can pick the offloading mode as often as you wish. In conclusion, our study offers a practical method for creating a realistic complicated structure.

References

1. Hu, S., Li, G.: Dynamic request scheduling optimization in mobile edge computing for IoT applications. IEEE Internet Things J. **7**(2), 1426–1437 (2020). https://doi.org/10.1109/JIOT. 2019.2955311
2. Smith, M., Maiti, A., Maxwell, A.D., Kist, A.A.: Object detection resource usage within a remote real-time video stream. In: Auer, M.E., Zutin, D.G. (eds.) Online Engineering & Internet of Things. LNNS, vol. 22, pp. 266–277. Springer, Cham (2018). https://doi.org/10. 1007/978-3-319-64352-6_25
3. Mach, P., Becvar, Z.: Mobile edge computing: a survey on architecture and computation offloading. IEEE Commun. Surv. Tutor. **19**(3), 1628–1656 (2017). 3rd Quart.
4. Mao, Y., You, C., Zhang, J., Huang, K., Letaief, K.B.: A survey on mobile edge computing: the communication perspective. IEEE Commun. Surv. Tutor. **19**(4), 2322–2358 (2017). 4th Quart.

5. Alameddine, H.A., Sharafeddine, S., Sebbah, S., Ayoubi, S., Assi, C.: Dynamic task offloading and scheduling for low-latency IoT services in multi-access edge computing. IEEE J. Sel. Areas Commun. **37**(3), 668–682 (2019)
6. Chen, M., Hao, Y.: Task offloading for mobile edge computing in software defined ultra-dense network. IEEE J. Sel. Areas Commun. **36**(3), 587–597 (2018)
7. Lyu, X., Tian, H., Sengul, C., Zhang, P.: Multiuser joint task offloading and resources optimization in proximate clouds. IEEE Trans. Veh. Technol. **66**(4), 3435–3447 (2017)
8. Wang, Q., Guo, S., Liu, J., Yang, Y.: Energy-efficient computation offloading and resource allocation for delay-sensitive mobile edge computing. Sustain. Comput. Inf. Syst. **21**, 154–164 (2019)
9. Tran, T.X., Pompili, D.: Joint task offloading and resource allocation for multi-server mobile-edge computing networks. IEEE Trans. Veh. Technol. **68**(1), 856–868 (2019)
10. Shojafar, M., Cordeschi, N., Baccarelli, E.: Energy-efficient adaptive resource management for real-time vehicular cloud services. IEEE Trans. Cloud Comput. **7**(1), 196–209 (2019)
11. Islam, S.M.R., Avazov, N., Dobre, O.A., Kwak, K.-S.: Powerdomain non-orthogonal multiple access (NOMA) in 5G systems: potentials and challenges. IEEE Commun. Surv. Tutor. **19**(2), 721–742 (2017). 2nd Quart.
12. Kamel, M., Hamouda, W., Youssef, A.: Ultra-dense networks: a survey. IEEE Commun. Surv. Tutor. **18**(4), 2522–2545 (2016). 4th Quart.
13. López-Pérez, D., Ding, M., Claussen, H., Jafari, A.H.: Towards 1 Gbps/UE in cellular systems: Understanding ultra-dense small cell deployments. IEEE Commun. Surv. Tutor. **17**(4), 2078–2101 (2015). 4th Quart.
14. Yu, B., Pu, L., Xie, Q., Xu, J.: Energy efficient scheduling for IoT applications with offloading, user association and BS sleeping in ultra dense networks. In: Proceedings of the 16th International Symposium on Modeling and Optimization in Mobile, Ad Hoc, and Wireless Networks (WiOpt), Shanghai, China, pp. 1–6 (2018)
15. Ma, C., Liu, F., Zeng, Z., Zhao, S.: An energy-efficient user association scheme based on robust optimization in ultra-dense networks. In: Proceedings of the IEEE/CIC International Conference on Communications in China (ICCC Workshops), Beijing, China, pp. 222–226 (2018)
16. Chen, X., Jiao, L., Li, W., Fu, X.: Efficient multi-user computation offloading for mobile-edge cloud computing. IEEE/ACM Trans. Netw. **24**(5), 2795–2808 (2016)
17. Do, T.V., Do, N.H., Nguyen, H.T., Rotter, C., Hegyi, A., Hegyi, P.: Comparison of scheduling algorithms for multiple mobile computing edge clouds. Simul. Model. Pract. Theory **93**, 104–118 (2019)
18. Gu, L., Cai, J., Zeng, D., Zhang, Y., Jin, H., Dai, W.: Energy efficient task allocation and energy scheduling in green energy powered edge computing. Future Gener. Comput. Syst. **95**, 89–99 (2019)
19. Jie, Y., Tang, X., Choo, K.-K.R., Su, S., Li, M., Guo, C.: Online task scheduling for edge computing based on repeated Stackelberg game. J. Parallel Distrib. Comput. **122**, 159–172 (2018)
20. Kiani, A., Ansari, N.: Toward hierarchical mobile edge computing: an auction-based profit maximization approach. IEEE Internet Things J. **4**(6), 2082–2091 (2017)

Numerical Simulation and Mathematical Modelling of Machine Learning Based Improved Crypto Currency Forecasting System

Ravi Bhushan Sharma[1]([✉]), Himani Goyal Sharma[2], and Md. Asif Iqbal[3]

[1] Department of Computer Science Engineering, Chandigarh University, Chandigarh, India
`Ravibohara12@gmail.com`
[2] Department of Electrical Engineering, Chandigarh University Gharuan, Chandigarh, India
[3] Department of Electrical Engineering, Vivekananda Global University, Jaipur, India

Abstract. The crypto currency market is a rapidly growing trading and investment industry that has attracted merchants, investors, and entrepreneurs on a global scale never seen before in this century. By providing comparison studies and insights from the pricing data of crypto currency marketplaces, it will aid in documenting the behavior and habits of such a lucratively demanding and rapidly growing sector. The bitcoin market is at one of its all-time highs in 2021. The introduction of new exchanges has made crypto currencies more accessible to the general public, enhancing their attractiveness. This, together with the launch of several genuine crypto initiatives by some of the founders, has resulted in a surge in crypto currency users and interest. Virtual currencies are growing in popularity, with corporations like Microsoft, Dell, and Tesla all accepting them. As the number of individuals using decentralised digital currencies grows, As new currencies gain popularity, it's more important than ever to properly educate the public about them so that they understand what they possess and how their money is being invested. The algorithm predicts that the high, low, and open prices will all be close to the same value on the same day. The coefficients indicate that the high price has the biggest influence on the closing price. Contrary to popular assumption, "volume" does not add to the data on the closing price provided by the other factors. We also observed that the "marketcap" argument offers no more information. This is odd because market cap is often determined by the price of a product. After removing the two previously mentioned factors, we found no discernible difference in adjusted R2. It's worth mentioning that the model was built using data from the same time period. At the same moment as the closing price, the variables we obtained are made public. We are hopeful that the model will be able to forecast the closing price based on the existing high and low values for a given day.

Keywords: Crypto currency · Bit coin · Machine Learning · Linear Regression

1 Introduction

The crypto currency market is a rapidly growing trading and investment industry that has attracted merchants, investors, and entrepreneurs on a global scale never seen before in this century. By providing comparison studies and insights from the pricing data of crypto currency marketplaces, it will aid in documenting the behaviour and habits of such a lucratively demanding and rapidly growing sector. The bitcoin market is at one of its all-time highs in 2021. The introduction of new exchanges has made crypto currencies more accessible to the general public, enhancing their attractiveness. This, together with the launch of several genuine crypto initiatives by some of the founders, has resulted in a surge in crypto currency users and interest. Virtual currencies are growing in popularity, with corporations like Microsoft, Dell, and Tesla all accepting them. As the number of individuals using decentralised digital currencies grows, it's more important than ever to properly educate the public about them so that they understand what they possess and how their money is being invested. The algorithm predicts that the high, low, and open prices will all be close to the same value on the same day. The coefficients indicate that the high price has the biggest influence on the closing price. According to the model, the high-price, low-price, and open-price are all indicative of the same-day closing price. We may deduce from the coefficients that the high-price has the greatest impact on the closing price (Fig. 1).

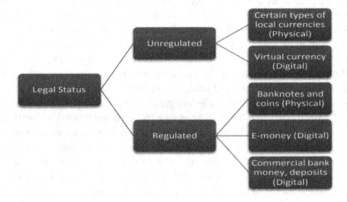

Fig. 1. Money Matrix

Bitcoin is a sort of virtual currency. It's the most contentious coin on the internet. Bitcoin is the market's poster child and the first and most well-known cryptocurrency. It was invented by an anonymous internet user known only as Satoshi Nakamoto, a person who has stayed anonymous since the creation of Bitcoin. In 2008, Bitcoin first became accessible. It became the first completely decentralised cryptocurrency in 2009. As a result, bitcoin is unrelated to any central bank or other organization, including the government. Instead, "the Blockchain", a peer-to-peer network, underpins Bitcoin's ability to function as a medium of trade. This network is in charge of validating transactions and issuing new bitcoins. According to Satoshi Nakamoto, the project's founder (a pseudonym for an individual or group of programmers), bitcoin was created to replace existing payment methods. Bitcoin allows cross-currency and cross-national transactions to take place without the intervention of central banks or sovereign governments. According to bit coin's inventor, traditional financial middlemen should not be allowed to benefit from bit coin transactions. Finally, bit coin is pseudo-anonymous, meaning no one knows who is purchasing or selling it. Numerical simulation and mathematical modeling can be applied to develop and improve machine learning-based crypto currency forecasting systems. These techniques can help in understanding the behavior of crypto currency markets, validating the accuracy of forecasting models, and optimizing their performance. Numerical simulation involves using mathematical algorithms and computer simulations to analyze and predict the dynamics of crypto currency markets. This can be done by creating virtual environments that mimic real-world market conditions and conducting experiments to observe the behavior of crypto currencies and their prices under different scenarios. Numerical simulations can help in testing the robustness and effectiveness of machine learning models for crypto currency forecasting, as well as in optimizing parameters and settings to improve their accuracy. Mathematical modeling involves using mathematical equations and statistical techniques to represent the dynamics of crypto currency markets and develop predictive models. These models can capture the relationships between various factors that influence crypto currency prices, such as market sentiment, trading volume, historical price patterns, and external factors like news and regulatory changes. Mathematical models can be used to simulate the behavior of crypto currencies and forecast their future prices based on historical data and other relevant information. By combining numerical simulation and mathematical modeling with machine learning techniques, such as regression, time series analysis, and artificial neural networks, it is possible to develop improved crypto currency forecasting systems. These systems can be trained on historical data to learn patterns and trends, and then used to predict future crypto currency prices with higher accuracy. However, it's important to note that crypto currency markets are highly volatile and influenced by various unpredictable factors, so even with advanced forecasting systems, there are inherent risks and uncertainties involved in predicting crypto currency prices.

2 Literature Review

(AshutoshShankhdhar, Akhilesh Kumar Singh, SuryanshNaugraiya and Prathmesh Kumar Saini. 2021 [1]) Investing in cryptocurrency, particularly Bitcoin (Bitcoin), has been popular for many years since it is one of the most popular and decentralized digital currencies. However, its prices are constantly fluctuating, making it impossible to anticipate. So, the goal of our research is to create the quickest and most accurate model for Bitcoin price prediction using machine learning models such as (Multivariate Linear Regression, Theil-Sen Regression, Huber Regression) and deep learning techniques such as (LSTM, GRU). Because it contains a large number of data points, the dataset we'll utilize for prediction will be saved in MongoDB (Big-Data Tool). We've also integrated IoT into our system to develop an alert system that notifies users when the price of bitcoin hits a certain threshold.

(Uras N, Marchesi L, Marchesi M, Tonelli R. 2020 [2]) In this paper We anticipate daily closing prices of Bitcoin, Litecoin and Ethereum coins using data on prices and volumes from prior days. Cryptocurrencies' price behavior is still totally unknown and offers researchers and economists the chance to identify comparisons and differences with traditional financial assets. In addition, we compared our findings with a number of benchmarks such as a recent study on Bitcoin price prediction using different methodologies. We also compared a well-known paper on Intel, National Bank shares, and the

Microsoft daily closing prices NASDAQ over a three year term. At the same time we employed a simple linear regression model (SLR) for univariate series forecasting using closed prices, and a multivariate series prediction model employing both price and volume data. Also used as artificial neural networks were Multilayer Perceptron (MLP) and Long Short-Term Memory (LSTM) (LSTM). While the complete time range could not be distinguished from a random walk, it broke data sets into shorter sequences, each of which reflect a "regime" pricing difference,' allowing a more exact forecast, as evaluated in MAPE and RMSE (relativeRMSE). The greatest outcomes of this scenario are produced by mixing several previous prices, which prove other than random walks that time regimes exist. Our models are also successful in terms of time complexity, providing superior overall results in benchmark tests that advance state-of-the-art performance.

(S M Raju and Ali Mohammad Tarif. 2020 [3])Bitcoin is the first decentralized digital cryptocurrency that have experienced a significant gain in market value in recent years. The aim of this study is for the prediction of the price direction of Bitcoin in US$ with the use of machine learning techniques and feeling analyses. In order to analyze the public mood, researchers paid special attention to Twitter and Reddit. We studied the connection between bitcoin fluctuations in tweets with feeling analysis and supervised machine learning ideas on Twitter and Reddit tweets. In order to create a prediction model and to provide informative analyses of future market prices, we have employed supervised training to study different machine learning technologies. The complexity of understanding the precise nature of a Time Series(ARIMA) model is usually tough to create good forecasts. We then continue to build recurrent neural networks (RNNs) through the use of long-term memory cells (LSTM). We therefore compared bitcoin price forecasting and bitcoin tweet feeling analysis to the normal procedure, and analyzed the time series model predictions for bitcoin prices using long-term memory (LSTM) technology with better efficiently (ARIMA). LSTM (single feature) and 197.515(multi-feature) RMSE (roots-mean-square error) show that the LSTM with a multi feature delivers more accurate results, respectively, 198.448 (single feature) and 209.263 (ARIMA model).

(Phaladisailoed T, Numnonda T. 2018 [4])In recent years Bitcoin has grown to be the most precious cryptocurrency. On the other side, Bitcoin values were highly volatile, making it incredibly hard to predict. The objective of this work is therefore to find the best effective and accurate model to predict Bitcoin values utilizing several techniques of machine learning. Researchers tested a few regression models with the scientific library of Scikit-Iearn and Keras from 1 January 2012 to 8 January 2018 by using interval data for one minute on the Bitcoin exchange website bitstamp. The MSF was 0.00002, and the RSQ (R 2) was 99.2% in the highest finds of the results.

(Aggarwal A, Gupta I, Garg N, Goel A. 2019 [5])Cryptocurrency investment has been popular for some years. One of the most popular and valuable cryptocurrencies is Bitcoin. Many research on bitcoin price prediction have been conducted utilizing various indicators such as bitcoin variables, social media, and so on. In this paper, utilizing multiple deep learning models such as Convolutional Neural Networks (CNN), Long Short Term Memory (LSTM), and Gated Recurrent Units, a comparative assessment of the many aspects affecting bitcoin price prediction is conducted using Root Mean Square Error (RMSE) (GRU). We looked into the impact of the price of gold on the price of bitcoin.

(Rane PV, Dhage SN. 2019 [6]) Bitcoin (BTC) is the most popular cryptocurrency on the internet. Because of the secrecy and openness of the system, Bitcoin is the most widely used cryptocurrency on the market. The popularity of daily trends in the Bitcoin market has grown among observers, speculators, customers, and others. Bitcoin price data have favorable qualities, which are used by some traditional time series prediction methods, resulting in poor predictions and a lack of a probabilistic interpretation. This research examines the evolution of Bitcoin in depth, as well as a comprehensive assessment of various machine learning methods for price prediction. The goal of comparative analysis is to find the best method for forecasting prices more accurately.

3   Proposed Methodology

Many methods for forecasting time series in stock markets have been developed over the years. The most extensively used are those that are based on historical market movements. Among the others, offered a prediction system based on a hybrid of genetic and neural techniques, with technical analysis elements and daily prices as inputs. A hybrid prediction model that performs an index level forecast by combining differential evolution-based fuzzy clustering with a fuzzy inference neural network. As a result, we were able to train and test our models, taking into account both bull and bear market circumstances at each stage. As a result, our work adds to the state-of-the-art because it is the most recent and deals with the largest and most comprehensive dataset.

The methodology for developing a numerical simulation and mathematical modeling-based machine learning cryptocurrency forecasting system typically involves the following steps:

Data collection: Historical data on cryptocurrency prices, trading volumes, market sentiment, and other relevant factors are collected from various sources, such as cryptocurrency exchanges, financial news websites, and social media platforms. The data should be cleaned, pre-processed, and organized into a suitable format for analysis.

Numerical simulation: Virtual environments are created to simulate cryptocurrency market conditions, taking into account factors such as market structure, trading dynamics, and investor behaviors. Numerical simulations are conducted using mathematical algorithms and computational techniques to model the behavior of cryptocurrencies under different scenarios, such as varying market conditions, trading strategies, and risk factors. The simulations may involve stochastic processes, Monte Carlo simulations, or other numerical methods to capture the uncertainty and randomness of cryptocurrency markets.

Mathematical modeling: Mathematical equations and statistical techniques are used to develop mathematical models that represent the dynamics of cryptocurrency markets. These models may include time series analysis, regression analysis, or other statistical methods to identify patterns, trends, and relationships in the data. Machine learning techniques, such as artificial neural networks, decision trees, or support vector machines, may also be used to build predictive models that can learn from the data and make forecasts.

Model training and validation: The machine learning models are trained using historical data, where the data is split into training and testing sets to evaluate the model's performance. The models are optimized by tuning hyperparameters, feature selection, and other techniques to improve their accuracy. The models are validated using backtesting or other validation methods to assess their performance in predicting cryptocurrency prices.

Model integration and optimization: The numerical simulation and mathematical modeling components are integrated into a cohesive system that combines the insights from both approaches. The system is optimized by adjusting parameters, settings, or algorithms to improve its performance and accuracy in forecasting cryptocurrency prices.

Model evaluation and refinement: The performance of the numerical simulation and mathematical modeling-based machine learning cryptocurrency forecasting system is evaluated using various metrics, such as accuracy, precision, recall, or profit/loss measures. The system is refined based on the evaluation results and feedback from users or stakeholders, and further improvements are made as needed.

Deployment and monitoring: Once the system is developed and refined, it can be deployed for real-time or near-real-time cryptocurrency price forecasting. The system may be monitored and updated regularly to adapt to changing market conditions, incorporate new data, or refine the models further.

It's important to note that the specific methodology may vary depending on the complexity of the cryptocurrency market, the type of data available, and the machine learning algorithms used. Rigorous testing, validation, and evaluation of the system's performance are critical to ensure its accuracy and reliability in forecasting cryptocurrency prices (Fig. 2).

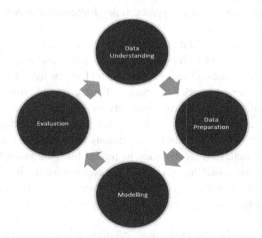

Fig. 2. Process Flow Chart

The four phases of the CRISP-DM Model are depicted in Fig. 3: data interpretation, data preparation, modeling, and evaluation. The cycle may be repeatable, meaning that it is possible to repeat the cycle with the newly reviewed results from the previous iteration. The features of the dataset were analyzed in the data interpretation step using reasoning from previous literature. In terms of data preparation, the dataset is received and processed in order to proceed with the modeling phase, which will yield findings that will be assessed and will lead to a better knowledge of the data and whether adjustments to the dataset can be made for a better outcome.

As one of the regression-based analysis tools, the experiments used linear regression. Note that typical analytical regression attempts to shape an objective value based on separate forecasts. These regression-based analytical tools are also commonly used to detect cause and effect links between variables or characteristics in the prediction of applications.

The linear regression is designed to represent a relation between variables, a dependent variable and an explanatory variable by building a linear equation with the data. A linear regression line is equated using Eq. 1. X is an explanatory variable and Y a dependent variable, and the pitch of the line with an intercept is b. The final objective is to discover the best possible a and b values to provide the best match for a certain number of data points.

$$Y = a + bX \tag{1}$$

Adaptive weights for approximating non-linear input functions are utilized in the neural network regression. It is a neural feed network, because the data is processed from one layer to another without any feedback. It responds to an input pattern. Further information in Bayesian Linear Regression complements the linear regression as a previous probability distribution. Previous parameter information is combined with a likelihood function to get estimates for the parameters. Boosted Decision Tree Regression, sometimes called Gradient boosting, creates a defined loss function for each step to measure and repair each regression tree step by step. Linear regression experiments are being conducted. The beginning daily price is marked 'Open,' the highest price is marked 'High,' the lowest price is marked 'Low' and the closing price is marked 'Close' in the date set.

4   Result Analysis

In 2021, the bitcoin market is at one of its highest points ever. More exchanges have been added, making cryptocurrencies more widely available to users and boosting their appeal. This has led to an increase in cryptocurrency users and interest, along with the several successful crypto initiatives headed by some of the founders. Microsoft, Dell, and Tesla are just a few of the companies who have already realised how popular virtual currencies are becoming and have begun to accept them. It is crucial to effectively inform the public about the new currencies as they grow in use by more people, as decentralised digital currencies, so that people are aware of what they own and where their money is invested.

Cryptocurrencies are relatively new in comparison to traditional fiat currencies such as the US Dollar or the British Pound. Cryptocurrencies are stored in digital wallets and cold storage devices rather than having a physical form (e.g. hard drives). A cryptographic object, such as Bitcoin, is represented as a chain of digital signatures spanning the transactions in which the coin was utilized. All cryptocurrencies are decentralized, which implies that the government has no power over the market and that the money cannot be inflated. Cryptocurrency marketplaces are governed purely by the buyers and sellers of the currency: they allow peer-to-peer direct electronic payment, without the need for a middleman like banks. The cryptocurrency market is extremely volatile due to its decentralized nature: the price of crypto can fluctuate dramatically. Traders can either make a lot of money or lose a lot of money.

Because of the growing popularity of crypto currencies like Bitcoin, Many people are looking for resources to aid with their currency investments. Many publicly accessible price indicators are available, but not all of them are likely to be helpful in forecasting the closing price on a particular day.

4.1 Dataset

The most well-known and established cryptocurrency is Bitcoin, which was first released in 2009 as an open source project by an as-yet-unidentified Satoshi Nakamoto. Bitcoin is a decentralised digital currency that eliminates the need for a central mediator or trusted record-keeping authority by enabling transactions to be validated and recorded in a public distributed ledger (the blockchain). Transaction blocks serve as an immutable record of all transactions ever made since they are connected by a SHA-256 cryptographic hash of earlier transaction blocks. Bitcoin trade and financial instruments, like any other currency/commodity on the market, quickly followed public adoption of bitcoin and continue to rise. Here you'll find historical bitcoin market data at 1-min intervals for a few of the most popular bitcoin exchanges.

CSV files with minute-by-minute updates of OHLC (Open, High, Low, Close), Volume in BTC and specified currency, and weighted bitcoin price for select bitcoin exchanges from January 2012 to December March 2021. Unix time is used for timestamps. The data fields of timestamps with no trades or activity are filled with NaNs. If a timestamp is missing or there are jumps, it's possible that the exchange (or its API) was down, that the exchange (or its API) didn't exist, or that there was some other unforeseeable technical problem in data reporting or gathering. To the best of my ability, I have attempted to deduplicate entries and check the contents are correct and comprehensive, but trust at your own risk.

4.2 Flow Chart of Simulation

The purpose of this statistical analysis was to determine the relationship between several price indicators and the closing price of the crypto currency Bitcoin. A regression model was utilized for this. There's a lot of evidence showing the opening price, high price, and low price are good predictors of the closing price. The fact that volume has no statistical significance in influencing the closing price is striking. This model will eventually be able to anticipate what price Bitcoin will close at on a particular day. Data Preparation Obtaining a Daily Price Data Set Cross-validation and model fitting Visualization Evaluation of the model Predicted Price Visualization is the end result.

Step 1. **Data Loading**
Step 2. **Getting Daily Price Data frame**
Step 3. **Model Fitting & Cross validation**
Step 4. **Visualization**

Step 5. *Model evaluation*
Step 6. *Output: Predicted Price Visualization*

4.3 Result Discussion

The simulation is initialized with the loading of dataset. The process has been discussed with the analysis of historical data in tabular form (Tables 1 and 2).

Table 1. Analysis of Bit Coin Historical Data

Timestamp	Open	High	Low	Close	Volume (BTC)	Volume (Currency)	Weighted Price
1325317920	4.39	4.39	4.39	4.39	0.455581	2.0	4.39
1325317980	NaN	NaN	NaN	NaN	NaN	NaN	NaN
1325318040	NaN	NaN	NaN	NaN	NaN	NaN	NaN
1325318100	NaN	NaN	NaN	NaN	NaN	NaN	NaN
1325318160	NaN	NaN	NaN	NaN	NaN	NaN	NaN

Table 2. Analysis of Day Wise Closing Value

S. No.	Date	Close
1	2011–12-31	4.471603
2	2012–01-01	4.806667
3	2012–01-02	5.000000
4	2012–01-03	5.252500
5	2012–01-04	5.208159

Figure 3 indicates the analysis of historical data collected from kaggle for statistical analysis as an input for design of linear regression. The analysis of cross validation has been analysed in Fig. 4. Figure 4 indicates the performance of cross validation of linear regression. It is evident that the performance of the linear regression is optimal for forecasting of the futuristic data of Bitcoin.

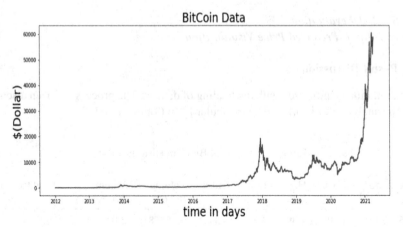

Fig. 3. Analysis of Historical Data from 2012–2021 (31st March)

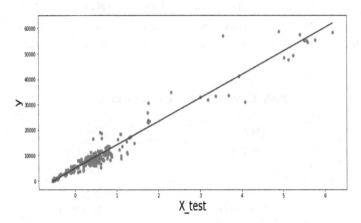

Fig. 4. Cross Validation of Predicted Data Based on Improved Linear Regression

Figure 5 indicates the analysis of forecasted data for the month of April obtained from linear regression. Figure 6 indicates the forecasted value designed from linear regression including forecasted value for the month of April which has been extrapolated in the graph of forecasting indicated as red coloured. It is evident that the performance of the linear regression is efficient for forecasting of the futuristic data of Bitcoin.

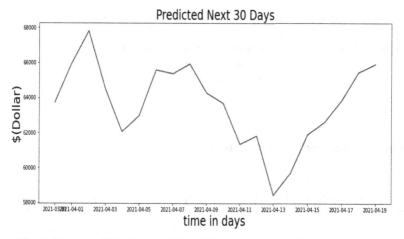

Fig. 5. Forecasted Data for April Month from the Designed Regression Model

Table 3. Analysis of Performance Parameters

Parameters	Value
F-Score	0.9623
RMS Value	1656.2467724223852

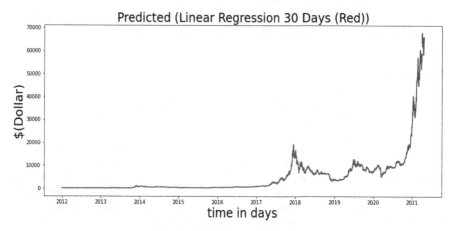

Fig. 6. USD Prices of Bitcoin

The crypto currency market is a rapidly growing canvas of trade and investment that has attracted merchants, investors, and entrepreneurs on a worldwide scale that has never been seen before in this century. By providing comparison studies and insights from the pricing data of crypto currency marketplaces, it will aid in documenting the behavior and habits of such a lucratively demanding and rapidly growing sector (Tables 3 and 4).

Table 4. Comparative Analysis of Performance Parameters

Parameters	Value (Proposed)	Automated Bitcoin Trading Via Machine Learning Algorithms [10]	Using the Bitcoin Transaction Graph to Predict the Price of Bitcoin [9]
Accuracy	96%	55%	78%

5   Conclusion and Future Scope

Price signals can be utilised to forecast the ultimate price of Bitcoin on a specific day? can be answered based on the information supplied above. The algorithm forecasts that on the same day, the high, low, and open prices will all be roughly equal in value. Based on the calculated factors, we conclude that the high price has the biggest impact on the final price. Contrary to popular belief, the variable "volume" does not contribute any new information to what the other variables already reveal about the closing price. We also found that the "marketcap" field offers no additional information. This is unusual because marketcap is typically determined by the price of a commodity. After removing the two previously mentioned factors, we found no discernible change in adjusted R2. The price of Bitcoin is unlikely to be completely determined by the factors we've discussed. Market sentiment and a variety of other factors, like with any other product, are likely to affect price changes. In practice, this means that statements made by powerful people can affect pricing, but this is not reflected in our data. As a result, our model is only dependent on actual data, and factors that cannot be described quantitatively are excluded. Other forecasting strategies can be used, and performance measures can be compared to discover the optimum model for price prediction.

References

1. Alesna, A., Venturini, M.G.: Analysis and design of optimum-amplitude 9-switch direct AC-AC converters. IEEE Trans. Power Electron. 4(1), 101–112 (1989). https://doi.org/10.1109/63.21879
2. Yan, F.: MC Based on asymmetric regular sampling method SPWM control strategy. Procedia Eng. 29, 2083–2087 (2012). https://doi.org/10.1016/j.proeng.2012.01.266
3. Iqbal, M.A., Sangtani, V.: Investigation of AC-AC converter technology for electric vehicle motor control and fast battery charging. In: 2022 First International Conference on Electrical, Electronics, Information and Communication Technologies (ICEEICT), Trichy, India, pp. 1–4 (2022). https://doi.org/10.1109/ICEEICT53079.2022.9768476
4. Iqbal, M.A., Gupta, S.K.: Comparative analysis between numerical simulation of PPV/PCBM and InGaN based solar cells. Mater. Today: Proc. 30, 168–173 (2020)
5. Iqbal, M.A., Sharma, S.: Analysis and comparison of various control strategy of hybrid power generation a review. In: 2014 1st International Conference on Non Conventional Energy (ICONCE 2014), pp. 184–189 (2014). https://doi.org/10.1109/ICONCE.2014.6808717
6. Iqbal, M.A.: Performance optimization assessment of different polymer based PV cells. Int. J. Modern Agric. 10(2), 3983–3989

7. Chimnani, M., et al.: Efficiency improvement approach of InGaN based solar cell by investigating different optical and electrical properties. In: Proceedings of International Conference on Sustainable Computing in Science, Technology and Management (SUSCOM), Amity University Rajasthan, Jaipur-India (2019)

8. Iqbal, M.A., Dwivedi, A.D.: Modelling & efficiency analysis of ingap/gaas single junction PV cells with BSF. Int. J. Eng. Adv. Technol. **8**(6), 623–627 (2019)

9. Iqbal, M.A., Dwivedi, A.D.D.: A comparative study of microgrid load frequency control techniques with incorporation of renewable energy. In: Published in International Conference on Recent Innovation and Trends in Engineering, Technology and Research (ICRITETR-2017), pp. 23–24 (2017)

10. Rizwan, M., Narejo, S., Javed, M.: Bitcoin price prediction using deep learning algorithm. In: 13th International Conference on Mathematics, Actuarial Science, Computer Science and Statistics (MACS), pp. 1–7. IEEE (2019)

11. Radityo, A., Munajat, Q., Budi, I.: Prediction of Bitcoin exchange rate to American dollar using artificial neural network methods. In: International Conference on Advanced Computer Science and Information Systems (ICACSIS), pp. 433–438. IEEE (2017)

12. Jain, A., Tripathi, S., Dwivedi, H.D., Saxena, P.: Forecasting price of cryptocurrencies using tweets sentiment analysis. In: 11th International Conference on Contemporary Computing (IC3), pp. 1–7. IEEE (2018)

13. Singh, H., Agarwal, P.: Empirical analysis of bitcoin market volatility using supervised learning approach. 11th International Conference on Contemporary Computing (IC3), pp. 1–5. IEEE (2018)

14. Akcora, C., Dey, A.K., Gel, Y.R., Kantarcioglu, M.: Forecasting Bitcoin price with graph chainlets. In: Pacific-Asia Conference on Knowledge Discovery and Data Mining (2018)

15. Bakar, N., Rosbi, S.: Autoregressive integrated moving average (ARIMA) model for forecasting cryptocurrency exchange rate in high volatility environment: a new insight of Bitcoin transaction. Int. J. Adv. Eng. Res. Sci. **4**(11), 130–137 (2017). https://doi.org/10.22161/ijaers.4.11.20

16. Catania, L., Grassi, S., Ravazzolo, F.: Forecasting cryptocurrencies financial time series. In: Centre for Applied Macro- and Petroleum Economics (CAMP), BI Norwegian Business School, Working Papers No. 5/2018 (2018). https://ideas.repec.org/p/bny/wpaper/0063.html

17. Cocco, L., Tonelli, R., Marchesi, M.: An agent-based artificial market model for studying the bitcoin trading. IEEE Access **7**, 42908–42920 (2019). https://doi.org/10.1109/ACCESS.2019.2907880

18. Cocco, L., Tonelli, R., Marchesi, M.: An agent based model to analyze the bitcoin mining activity and a comparison with the gold mining industry. Future Internet **11**(1), 8 (2019). https://doi.org/10.3390/fi11010008

19. Mallqui, D., Fernandes, R.: Predicting the direction, maximum, minimum and closing prices of daily Bitcoin exchange rate using machine learning techniques. Appl. Soft Comput. **75**, 596–606 (2018). https://doi.org/10.1016/j.asoc.2018.11.038

Reinforcement Learning in Blockchain-Enabled IIoT Networks

Dema Daoun(ID), Zulfikar Alom(ID), and Mohammad Abdul Azim(✉)(ID)

Department of Computer Science, Asian University for Women,
Chittogram, Bangladesh
{dema.daoun,zulfikar.alom}@auw.edu.bd, azim@ieee.org

Abstract. Blockchain-Enabled Industrial Internet of Things (IIoT) networks are a new norm in global developments. This paper discusses Blockchain-Enabled IIoT network challenges and the role of Reinforcement Learning techniques in offering solutions for those challenges. This paper provides (i) fundamental frameworks of Blockchain and IIoT networks, (ii) a sketch of RL techniques, e.g., Q-Learning, Multi-armed Bandit Learning, and Actor-Critic Learning, (iii) demonstrates Blockchain-Enabled IIoT networks concerning IIoT challenges, and (iv) Blockchain realizable solutions that improve IIoT. This study finds that Blockchain improves security, data integrity, and autonomy in IIoT networks. Moreover, it reduces the cost of instrument IIoT networks and builds trust among users. A blockchain-enabled most crucial solution materializes that Smart contracts facilitate transactions between parties. However, the Blockchain-Enabled IIoT network nevertheless faces diverse issues. Most importantly, the system needs to be optimized regarding forking events, energy, time to finality, transaction throughput, link security, and average Blocktime. Consequently, RL techniques such as Q-Learning plausibly provide solutions for these issues and improve the performance and efficiency of networks.

Keywords: Blockchain · IIoT · Reinforcement Learning · Deep Reinforcement Learning · Q-Learning

1 Introduction

Blockchain, Artificial Intelligence, and the Industrial Internet of Things (IIoT) are the hottest technology trends, even though they differ in applications, development processes, and many others. These technologies are essential in business and industry because they move them to more advanced stages in numerous aspects. First, Blockchain introduces a new way to make transactions, and it is beneficial in achieving efficiency, improving supply chain management, and increasing trust and transparency [35]. Second, IIoT drives the industrial sector to a new era through the practical usage of sensors and intelligent devices [29]. Furthermore, finally, AI transforms businesses through its ability to process and analyze data faster and better than humans, improving business outcomes [6].

R. S. Tomar et al. (Eds.): CNC 2022, CCIS 1894, pp. 226–240, 2023.
https://doi.org/10.1007/978-3-031-43145-6_19

Many applications or techniques that combine two of these techniques, like Blockchain-Enabled IIoT networks, will be discussed in this paper. Unfortunately, only some applications combine all three approaches. Enabling all these technologies will provide promising solutions to manage data and automate business processes.

Blockchain provides many solutions to IIoT networks, like trust, privacy, security, and other challenges. This paper aims to discuss some of the Blockchain-Enabled IIoT network challenges and how they can be solved using AI methods.

The organization of this paper is as follows: In Sect. 2, a brief about the interconnection between Blockchain and IIoT is given. In Sect. 3, a background about Blockchain and IIoT is provided. Section 4 presents the techniques of RL. Section 5 provides a discussion about Blockchain-Enabled IIoT networks is highlighted. In Sect. 6, the application of RL techniques in Blockchain-Enabled IIoT networks is highlighted. The paper concludes in Sect. 6 with a summary of the paper (Table 1).

Table 1. Abbreviation Table

Abbreviation	Explanation
RL	Reinforcement Learning
AI	Artificial Intelligence
IIoT	Industrial Internet of Things
IoT	Internet of Things
P2P	Peer-to-peer
PoW	Poof-of-Work
DQN	Deep Q-network
DRL	Deep Reinforcement Learning

2 Interconnection Between Blockchain, IIoT, and AI

For years, Blockchain has been a primary mechanism of popular cryptocurrencies such as Bitcoin and Ether [16]. Little research is done on other Blockchain (non-financial applications) rather than financial ones. Recently, this technology has been used widely in many fields and combined with other technologies, such as IoT and AI, to discover more innovations and solutions. After the increase in the number of IIoT devices, Blockchain technology attracted the attention of researchers as a promising potential technology that can play an essential role in improving the performance of IIoT devices, especially regarding transaction speed [63]. Conversely, Blockchain technology and AI are combined so both can exchange benefits. The decentralization feature of Blockchain with the intelligence and decision-making capabilities creates a new innovative technology [48]. Some studies have discussed the convergence of Blockchain, AI, and IoT. One of the studies by Kumar Singh et al. provides a design for IoT architecture with the support of Blockchain and AI [50]. As IIoT is a branch of IoT, it can also combine with Blockchain and AI (Fig. 1).

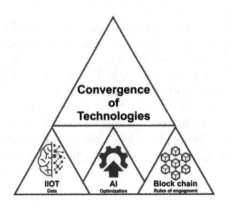

Fig. 1. Convergence of Technologies.

3   Blockchain Technology and IIoT

Blockchain is a distributed ledger that records transactions between parties and ensures safety and efficiency [33]. Blockchain has been used widely in the industry of payment and finance [44]. Recently, Blockchain technology has been introduced as a critical enabler of Industry 4.0. This industry includes IIoT, which aims to establish a suitable environment for companies to improve manufacturing and supply chain processes through devices, machines, and people using data analytics to enable intelligent industrial operations [9, 30]. Industry 4.0 has three patterns: innovative products, intelligent machines, and augmented operation. The intelligent product controls and organizes the manufacturing process from the beginning until the end. The intelligent machine works in transiting the traditional manufacturing processes to the production lines. Finally, the augmented operation ensures successful human-machine interaction by creating an ecosystem where humans and machines participate in the production process, each due to its ability [9]. Moreover, the number of IIoT devices is increasing because of the continued improvements in sensor network technologies and wireless communication. Those devices can be connected and share information without human intervention [4]. Information and connection must be secured and reliable to ensure data integrity, and blockchain can play an important role here. Blockchain depends on transactions and provides a new way to deal with security and integrity issues in IIoT industries. This technology follows a decentralized approach to sharing data, unlike the traditional approaches, which are expected to be important in developing IIoT networks [9]. In other words, sharing and storing data will be more accessible as devices and sensors do it without going through any centralized processes.

In Blockchain, transactions are controlled by specific intelligent contracts, which determine the conditions of applying a transaction and what will happen when the transaction is done [5]. The Blockchain system is based on consensus algorithms which are a protocol between users who agree about data on a ledger, and this algorithm determines the system's performance and behavior [21]. Once all required conditions are satisfied, the intelligent contracts enforce their rules, and all users can see any change after confirming the transaction process in this network [5]. This process is essential for building trust between users where transactions are cryptographical and automated. Thus, the transactions can be done by users or devices transparently without needing third parties.

4   Reinforcement Learning Techniques

Reinforcement Learning is a category of machine learning that solves problems based on experience. A learner in RL goes through many trials and errors and learns from them the best policy that should be followed to maximize the rewards. An agent aims to maximize its rewards; for that, it interacts with the environment, observes the rewards, and adjusts its policy to get the highest rewards [54]. To understand reinforcement learning, knowing the Markov decision process is essential, which plays a vital role in solving reinforcement learning problems. MDP has four components: states, actions, transitions, and reward functions. An agent has a goal within an environment, taking a series of actions from a start state to a goal state. The agent uses all those actions to decide which optimal action gives maximum reward [57]. This is a sequential decision-making process because the agent transits from state to state and learns from this experience to reach the optimal action.

Reinforcement Learning is located between supervised and unsupervised learning regarding dealing with data. In supervised learning, outputs are known by the system, and data should be labeled, unlike unsupervised learning, where data are unlabeled and outputs are based on perceptions. In contrast, Reinforcement learning does not need any labeled data or previous information about the environment. Reinforcement Learning depends only on the information taken from previous actions [54]. This feature allows it to be used in Blockchain techniques that care about transaction information.

Reinforcement learning techniques are divided into two categories which are model-based RL and model-free RL. In model-based RL, an agent uses the environment model to learn the optimal action, and this model helps predict outcomes and rewards of the action [1]. This approach helps improve the agent's efficiency because when the agent understands the environment's model, it can predict the available choices and find the optimal policy. Model-based RL is very popular in play-two-player games and spoken dialog systems. Recently, it has been used to fly a remote-controlled helicopter [1]. Many techniques have been introduced for model-based RL; one is model-predictive control, where an agent changes its plan after each interaction with the environment until it formulates the optimal policy [20]. Another technique is data augmentation which does not need any pre-training [32]. Model-based RL has many benefits in achieving data efficiency, targeted exploration, safety, explainability, and transfer [41]. However, this technique requires extra computation to train the model, and it might face instability when it works with a learned model. Model-based RL, unlike model-free RL, uses more tunable hyperparameters [41] to solve uncertainty and other issues. Those disadvantages make model-free RL a better approach to be used in order to improve the performance in the environment.

In model-free RL, an agent learns directly from its experience, estimating its actions' values and using them again to find the optimal policy [42]. Using this approach helps get better asymptotic performance and control the computational complexity, even though it requires much experience to have better performance [12]. Model-free RL includes two algorithms: a value-based algorithm where an agent keeps updating its value until it learns the optimal policy. The second is a policy-based algorithm where an agent updates its policy due to rewards without storing state value [18]. Model-free RL includes the following techniques:

4.1 Q-Learning

It is a value-based RL used widely to solve various RL problems. It has three components: state, action, and reward. It works by establishing a Q-table to find the Q-value. In this algorithm, the agent takes actions based on the predefined policy at each state, and each action-state pair gives a different Q-value. The agent compares those values to adopt the policy that gives maximum reward [40].

4.2 Multi-armed Bandit Learning

In this algorithm, an agent chooses an arm (action) in a specific round without having information about the environment and then gets a reward. The algorithm observes only the rewards of a chosen arm, not the rewards of other possible arms. Therefore, exploring other actions and exploiting the same action is in-between because it aims to find the best action in less time [51].

4.3 Actor-Critic Learning

It combines two methods: policy research and learned value function, combining the role of actor and critic [11]. The actor works with parameterized policies to compute actions without any need to improve the value function. The critic works with the value function to learn the optimal policy, which improves and speeds up the learning process [24,31] (Fig. 2).

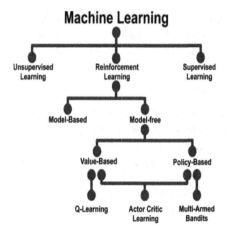

Fig. 2. Machine Learning Branches.

5 Blockchain-Enabled IIoT Network

The fourth revolution in our world is made in manufacturing, where the production process is transformed into a new shape, and this revolution is called Industry 4.0. One of the significant achievements of this revolution is improving IIoT, which aims to invest in intelligent manufacturing in the production process. This technology is based on collecting and sharing data with different parties involved in the manufacturing process [64]. In IIoT networks, data are streaming from sensors that require to be connected to centralized servers [56,64]. Due to the involvement of third parties in IIoT networks, many security concerns arise, which might cause severe issues in industrial facilities [17]. For that, using decentralized servers in IIoT networks will help solve the security issue. As discussed before, Blockchain technology depends on decentralization. Thus this technology solves the problem of security as well as other issues such as:

5.1 Security

The decentralized nature of blockchain technology provides security infrastructure to IIoT networks. It solves the issue of a single point of failure, which is associated with centralized servers [63]. Instead of depending on a third party for transactions, decentralization makes this process done between only two parties with the help of nodes located in the peer-to-peer network. Moreover, transactions done with the help of Blockchain are encrypted and need approval to be documented. Furthermore, the system uses asymmetrical cryptography to ensure that data is protected. Therefore, it is difficult to formulate the private key from a public key [56]. e.g., Data integrity.

Blockchain uses cryptography on its peer-to-peer network, allowing users to check and verify the correctness by giving them fair validation rights [56].

Therefore, transactions cannot be changed until the user in the network confirms that. This property makes Blockchain tamper-proof because transactions are done correctly and securely. Thus data integrity is achieved [63].

5.2 Cost Effectiveness

Blockchain dispenses with the third party. Therefore, it reduces the cost because it does not require installing servers or infrastructures to ensure the success of transaction processes. Moreover, this process removes the role of server monopolists who charge extra money for providing such services. Both parties in the network have access to transaction history and ledger without any need to do other processes than confirming it [56]. This feature helps in spreading the technology of Blockchain among people if security is ensured.

5.3 Trustless

Even though Blockchain does not have a third party, it helps build trust among users in the network. Transactions are encrypted where a private key is established from random numbers, and a public key is derived in alphanumeric. The function of the public key is to encrypt and sign messages, so other users in the network can recognize this key, while the private key is used to decrypt sent messages and for signing the transactions. This method makes transaction cracking difficult because it is almost impossible to guess the private and public keys as they are related by complex math [28].

5.4 Autonomy

Blockchain technology helps the IIoT system to be autonomous and independent. Devices on the network can interact with each other without using any server or central authority [45]. That means trust is shifted from a centralized authority to the whole network. This process helps establish decentralized autonomous corporations (DAC) that follow specific rules called smart contracts, which are recorded as blocks in Blockchain [28].

5.5 Smart Contracts

The critical component of Blockchain technology is computer programs used to create agreements in specific conditions through nodes in the network without any central authority. It is recorded as blocks [14, 28]. Blockchain technology is used in two popular platforms: Bitcoin and Ethereum. Ethereum is a platform of smart contracts that offers Ether cryptocurrency and provides a new generation for Blockchain systems in various applications [47]. It can be used for storing valuable data, automating processes, service provision, fair payments, and others [15, 23].

Blockchain technology provides a new design to solve IIoT problems by building trust, transparency, and accountability in a system. Therefore, it enables IIoT networks to be used in more fields like health care, supply chain/logistics, power industry, agriculture industry, manufacturing industry, and E-commerce [9]. With the increase in the number of IIoT devices due to recent developments in wireless communications and sensor network technologies, there will be a huge need to make the data-sharing process more secure and effective [46] (Fig. 3).

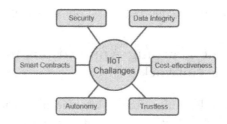

Fig. 3. How Blockchain solves IIoT challenges.

5.6 Blockchain-Enabled IIoT Layers

Each technology, Blockchain and IIoT, has its specific layers. Blockchain has six layers: Data Layer, Network Layer, Consensus Layer, Incentive Layer, Contract Layer, and finally, Application Layer [61]. While IIoT has only three common layers: Perception Layer, Network Layer, and Application Layer [19]. We will discuss how these layers help interact between Blockchain and IIoT.

5.7 Physical Layer

In IIoT, It is also called the perception layer or sensor layer. Its main objectives are to collect information and identify things from the surrounding environment. Then, it transfers that information to the network layer. As it is the first layer, attackers aim to replace their sensors with their devices [19]. Blockchain technology can deal with those attacks effectively [53]. The physical layer in Blockchain technology consists of servers, nodes, and devices on the network, and it works as a medium that transfers bits from the network layer to the following layer [25].

5.8 Network Layer

It is a transmission layer in IIoT networks that connects the physical and application layers. It also connects smart things, network devices, and networks [19]. It does similar work in Blockchain technology where the network layer here is called peer-to-peer that provides internode connections to make transactions in the network [43].

5.9   Application Layer

It is the layer that makes applications live. In Blockchain, the application layer consists of two sub-layers: the application layer, which includes end-user applications, and the execution layer, which has intelligent contracts and chaincode [3]. In IIoT it refers to all applications that use the technology of IIoT networks. It provides services to those applications, and those services differ from one application to another due to the collected data from sensors devices [19].

6   Reinforcement Learning Applications in Blockchain-Enabled IIoT Network

As discussed in Sect. 4, RL differs from other machine learning techniques. It is based on the interaction between an agent and an environment. Agent's experience in RL is significant for decision making, where this experience leads to rewards, and it decides the optimal action. To increase an agent's wealth, the agent has to expand its activities through trial and error actions. The nature of RL techniques, dealing with an environment that does not provide training data, helps improve Blockchain-Enabled IIoT networks' performance. That can be done through various applications, which are briefly discussed below.

6.1   Minimizing Forking Events

In Blockchain, forks happen because of a split in the Blockchain network where miners find and publish a new block independently and cause changes in the existing rules. Forks occur because miners have different views and disagree with the consensus agreement or because of delay or deviating mining strategies [60]. This event threatens Blockchain applications' security, especially if miners do not solve the issue of disagreement. For that, forking events should be minimized, which can be done with the help of RL techniques. Q-Learning algorithm, one of the most popular RL algorithms, is used to find the optimal mining strategy without knowing the environment's parameters [58]. Therefore, transmission delays can be minimized through training agents in the environment (Fig. 4).

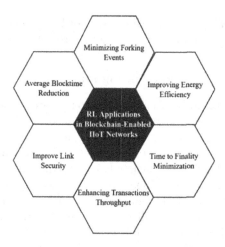

Fig. 4. RL applications in Blockchain-Enabled IIoT networks.

6.2 Improving Energy Efficiency

Achieving energy efficiency in Blockchain-Enabled IIoT networks is very important [7]. The mining process in Blockchain requires a tremendous amount of energy [13]. That is because consensus algorithms like PoW need to be executed multiple times [22]. In non-PoW Blockchains, the mining process requires energy for redundant operations [49]. That means it needs more time for mining which causes more energy consumption. Reducing redundancy can improve energy consumption, thereby improving Blockchain-Enabled IIoT network efficiency. Applying RL techniques in Blockchain-Enabled IIoT networks such as DQN helps choose the optimal decision for aching servers, computing servers, and Blockchain systems. That maximizes the system rewards through achieving higher efficiency during data processing, reducing network costs, and improving data interaction security [34].

6.3 Time to Finality Minimization

Blockchain finality is the time needed to ensure that appended blocks are not changed, reversed, or tampered with [10]. Thus, users in the network will be sure that their transactions will not be manipulated after it goes through. The consensus protocols in Blockchain are divided into two categories: probabilistic-finality consensus protocols and absolute-finality consensus protocols. These protocols are applied to avoid any issue and ensure that nothing affects the final consensus result in less time [62]. However, consensus mechanisms are exposed to be attacked by selfish mining, which aims to divert its behavior to hide the mined block. Thus they drain the resources. If the time needed to include a new block and its effect on the consensus mechanism is known, the selfish miners can be detected [27]. Using DRL techniques helps in Blockchain-Enabled IIoT networks reducing the probabilistic time to the finality of PoW; thereby, agents will learn from their experience in improving the probabilistic time to finality [36].

6.4   Enhancing Transaction Throughput

Transaction throughput in Blockchain refers to the rate of total committed transactions per second at the network size [2]. In Blockchain-Enabled IIoT networks, scalability is challenging because only a few transactions can be processed in a second. One suggested solution is to increase the bandwidth and decrease transactions' latency by adapting Blockchain [45]. Applying that requires more energy and time to record more transactions [26]. As RL techniques are based on finding the optimal policy, they can play an essential role in increasing the throughput with fewer issues regarding scalability and decentralization and using algorithms like Double DQN in Blockchain-Enabled IIoT networks that allow identifying the tradeoffs between transaction throughput and decentralization [38].

6.5   Improving Link Security

As discussed in previous sections, security is an essential aspect of Blockchain-Enabled IIoT networks. Security is critical to ensure that transactions between trusted parties cannot be manipulated or changed for any reason. For that, there must be a communication link between devices in the network to avoid eavesdropping nodes that aim to intercept the transmissions [8]. That can be done by using physical layer security techniques like exploiting the randomness of a wireless channel to confuse the eavesdroppers or by injecting artificial noise to protect the communication channel [52]. In general, AI techniques can distinguish between eavesdropping and jamming attacks. DRL techniques can be applied against jamming attacks by considering anti-jamming communication efficiency as a reward. Also, DQL algorithms train the agents in an environment to deal with different kinds of attacks [59].

6.6   Average Blocktime Reduction

Blocktime in Blockchain technology means the average time needed to create a new block in a Blockchain network and validate it. Its unit differs from the human time system, measured by transaction block confirmation times. The algorithms used in Blockchain-Enabled IIoT networks like PoW are complex and require lots of energy. Thus it causes an increase in the average blocktime [55]. Multi-arme https://www.overleaf.com/project/6125040312219565813a5b08d bandit algorithms can be used to reveal nodes in the network [39]. Therefore, it can determine the complexity of Blockchain algorithms. Therefore, the blocktime can be adjusted to suit the complexity. That means DRL can help improve the Blockchain-Enabled IIoT network's performance by designing a modulable system that allows adjusting the blocktime in the network [37].

7   Conclusion

In this paper, we have reviewed the current challenges of Blockchain-enabled IIoT networks and the usage of RL features in optimizing those networks. Using the conventional model-driven methods in the optimization process does not give satisfactory results as RL techniques do. This paper summarized the various features of the following technologies: RL, Blockchain, and IIoT, and used all this information to give an extensive analysis of RL applications in Blockchain-enabled IIoT networks. RL techniques are a viable solution for Blockchain-enabled IIoT networks. They can minimize forking events, improve energy efficiency, minimize time to finality, enhance transaction throughput, improve link security, and reduce average blocktime.

References

1. Ray, S., Tadepalli, P.: Model-based reinforcement learning. In: Sammut, C., Webb, G.I. (eds.) Encyclopedia of Machine Learning, pp. 690–693. Springer, Boston (2010). https://doi.org/10.1007/978-0-387-30164-8_556
2. Hyperledger blockchain performance metrics. Hyperledger (2018). https://www.hyperledger.org/learn/publications/blockchain-performance-metrics#transaction
3. Acharya, V., Yerrapati, A.E., Prakash, N.: Oracle Blockchain Quick Start Guide: A Practical Approach to Implementing Blockchain in your Enterprise. Packt Publishing Ltd., Birmingham (2019)
4. Adnan, M.H., Ahmad Zukarnain, Z.: Device-to-device communication in 5G environment: issues, solutions, and challenges. Symmetry **12**(11), 1762 (2020)
5. Aggarwal, S., Kumar, N.: Chapter fifteen - blockchain 2.0: Smart contracts working model. In: Aggarwal, S., Kumar, N., Raj, P. (eds.) The Blockchain Technology for Secure and Smart Applications across Industry Verticals, Advances in Computers, vol. 121, pp. 301–322. Elsevier (2021). https://doi.org/10.1016/bs.adcom.2020.08.015, https://www.sciencedirect.com/science/article/pii/S006524582030070X
6. Al-Zahrani, A., Marghalani, A.: How artificial intelligent transform business. In: SSRN 3226264 (2018)
7. Alghamdi, N.S., Khan, M.A.: Energy-efficient and blockchain-enabled model for internet of things (IoT) in smart cities. CMC-Comput. Mater. Continua **66**(3), 2509–2524 (2021)
8. Alkurd, R., Shubair, R.M., Abualhaol, I.: Survey on device-to-device communications: challenges and design issues. In: 2014 IEEE 12th International New Circuits and Systems Conference (NEWCAS), pp. 361–364. IEEE (2014)
9. Alladi, T., Chamola, V., Parizi, R.M., Choo, K.K.R.: Blockchain applications for industry 4.0 and industrial IoT: a review. IEEE Access **7**, 176935–176951 (2019). https://doi.org/10.1109/ACCESS.2019.2956748
10. Anceaume, E., Pozzo, A., Rieutord, T., Tucci-Piergiovanni, S.: On finality in blockchains. arXiv preprint arXiv:2012.10172 (2020)
11. Arulkumaran, K., Deisenroth, M.P., Brundage, M., Bharath, A.A.: A brief survey of deep reinforcement learning. arXiv preprint arXiv:1708.05866 (2017)
12. Asadi, K.: Strengths, weaknesses, and combinations of model-based and model-free reinforcement learning. Department of Computing Science University of Alberta (2015)

13. Atlam, H.F., Azad, M.A., Alzahrani, A.G., Wills, G.: A review of blockchain in internet of things and AI. Big Data Cogn. Comput. **4**(4), 28 (2020)
14. Atzei, N., Bartoletti, M., Cimoli, T.: A survey of attacks on Ethereum smart contracts (SoK). In: Maffei, M., Ryan, M. (eds.) POST 2017. LNCS, vol. 10204, pp. 164–186. Springer, Heidelberg (2017). https://doi.org/10.1007/978-3-662-54455-6_8
15. Augusto, L., Costa, R., Ferreira, J., Jardim-Gonçalves, R.: An application of Ethereum smart contracts and IoT to logistics. In: 2019 International Young Engineers Forum (YEF-ECE), pp. 1–7 (2019). https://doi.org/10.1109/YEF-ECE.2019.8740823
16. B Rawat, D., Chaudhary, V., Doku, R.: Blockchain technology: emerging applications and use cases for secure and trustworthy smart systems. J. Cybersec. Priv. **1**(1), 4–18 (2021)
17. Bajramovic, E., Gupta, D., Guo, Y., Waedt, K., Bajramovic, A.: Security challenges and best practices for IIoT. In: INFORMATIK 2019: 50 Jahre Gesellschaft für Informatik-Informatik für Gesellschaft (Workshop-Beiträge). Gesellschaft für Informatik eV (2019)
18. Bennett, D., Niv, Y., Langdon, A.: Value-free reinforcement learning: policy optimization as a minimal model of operant behavior (2021)
19. Burhan, M., Rehman, R.A., Khan, B., Kim, B.S.: IoT elements, layered architectures and security issues: a comprehensive survey. Sensors **18**(9), 2796 (2018)
20. Ernst, D., Glavic, M., Capitanescu, F., Wehenkel, L.: Reinforcement learning versus model predictive control: a comparison on a power system problem. IEEE Trans. Syst. Man Cybern. Part B (Cybernetics) **39**(2), 517–529 (2008)
21. Ferdous, M.S., Chowdhury, M.J.M., Hoque, M.A., Colman, A.: Blockchain consensuses algorithms: A survey. arXiv preprint arXiv:2001.07091 (2020)
22. Ghosh, E., Das, B.: A study on the issue of blockchain's energy consumption. In: Chakraborty, M., Chakrabarti, S., Balas, V.E. (eds.) eHaCON 2019. AISC, vol. 1065, pp. 63–75. Springer, Singapore (2020). https://doi.org/10.1007/978-981-15-0361-0_5
23. Gong, X., Liu, E., Wang, R.: Blockchain-based IoT application using smart contracts: case study of M2M autonomous trading. In: 2020 5th International Conference on Computer and Communication Systems (ICCCS), pp. 781–785 (2020). https://doi.org/10.1109/ICCCS49078.2020.9118549
24. Grondman, I., Busoniu, L., Lopes, G.A., Babuska, R.: A survey of actor-critic reinforcement learning: standard and natural policy gradients. IEEE Trans. Syst. Man Cybern. Part C (Applications and Reviews) **42**(6), 1291–1307 (2012)
25. Honar Pajooh, H., Rashid, M., Alam, F., Demidenko, S.: Multi-layer blockchain-based security architecture for internet of things. Sensors **21**(3), 772 (2021)
26. Javaid, U., Sikdar, B.: A checkpoint enabled scalable blockchain architecture for industrial internet of things. IEEE Trans. Ind. Inform. **17**(11), 7679–7687 (2020). https://doi.org/10.1109/TII.2020.3032607
27. Jesus, E.F., Chicarino, V.R., de Albuquerque, C.V., Rocha, A.A.D.A.: A survey of how to use blockchain to secure internet of things and the stalker attack. Secur. Commun. Netw. **2018**, 9675050 (2018)
28. Joshi, A.P., Han, M., Wang, Y.: A survey on security and privacy issues of blockchain technology. Math. Found. Comput. **1**(2), 121 (2018)
29. Kamieniecky, G., Bennet, J.: Emerging use of industrial internet of things (IIoT). Investcorp Investment Insights, 1–22 (2019)

30. Kaya, S.K.: Industrial internet of things: how industrial internet of things impacts the supply chain. In: Internet of Things (IoT) Applications for Enterprise Productivity, pp. 134–155. IGI Global (2020)
31. Konda, V.R., Tsitsiklis, J.N.: Actor-critic algorithms. In: Advances in Neural Information Processing Systems, pp. 1008–1014. Citeseer (2000)
32. Kostrikov, I., Yarats, D., Fergus, R.: Image augmentation is all you need: regularizing deep reinforcement learning from pixels. arXiv preprint arXiv:2004.13649 (2020)
33. Lakhani, K.R., Iansiti, M.: The truth about blockchain. Harv. Bus. Rev. **95**(1), 119–127 (2017)
34. Li, M., Yu, F.R., Si, P., Wu, W., Zhang, Y.: Resource optimization for delay-tolerant data in blockchain-enabled IoT with edge computing: a deep reinforcement learning approach. IEEE Internet Things J. **7**(10), 9399–9412 (2020). https://doi.org/10.1109/JIOT.2020.3007869
35. Lim, M.K., Li, Y., Wang, C., Tseng, M.L.: A literature review of blockchain technology applications in supply chains: a comprehensive analysis of themes, methodologies and industries. Comput. Ind. Eng. **154**, 107133 (2021)
36. Liu, M., Teng, Y., Yu, F.R., Leung, V.C., Song, M.: Deep reinforcement learning based performance optimization in blockchain-enabled internet of vehicle. In: ICC 2019–2019 IEEE International Conference on Communications (ICC), pp. 1–6. IEEE (2019)
37. Liu, M., Yu, F.R., Teng, Y., Leung, V.C.M., Song, M.: Performance optimization for blockchain-enabled industrial internet of things (IIoT) systems: a deep reinforcement learning approach. IEEE Trans. Industr. Inf. **15**(6), 3559–3570 (2019). https://doi.org/10.1109/TII.2019.2897805
38. Luong, N.C., Anh, T.T., Binh, H.T.T., Niyato, D., Kim, D.I., Liang, Y.C.: Joint transaction transmission and channel selection in cognitive radio based blockchain networks: a deep reinforcement learning approach. In: ICASSP 2019–2019 IEEE International Conference on Acoustics, Speech and Signal Processing (ICASSP), pp. 8409–8413. IEEE (2019)
39. Madhawa, K., Murata, T.: A multi-armed bandit approach for exploring partially observed networks. Appl. Netw. Sci. **4**(1), 1–18 (2019). https://doi.org/10.1007/s41109-019-0145-0
40. Manju, S., Punithavalli, M.: An analysis of Q-learning algorithms with strategies of reward function. Int. J. Comput. Sci. Eng. **3**(2), 814–820 (2011)
41. Moerland, T.M., Broekens, J., Jonker, C.M.: Model-based reinforcement learning: a survey. arXiv preprint arXiv:2006.16712 (2020)
42. Morris, A., Cushman, F.: Model-free RL or action sequences? Front. Psychol. **10**, 2892 (2019)
43. Neudecker, T., Hartenstein, H.: Network layer aspects of permissionless blockchains. IEEE Commun. Surv. Tutorials **21**(1), 838–857 (2018)
44. Niforos, M.: Blockchain in financial services in emerging markets, part i (2017)
45. Reyna, A., Martín, C., Chen, J., Soler, E., Díaz, M.: On blockchain and its integration with IoT, challenges and opportunities. Future Gener. Comput. Syst. **88**, 173–190 (2018)
46. Rifi, N., Agoulmine, N., Taher, N.C., Rachkidi, E.: Blockchain technology: is it a good candidate for securing IoT sensitive medical data? Wirel. Commun. Mob. Comput. **2018**, 1–11 (2018)
47. Rouhani, S., Deters, R.: Security, performance, and applications of smart contracts: a systematic survey. IEEE Access **7**, 50759–50779 (2019). https://doi.org/10.1109/ACCESS.2019.2911031

48. Salah, K., Rehman, M.H.U., Nizamuddin, N., Al-Fuqaha, A.: Blockchain for AI: review and open research challenges. IEEE Access **7**, 10127–10149 (2019). https://doi.org/10.1109/ACCESS.2018.2890507

49. Sedlmeir, J., Buhl, H.U., Fridgen, G., Keller, R.: The energy consumption of blockchain technology: beyond myth. Bus. Inf. Syst. Eng. **62**(6), 599–608 (2020)

50. Singh, S.K., Rathore, S., Park, J.H.: BlockIoTIntelligence: a blockchain-enabled intelligent IoT architecture with artificial intelligence. Futur. Gener. Comput. Syst. **110**, 721–743 (2020)

51. Slivkins, A.: Introduction to multi-armed bandits. arXiv preprint arXiv:1904.07272 (2019)

52. Sun, L., Du, Q.: A review of physical layer security techniques for internet of things: challenges and solutions. Entropy **20**(10), 730 (2018)

53. Sun, Y., Zhang, L., Feng, G., Yang, B., Cao, B., Imran, M.A.: Blockchain-enabled wireless internet of things: performance analysis and optimal communication node deployment. IEEE Internet Things J. **6**(3), 5791–5802 (2019). https://doi.org/10.1109/JIOT.2019.2905743

54. Sutton, R.S., Barto, A.G.: Reinforcement Learning: An Introduction. MIT press, Cambridge (2018)

55. Swan, M.: Blockchain temporality: smart contract time specifiability with block-time. In: Alferes, J.J.J., Bertossi, L., Governatori, G., Fodor, P., Roman, D. (eds.) RuleML 2016. LNCS, vol. 9718, pp. 184–196. Springer, Cham (2016). https://doi.org/10.1007/978-3-319-42019-6_12

56. Uddin, M.A., Stranieri, A., Gondal, I., Balasubramanian, V.: A survey on the adoption of blockchain in IoT: challenges and solutions. Blockchain Res. Appl. **2**, 100006 (2021)

57. Van Otterlo, M., Wiering, M.: Reinforcement learning and Markov decision processes. In: Wiering, M., van Otterlo, M. (eds.) Reinforcement Learning, Adaptation, Learning, and Optimization, vol. 12, pp. 3–42. Springer, Berlin (2012). https://doi.org/10.1007/978-3-642-27645-3_1

58. Wang, T., Liew, S.C., Zhang, S.: When blockchain meets AI: optimal mining strategy achieved by machine learning. arXiv preprint arXiv:1911.12942 (2019)

59. Wang, Xiaofei, Han, Yiwen, Leung, Victor C. M.., Niyato, Dusit, Yan, Xueqiang, Chen, Xu.: Artificial intelligence for optimizing edge. In: Edge AI, pp. 117–134. Springer, Singapore (2020). https://doi.org/10.1007/978-981-15-6186-3_8

60. Yiu, N.C.: An overview of forks and coordination in blockchain development. arXiv preprint arXiv:2102.10006 (2021)

61. Zhang, R., Xue, R., Liu, L.: Security and privacy on blockchain. ACM Comput. Surv. (CSUR) **52**(3), 1–34 (2019)

62. Zhang, S., Lee, J.H.: Analysis of the main consensus protocols of blockchain. ICT Express **6**(2), 93–97 (2020)

63. Zhao, S., Li, S., Yao, Y.: Blockchain enabled industrial internet of things technology. IEEE Trans. Comput. Soc. Syst. **6**(6), 1442–1453 (2019)

64. Zhong, R.Y., Xu, X., Klotz, E., Newman, S.T.: Intelligent manufacturing in the context of industry 4.0: a review. Engineering **3**(5), 616–630 (2017)

Practical Challenges in Implementation of Information and Communication Technology

Balbir Singh Dhol, Surjeet Singh Chauhan Gonder[✉], and Naveen Kumar

Department of Mathematics, University Institute of Sciences (UIS), Chandigarh University,
Gharuan, Mohali 140413, India
surjeetschauhan@yahoo.com

Abstract. The Information and Communication Technology (ICT) based math's education is having several technological, infrastructure-based, teacher and student-related challenges. The United States of America is the leader in the research on this topic, but the leading affiliations and sponsors are from China. This paper is based on Scopus resources and the study of major challenges by thematic and bibliometric analysis. Several promising themes for further research have been identified including research on individual challenges and working for developing optimum solutions for these challenges. Further research can be for better implementation, integration with improved access, and equality in digital education platforms for teaching and learning mathematics.

Keywords: Systematic Study · Challenges · Information technology · Communication Technology · ICT · Mathematics

1 Introduction

Mathematics Math's is often considered one of the difficult subjects to learn. Conventional math's education has several challenges in teaching, technology, and pedagogy. Technology offers different solutions for this challenge. ICT-based math's education can be a good solution in this regard, but the ICT-based math's education itself has a variety of challenges. A deep understanding of these challenges and inquiry for scientific solutions for the same is the central theme of this study. The ICT can be integrated with a variety of modules in math's learning, especially for the teaching and learning of trigonometric lessons, geometric lessons (Arvanitaki and Zaranis, 2020); numerical series (Baran, Frausin and de Los Milagros Gutierrez, 2019), and also helps in stimulating, mathematical competencies and thinking skills (Baran, Frausin and de Los Milagros Gutierrez, 2019); logical reasoning and concrete problem-solving among children (Alarcon and Angotti, 2020).

Among various challenges, the challenges associated with teachers (Carmen Ricoy and Couto, 2011; Barrientos and Mogollon, 2019; Addimando and Casabianca, 2014; Anghel and Anghel, 2017; Dominguez Castillo and Morcillo Baquedano, 2016; Dofkova and Uhlirova, 2017; Saltan and Arslan, 2017; Alarcon and Angotti, 2020; Barton and Dexter, 2020); and students (Desiron and Petko, no date; Colley and Comber, 2003;

Delen and Bulut, 2011; Ivan and Schiau, 2016) need prime attention, followed by the technical issues (Baldaque, 2014; Bel and Jarque Fernandez, 2014; S Kim, 2018; Sunha Kim, 2018); integration and implementation challenges (Carmen Ricoy and Couto, 2011; Awodeyi and Tiamiyu, 2012; Ndlovu and Mostert, 2014; Ghavifekr et al., 2017; Alarcon and Angotti, 2020). The other challenges related to ICT-based math's education include the financial challenges and gender challenges specific to the societies and communities.

This paper has the purpose to consolidate the scientific findings related to practical challenges confronted by ICT-based math's education, understanding the bibliometric and thematic features, and spot promising research themes for further research. This study has used the following questions for a better focus on the practical challenges of ICT-based math's education and promising research themes on this topic.

a) What is the variety of challenges associated with ICT integrated math's learning?
b) What are the future themes of the research related to challenges associated with the ICT integration in learning maths?

Very few study has focused on the practical challenges associated with ICT-based math's education. This study is unique by addressing the real challenges of ICT integrated math's learning and the discussion is arranged in four sections, including the introductory section and research methodology discussion. These two sections are followed by a discussion about leading authors, affiliations, document sources, collaborations, and sponsorship is included. The promising themes for further research are discussed in the thematic analysis, and the last section is the conclusion.

2 Research Methodology

The guidelines and motivation from works (Tranfield, Denyer, and Smart, 2003; Tawfik et al., 2019) (Bown and Sutton, 2010) are followed for developing this systematic study of practical challenges of the ICT-based math's education. The software "VOS Viewer" is used for developing the bibliometric analysis for this paper, by focusing on the leading authors, document sources, countries, affiliations, and sponsors. The Scopus resources are used for this paper and the resources are downloaded using the Boolean "TS = ((ICT OR information and communication technology) AND MATHS challenges)" on 10/08/2022. This paper also includes a thematic discussion, where each practical challenge of ICT-based math's education is taken as the research theme of this paper. The thematic analysis is conducted by following the PRISMA guidelines. Variety of documents including articles and conference papers used for this analysis. As the initial step, the anonymous publications and duplicates are removed and an analysis is prepared by reading the title and abstract. The detailed steps followed in the article selection process by using the PRISMA guidelines for systematic analysis are shown in Fig. 1:

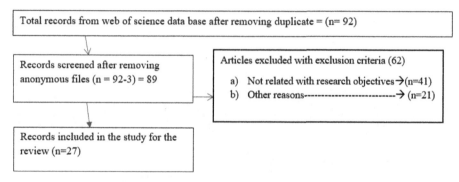

Total records from web of science data base after removing duplicate = (n= 92)

Records screened after removing
anonymous files (n = 92-3) = 89

Articles excluded with exclusion criteria (62)
  a) Not related with research objectives→(n=41)
  b) Other reasons--------------------------→ (n=21)

Records included in the study for the
review (n=27)

Fig. 1. Journal Selection by PRISMA Guidelines.

3 Bibliometric Details

3.1 Authors

The leading authors on this research topic based on document publications are Caboni A, Huang A, Koleszar V, TejeraG, Viera M and Wagner J. Very strong research collaboration exists among authors, and the details of the leading authors and their research collaborations are visualized in Fig. 2:

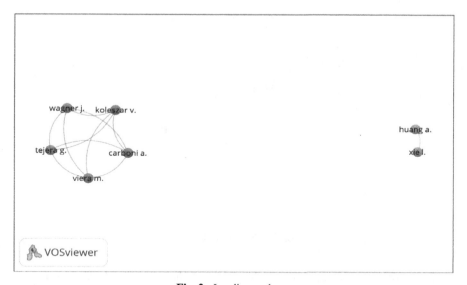

Fig. 2. Leading authors.

3.2 Source Documents and Keywords

The leading document sources include Journal of Physics Conference Series, Computers and Education, Journal of Computer Assisted Learning, Communications in Computer

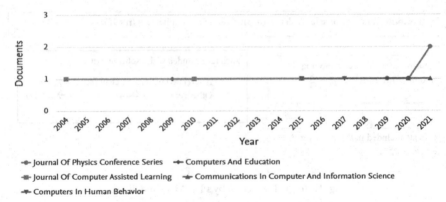

Fig. 3. Leading source documents.

and Information Science, and Computers in Human Behaviour. The leading document sources are shown in Fig. 3:

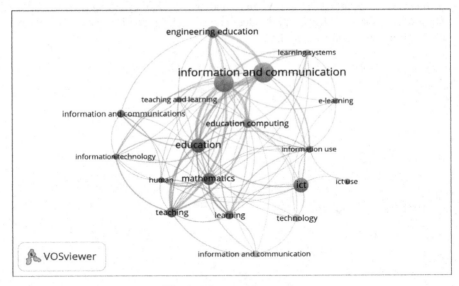

Fig. 4. Most used keywords.

The most occurred keywords on this topic are shown in Fig. 4. The most popular keywords include information and communication; learning systems, engineering education, education, mathematics, teaching, learning, human, ICT, and e-learning.

3.3 Countries, Sponsors, and Affiliations

The United States of America leads the research on challenges related to ICT-based math's education. The USA has twelve document publications on this topic, followed by Spain, Indonesia, Turkey, the United Kingdom, and Australia. The leading research affiliations include Colegio Nacional José Pedro Varela and Peking University. The major funding agencies engaged in the research on challenges related to ICT-based math's education are the Bulgarian National Science Fund, followed by the Economic and Social Research Council, and the European Regional Development Fund. Future researchers can focus on these leading institutions for building collaborations and research funding in research on challenges related to ICT-based math's education.

4   Thematic Discussion

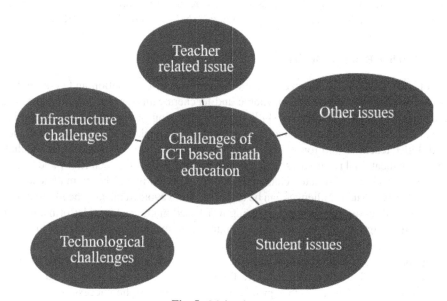

Fig. 5. Major themes.

4.1   Technological and Implementation Challenges

Other than pure technological challenges associated with ICT-based math education, the poor implementation at school levels should be monitored and avoided for better outcomes from an ICT-based math's education (Baldaque, 2014). The technology-related challenges include the e-learning platform and its ability to cater to the needs of students. It should facilitate personalized learning and should cope with diversified learning styles (Bel and Jarque Fernandez, 2014). The ICT access and the gap between various classes of students related to technology access and affordability is a challenge for ICT-based math's education (S Kim, 2018) (Sunha Kim, 2018).

4.2 Infrastructure Based Challenges

Even though the ICT-based math's learning platforms are better teaching aids for teaching maths, the infrastructure for the same is a big challenge in many educational institutions (Alarcon and Angotti, 2020). The software adoption, availability of computers, and upgradation of software can also be challenging tasks for providing ICT-based maths education. The poor internet coverage, overpopulated classrooms, and high student-to-teacher ratio can create negative outcomes for ICT-based math's education (Awodeyi and Tiamiyu, 2012). The other infrastructure-related challenges for ICT-based math's education are time limitations (Ghavifekr et al., 2017) (Carmen Ricoy and Couto, 2011), lack of sufficient and proper equipment, and lack of technical support systems (Carmen Ricoy and Couto, 2011). Challenges were also related to internet services, and speed (Ghavifekr et al., 2017); connectivity challenges (Ndlovu and Mostert, 2014).

4.3 Teacher Related Challenges

In a highly technology-oriented education environment, information and communication technology integration is inevitable and teachers cannot avoid such integrations, but self-adapt and upgrade their skills for better catering of knowledge to the coming generation with the help of technology (Anghel and Anghel, 2017). The lack of trained and skilled teaching staff for ICT-based math education is a major teacher-oriented challenge in educational institutions (Alarcon and Angotti, 2020) (Carmen Ricoy and Couto, 2011). Several teacher-related challenges can be expected in ICT-based math teaching. The majority of such challenges can be anticipated and avoided through better planning, training, and monitoring of teachers using ICT-based math teaching platforms. For the successful usage of information and communication technology in math teaching and learning, proper modeling, mentoring, and supervision of teachers during training sessions are very essential for better adoption of the technology and for removing all kinds of hesitance and confusion in using ICT platforms for teaching math's (Addimando and Casabianca, 2014). Teacher profile has a great role in the success of ICT-based maths education (Dofkova and Uhlirova, 2017), and the experience, skills, work tools, and expectations of teachers is an important determinants in this aspect (Dominguez Castillo and Morcillo Baquedano, 2016). The teachers' technological pedagogical content knowledge and self-confidence are another challenge for succeeding in ICT-based math's education (Saltan and Arslan, 2017).

Adverse outcomes can happen due to inexperienced and poor handling of ICT tools for math's education by teachers. Proper training is essential before such tools are used for teaching students (Barrientos and Mogollon, 2019). Teacher efficiency and teacher integration with ICT platforms are also major concerns for the success of ICT-based math's education (Barton and Dexter, 2020). Moreover, student management in the internet environment during math's class is also a challenge, especially for teachers with limited time and training (Carmen Ricoy and Couto, 2011).

4.4 Student Related Challenges

Learning difficulties of students is a serious challenge, even in ICT-based math's education and this factor should be considered while planning and designing the technology-based math's education. The age and gender difference among students is also an important student-related factor to be considered for better performance in ICT-based math's education (Colley and Comber, 2003). Several studies have identified the role of student familiarity and exposure to technology can be determinants affecting the success of ICT integration in ICT-based math's learning environments (Delen and Bulut, 2011). The other student-related challenges include academic dishonesty by students in technology-based learning environments (Desiron and Petko, no date); computer anxiety among students (Ivan and Schiau, 2016). The student-oriented challenges would be stronger in cases involving disabled students.

4.5 Other Challenges

Among various challenges related to ICT-based math's education, a lower level of women's participation in ICT-based math's teaching and learning environment is a serious issue to be attended to. Even though, this issue is not limited to ICT-based math's learning, but general to other science and technology courses. Spain can be the best epitome of this crisis (Alastruey Benede et al., 2019) (Marzolla and Mirandola, 2019) (Meggiolaro, 2017) (Sainz and Eccles, 2012) and strong policy actions and motivational measures are essential for encouraging gender-free technology-based education of math's and science courses. The equally important and challenging task is to ensure that the ICT-based math education enhances the reach to vulnerable students (Atkins, May, and Marks-Maran, 2005). The digital divide in the education sector is another challenge to be addressed for better integration of ICT-based math's education (Pick and Azari, 2007). Very few researches focus on the outcomes of ICT investments and the various ICT investments have a different levels of outcomes (Piper et al., 2016).

5 Future Research Agenda

5.1 Other Challenges

The research on ICT-based math's education and practical challenges opens various promising themes for further research. Future researchers can focus on the individual challenges faced in ICT-based math's education. Systematic study can be planned for each challenge on this topic. It's not only the challenge, researchers can work for developing optimum solutions for these challenges. Future researchers can focus on the most important challenges like technological challenges, integration challenges, teacher-related challenges, and student-related challenges. The infrastructure challenges of ICT-based math's education are also topics with good prospects for further research.

Recommended Themes
1. Teacher related challenges
2. Student related challenges
3. Infrastructure related challenges
4. Technological challenges

Focus areas for further research
1. Access and better implementation
2. Personalised learning systems
3. Software, hardware, and network challenges
4. Poor teacher student ratio, teacher skill, teacher training,
5. Personal challenges of students and teachers, gender and age differences
6. Academic dishonesty and disability of children
7. Reach and digital divide

Fig. 6. Future agenda for research.

5.2 Research Niches

One of the major issues faced in ICT-based math's education is related to inequality and access limitations. The inequality can be due to several reasons including economic reasons, gender, etc. Access to technology-based education can happen due to these. The other reasons for the limitation of technology-based math's education can be related to internet-related issues, poor implementation, etc. Future researchers can work on these issues and for developing solutions. The learning capabilities of individual students differ and future ICT-based math's education should look for the individual learning needs of students and also personalization of technology for better learning.

Future researchers should focus on resolving issues associated with the software, hardware, and network issues of ICT-based math's education. The focus should also be on challenges associated with slow network connections, network intrusions, and misuses by stakeholders and outsiders. Further research is essential for resolving poor teacher-student ratio, poor teaching skills in technology platforms, and poor adaptation of teachers to technology-based math's teaching. The researchers can also work on resolving inequality in ICT-based math's education. The focus can be on inequality due to individual challenges of teachers and students, gender, age, digital access, etc. The other research niches to be focused on for further research include the issues of reach and academic dishonesty among students in ICT-based math's education.

6 Conclusion

The research on challenges associated with ICT-based math's education is relatively new and offers good potential for further research. The majority of the research on this topic is in the United States of America and Spain. However, most of the research organizations and funding agencies are from China. The other peculiarity of bibliometric patterns of this research topic is the limited collaboration among countries and research organizations.

Future researchers should focus on collaborated research for further development of the topic and better funding options.

Even though math's is a difficult subject to teach and learn, technology integration, especially, ICT-based on math's education can revolutionize the math's learning environment. However, this technology integration in math's learning is limited by several challenges. The major challenges associated with ICT-based math's education are technological, infrastructure challenges, teacher-based challenges, and student-based challenges. These challenges have been taken up for the thematic discussion in this paper. These themes offer promising opportunities for further research.

Poor implementation and monitoring is a major challenge in ICT-based math's education and also the monotonous style. Future researchers can take up the challenge to personalize technology-based math's education with professional implementation and monitoring. Future researchers can take up the issues of the gender divide, digital divide, inequality due to age, and economic resources in the ICT-based math's education. The solution for these challenges offers better reach and access to ICT-based math's education among students from diversified backgrounds.

Future researchers can also work on developing solutions for issues of software, hardware, network challenges, and poor connectivity. The solutions are essential for the poor student-teacher ratios, poor teaching skills, and lack of teacher training. The researchers should take interest in challenges associated with student challenges and student dishonesty and misutilizations in the digital education platforms. Equally important are the solutions for children suffering from disabilities in the digital education platforms, especially ICT-based math's education. Proper planning and coordination, along with technology integration and upgrading are essential for overcoming these challenges associated with the ICT-based math's education for the student community.

References

Addimando, L., Casabianca, E.: Integration of information and communication technologies in teaching mathematic with a new software (cabri elem): lessons from Switzerland. In: Chova, L.G., Martinez, A.L., Torres, I.C. (eds.) INTED 2014: 8th International Technology, Education and Development Conference, INTED Proceedings, Valenica, Burjassot, Spain, pp. 886–901. IATED-International Association of Technology Education & Development (2014)

Alarcon, D.F., Angotti, J.A.: Educational software in math teaching: scientific and technological training of public schools teachers in the santa catarina state – Brazil. In: Chova, L.G., Martinez, A.L., Torres, I.C. (eds.) 14th International Technology, Education and Development Conference (INTED2020), INTED Proceedings, Valenica, Burjassot, Spain, pp. 5411–5417. IATED-International Association of Technology Education & Development (2020)

Benede, I.A., et al.: Encouraging the role of women in the ICT sector. In: 2019 24th IEEE International Conference on Emerging Technologies and Factory Automation (ETFA), New York, NY, USA, pp. 1831–1835. IEEE (2019)

Anghel, G., Anghel, I.A.: Learning maths on the internet. In: Roceanu, I., et al. (eds.) Rethinking Education by Leveraging the Elearning Pillar of the Digital Agenda for Europe! Bucharest, Romania, vol. II, pp. 453–458. Carol I Natl Defence Univ Publishing House (2017). (eLearning and Software for Education). https://doi.org/10.12753/2066-026X-15-159

Arvanitaki, M., Zaranis, N.: The use of ICT in teaching geometry in primary school. Educ. Inf. Technol. **25**(6), 5003–5016 (2020). https://doi.org/10.1007/s10639-020-10210-7

Atkins, N., May, S., Marks-Maran, D.: Widening participation in subjects requiring data handling skills: the MathsAid Project. J. Further High. Educ. **29**(4), 353–365 (2005). https://doi.org/10.1080/03098770500353607

Awodeyi, T.O., Tiamiyu, M.A.: The development of mathematics e-learning tool for Nigerian senior secondary schools. Afr. J. Libr. Arch. Inf. Sci. **22**(2), 99–116 (2012). https://www.scopus.com/inward/record.uri?eid=2-s2.0-84872414864&partnerID=40&md5=25ac1a247c95b607d60cddc3e6894c99

Baldaque, A.: Innovative good practices for using ICT in the classroom. In: Chova, L.G., Martinez, A.L., Torres, I.C. (eds.) INTED 2014: 8th International Technology, Education and Development Conference, INTED Proceedings, Valenica, Burjassot, Spain, pp. 5175–5183. IATED-International Association of Technology Education & Development (2014)

Baran, V., Frausin, A., de los Milagros Gutierrez, M.: Software tools for teaching numerical series at the university level. In: 2019 38th International Conference of the Chilean Computer Science Society (SCCC), New York, NY, USA. IEEE (2019)

Barrientos, J., Mogollon, E.: Mathematical interactive learning strategies with the use of information and communication technologies for general secondary education students. Redhecs-Revista Electronica de Humanidades Educacion y Comunicacion Social **14**(8), 24–39 (2019)

Barton, E.A., Dexter, S.: Sources of teachers' self-efficacy for technology integration from formal, informal, and independent professional learning. Educ. Technol. Res. Dev. **68**(1), 89–108 (2020). https://doi.org/10.1007/s11423-019-09671-6

Bel, M., Fernandez, M.J.: First European experience in PCP process applied to education: imaile (innovative methods for award procedures of ICT learning in Europe). In: Chova, L.G., Martinez, A.L., Torres, I.C. (eds.) EDULEARN 2014: 6th International Conference on Education and New Learning Technologies, EDULEARN Proceedings, Valenica, Burjassot, Spain, pp. 3124–3125. IATED-International Association of Technology Education & Development (2014)

Bown, M.J., Sutton, A.J.: Quality control in systematic reviews and meta-analyses'. Eur. J. Vasc. Endovasc. Surg. **40**(5), 669–677 (2010). https://doi.org/10.1016/j.ejvs.2010.07.011

Ricoy, M.C., Couto, M.J.V.S.: ICT in secondary education in mathematics at Portugal: the perspective of teachers. Revista latinoamericana de investigacion en matematica educativa-relime **14**(1), 95–119 (2011)

Colley, A., Comber, C.: Age and gender differences in computer use and attitudes among secondary school students: what has changed? Educ. Res. **45**(2), 155–165 (2003). https://doi.org/10.1080/0013188032000103235

Delen, E., Bulut, O.: the relationship between students' exposure to technology and their achievement in science and math. Turk. Online J. Educ. Technol. **10**(3), 311–317 (2011)

Désiron, J.C., Petko, D.: Academic dishonesty when doing homework: how digital technologies are put to bad use in secondary schools. Educ. Inf. Technol/ **28**(2), 1251–1271 (2022). https://doi.org/10.1007/s10639-022-11225-y

Dofkova, R., Uhlirova, M.: The profile of a freshman year student of a teacher training course in terms of his/her attitude to mathematics. In: Chova, L.G., Martinez, A.L., Torres, I.C. (eds.) 9th International Conference on Education and New Learning Technologies (EDULEARN 2017), EDULEARN Proceedings, Valenica, Burjassot, Spain, pp. 9071–9076. . IATED-International Association of Technology Education & Development (2017)

Dominguez Castillo, J.G., Morcillo Baquedano, J.S.: Evaluation of an online course for skills training in the use of ICT in science teachers in public secondary Southeast Mexico. Red-Revista de Educacion a Distancia (51) (2016). https://doi.org/10.6018/red/51/2

Ghavifekr, S., et al.: Challenges facing maths teachers in ICT integration: a comparative study on secondary schools in Kuala Lumpur and Kota Kinabalu. Adv. Sci. Lett. **23**(3), 2159–2162 (2017). https://doi.org/10.1166/asl.2017.8583

Ivan, L., Schiau, I.: Experiencing computer anxiety later in life: the role of stereotype threat. In: Zhou, J., Salvendy, G. (eds.) ITAP 2016. LNCS, vol. 9754, pp. 339–349. Springer, Cham (2016). https://doi.org/10.1007/978-3-319-39943-0_33

Kim, S.: ICT and the UN's sustainable development goal for education: using ICT to boost the math performance of immigrant youths in the US. Sustainability 10(12) (2018). https://doi.org/10.3390/su10124584

Kim, S.: ICT for children of immigrants: indirect and total effects via self-efficacy on math performance. J. Educ. Comput. Res. 55(8), 1168–1200 (2015). https://doi.org/10.1177/0735633117699954

Marzolla, M., Mirandola, R.: Gender balance in computer science and engineering in Italian universities. In: Duchien, L., et al. (eds.) 13th European Conference on Software Architecture (ECSA 2019), vol. 2, pp. 82–87. Association Computing Machinery, New York (2019). https://doi.org/10.1145/3344948.3344966

Meggiolaro, S.: Information and communication technologies use, gender and mathematics achievement: evidence from Italy. Soc. Psychol. Educ. 21(2), 497–516 (2017). https://doi.org/10.1007/s11218-017-9425-7

Ndlovu, M., Mostert, I.: The potential of moodle in a blended learning management system: a case study of an in-service programme for secondary mathematics teachers. In: Chova, L.G., Martinez, A.L., Torres, I.C. (eds.) EDULEARN 2014: 6th International Conference on Education and New Learning Technologies, EDULEARN Proceedings, Valenica, Burjassot, Spain, pp. 3715–3724. IATED-International Association of Technology Education & Development (2014)

Pick, J.B., Azari, R.: Worldwide digital divide: influences of education, workforce, economic, and policy factors on information technology. In: SIGMIS CPR 2007: Proceedings of the 2007 ACM SIGMIS CPR Conference Global Information Technology Workforce, pp. 78–86. Association Computing Machinery, New York (2007)

Piper, B., et al.: Does technology improve reading outcomes? Comparing the effectiveness and cost-effectiveness of ICT interventions for early grade reading in Kenya. Int. J. Educ. Dev. 49, 204–214 (2016). https://doi.org/10.1016/j.ijedudev.2016.03.006

Sainz, M., Eccles, J.: Self-concept of computer and math ability: gender implications across time and within ICT studies. J. Vocat. Behav. 80(2), 486–499 (2012). https://doi.org/10.1016/j.jvb.2011.08.005

Saltan, F., Arslan, K.: A comparison of in-service and pre-service teachers' technological pedagogical content knowledge self-confidence. Cogent Educ. 4 (2017). https://doi.org/10.1080/2331186X.2017.1311501

Tawfik, G.M., et al.: A step by step guide for conducting a systematic review and meta-analysis with simulation data. Trop. Med. Health 6, 1–9 (2019)

Tranfield, D., Denyer, D., Smart, P.: Towards a methodology for developing evidence-informed management knowledge by means of systematic review. Br. J. Manag. 14, 207–222 (2003)

Facial Analytics or Virtual Avatars: Competencies and Design Considerations for Student-Teacher Interaction in AI-Powered Online Education for Effective Classroom Engagement

Ashraf Alam[(✉)] [iD] and Atasi Mohanty [iD]

Rekhi Centre of Excellence for the Science of Happiness, Indian Institute of Technology Kharagpur, Kharagpur, West Bengal, India
`ashraf_alam@kgpian.iitkgp.ac.in`

Abstract. Artificial intelligence (AI) technologies provide useful assistance for online learning and teaching, such as individualized instruction for students, automation of faculty responsibilities, and adaptive learning assessment. Although AI has promising applications, it is yet unclear how these technologies will affect the norms and expectations of the student-teacher dynamic. Interaction between teachers and students is a key factor in the success of online courses (including communication, assistance, and presence). Understanding how students and teachers see the influence of AI systems on their interactions is crucial for locating any gaps, hurdles, or constraints preventing AI systems from reaching their full potential and jeopardizing the sanctity of these interactions. For this foresightful investigation, we conducted a storyboard study of the opinions of 9 students and 8 professors about various use cases of potential AI systems in online learning. Participants predict the widespread use of AI systems in online education to promote individualized learner-instructor engagement, despite the fact that doing so carries the potential for ethical violations. Even though AI systems have been lauded for improving both the quantity and quality of communication, for providing large-scale settings with just-in-time, customized assistance, and for fostering a greater sense of connection, worries have been raised about accountability, agency, and surveillance. These results have important implications for the development of AI systems, particularly with regard to facilitating their explicability, interaction with humans, and comprehensiveness of data collection and display.

Keywords: Artificial Intelligence · Facial Analytics · Virtual Avatars · Educational Technology · Online Learning · Student-Teacher Interaction · Classroom Engagement · E-Learning

1 Introduction

Artificial Intelligence (AI) powered assessments, individualized student learning, and the automation of instructors' mundane responsibilities are just a few of the potential applications of AI in online learning and teaching [1]. For instance, AI-powered tutoring

R. S. Tomar et al. (Eds.): CNC 2022, CCIS 1894, pp. 252–265, 2023.
https://doi.org/10.1007/978-3-031-43145-6_21

systems may cater to each student's needs by tailoring lessons to their own learning preferences and strengths [2]. Automatically responding to student queries in online discussion forums, performing repetitive tasks that can be automated by AI teaching assistants thus giving educators more time to focus on other important tasks [3]. AI analytics decodes clickstream data to aid educators in gauging student achievement, growth, and potential [4]. Though AI has many possible uses, some teachers and students may not enjoy the work that AI does [5]. Students may feel their privacy is being invaded when AI systems gather and analyze their data without their knowledge or consent. Unless AI robots resolve the possibility of bias arising from data or algorithm, its actions may be seen as biased by the students using it [6]. Teachers worry that if their students rely too much on AI systems, they may lose their ability to think for themselves and develop their critical thinking skills [7]. Thus, understanding the influence that AI technologies have on both teachers and students in virtual classrooms is crucial. The scientists who are working on applications of AI in Education (AIEd) are now looking at the potential effects that AI systems might have on distance learning [8]. For example, the risks and ethical implications of AI systems in the student-teacher dynamic have not been given enough consideration [9]. Conflicts between students and professors may arise over a variety of issues, including but not limited to privacy concerns, shifting power dynamics, and overbearing control [10]. Further investigation into how AI systems affect learner-instructor interactions is required to uncover any gaps, difficulties, or impediments stopping AI systems from attaining their full potential [11]. The ability of students and instructors to communicate and collaborate online is essential. Students are more engaged and succeed more in class when teacher-student interactions include elements like communication, support, and physical presence [12]. Students' sense of self-worth, motivation to study, and bravery in trying new things are all influenced by the bonds they form with their teachers [13]. The influence of Artificial Intelligence technologies on student-teacher dynamics in internet-based teaching-learning is less clear. It is widely expected that AI systems will have far-reaching consequences for the future of education, particularly regarding the dynamic between teachers and pupils [14]. Further research is required to comprehend why and how different kinds of Artificial Intelligence systems affect teacher-student interactions in internet-based education [15]. We used storyboards to provide participants with several potential situations in order to get insight into their instant emotions [16]. By conducting these interviews, we were able to get a comprehensive understanding of how teachers and learners evaluate the effects of Artificial Intelligence systems on student-teacher interactions and the points at which students and professors begin to see AI as 'intrusive' [17]. Many original additions this study brings to the existing corpus of knowledge in AIEd research. In the current investigation, we started by sketching up the potential scenarios that may be used in follow-up studies of AI's impact on online and distance education (ODE). Second, the research summarizes the main benefits and drawbacks of Artificial Intelligence in internet-based learning from the perspectives of both students and teachers in higher education. Lastly, we discussed how AI-based systems could affect online education in terms of both design and implementation. Emphasis is placed on including both students and professors in the process, ensuring their questions and concerns are addressed, and collecting and presenting data thoroughly.

2 Background

This study investigates the effects of AI on the dynamics between online teachers and their students. To begin, we introduced a theoretical framework based on research on the dynamics of teacher-student relationships in virtual classrooms. Then, we looked at the AI software currently employed in virtual classrooms.

3 Conceptual Foundation

Online education can only be effective when there is heart-to-heart and soul-to-soul student-teacher communication [18]. Students learn from one another and create fresh insights via dialogue. Interactions in online learning may be broken down into three broad categories: those between students and course materials, between students, and between students and teachers [19]. Such communications motivate students to participate in online classes and develop a feeling of belonging among them [20]. These two factors, i.e., participation and belongingness, are crucial to the sustainability of e-learning environments [21]. The relationship between students and teachers is crucial. Teachers may improve their students' motivation and performance by offering several means of contact, as well as guidance, motivation, and timely feedback [22]. A feeling of community among students might be fostered by instructors' participation in and encouragement of online dialogues [23]. Overall, the amount of interaction between students and teachers is a major factor in determining whether students succeed as distance learners [24]. Online student-teacher interactions may be examined via the perspective of the five-factor model of student-teacher collaborative communication. When designing internet-based collaborative education methodologies, effective communication and support between students and teachers are vital. Perceived teacher presence during learner-instructor interaction in online courses has a beneficial impact on student engagement, pleasure, learning, and retention. Increasing student success and satisfaction requires a combination of open lines of communication, positive reinforcement, and physical presence. This analysis is focused on the interactions between students and teachers in terms of both their physical presence and their level of support and communication. The use of AI is expected to change the dynamics of online classrooms in the future. Despite the obvious advantages, such systems would not be adopted if students and teachers had serious worries about how AI technology may impact their relationships. There have been very few empirical studies on how AI systems affect student-teacher relationships and thus arose the need to carry out the current research.

4 AI-Powered Online Learning

The anticipated consequences of different artificial intelligence (AI) systems on virtual interactions between educators and students are uncertain, as opinions on the matter are varied. Automated responses to student introductions, weekly announcements, and commonly asked questions are just a few ways in which AI may be used as a teaching assistant to help instructors feel more connected to their classes. In the near future, educational institutions may have access to artificial intelligence (AI) tools that offer continuous assessments of students' learning progress and growth, assisting both teachers and learners in achieving their academic goals. The goal of offering adaptive quizzes online is to boost student motivation and engagement by personalizing the learning experience for each individual student. Virtual avatars make it easier for people in different locations to work together because they provide the impression that they are in the same room. In today's tech-enhanced classrooms, AI-powered face analytics are being used to further facilitate teachers' roles as mentors and guides. To thoroughly analyze the diverse artificial intelligence (AI) systems, it is crucial to consider the perceptions of both learners and instructors regarding their influence. The emergence of commercial AI solutions for virtual education has brought to light the challenges posed by these systems to the dynamic of teacher-student communication. Example: 'Proctorio' is a gadget that watches students' screens during tests in an effort to detect any instances of cheating. Although it appears like a foolproof way to keep tabs on online students, some students have complained that it makes them more nervous before exams. Students who know that Proctorio will be recording their exams tend to be distracted and anxious during such times. Similarly, 'Squirrel AI', which intends to give adaptive learning, automatically modifies teaching methodology to best suit each student's requirements, which may consequently stifle students' creative and imaginative growth. In such settings, AIs are gaining more independence in data evaluation, inferring learning, and even making certain pedagogical judgments on their own.

5 Methods and Methodology

The purpose of this research is to discover more about how students and teachers feel AI systems have altered their presence, support, and communication during online learning. Teachers and learners both have a newfound respect for the benefits of online education, especially during the recent online course experiences that they experienced during the COVID-19 outbreak. Our goal was not to conduct a systematic assessment of AI technology, but rather to identify how AI systems may improve student-instructor interactions and identify areas in need of further study. To promote critical examination of the consequences of various aspects of AI in Education (AIEd), we employed a research method called "Speed Dating" with "storyboards." This approach allowed participants to explore a diverse range of potential AI systems through the use of visual storyboards. By experiencing possible AI domains in this way, participants gained a more comprehensive understanding of the systems and developed informed opinions about their potential impacts. Using storyboards, we conducted "Speed Dating" sessions with students and teachers, covering a broad spectrum of hypothetical AI applications in online education. Our primary research question addressed the effects of AI systems on communication, support, and physical presence in online classrooms.

5.1 Creation of a Storyboard

To create storyboards that depict AI systems for online learning environments that are technically feasible and enhance learner-instructor interaction, our design team conducted an online brain writing exercise. This involved eight designers with an average experience of 9.7 years (SD = 2.8 years) in the field of human-computer interface (HCI) design, who were employed by an AI laboratory located in Bangalore. Each member of the team shared a Google Slides file including an incident log with the rest of the group. This cycle was performed four times until the designers reached a consensus that the AI system scenarios were technically possible and would facilitate learner-instructor interaction in online education. The initial versions of the scenarios were created by HCI designers, but to ensure the technical feasibility and beneficial effects on learner-instructor interaction, we conducted follow-up interviews with eight AI experts. On average, these experts had 13.6 years (SD = 9.1 years) of research experience and 6 years (SD = 4.7 years) of teaching experience. The researchers used video conferencing to conduct semi-structured interviews with experts in the field of AI. We asked whether there was any way to improve its technical viability. Given their background in online education, we then questioned AI experts, whether they think they could make changes to this situation that would have a net beneficial effect on the interaction between the students and the teacher. We also asked whether they can think of any scenarios where such research ideas can be put into action. As suggested by AI specialists, the scenario was updated to add AIEd-related details. The average time of each interview was 39 min (SD = 9.1 min). Every AI professional who contributed to the study was paid 11,000 Indian Rupees. Finally, we devised nine scenarios that promote communication, presence, and facilitation between students and instructors during online learning. Researchers made use of factors affecting student-teacher relationships to classify specific cases. However, the AI's 'Teaching and Grading Support' might be seen as systems that help the instructor, the term 'support' in the context of student-teacher interaction refers to assistance for the learner. The scenarios of AI systems categorized as "Teaching and Grading Support" are more appropriately considered as communication tools rather than direct forms of student assistance due to their capacity to facilitate faster and more effective communication between learners and instructors. Research suggestions from AI specialists were used to develop the following four scenarios: (1) AI as a companion, (2) AI as a peer reviewer, (3) AI as a group project organizer, and (4) AI as a breakout room matching tool. The goal of these scenarios was not to conduct a comprehensive exploration of all the AI systems available in online learning or to delve deeply into every issue, but instead to demonstrate the diverse situations that may arise when implementing AI systems in online education. To eliminate gender and racial biases and encourage participants to identify with the characters, we utilized four-cut storyboards with consistent visual styles for all the characters.

5.2 Participants

We then engaged in 'Speed Dating' using storyboards. To our 'Speed Dating' event, we invited five professors and eight students. In order to increase diversity, we hired professors from three distinct fields and students from five distinct academic tracks. Because of the COVID-19 pandemic, it was made mandatory that all students and instructors have at least 100 days of experience with internet-based teaching and learning. The average tenure of the teachers was three years, while the average time spent in college was one year. Both students and faculty members needed to have previous experience with online learning and teaching in order to handle the anticipated levels of student-instructor involvement within online university courses. Our focus was not on the participants' familiarity with AI systems, but rather on their perspectives on the planned human-AI interactions and their possible consequences. Given that recent studies have proven that Speed Dating is successful even for those without any erstwhile expertise or acquaintance with Artificial Intelligence systems, participation in this study needed neither specialized information nor experience. Professors and students received 3,000 Indian Rupees each as payment for participation.

5.3 Procedure

Semi-structured interviews were performed with participants through video conferencing application software 'Zoom'. The interview questions were crafted with the respondents' perceptions of the AI systems, keeping in mind, the storyboards that were shown. After reading each storyboard aloud, participants discussed how they saw AI applied to digital teaching. We posed the question, "Would you want to experience the implications of adding an AI system to an online course?" to the participants to get them thinking critically about the potential impacts of this technology on the learner-instructor dynamic. We also had students choose AI systems they thought would and would not be effective in order to acquire a fuller picture of the pros and cons of AI. Each participant was given a storyboard and was asked several questions that revolved around its importance with 'student-professor interaction' at the fore, for an average of 39.6 min (SD = 8.2 min) of interview time.

5.4 Data Analysis

Each interview was recorded and transcribed so that data could be analyzed. As a method, we used Reflexive Thematic Analysis. After spending some time getting to know the interview data, we created a set of semantic codes for notable words or remarks. After that, we moved on to the inductive coding phase. After carefully reviewing the data, we coded each transcript individually by highlighting and annotating it in Google Docs. We were able to put right the differences of opinion on these matters via prolific and industrious discussions. The collected data was classified and structured into themes using a deductive approach based on the variables that were found to impact the interaction between learners and instructors, and this process was carried out in a separate MS Word document. After having three rounds of dialogs, we were able to organize the data into meaningful thematic units, generating recurrent problems and themes.

6 Findings

The dominating theme in the replies to our survey was that the use of AI systems in online learning might allow for scalable learner-instructor personalization but at the risk of breaking societal norms. Participants were concerned that problems regarding accountability, agency, and supervision in online learning would be raised if AI systems violated social norms in any aspect of student-teacher collaborative communication (i.e., presence, support, and communication).

6.1 Communication

In virtual classrooms, students ask each other questions and provide answers on course materials including readings, debates, and quizzes. There is hope that AI systems would improve communication between students and teachers, but there is also concern that it might lead to misunderstandings and accountability problems.

6.2 Quantity and Quality

The pupils think that the anonymity provided by AI will make them less shy about asking questions. Online students sometimes refrain from asking questions in lectures because they worry that the instructor has already addressed the topic or because they do not want to seem ignorant in front of their peers. They believe that if they had an AI Teaching Assistant, they would feel more comfortable asking questions, less guilty about taking up too much of the teacher's time, and less disruptive in the classroom. One student even joked, "If the question is deemed foolish, I have an AI available to handle it for me." Questions directed to an Artificial Intelligence robot eliminate the awkwardness that might be part of instructional conversations. According to another student, "Asking questions is not a burden anymore. Because AI does not get frustrated, we feel free to bombard it with questions." All the students surveyed had the same opinion that adding AI into online education will encourage greater student inquiry. Professors believe that AI might deliver short, repeated replies, thus freeing up their time to have deeper conversations with pupils. Students' incessant probing requires much time and effort to respond. Teachers hoped that if they spent less time on mundane duties like responding to administrative queries, they would have more time to address students' concerns about the course material. Teachers may better interact with students by focusing on fresh questions or allocating more time for in-depth or atypical queries if an AI Teaching Assistant handles students' simple, routine, and repetitious questions. The AI systems of Grading Assistance and Peer Review provide prompt feedback loops.

6.3 Responsibility

Despite believing that AI systems would increase the amount and quality of instructional communication, students are afraid that AI systems may offer inaccurate answers that may have a detrimental effect on their marks. Several concerns were voiced by students. Because if the AI is answering queries from learners and improvising itself accordingly, students may utilize that response in their future work, and it may be labelled erroneous. Students want to make sure that it is an authentic source from where AI systems learn. This might make it challenging for teachers as well because teachers may mark an answer incorrect, however, students may claim that it was the AI system that gave them that answer. While AI may be held accountable in some cases, such as when providing definitive answers to questions, the majority of students believe it would be hard to hold AI accountable due to its incomprehensibility. As another student put it, understanding the reasoning behind an answer given by an AI whose inner workings are not completely known makes it more challenging to comprehend. Due to their reliance on AI, students worry about how teachers will respond in an emergency. A student makes the following observation: "Many of my engineering classmates will have greater leeway to justify their grades, I can see. I can see people being less accepting of their destinies under such a system." Teachers expected conflicts with pupils because of AI-based misunderstandings or dishonesty. For instance, if the professor, the AI, and the TAs all come up with different answers, a disagreement may emerge. If students do not perform well in exams, many of them would claim that AI is wrong. Teachers and TAs in positions of authority may find this challenging. Another professor has pointed out that there may be problems on the opposite side of the equation: "if an AI gives students a brilliant thought and the teacher and TA decide to regrade, then there would be lots of difficulties." Since there might be room for interpretation in the questions students ask, one professor remarked: "This problem stems from the poor quality of the answer. I worry that the algorithm will react in some roundabout way." A second academic voiced concern about the potential for AI-based misinterpretation: "Misunderstandings and other problems can usually be solved with a face-to-face conversation. I do not think a machine will ever be able to do it. There is a risk that the students may be misinformed and confused."

6.4 Support

Aiding in an online classroom means that the teacher is in charge of the learning process for the students and is making sure that they are getting what they need. AI systems will be capable of providing personalized and timely support to a large number of students in the future, but both students and teachers worry that too much support might undermine students' agency and control over their education. Many students feel that AI will make it easier to get individualized instruction, especially in group settings. All the interviewed students agreed that AI has the potential to help them focus on what they do, especially in student-led activities like group projects and independent study. Some students opined that adaptive technology might make learning more efficient by allowing them to concentrate and improve their weaker areas of knowledge. A student who was asked about the Adaptive Quiz system's potential as a source of advice, replied: "I believe that being able to take quizzes is motivating and guiding for me, and I think it would be beneficial for my learning." A second student liked having an AI's 'Group Project Organizer' as a mentor, by his side. Students believed that they would then have more time to devote to essential project-related activities like researching, writing, and submitting their work on time. Many educators hold the view that AI might be used to provide pupils with timely, individualized help. A professor observed, "one of the most effective learning tactics is to be presented immediately with the proper answer or the suitable means to discover the correct answer," which is especially helpful while taking quizzes and completing projects. An AI-based solution for adaptive assessments and intelligent suggestions has received rave reviews from several educators. All the teachers were happy to hear that AI might help pupils keep up with their studies and quickly identify any gaps in their knowledge, especially while they were absent. Two educators saw the potential for AI to help students who want to learn at their own pace. For example, in an online synchronous learning setting where students may not be in the same time zone, the availability of instantaneous responses from AI systems might increase student engagement.

6.5 Agency

Despite their excitement about the support that AI may give, students are worried that standardized help would hamper their capacity to learn independently. For instance, one student worryingly stated, "over-standardizing the educational process would result in using only the standardized tools. Gathering data on students' involvement would eventually dictate students' behaviour, and an engaged student would start exhibiting a standardized demeanour over time." While learning should include "discovering yourself and proceeding at your own pace," he said that instruction provided by an AI may arbitrarily boost a student's learning speed. Several students expressed apprehension regarding the probable consequences of a tool such as the Group Project Organizer powered by AI, citing concerns that they might not be as dedicated to their group assignments if the decision-making authority was held by an artificial intelligence system. Another student voiced concern that AI would reduce the importance of hands-on learning. It lulls them into a sense of complacency because they grow accustomed to working with an AI assistant and are thus ill-equipped to handle challenges when they ascend into the real world. To put it plainly, they will be unprepared. Instructors share students' concerns that too much reliance on AI might stifle students' curiosity and prevent them from learning on their own. There was worry among educators that students would not have the chance to develop their talents and grow from their failures. A professor said that she would like not to have all of her students working on the same kind of project and that the AI Group Project Organizer would prevent her from doing so. Others in the teaching community, especially those in the humanities, have voiced similar concerns, pointing out that students' final projects can vary widely while still being of high quality, and that giving students advice based on historical data could steer them in a particular direction, potentially stifling their creativity. A professor said that he does not like to show students their old assignments because he thinks it kills their ability to think outside the box. A professor had an important question after seeing the AI-powered storyboards: "At what point is it students' work and at what point is it the AI's algorithm?".

6.6 Connection

'Presence' is a feature of online classrooms that allows teachers and students to be aware of one another and collaborate effectively. Both students and educators expect AI technologies to increase their sense of connectedness while decreasing the risk of privacy issues. Students speculate that AI might alleviate learner-instructor interactions by passing on social interaction signals without using camera data, hence protecting students' privacy. Numerous students have expressed their reluctance to activate their cameras during online lectures, citing concerns about appearing disheveled, being in casual clothing or feeling too exposed. According to one student, filming oneself induces self-awareness and anxiety, which can impede the ability to engage with course content. To overcome these challenges, students have shown a preference for using AI-driven virtual avatars that convey emotions and body language to instructors. They believe that virtual avatars enable them to exhibit a broader range of emotions and convey confusion or understanding without feeling intrusive, making at-home studying more comfortable. One student expressed optimism about AI systems, stating that virtual avatars offer a solution to the problem of avoiding exposure while still conveying sentiments to instructors. Teachers will be able to meet the needs of their students more effectively with the help of AI, proponents say. Many educators, especially those who have taught at the university level, claim that students frequently turn off their cameras in online learning situations, making it hard for professors to detect their body language. One educator praised the potential of AI Facial Analytics to scan pupils' faces automatically to evaluate whether they understand the information being taught. A second professor agreed, saying that it was hard to detect whether students were paying attention, particularly when she was making a joke, and that an avatar may help. A professor also stressed that activating the camera could prove advantageous for both the instructor and the pupils as it is highly probable that the students would engage in other activities if the camera remained off. The capacity of AI to deliver critical data on students' performance and students' sentiments in online classes was widely praised by educators.

6.7 Surveillance

While technologies like AI have the potential to improve communication between lecturers and their students, the evaluation of non-conscious behaviors like eye tracking and facial expression analysis has the opposite effect, making students feel as if they are under surveillance. Students who took part in this study unanimously reported feeling uneasy about having their unauthorized eye movements recorded. "I become anxious when it comes to taking and passing tests or other similar quizzes and assignments. I could be worried that I cheated unintentionally", one student stated. Another student conveyed feeling heightened levels of anxiety when interacting with educators either through electronic mail or in person due to apprehensions about the potential evaluation of his subconscious actions prior to receiving feedback. A majority of students are uneasy with facial analysis utilizing AI. Because an individual's facial expressions are "something that takes place which may be outside of one's influence," a student is concerned that AI could disregard the intricacies of authentic human emotions in favor of generalizations that could result in greater confusion. Despite the benefits, students have voiced concerns about using AI for assessing unconscious behavior. Using AI interpretation to analyze students' social indicators has been criticized by many teachers. Since not all students are comfortable providing personal information to teachers, all educators were wary of using AI to detect students' eye movements and facial expressions. One educator worried that students would start smiling more in online classes if they knew that doing so would increase their engagement scores generated by AI Facial Analytics. Several educators have expressed strong opposition to using AI-based tools that monitor online students' eye movements and analyze their facial expressions. One educator expressed his preference for avoiding reliance on AI by maintaining face-to-face interactions with his students. A number of educators also expressed doubt that the data accurately reflected students' responses to course material as opposed to extraneous environmental stimuli, citing a lack of time and/or technical resources. It is anticipated that the implementation of AI technology will enhance the level of interaction between instructors and learners in web-based education by amplifying the quantity and caliber of communication, providing customized and timely assistance to students on a large scale, and heightening the sense of belonging among students. Despite this, both students and instructors were worried that AI systems would violate social boundaries in online education, leading to problems with accountability, agency, and surveillance.

7 Analysis and Conclusion

In this research, we intended to explore how both students and teachers feel AI systems have altered their face-to-face and virtual classroom experiences in terms of communication, assistance, and instructor presence. Even while there is a growing amount of AIEd research exploring the beneficial features of AI systems, not much has been done to understand the worries of students and teachers. Recent developments in the field of AI in online education have shown how haphazard use may lead to disturbing privacy and surveillance implications for students. The results of this investigation showed that both educators and their pupils see AI systems as having positive and negative effects. Although AI systems were praised for enhancing communication by providing personalized assistance to a large number of students in a timely and efficient manner, improving the sense of connection, and elevating the overall quality of communication, concerns remained regarding the issues of accountability, autonomy, and surveillance. The presence of AI systems has resulted in many of the desirable qualities that students and teachers find objectionable. Teachers and students alike have praised AI for its efficient communication, but they have also voiced concerns about the potential for dishonesty and misinterpretation while dealing with AI. Both teachers and students appreciated AI's tailored, on-demand support, but many were concerned it might impede their capacity for autonomous learning. However, they fret over the AI's intrusive data collection, which they fear will compromise their privacy. The social signals that AI gave for student and teacher participation were well received. This study has presented several opportunities to determine the points at which AI systems can be considered intrusive. Although AI systems have enhanced communication between students and teachers by enabling users to remain anonymous, some students have raised concerns about accountability when the AI's erroneous and unexplained responses lead to negative outcomes. Due to the opaque nature of AI systems, students have no means of verifying the accuracy of the responses they receive from an AI Teaching Assistant, and they perceive it as difficult to comprehend the reasoning behind the AI's response. There could be serious assessment and evaluation implications if students use AI-generated answers on exams and their professors mistakenly mark them as incorrect. Since AI is inherently unreliable, students would have more leeway to challenge their grades. Realizing that AI systems do not always get things right, it could be feasible to get around this by making the system more explicable. The capacity of an AI to provide human-understandable explanations for its results or procedures is known as 'explainability.' The ability to explain the reasoning behind an AI's answer empowers students to evaluate the accuracy of the system on their own, which may increase the system's credibility and transparency. In order for students to have faith in and embrace AI systems, they must be explicable. It would be quite interesting to look at how to make sure that AI systems can be explained in the context of online education. AI systems should not provide students with incorrect answers that could confuse or mislead them, but rather point them in the direction of credible, independently-accessible sources of information. Second, even though AI systems can be tailored to the needs of each individual student, they run the risk of standardizing the learning process too much by dictating what a motivated student must or must not do. Although students welcome whatever help they may obtain from AI systems, many are wary of the pre-packaged, standardized support it provides for fear that it would diminish their control over their own education. Educators share the apprehensions of students regarding the potential drawbacks of excessive reliance on AI systems, as it could potentially hinder students' capacity for self-directed learning. They are concerned that learners might not have the opportunity to hone their abilities and learn from their errors. Rather than limiting students' autonomy by imposing standardized approaches, AI technology should be leveraged to enhance human reasoning and accelerate the learning process in online education. To create an effective learning environment, AI systems should work in conjunction with human facilitators, including teachers and peers. With a mix of human and AI tutoring systems, it is possible to bring harmony between the two kinds. While AI systems excel at quickly analyzing big datasets, they often falter when presented with novel or complex problems. Humans are versatile and smart, but AI systems can process information quickly and accurately. Humans learn more effectively and efficiently when they are involved in decision-making. If we want our online learners to feel safe and in charge, we need to keep a human-teacher in loop. Studying how to combine human intelligence and AI to encourage student independence is important. It is possible that AI systems may be seen as 'invasive' if they begin to make judgments about social interaction based on unconscious behavior. Students worried about the impression they were giving since they had no idea what their expressions and gazes were like. Regulating and monitoring facial recognition is problematic and racist. Several learners voiced displeasure with the AI system's depiction of their presence. The educators expressed similar feelings regarding the function of the AI system in assessing the significance of students' activities. It is imperative that clear and unambiguous data regulations and agreements be established, delineating the nature of data collection from students and the kinds of data that can be accessed by instructors. This should be an area of emphasis in upcoming research. More research on various AI systems is possible and much needed. After that, the viewpoints of AI systems among educators and their students may be gathered across several academic disciplines. We included participants from a wide variety of majors and fields of study. Even while this enabled us to generalize our findings from people of varied backgrounds, further research into how students and teachers from other disciplines see AI systems might be fruitful. Our research found anecdotally that humanities-based teachers cared more about their students' connections with them and their creativity in class than did instructors from engineering and pure science disciplines. The research had another flaw in that it was performed through reading storyboards rather than having participants interact with actual AI systems. Therefore, it is possible that the participants' perspectives on AI systems were narrowed as a result. Participants' perspectives may shift if they are exposed to AI systems on a regular basis in the actual world. Studies on the effects of AI on pupils' behavior should be carried out in the future. Longitudinal studies would help determine if and how student attitudes shift over time. The findings of this study may prove useful in the classroom and in the real world. Most unfavorable experiences with AI systems may be traced back to student misconceptions and unreasonable expectations.

Even though the AI system is only an algorithm trained on collected data, students often assume that its result would be absolutely and completely true. These misunderstandings might prevent both students and teachers from making effective use of AI. Therefore, it is essential to raise AI literacy levels among non-technical students and teachers in order to address this challenge. Studies have recently released how-to guides on incorporating AI into K-12 curriculum, and researchers are looking at ways to get young children involved in creative programming activities including AI. Resolving disputes when AI systems break the boundaries between students and instructors is also crucial for mitigating the negative consequences of these technologies on learner-instructor interaction. Our suggestion is that in the future, AI systems should be designed to ensure that their actions can be explained by humans, that human input can be solicited, and that data is collected and presented meticulously. This will allow for a more seamless integration of AI technologies into future iterations of online learning. Because of the inevitably tight collaboration between AI systems and humans in the future of online learning, it is crucial to implement such systems while keeping in mind their obvious benefits and limitations.

References

1. Alam, A.: Challenges and possibilities in teaching and learning of calculus: a case study of India. J. Educ. Gifted Young Sci. **8**(1), 407–433 (2020)
2. Franzoni, V., Milani, A., Mengoni, P., Piccinato, F.: Artificial intelligence visual metaphors in e-learning interfaces for learning analytics. Appl. Sci. **10**(20), 7195 (2020)
3. Alam, A.: Pedagogy of calculus in India: an empirical investigation. Periódico Tchê Química **17**(34), 164–180 (2020)
4. Raj, N.S., Renumol, V.G.: Early prediction of student engagement in virtual learning environments using machine learning techniques. E-Learn. Digit. Media **19**(6), 537–554 (2022). https://doi.org/10.1177/20427530221108027
5. Alam, A.: Possibilities and challenges of compounding artificial intelligence in India's educational landscape. Int. J. Adv. Sci. Technol. **29**(5), 5077–5094 (2020)
6. Bagunaid, W., Chilamkurti, N., Veeraraghavan, P.: AISAR: artificial intelligence-based student assessment and recommendation system for E-learning in big data. Sustainability **14**(17), 10551 (2022)
7. Alam, A.: Test of knowledge of elementary vectors concepts (TKEVC) among first-semester bachelor of engineering and technology students. Periódico Tchê Química **17**(35), 477–494 (2020)
8. Alam, A.: Should robots replace teachers? Mobilisation of AI and learning analytics in education. In: 2021 International Conference on Advances in Computing, Communication, and Control (ICAC3), pp. 1–12. IEEE (2021)
9. Ayouni, S., Hajjej, F., Maddeh, M., Al-Otaibi, S.: A new ML-based approach to enhance student engagement in online environment. PLoS ONE **16**(11), e0258788 (2021)
10. Alam, A.: Possibilities and apprehensions in the landscape of artificial intelligence in education. In: 2021 International Conference on Computational Intelligence and Computing Applications (ICCICA), pp. 1–8. IEEE (2021)
11. Alam, A.: Educational robotics and computer programming in early childhood education: a conceptual framework for assessing elementary school students' computational thinking for designing powerful educational scenarios. In: 2022 International Conference on Smart Technologies and Systems for Next Generation Computing (ICSTSN), pp. 1–7. IEEE (2022)

12. Yin, W.: An artificial intelligent virtual reality interactive model for distance education. J. Math. **2022**, 7099963 (2022)
13. Alam, A.: A digital game based learning approach for effective curriculum transaction for teaching-learning of artificial intelligence and machine learning. In: 2022 International Conference on Sustainable Computing and Data Communication Systems (ICSCDS), pp. 69–74. IEEE (2022)
14. Alam, A.: Investigating sustainable education and positive psychology interventions in schools towards achievement of sustainable happiness and wellbeing for 21st century pedagogy and curriculum. ECS Trans. **107**(1), 19481 (2022)
15. Schiff, D.: Out of the laboratory and into the classroom: the future of artificial intelligence in education. AI Soc. **36**(1), 331–348 (2020). https://doi.org/10.1007/s00146-020-01033-8
16. Alam, A.: Social robots in education for long-term human-robot interaction: socially supportive behaviour of robotic tutor for creating robo-tangible learning environment in a guided discovery learning interaction. ECS Trans. **107**(1), 12389 (2022)
17. Greenhow, C., Graham, C.R., Koehler, M.J.: Foundations of online learning: challenges and opportunities. Educ. Psychol. **57**(3), 131–147 (2022)
18. Alam, A.: Positive psychology goes to school: conceptualizing students' happiness in 21st century schools while 'minding the mind!' Are we there yet? Evidence-backed, school-based positive psychology interventions. ECS Trans. **107**(1), 11199 (2022)
19. Yildirim, Y., Celepcikay, A.: Artificial intelligence and machine learning applications in education. Eurasian J. High. Educ. **2**(4), 1–11 (2021)
20. Alam, A.: Mapping a sustainable future through conceptualization of transformative learning framework, education for sustainable development, critical reflection, and responsible citizenship: an exploration of pedagogies for twenty-first century learning. ECS Trans. **107**(1), 9827 (2022)
21. Chung, Y., Kim, J.R.: Is artificial intelligence (AI) lecturer acceptable for adult learners in distance education?: An exploratory study on a cyber university, South Korea (2020)
22. Alam, A.: Employing adaptive learning and intelligent tutoring robots for virtual classrooms and smart campuses: reforming education in the age of artificial intelligence. In: Shaw, R.N., Das, S., Piuri, V., Bianchini, M. (eds.) Advanced Computing and Intelligent Technologies, vol. 914, pp. 395–406. Springer, Singapore (2022). https://doi.org/10.1007/978-981-19-2980-9_32
23. Greener, S.: The tensions of student engagement with technology. Interact. Learn. Environ. **30**(3), 397–399 (2022)
24. Alam, A.: Cloud-based E-learning: scaffolding the environment for adaptive E-learning ecosystem based on cloud computing infrastructure. In: Satapathy, S.C., Lin, J.C.W., Wee, L.K., Bhateja, V., Rajesh, T.M. (eds.) Computer Communication, Networking and IoT, vol. 459, pp. 1–9. Springer, Singapore (2023). https://doi.org/10.1007/978-981-19-1976-3_1

Vehicular Technology and Applications

Real Time Connectivity Analysis of Vehicles in Different City Dense Environment

Mayank Sharma$^{(\boxtimes)}$, Ranjeet Singh Tomar, Bhupendra Dhakad,
Shailendra Singh Ojha, and Sadhana Mishra

ITM University Gwalior, Gwalior, India
{mayanksharma.ec,ranjeetsingh,bhupendradhakad.ece,
Shailendraojha.ec,sadhanamishra.ec}@itmuniversity.ac.in

Abstract. Today, wireless communication systems play a significant role in our
daily lives. Cellular mobile networks have been helping billions of people all over
the world with this wireless technology. Vehicle ad hoc networks (VANETs) are
gaining popularity because it is based on dynamic in nature. Many simulators
software programs to permit simulation of routing and media access protocols.
Additionally, Vehicular Ad Hoc Networks (VANETs) presented safety and security
risks to users as well as monolithic advantages in traffic safety. Verifying new
safety technique to address this issue is stimulating. Simulates the application
level of security and privacy issues in VANET by using an event-driven simulation
platform. A VANET simulator has a small message size and a limited time value.
A method is presented in this paper through which RSU will be used for different
city paths and the communication range of vehicles will be measured. Using RSU
along different routes through a city, this paper proposes a method for measuring
vehicle communication range. We distribute RSU into clusters in this case. This
work proposes a concept that is based on safety. Examine three city maps on the
basis of some key factor like current time, throughput, average speed, average
travel time, and average travel distance. For security purpose we have measured
the post-crash notification with time.

Keywords: Vehicular Ad hoc Network (VANET) · Road Side Unit (RSU) ·
VANETsim · OSM

1 Introduction

VANET is a network of moving vehicle on the road. In VANET, vehicles are equipped
with communication devices, processors, micro controller along with the sensors and
global positioning system. Integration of these devices enables vehicles to communicate
with each other's as well as road side units known as RSUs. These RSUs placed at a
fixed optimal place. The RSUs are connected to backbone network to support many
other network application and services like internet access and portal-based services.
Communication between vehicles is known as inter-vehicle communication (IVC or
V2V) and communication between vehicles and road side unit is known as vehicle-to-
roadside communication (V2R).

© The Author(s), under exclusive license to Springer Nature Switzerland AG 2023
R. S. Tomar et al. (Eds.): CNC 2022, CCIS 1894, pp. 269–278, 2023.
https://doi.org/10.1007/978-3-031-43145-6_22

A vehicle to everything (V2X) communication system is at the top of the vehicular communication system hierarchy. A connected car is not a new concept, but it took a few years for the automotive industry to have the technology and communication standards to make it possible. The goal of connecting vehicles with the surrounding world can be achieved through the use of a broader set of communication technologies known as V2X. Literally.

Similar to communication itself, V2X technologies are constantly evolving and adapting to meet emerging challenges, so it should not be regarded as static technologies. In this respect, every subcategory has its own concerns, strengths, and weaknesses. A powerful feature of V2X is that it makes the whole greater than the sum of the parts by taking advantage of the synergy between the various technologies.

There are no widely available criteria or specifications for higher level communications at the moment, although car manufacturers and research institutes are already testing and improving communication links. Researchers must therefore rely on abstract modeling and simulations to evaluate their proposals for improving traffic security and privacy.

2 Problem Description

A simulation engine is based on specifically on the distinctive characteristics of VANETs will be useful in future research areas. Research community proposals on security and privacy are easily incorporated. The privacy and security aspects of VANETs are not adequately modelled in any simulator to our knowledge. Virtualized networks are a vital topic of research in VANETs generally, and existing simulators typically focus on a network layer simulation. Security threats that exploit the specific characteristics of the vehicular setting originate at the application layer, even though VANETs inherit the security issues of other wireless networks. The purpose of this simulator is to simulate application layer protocols [1, 9].

VANET's unique requirements must be verified by a MAC protocol. There are several peculiar characteristics that characterize a VANET in a situation where vehicles are highly mobile, roadside infrastructure is half supported. Speed is determined by a predefine road path, small parts of vehicles are autonomous of the predefined network within the RSU area, and dangerous messages must be delivered in a timely manner. The several number of vehicle in RSU area can modtfy from a small amount to a large amount. Vehicles stay in RSU areas for a very short amount of time. To satisfy these characteristics, a protocol needs to be identified or requires some RSU support with efficient hand-offs from one road side unit to another. In wireless communication, the connection is delayed because the data is being transmitted over a shared wireless channel [1, 9].

2.1 VANET Scenario

Essentially, VANETsim is the first and foremost simulation tool that analyzes and counteracts security threats at the application level. Because VANETsim provides top-level access to all similar data structures, it can easily deal with new attacks as well. With an efficient Graphical User Interface, the simulation process can be visualized intuitively, and a lightweight terminal interface can also be experimented with to debug the simulation [1, 9].

2.2 VANETsim Overview

An example of an event-driven simulator is VANETsim. It is designed specifically for vehicular communication. Using vehicular communication will reduce transport impairments in a smart city scheme. The main purpose of Venetism is to provide security and privacy for vehicular networks. Using the Post Processing Engine, the simulation core embeds the topology devices supporting the infrastructure and the privacy and security modules that assure the GUI of the network's security [1, 9].

3 Performance Evaluation

In developing VANETsim, high performance on off-the-shelf hardware is a central goal. Our Open Street Map (OSM) solution allows us to show different routes as well as self-created tracks by using different cities. There are different lengths and capacities for vehicles in different cities or paths. Using VANETsim, the beacon interval message is set to 240 ms, the range of each vehicle is set to 100 m, and the simulation step is every 40 ms. As soon as the vehicle configuration changes, the traffic situation changes as well. Two open street maps need to be used; both are self-designed open street map. A simulation of this scenario is conducted by using VANET simulator, which also takes three different paths and makes different measurements and predictions, according to the active vehicle, current time, speed, average travel distance, and post-crash notifications, as well as correct analysis of different roadside maps based on throughput and delay parameters. A simulation run lasts 10,000,000 ms. As a result of this analysis, we find the average distance time, average travel distance, active vehicle, current speed, simulation time, as well as the post-crash warning [1, 9].

4 Results and Discussion

Using VANET simulator, we created the scenario shown in Figs. 1 and Fig. 2. The simulation included 500 vehicles, and we obtained results about the active vehicle, the active travel distance, and the post-crash notification, throughput.

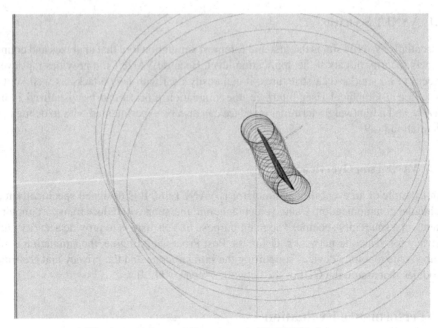

Fig. 1. Vehicle's mobility pattern in VANET Environment

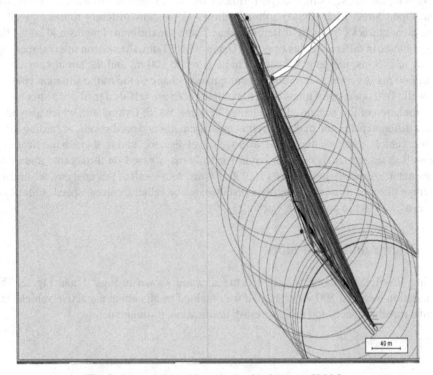

Fig. 2. Movement and interconnection between Vehicles

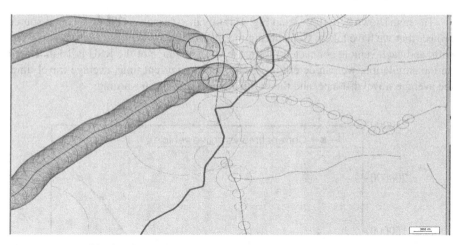

Fig. 3. Vehicle Mobility on Different Road Paths in the City

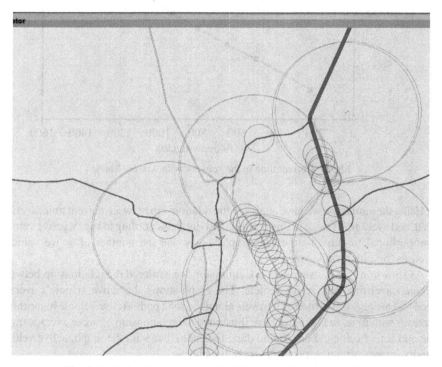

Fig. 4. Vehicles Connectivity with RSU during Travelling on Road

The map shown here (Fig. 3 and Fig. 4) is city map scenario. OSM is an open-source project that we have taken. Considering the map size, only vehicles can run along this path, and each vehicle connected through RSU. The range of the RSU is 1 km. Based on the simulation, we can determine active vehicle, current time, average travel time, the average travel distance, and the notification of post-crash warning.

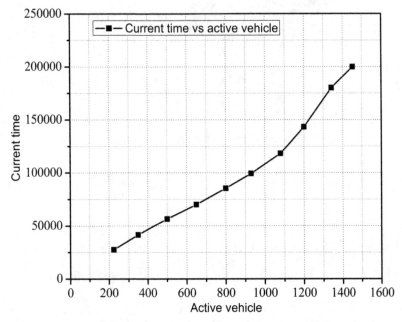

Fig. 5. Current time in the network with Active Vehicle

Using the simulator, we have analyzed the relationship between current time, average speed, and average distance in Fig. 5, Fig. 6 and Fig. 7. According to Fig. 5, active vehicle is proportional to current time The graph shows that the number of active vehicles increases logarithmically over time.

As shown in Fig. 5, using network simulator, we explored the relationship between average travel time and active vehicle. The graph shows the active vehicle's average speed and average travel time as it travels along the road path. Active vehicle logarithmic increases with time. In Fig. 6, we have illustrated the relationship between average travel time and active vehicle. For specific data. In accordance with the graph, active vehicle initially increases with respect to average travel time.

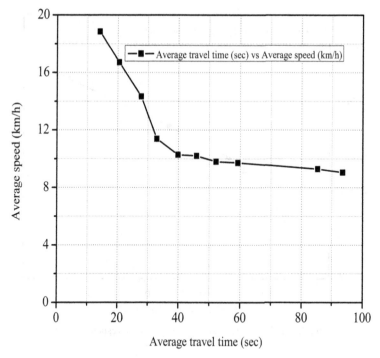

Fig. 6. Vehicle speed analysis with respect to time

As shown in Fig. 6. Using the network simulator, we have described the relationship between travel speed and travel time. An average speed and average travel time are shown in this graph for the active vehicle traveling along the track. As a analysis, average travel time increases while average vehicle speed decreases logarithmically. As shown in Fig. 6 Here, we show the connection between time and speed. There are several active vehicles moving in a network to travel distance, graph is indicated the travel time and speed for particular data set. After some time, average travel speed becomes decreases and constant with respect to average travel time as shown in the Fig. 6.

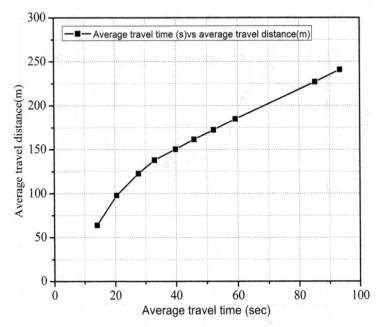

Fig. 7. Vehicle travel distance analysis with respect to time

As shown in Fig. 7, the graph shows the connection between travel distance and current time. According to Fig. 7 vehicle average distance increases logarithmically with time.

As shown in Fig. 8, we have explained the relation between post-crash notifications and current time, implying that some vehicles are involved in accidents or communications are impaired. According to the graph, post-crash notifications increase logarithmically with respect to current time.

In Fig. 9, We have analyzed the connection between throughput and average travel distance during the vehicle's connectivity.

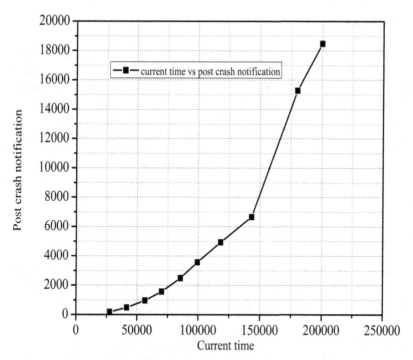

Fig. 8. Vehicle Post-crash information with current time

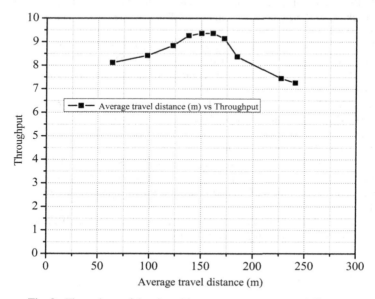

Fig. 9. Throughput of the city with respect to average travel distance

5 Conclusion

The paper presents a communication system based on vehicle connectivity for road traffic safety using simulator. With this simulator, we can analyze privacy, security, and safety issues within transportation systems. In order to run the vehicles and analyze the results, we used VANETsim to simulate many different paths and streets. We compared the paths taken by the simulator and noted the differences between them. As a result of this analysis, we have a better understanding of the safety concerns associated with transportation communication systems. Moreover, we have explored how these systems may be used to improve transportation safety and security. We believe that our work has shown that VANETsim is a valuable tool for understanding the complexities of communication technique for road safety.

References

1. Tomar, R.S., Sharma, M.S., Jha, S., Sharma, B.: Vehicles connectivity-based communication systems for road transportation safety. In: Ray, K., Sharma, T., Rawat, S., Saini, R., Bandyopadhyay, A. (eds.) Soft Computing: Theories and Applications. AISC, vol. 742, pp. 483–492. Springer, Singapore (2019). https://doi.org/10.1007/978-981-13-0589-4_45
2. Moreno, M.T., Jiang, D., Hartenstein, H.: Broadcast reception rates and effects of priority access in 802.11-based vehicular Ad-hoc networks. IEEE Trans. Veh. Technol. **61**, 1 (2012)
3. Peng, J., Cheng, L.: A distributed MAC scheme for emergency message dissemination in vehicular ad hoc networks. IEEE Trans. Veh. Technol. **56**(6), 3300–3308 (2007)
4. Yu, F., Biswas, S.: Self-configuring TDMA protocol for enhancing vehicle safety with DSRC based vehicle-to-vehicle communications. IEEE J. Sel. Areas Commun. **25**(8), 1526–1537 (2007)
5. Williams, B., Mehta, D., Camp, T., Navidi, W.: Predictive models to rebroadcast in mobile ad hoc networks. IEEE Trans. Mob. Comput. **3**(3), 295–303 (2004)
6. Zhang, H., Jiang, Z.-P.: Modeling and performance analysis of ad hoc broadcasting scheme. Perform. Eval. **63**(12), 1196–1215 (2006)
7. Fracchia, R., Meo, M.: Analysis and design of warning delivery service in inter-vehicular networks. IEEE Trans. Mob. Comput. **7**(7), 832–845 (2008)
8. Ma, X., Chen, X.: Saturation performance of the IEEE 802.11 broadcast networks. IEEE Commun. Lett. **11**(8), 686–688 (2007)
9. Tomandl, A., Herrmann, D., Fuchs, K.P., Federrath, H., Scheuer, F.: VANETsim: an open source simulator for security and privacy concepts in VANETs. In: 2014 International Conference on High Performance Computing & Simulation (HPCS), 21 July 2014, pp. 543–550. IEEE (2014)
10. Lou, W., Wu, J.: Toward broadcast reliability in mobile Ad hoc networks with double coverage. IEEE Trans. Mob. Comput. **6**(2), 148–163 (2007)

Design and Analysis of Energy Efficient Wireless Senor Network with 6LoWPAN IoT Gateway

Sadhana Mishra[✉], Ranjeet Singh Tomar, Bhupendra Dhakad, Shyam Akashe, Mayank Sharma, and Shailendra Singh Ojha

ITM University Gwalior, Gwalior, MP, India
{sadhanamishra.ec,ranjeetsingh,bhupendradhakad.ece,shyam.akashe,
mayanksharma.ec,shailendraojha.ec}@itmuniversity.ac.in

Abstract. Internet of Things (IoT) is an emerging paradigm in the interdisciplinary field of technologies. Integration of IoT with Wireless Sensor Network is playing a great role to not only to enhance the society demands but for defense and surveillance. With increase in IoT devices there is a greater demand of self-powered devices so Energy Harvesting techniques are required with rapid rate. In this proposed work, the effect of Energy Harvesting and 6 LowPAN IoT Gateway is analyzed for Wireless Sensor Network. NetSim WSN module and 6LowPAN IoT Gateway are considered in this work to illustrate the effect of Energy Harvesting on WSN with varying number of sensor nodes. Different performance parameters are expressed and extensive simulation results are drawn to show the effectiveness of the network with and without 6LoWPAN IoT Gateway in the proposed system. In this paper, a simulation framework of WSN is proposed which is based on NetSim Version 9.0 simulator. This framework can be used to investigate and evaluate the impact of energy harvesting on the proposed system with 6LowPAN IoT Gateway. This work also demonstrates some important sensor network parameters such as packet transmitted, payload transmitted, and overhead transmitted. Individual Link throughputs and application throughputs are also demonstrated by enabling the real-time trace in NetSim.

Keywords: Energy Harvesting · 6LowPAN IoT Gateway · Wireless Sensor Network · Network Simulator

1 Introduction

Integration of Internet of Things (IoT) with Wireless Sensor Network (WSN) is an area of research which is demanding nowadays as real-time remote monitoring and controlling of the parameters is provided by the IoT supported module/devices in a wireless sensor network. In WSN, sensor nodes demand a huge amount of wireless energy to extend their lifetime. It's a challenging task for wireless sensor nodes that they remain charged for a long time because most of the sensor motes are battery operated and as battery goes down either the battery should be charged or replaced. Due to circumstances like forest, mines seas it's not possible to replace the battery of a sensor node so there is a great need

© The Author(s), under exclusive license to Springer Nature Switzerland AG 2023
R. S. Tomar et al. (Eds.): CNC 2022, CCIS 1894, pp. 279–290, 2023.
https://doi.org/10.1007/978-3-031-43145-6_23

of wireless energy harvesting techniques for practical implementation. A generalized framework of WSN is represented in Fig. 1 where some of the nodes are transmitting nodes and some are receiving and others are base stations which are represented with PU1 and PU2. Different scenarios can be drawn based on the proposed system architecture.

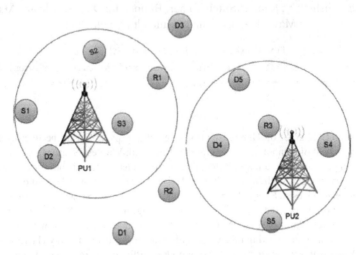

Fig. 1. A generalized Sensor Network consisting of different Users [7]

In Fig. 2 different IEEE standards with different network topologies are shown. WSN follows the IEEE standard of 802.15.4 which is basically for personal area network. WSN mostly implemented with ZigBee communication technology it also supports other communication technologies such as Z-Wave, SigFox etc. for wireless communication.

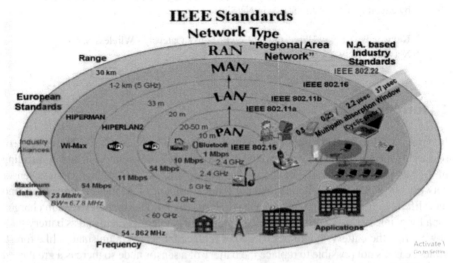

Fig. 2. Different IEEE standards for different Networks with frequency bands [9]

Energy Harvesting is essential technique to power battery operated IoT devices authors in [1, 2] have discussed the tools, techniques and implementation issues along with future challenges faced by Energy Harvesting techniques to implement IoT applications or to deploy IoT systems [12]. Further, authors in [3–6] presented the cognitive radio concepts along with relay selection to improve the spectrum efficiency of the cognitive radio networks which comes under Wireless Regional Area Networks (WRAN) demonstrated in Fig. 2. Moreover, two way relay channel analysis is discussed and simulation results are presented in [8] to show the better performance with the proposed two way Gaussian relaying for optimal resource allocation.

2 Wireless Energy Harvesting and Implementation Techniques

Wireless energy harvesting is a challenging task in WSN and number of researches have presented number of techniques for wireless energy harvesting. Other energy harvesting can be achieved from different sources such as vibration, thermal, light, motion which has been implemented in the systems as well. RF energy harvesting is also a method to extend the lifetime of a battery-operated sensor nodes. Power management in WSN is another very important aspect, a wireless energy harvesting system of sensor mote generally consists of an antenna, a wireless energy harvesting unit, transceiver, power management unit, number of sensors, and onboard battery. The amount of harvested power is directly proportional to some important parameters like transmitted power, path loss, antenna gain both transmit and receive and inversely proportional to the distance between source and destination nodes. Mainly, the energy consumption involves the receiving energy, listening energy of a sensor node, transmitting energy, processing energy and sensing energy. In WSN, IEEE802.15.4 ZigBee communication protocol is utilized for short range communication among wireless sensor motes which are distributed randomly in a specific geographic area. The sink node or personal area network coordinator node can be configured with super frame and beacon frames. In NETSIM 2.4 GHz frequency band and 5 MHz bandwidth is used. Single channel is supported and it does not support multiple channels. Data rate is defined as the number of bits processed in unit time it is 250 kbps for personal area networks. Reliability of the system is directly affected by the amount of transmitted power. Power can be main line or battery when battery is power source then range is 0–1 mA in simulations. Energy is derived from external sources such as light, thermal etc. and is captured and stored. Battery energy is 0–1000 mW in simulations. Ideal mode current range is 0–20 mA. Voltage is 0–10 V, sleep mode current is 0–20 mA.

2.1 Role of Performance Parameters in the Proposed System

In this sub-section network performance parameters such as link throughput, application throughput, average throughput, average spectral efficiency, lifetime of a sensor node, energy efficiency, delay will be discussed. Performance parameters are very important metrics for any kind of system with these parameters performance at every layer can be visualized and analyzed and then some important decisions can be drawn based on the every layer performance. Delay is defined as a average time required to transmit/receive all the packets in the system, whereas lifetime of a sensor node is for how much duration the sensor node can survive in the system. Similarly, other parameter link throughput is the total number of bytes successfully transmitted over the particular link. Average parameter is calculated by considering all the links/applications throughput of the wireless system.

3 Proposed System Model of Wireless Sensor Network with 6LoWPAN Gateway

This section presents the proposed system design of wireless sensor nodes with 6LoW-PAN Gateway. 6LoWPAN IoT Gateway is a networking device which is very appropriate choice in IoT systems for aggregating the sensor data from the surrounding sensor nodes in the system and the forwarding or relaying the aggregated data to a router or any other network. 6LoWPAN IoT Gateway is a device which works with low power for personal area network over IPv6 to connect to the internet. Sensors are connected wirelessly which are represented with wireless ad-hoc links. The considered network is assumed ad-hoc as it does not rely on any preexisting infrastructures. As shown if Fig. 3 total nine sensor nodes are distributed randomly in the scenario. IoT Gateway is placed to collect data from these sensors and further two routers and one access point is forwarding this sensor information into another network. Three applications are established among sensor nodes and another network. Total five types of links are created to connect each and every node in the system. Packet trace is enabled in the scenario of Fig. 9 so visualization of packets successful transmission/dropped can be noticed and can be recorded in the data sheet.

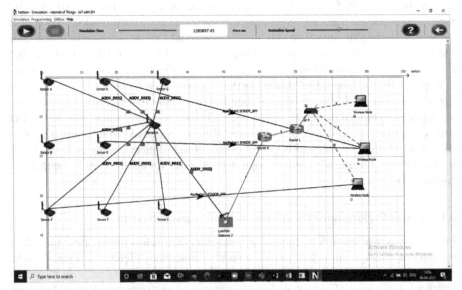

Fig. 3. Proposed Wireless Sensor Network Scenario with 9 Sensor Nodes by enabling the packet trace in the Netsim.

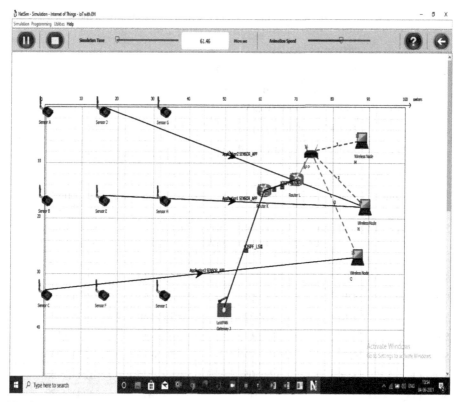

Fig. 4. Proposed Wireless Sensor Network Scenario with 9 Sensor Nodes and 6LoWPAN Gateway in the Netsim.

In Fig. 4 scenario energy harvesting parameter is turned on and off during simulation of the two cases. NETSIM has a power model which is dedicated for sensor nodes. This power model can be configured through users and can be in the ZigBee communication interface file.

4 Simulation Results and Discussion

This section presents simulation results of the considered scenarios and discuss the findings of this proposed work. Network Simulation parameters such as Simulation time, packets transmitted packets collided, payload transmitted, bytes transmitted are shown in Table 1.

Further, power model metrics without energy harvesting and with energy harvesting are illustrated in Table 2 and Table 3, respectively. In Table 2 total number of sensor nodes are nine which are represented with Sensor A, Sensor B, Sensor C, Sensor D, Sensor E, Sensor F, Sensor G, Sensor H, Sensor I. Total energy consumption is the sum of the transmitted energy, receive energy, idle energy and sleep energy in both the results of the power model metrics. Here, sleep energy is not shown in both the tables as it is zero in both the considered scenarios since sensor node is considered active all the time.

Table 1. Representation of the network metrics for the considered scenarios of the 9 sensor nodes

#Network Metrics
Simulation Time (ms) = 100000.00
Packets Transmitted = 28790
Packets Collided = 4833
Bytes Transmitted (Bytes) = 1223978.00
Payload Transmitted (Bytes) = 273060.00

Table 2. Illustration of the Power Model Metrics without Energy Harvesting

Sensor Node	Transmission Energy Consumed (mW)	Receiving Energy Consumed (mW)	Idle Energy Consumed (mW)	Total Energy Consumed (mW)
Sensor A	33.9421	19.6290	1165.5542	1219.1254
Sensor B	39.0549	22.2201	1162.7462	1224.0213
Sensor C	277.9904	21.7822	1073.2960	1373.0686
Sensor D	28.0145	17.6969	1168.4412	1214.1527
Sensor E	42.0927	30.1197	1158.8916	1231.1040
Sensor F	24.5336	17.6505	1169.7625	1211.9466
Sensor G	48.9370	39.3575	1153.1495	1241.4439
Sensor H	270.7774	252.8664	996.5656	1520.2095
Sensor I	272.3679	248.4637	997.4826	1518.3143

All the simulations are run for 100 s. Packet trace is turned on while simulation. 6LoWPAN Gateway properties are turned on for all the simulations. As the super frame order is kept equal to beacon order (assumed SO = BO = 10) so sleep energy consumption is zero. Further, by changing the super frame order and beacon order between 0–14 and rerunning the simulation can result in sleep energy consumption.

It is noticed from the Table 2 and Table 3 that the remaining energy is more as compared to without Energy Harvesting mode which ultimately extend the lifetime of sensor nodes so sensor node can survive for more time with Energy Harvesting approaches.

Figure 5 and Fig. 6 are demonstrating the link 1 and link 2 throughput with maximum throughput of 2.05 Mbps and minimum is zero whereas it is 0.624 Mbps and zero for link 2, respectively. Next, Fig. 7 and Fig. 8 are representing throughput of Sensor Application 1 and sensor Application 2, respectively. Though three applications are considered in the proposed system but only two are demonstrated here.

Table 3. Illustration of the Power Model Metrics with Energy Harvesting

Sensor Node	Transmission Energy Consumed (mW)	Receiving Energy Consumed (mW)	Idle Energy Consumed (mW)	Total Energy Consumed (mW)
Sensor A	23.1570	17.3165	1167.7800	1208.2535
Sensor B	1010.1015	94.9300	770.9962	1876.0276
Sensor C	28.8366	24.1378	1163.3053	1216.2797
Sensor D	22.1353	12.2304	1169.9115	1204.2771
Sensor E	1310.1736	22.7244	683.2898	2016.1878
Sensor F	8.1259	16.9117	1173.5558	1198.5934
Sensor G	42.4176	38.5236	1153.2673	1234.2085
Sensor H	241.9337	226.4128	1013.8619	1482.2084
Sensor I	243.3466	220.9429	1015.2123	1479.5018

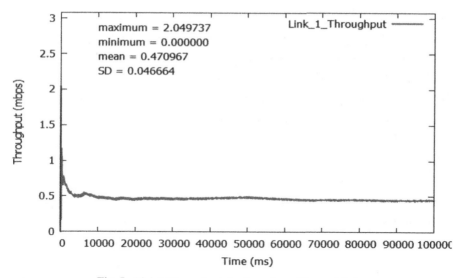

Fig. 5. Link 1 Throughput for 9 number of Sensor Nodes

Further, rest performance parameters such as payload transmitted is demonstrated in Fig. 9. It is noticed in the figure that the increase in number of sensor nodes results in increased payload. For one sensor node in the system payload transmitted is 110500 bytes whereas it is 5541680 with 15 number of sensor nodes considered in the system.

In Fig. 10 delay parameter in microsecond is graphically demonstrated with number of sensor nodes in the proposed system.

Further, Fig. 11 represents the average throughput of the proposed system in Mbps with varying number of sensor nodes which are one, five, ten and fifteen. Figure 12

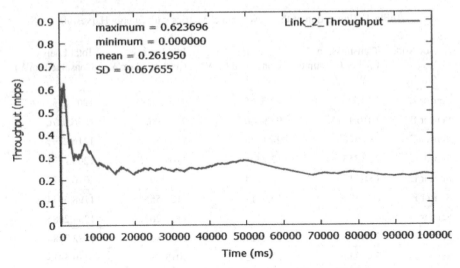

Fig. 6. Link 2 Throughput for 9 number of Sensor Nodes

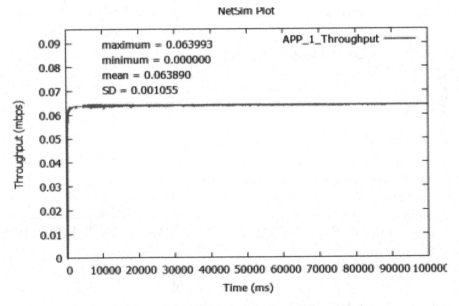

Fig. 7. Sensor APP_1 Throughput for 9_no of Sensor Nodes

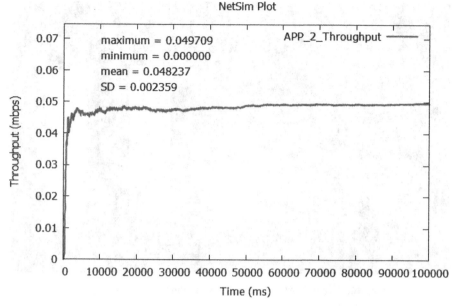

Fig. 8. Sensor APP_2 Throughput for 9_no of Sensor Nodes

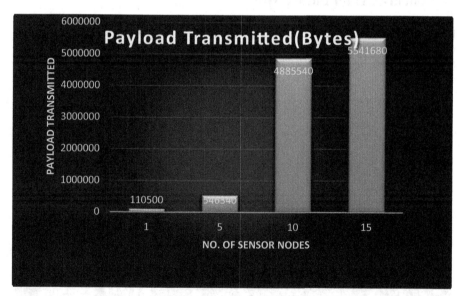

Fig. 9. Payload Transmitted verses Number of Sensor Nodes
demonstrating the spectral efficiency of the proposed system which is increasing with
the number of nodes in the system as more sensor nodes will utilize more spectrum
efficiently.

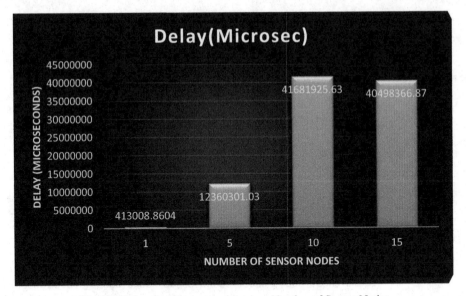

Fig. 10. Delay (in Microseconds) verses Number of Sensor Nodes

5   Conclusion and Future Work

In this work, performance of proposed Wireless Sensor Network with 6LoWPAN Gateway is analysed through simulation carried out using network and traffic simulator NetSim. Power model metrics of the proposed system is discussed with enabling Energy

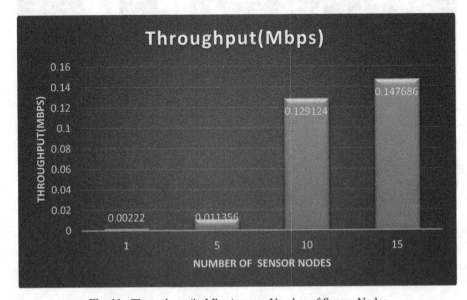

Fig. 11. Throughput (in Mbps) verses Number of Sensor Nodes

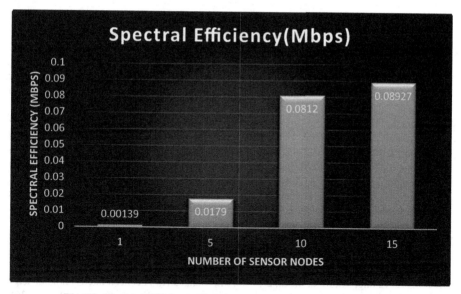

Fig. 12. Spectral Efficiency (in Mbps) verses Number of Sensor Nodes

Harvesting and without Energy Harvesting for the proposed system of WSN. Parameters of the proposed system such as payload transmitted, application throughput, link throughput, spectral efficiency, delay with varying number of sensor nodes are graphically plotted and discussed. It is observed through the results that increase in number of available sensor nodes increases the throughput and spectral efficiency because with this increase sensor noes are getting better opportunity to transmit/receive their sensor data. In future this work can be extended by implementing it with the IoT applications such as smart city, smart agriculture, smart healthcare by considering the sensor nodes and 6LoWPAN IoT Gateway.

Acknowledgments. I would like to acknowledge my family and friends who consistently motivate me to do my best in every field of my life. Most importantly, I gratitude my God Sai Ji for blessing us.

References

1. Kamalinejad, P., Mahapatra, C., Sheng, Z., Mirabbasi, S., Leung, V.C., Guan, Y.L.: Wireless energy harvesting for the Internet of Things. IEEE Commun. Mag. **53**(6), 102–108 (2015). Haykin, S. (2005)
2. Mysorewala, M.F., Cheded, L., Aliyu, A.: Review of energy harvesting techniques in wireless sensor-based pipeline monitoring networks. Renew. Sustain. Energy Rev. **157**, 112046 (2022)
3. Mishra, S., Trivedi, A.: Relay selection with channel allocation for cognitive radio relay channels in CRN. In: IEEE Eleventh International Conference on Wireless and Optical Communications Networks (WOCN), pp. 1–4 (2014)

4. Mishra, S., Trivedi, A.: Exploiting opportunistic decode-and-forward cooperation for cognitive radio relay channels in multi-antenna cognitive radio networks. In: IEEE International Conference on Advances in Computing, Communications and Informatics (ICACCI), pp. 155–158 (2013)
5. Li, L., Zhou, X., Xu, H., Li, G.Y., Wang, D., Soong, A.: Simplified relay selection and power allocation in cooperative cognitive radio systems. IEEE Trans. Wirel. Commun. 10(1), 33–36 (2011)
6. Mishra, S., Trivedi, A.: Performance study of MIMO transmissions with joint channel allocation and relay assignment. Wirel. Pers. Commun. (WPC) 96, 2651–2665 (2017). https://doi.org/10.1007/s11277-017-4317-x
7. Mishra, S., Trivedi, A.: Performance study of an improved resource allocation scheme with full-duplex relaying. Wirel. Pers. Commun. (WPC) 98, 2819–2836 (2017)
8. Srinath, G., Mishra, S., Trivedi, A.: Hybrid cognitive gaussian two way relay channel: performance analysis and optimal resource allocation. Phys. Commun. 27, 106–115 (2018)
9. Network-Simulator-NetSim. www.tetcos.com
10. Saifuddin, K.M., Ahmed, A.S., Reza, K.F., Alam, S.S., Rahman, S.: Performance analysis of cognitive radio: NETSIM viewpoint. In: International Conference on Electrical Information and Communication Technology (EICT), pp. 7–9 (2017)
11. Teng, Z., Zhong, M., Mao, Y., Li, E., Guo, M., Wang, J.X.: A concentrated sunlight energy wireless transmission system for space solar energy harvest. Energy Convers. Manage. 261, 115524 (2022)
12. Sherazi, H.H.R., Zorbas, D., O'Flynn, B.: A comprehensive survey on RF energy harvesting: Applications and performance determinants. Sensors 22(8), 2990 (2022)

Energy-Efficient Data Routing Protocols for Sink Mobility in Wireless Sensor Networks

Neetu Sikarwar[✉] and Ranjeet Singh Tomar

ITM University, Gwalior, Gwalior, India
neetusik1@gmail.com

Abstract. Routing in sensor networks is very hard compared to modern communication & Wireless Ad-hoc Networks. Several distinguishing features set them apart from other networks in this way. Moreover, several WSNs applications need fast data transmission, like real-time target tracking in combat scenarios or developing event triggering in monitoring applications, requiring an efficient RP (Routing Protocol). This study overviews advanced routing approaches in WSNs under all three categories. The primary aim of this work was to determine the most effective energy-efficient routing protocols for sink mobility in WSN. This research examines the energy efficiency of various RPs across various performance metrics. All assessment measures, including Stability Period (SP), Network Lifetime (NL), & Residual Energy (RE), are surpassed by various routing protocols, as shown by simulation results. Results of the comparisons show that the energy efficiency of WSNs may be improved with the help of Multi-chain PEGASIS and GA-based sink mobility RPs.

Keywords: Wireless Sensor Networks · Sensor Nodes · Clustering · Energy Efficient · Data Routing · Routing Protocols · Sink Mobility

1 Introduction

Recent advancements in wireless communication, computers, & microelectronics have facilitated the fast creation of tiny, inexpensive, multifunctional sensors. Usually, these sensors are randomly put in target areas to monitor the environment's physical features, like humidity, temperature, and pressure. Monitored data is typically sent to data collector (sink) cooperatively (often multi-hop). The data collector may transfer data to distant server for more processing. Additionally, sensors may self-organize depending upon their local cooperation to build Wireless Sensor Networks (WSNs) [1]. In current years, WSNs have gained prominence due to technological advancements in wireless communication and the fast expansion of research in certain fields. WSN refers to the network of SNs connected over a wireless medium. Each node is equipped with Handling capability (minimum of one CPU, microcontroller, as well as DSP chips) and may include several types of memory (data, programs, & flash memories), a power supply (such as sun-powered cells & batteries), as well as various actuators and sensors. As SN contains limited non-rechargeable power sources, it isn't easy to replace nodes. Energy

© The Author(s), under exclusive license to Springer Nature Switzerland AG 2023
R. S. Tomar et al. (Eds.): CNC 2022, CCIS 1894, pp. 291–305, 2023.
https://doi.org/10.1007/978-3-031-43145-6_24

conservation is main concern in WSNs due to need to extend the nodes' lifetime. While transferring data, EE (Energy-Efficient) RPs are essential to limit energy consumption resources & increase network's lifetime [2]. The beneficial characteristics of WSNs, like quick deployment, self-organization, real-time data transport, high fault tolerance, etc., make them appropriate for deployment in hostile or extremely hostile situations, particularly for military or disaster monitoring. In addition, WSNs are widely used for industrial production line monitoring, healthcare, smart homes, agricultural & wildlife observation, and other applications [3–6].

The issue of energy efficiency & energy balance has received a lot of attention, and excellent comparison findings have been provided [7, 8]. The clustering technique drastically reduces WSNs' energy consumption by grouping sensors into clusters per certain rules. One or more CHs (Cluster Heads) are chosen as relay nodes for members of every cluster. Clustering simplifies the network's topological structure and prevents sensors from communicating directly with the sink. One of the fundamental clustering based RPs is LEACH. Although the method for selecting CHs is irrational, much extensive study depends on LEACH.

SM technology is an effective way to address imbalanced energy present in WSNs. It is common for intelligent vehicles or robots to transport the sink in mobile sink-supported WSNs, allowing it to move easily over the sensing field. The following benefits become available with the use of sink mobility technology. First, moving the sink may significantly reduce the "hot spots" issue. Typically, regions around sink are traffic hubs; when sink is moved, traffic hub also relocates. Sensors take turns as "hot spots" to equally disperse energy utilization. Next, if the SM pattern is properly thought out, reducing transmission distance among communication pairs may dramatically reduce overall energy use. Third, a mobile sink may decrease network latency and boost network throughput.

Last but not least, a network connection may be guaranteed even in disjointed or sparse sensor networks. There are numerous benefits to implementing sink mobility, but some obstacles to overcome [9]. Location of mobile sink must be broadcast regularly or anticipated by sensors that can increase load on network. In addition, sinks involved in this method should be thoughtfully crafted to facilitate information exchange with adjacent nodes.

The remaining paper is arranged as follows. Section II describes related work with review table. Section III presents research gaps in this research that remain to solve. The next section provides the challenges of energy consumption in WSN. Then, a theoretical description of RPs classification in WSN is discussed in section V, and section VI provides a comparison of major hierarchical routing protocols. Section VII presents the comparative results in terms of performance parameters like SP (Stability Period), RE (Residual Energy), and NL (Network Lifetime). Section VIII concludes this paper.

1.1 Motivation

WSNs gather data in various applications, like battlefield & civilian monitoring, that reduce the involvement of humans & users. In the last decade, the research community has paid growing attention to WSNs due to their many applications and features, which provide several issues in designing EE protocols for medium access, deployment, sensing, tracking, routing, fusion & data collecting, cross-layer, and coverage protocol design etc. Owing to the restricted power of SNs in WSN, a novel strategy is essential to extend NL. WSNs are difficult & costly to deploy on a broad scale due to their limited power of SNs. Multiple authors have worked to create an efficient RP that minimizes energy consumption. Self-configuring approaches, as shown by the Energy-Aware Protocol, have been shown to play a crucial part in ensuring that energy usage is kept under control. Therefore, the most significant factor in ensuring the long-term viability of WSN is an energy-efficient routing strategy. The strategy used in data routing and the method used to transmit data to BS (Base Station) are crucial concerns in WSN. In such a case, it would be ideal for WSNs to use a routing strategy that minimizes energy usage while selecting the most direct route for data transmission. In WSNs, each SN quickly and automatically gathers information about its environment, neighbours, & network topology. To implement EE routing in WSNs, key research methodology procedures must be followed.

- Energy consumption equalization across SNs to increase WSNs' overall lifetime.
- To determine the ideal routes among wireless SNs, intermediate nodes would be chosen depending on ratio of their maximum RE to distance between themselves and destination.
- EE optimization methods for determining the best path from every node to sink.

Self-organization, self-configuration, & dependability are featuring that wireless sensor networks must possess to meet the three requirements mentioned above.

2 Related Work

Since one of the primary functions of WSN is to gather data efficiently while using as few resources as possible, there has been a lot of work done in this area. Most data gathering algorithms are developed to decrease the issue of energy utilization.

Sujihelen et al. [10] introduced EERA (Energy Efficient Routing Approach) to discover routing paths where less energy is spent to increase NL. This work [11] provides an ensemble bio-inspired approach using Firefly & Spider Monkey Optimization (SMO) algorithms as a clustering-based RP for WSN. The simulation findings suggest that the average lifetime may increase by up to 30.91%, 32.12%, 12.4%, and 13.50% compared to bee colony, SFLA, GWO, and PSO, respectively, in various network circumstances.

This article [12] used the NS2 network simulator to evaluate the performance of FLNC-EE (Fuzzy Logic-Network Coding-Energy Efficient) RP against other EE clustering methods, including LEACH-FL, LEACH, FL-EE/D, and K Means-LEACH. Compared to other protocols addressed in this study, the FL-NC-EE protocol demonstrates superior NL and energy efficiency performance. Next, Kumar et al. [13] suggested that chain-based RP enhances "PEGASIS (Power-Efficient Gathering in Sensor Information Systems)". To improve performance, a modified PEGASIS protocol is presented that delivers more energy efficiency & longer lifetime sensor networks than the original PEGASIS protocol.

The paper [14] proposes a new routing protocol technique for wireless SN communications that is compatible with both isotropic & anisotropic network distributions.

This approach is based on a version of Prim's algorithm, which depends on the "MST (Minimum Spanning Tree)" graph theory. Simulation findings further demonstrate their proposed method's superior performance in reducing the total no. of transmissions in randomly distributed sensor networks, with both isotropic & anisotropic sensing areas being taken into account.

Researchers [15] have developed a method to save energy during cluster formation, which may be used in subsequent routing activities. Also, the proposed mechanism alternates the role of CH among nodes. This proposed algorithm for balancing energy usage forms new clusters at regular intervals, allowing for the use of other routes for data transmission. In addition, the suggested mechanism is evaluated, and its results are compared to those of the existing k-means method. The results of the comparison study validate the efficacy of the proposed method.

Haseeb, K., et al. [16] introduced the ESMR protocol, a multi-hop, energy-aware, and secure RP. The work proposed here presents a simpler way for safeguarding IoTbased restricted WSNs in constrained deployment environments. Compared to prior studies, the findings of the experiments and simulations demonstrate that the provided system delivers improvements of 34% in throughput, 38% in NL, 28% in average E2E delay (End-to-End Delay), 34% in energy efficiency, and 36% in routing overheads. Gap: Table 1 demonstrates that ESMR performance is only tested for static nodes & not for mobility SNs in heterogeneous network environment.

Table 1. A Concise Analysis of Secure & Efficient Routing Techniques.

Year	Title Name	Researchers	Findings	Limitations
2010	"On Energy Efficient Encryption for Video Streaming in WSNs" [17]	Wei Wang et al.	A wireless channel-aware selective encryption system that reduces overheads and enhances video quality and a resource allocation mechanism depend upon UEP that optimizes encoded video communication at lower layers	This encryption approach is only useful for use in WSN-based video surveillance applications. Emphasizing both secure storage and high-quality video
2013	"Energy-Efficient Routing Protocols in WSNs" [18]	N. A. Pantazis, et al.	This work presents a summary of protocols used in WSN, including LEACH, SPIN, HEED, DECA, & PEGASIS	WSN architectures, applications, security, and power management all have problems that require addressing
2013	"A Survey on Distributed Topology Control Techniques for Extending the Lifetime of Battery Powered WSNs" [19]	A. A. Aziz, et al.	After analyzing these methods for improving energy efficiency via topology control, the researchers have discovered a few areas where further work has to be done	While reviewing the protocols, security was not given enough attention. There are different research areas in the realms of security & resource preservation

(continued)

Table 1. (*continued*)

Year	Title Name	Researchers	Findings	Limitations
2014	"A Framework of Joint Mobile Energy Replenishment & Data Gathering in Wireless Rechargeable Sensor Networks" [20]	M. Zhao, et al.	"J-MERDG: Joint Design of Energy Replenishment and Data Gathering", anchor point selection method, rechargeable nodes allow flexibility for using energy to leverage complicated calculations and make it simpler to develop more secure and high-performance network applications	Performance drops solely for WSNs with rechargeable nodes when using non-symmetric network topology; more considerations are required for impediment alertness & SenCar battery restriction to assist realistic implementations
2016	"ActiveTrust: Secure and Trustable Routing in WSNs" [21]	Y. Liu et al.	ActiveTrust's ability to rapidly detect nodal trust with minimal energy consumption increases the chance of successful routing by 3 to 10 times	In the case of basic SNs applications, the hardware's minimal processing capabilities may be unable to handle the complexity of these approaches
2017	"Location-Based Key Management Strong Against Insider Threats in WSNs" [23]	J. Choi et al.	Position-based strategy for key management, particular considerations for inside hazards, and a lower network	Each SN must have a positioning system to use location-based routing methods. Utilized solely in certain applications
2017	"JAMMY: A Distributed and Dynamic Solution to Selective Jamming Attack in TDMA WSNs" [22]	M. Tiloca et al.	For selective jamming attacks in TDMA-based wireless sensor networks, JAMMY provides novel distributed approach with improved performance	Limited to TDMA on a single channel
2017	"Resilience of DoS Attacks in Designing Anonymous User Authentication Protocol for WSNs" [24]	P. Gope et al.	Each SN must have a positioning system to use location-based routing methods. Utilized solely in certain applications	As no. of nodes and overall network size grows, performance suffers
2017	"Research on Trust Sensing Based Secure Routing Mechanism for WSN" [25]	D. Qin et al.	Using semiring theory, TSSRM suggests a more efficient routing method that may evaluate the degree of trust, lessen routing overheads, and improve packet transmission dependability	A novel approach to trust degree assessment & pervasive routing may emerge from future studies aimed at developing distributed IDS (Intrusion Detection System) for WSN
2017	"SCOTRES: Secure Routing for IoT & CPS" [26]	G. Hatzivasilis et al.	Compared to other trust sense systems, SCOTRES offers to handle more attack types, less overhead costs, and more efficient routing	Only Cloud environments & IoT applications are supported

(*continued*)

Table 1. (*continued*)

Year	Title Name	Researchers	Findings	Limitations
2018	"Secure and Energy Efficient Path Optimization Technique in WSNs Using DH Method" [27]	T. A. Alghamdi	E2E node authentication at each hop, low packet loss, low delay, & increased NL are all features of this architecture	A separate authentication layer raises network complexity for static WSNs of significant size
2018	"Energy-efficient scheme using multiple antennas in secure distributed detection" [28]	Y. Lee, & J. Choi	Numerous antenna schemes, increased reliability, energy efficiency, & more security are the results of random beamforming	Considerations at the level of hardware design are required for a change in antenna scheme; particular hardware is required, but security and reliability are not enhanced
2019	"CREDND: A Novel_Secure_Neighbor Discovery Algorithm for Wormhole Attack" [29]	X. Luo et al.	Depending upon local monitoring and hop variation, CREDND is used to identify wormholes. Both external & internal wormholes may be detected with this device	Not a good match for mobile WSNs or nodes with varying transmission ranges. Not appropriate for the vast majority of real-time applications since it only operates with uniform distribution of nodes
2019	"Secret Sharing-based Energy-aware & Multi-hop Routing Protocol for IoT-based WSNs" [16]	K. Haseeb et al.	Lightweight resolution for secure multi-hop routing, quantitative analysis of connections, and ESMR (Efficient Secret Data Sharing Scheme)	Currently supports only IoT-based limited WSNs. Appropriate for the static, small-scale network. Inadequate for use in highly dynamic, large-scale, real-world networks

3   Research Gaps

Sensor networks are affected by problems such as routing, network failure owing to energy drainage and holes, etc. The issue of energy loss, in particular, must be treated with care since it may become the root cause of several other problems. As a result, the improved energy efficiency of SNs is very significant. A routing protocol's (RPs) most significant attribute for efficiency in WSNs is its ability to cut energy usage while increasing the network's lifetime. According to the literature, achieving sink mobility may significantly save energy on a large scale. The application under consideration determines the requirements for developing routing and other aspects of WSNs. The notion of sink mobility may be used in applications such as smart home environments or medical applications such as patient monitoring without causing significant issues. Additionally, the mobile sink boosts network performance [30]. Since mobile sink is capable of gathering data from SN as well as transmitting it to the computer, the mobile sink node must have strong computation, storage, including communications abilities [31–33].

Energy efficiency in WSNs is a hot study topic in which many approaches to improving EE are being investigated. Various strategies and procedures may be used to minimize energy consumption or make the most efficient use of the given energy to the greatest degree feasible. Each approach will be suitable for a particular purpose. Rendering literature, communication consumes a vast common of energy available rather than processing or sensing. As a result, the necessity for energy-efficient RP is critical for extending network's lifetime. Hierarchical category of RPs, in which the clustering notion is used, includes energy-efficient routing methods [18, 34, 35].

The bulk of existing sink mobility-based WSN RPs follow conventional paradigm, in which sink moves with constant velocity along predetermined movement route [36–38]. Data packets from nodes in area are sent to the sink in the multi-hop method. Sink mobility methods now in use do not contain any EE optimization techniques for determining ideal data collecting points along sink movement trajectory (SMT).

4   Classifications of Routing Protocols in WSN

Most RPs of WSN aim to maximize network lifetime by effectively using SN resources. It is possible to use various routing methods, each best suited to a certain set of needs. Applications may be time-sensitive or need periodic updates; they can demand exact data or a resilient, less precise network; also, they can have continuous data flow or event-driven output. Improvements and customizations to routing mechanisms are also possible.

Based on the network topology, RPs in WSNs may be classed as location-based, data-centric, or hierarchical-based, as seen in Fig. 1.

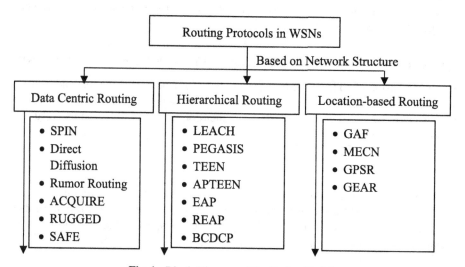

Fig. 1. Block Diagram of Prediction Model.

In a data-centric network, all nodes are functionally equal & collaborate to route query from BS to event. In the hierarchical method, certain nodes have additional tasks to alleviate the burden on other network nodes. In location-based routing, information on SN placements is employed to direct the query from base station to event [39].

In WSNs, network energy efficiency is an important challenge. Today's networks are growing in size, and as a consequence, the collected data is also growing, using a tremendous deal of energy and resulting in the early death of nodes. Thus, several EE protocols are generated to reduce power required for data sampling & gathering to increase NL [40].

Following are examples of energy-efficient RPs:

4.1 PEGASIS (Power-Efficient Gathering in Sensor Information Systems)

It is a "chain-based protocol" as well as improvement on "LEACH." In "PEGASIS," every node may only exchange & collect information with its nearest neighbours.

4.2 LEACH (Low-Energy Adaptive Clustering Hierarchy)

Most nodes in this form of hierarchical protocol connect with CH. It includes 2 phases: (i). During the Setup Phase, clusters are organized & CH is picked. CH is responsible for gathering, wrapping, & transmitting information to BS (Sink). (ii) Study State Phase: in the former condition, nodes, as well as CH, were arranged; however, in 2nd state of "LEACH," data is sent to BS (Sink).

4.3 TEEN (Threshold Sensitive Energy Efficient Sensor Network Protocol)

TEEN is hierarchical protocol developed for situations that include sudden shifts in values of measured parameters like temperature. TEEN was first protocol that was developed specifically for reactive networks.

4.4 APTEEN (Adaptive Threshold Sensitive Energy Efficient Sensor Network)

It is an extension of "TEEN" & purposes to gather episodic data and respond to time-sensitive rates. CH communicates features, threshold values, & transmission schedules to all nodes as soon as BS creates clusters. CH then conducts data accumulation, resulting in power conservation.

4.5 Directed Diffusion

In WSNs, data collection and dissemination are accomplished via a routing protocol known as directed diffusion. It was designed to solve the problem of transferring data from sink to sensors, which occurs when sink requests specific data from sensors. Its major aim is to reduce overall network energy consumption to lengthen NL.

4.6 EESR (Energy-Efficient Sensor Routing)

It is flat routing strategy meant to decrease energy consumption & data latency in WSNs, in addition to providing scalability. Manager Nodes (MNs), Gateway, SNs, and BS are its primary components. Their duties include: Gateway Delivers communications from MNs or other networks to BS, which has more specifications than standard SNs. It transmits & receives messages to and from Gateway.

5 Comparison of Main Hierarchical RPs in WSN

Table 2 demonstrates the energy efficiency & complexity of several protocols like "HEED (Hybrid Energy Efficient Distributed Clustering)", "LEACH (Low Energy Adaptive Clustering Hierarchy)", "PEGASIS (Power Efficient Gathering in Sensor Information Systems)", "EECS (Energy Efficient Clustering Scheme)", "TEEN (Threshold-sensitive Energy Efficient sensor Network)", "UCS (Unequal Clustering Size)", "HGMR (Hierarchical Geographic Multicast Routing)", "APTEEN (Adaptive Periodic Threshold-Sensitive Energy Efficient sensor Network)". Compared to HEED, LEACH, EECS, PEGASIS, UCS, TEEN, APTEEN, HGMR, & CCS, the TEEN protocol has high energy efficiency. Compared to EECS, PEGASIS, UCS, HEED, TEEN, APTEEN, & CCS, the complexity of LEACH and HGMR is minimal [41].

Table 2. Complexity and energy efficiency of key RPs.

Protocol Name	Energy Efficiency	Complexity
HEED	Moderate	Moderate
LEACH	Very Low	Low
UCS	Very Low	Moderate
TEEN	Very High	High
PEGASIS	Low	High
EECS	Moderate	Very High
HGMR	Low	Low
CCS	Low	Moderate
APTEEN	Moderate	Very High

6 Comparative Results and Discussion

Here, we assess the simulation outcomes used to analyze the efficacy of various RPs, such as those found in the genetic algorithm-based sink mobility, LEACH, Multi-chain PEGASIS, SEP, RAMSS, ECRP, & ECDRA etc., described in the literature as mentioned above review. Comparing network Stability Period (SP), Network Lifetime (NL), as well as Residual Energy (RE) is used to assess the performance of protocols. The most important factors for any given sensor network are its expected lifetime & stability period. We count no. of alive & dead nodes & count no. of packets sent to BS to determine how well these parameters work. There is a comparison of the parameters and their comparative values in Table 3.

The above Table 3 illustrates a comparative representation of RPs in terms of performance evaluation parameters, including SP, NL, & RE for multiple routing protocols such as GA-based sink mobility, LEACH, multi-chain PEGASIS, SEP, RAMSS, ECRP,

Table 3. Comparative results analysis of RPs in terms of performance parameters.

Protocol Name	Stability Period (SP)	Network Lifetime (NL)	Residual Energy (RE)
GA-based Sink Mobility [42]	1298	3158	3000
LEACH [43]	1095	2122	1500
Multi-chain PEGASIS [44]	1700	3000	3225
SEP [45]	527	2145	1650
RAMSS [46]	1233	2542	2275
ECRP [47]	1185	1765	1552
ECDRA [46]	1050	1200	1085
GA-based Sink Mobility [42]	1298	3158	3000
LEACH [43]	1095	2122	1500

ECDRA etc. The stability period performance of multi-chain PEGASIS is improved than SEP, LEACH, RAMSS, ECRP and &. Highest value of the network lifetime and residual energy is 3158 for GA-based sink mobility and 3225 for multi-chain PEGASIS, respectively.

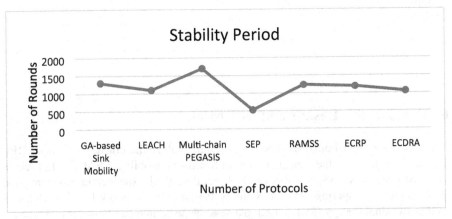

Fig. 2. Graph of Network Stability Period.

Figure 2 shows a line graph for the network stability period, demonstrating the performance of different RPs in network stability. NL consists of two continuous parts. The initial portion, from the network's creation until death of first node, is named stable phase. This phase continues until the last node in the network dies. In this graph, the x-axis demonstrates no. of RPs, & y-axis denotes no. of rounds for SP. From this comparative graph, we can observe that the SEP algorithm was not so stable for many rounds and ended up in less than 600 rounds. Other energy-efficient routing protocols like ECDRA and LEACH did not perform well, and more than 1100 rounds did not increase their stability periods. However, the RAMSS protocol was stable till 1200 rounds, but it was not exceeded than GA-based sink mobility algorithm, which was stable till 1300 rounds. But when looking at the Multichain-PEGASIS protocol, it presented the best stability period with 1700 rounds among all data routing protocols. The energy gain due to sink mobility is responsible for this phenomenon.

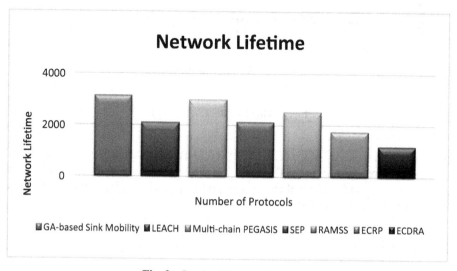

Fig. 3. Graph of Network Lifetime.

The NL for different protocols is shown in Fig. 3. To put it another way, the NL is the period that elapses from when the simulation begins until the last node in the network dies. Primarily, RPs exist to maximize network's availability over time. The network lifetime of the Multichain PEGASIS routing algorithm is higher than RAMSS protocol, similar to network stability period in this comparative graph. Whereas NL of SEP & LEACH RPs is approximately the same, NL of ECRP & ECDRA protocols were very low and did not survive up to 1600 to 1700 rounds. Based on comparative bar graph, it is evident that GA-based sink mobility has a longer NL than other protocols. This is because it distributes workload across SNs using fewer control packets. According to this graph, the GA-based sink mobility obtains greatest values of others.

Figure 4 displays the entire amount of energy still in the sensors' battery at a round R, which is RE. In WSNs, data routing is most energy-intensive task. As a result, routing protocol should extensively use smart methods to minimize energy consumption. The total amount of power used for sending & receiving packets during simulation. In this graph, the x-axis shows several protocols, & the y-axis shows no. of rounds, and residual energy is calculated in joule. This line graph demonstrates a comparison among various RPs and found that LEACH, SEP, ECRP and ECDRA routing protocols do not have so much residual energy, which is not more than 1700 rounds. However, RAMSS routing

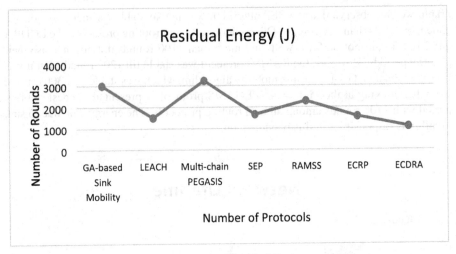

Fig. 4. Graph of Residual Energy.

protocol residual energy was more than 2000 rounds, but residual energy of GA-based sink mobility reached up to 3000 rounds. The highest value of the residual energy is 3225 of multi-chain PEGASIS than the other protocols, and there is a minimal difference from GA-based sink mobility.

7   Conclusion

In recent decades, the rise of WSNs enabling a broad range of applications has encouraged academics and garnered substantial interest. In this work, we provide a brief analysis of existing routing techniques & protocols. We used our taxonomy to categorize the most popular recently proposed protocols into distinct types of protocols. A detailed energy consumption challenge in WSN is discussed in this paper, and the classification of routing protocols is also presented.

Furthermore, a comparison of major hierarchical RP is provided in this research. This paper presents comparative results of some routing protocols such as GA-based sink mobility, LEACH, Multi-chain PEGASIS, SEP, RAMSS, ECRP, and ECDRA. The obtained findings indicate that GA-based Sink Mobility, Multi-chain PEGASIS, & RAMSS protocols enhance NL, SP, and RE compared to other protocols, leading us to infer that the use of smart approaches increases NL and ensures improved coverage in the sensing region. But Multi-chain PEGASIS outperforms all of these three best routing protocols in all cases.

A novel energy-efficient clustering strategy may be used to improve this work further. In addition, in future studies, we may analyze routing attacks & security mechanisms in WSNs, with demonstrated analysis by simulations, to make it easier for researchers to think of smart & secure RPs.

References

1. Zeng, D., Dai, Y., Li, F., Sheratt, S., Wang, J.: Adversarial learning for distant supervised relation extraction. Comput. Mater. Contin. **55**, 121–136 (2018)
2. Gupta, S.K., Kumar, S., Tyagi, S., Tanwar, S.: Energy efficient routing protocols for wireless sensor network. Adv. Intell. Syst. Comput. **1132**(12), 275–298 (2020)
3. Chanak, P., Banerjee, I., Wang, J., Sheratt, R.: Obstacle avoidance routing scheme through optimal sink movement for home monitoring and mobile robotic consumer devices. IEEE Trans. Consum. Electron. **60**, 596–604 (2014)
4. Wang, J., Zhang, Z., Li, B., Lee, S.: An enhanced fall detection system for elderly person monitoring using consumer home networks. IEEE Trans. Consum. Electron. **60**, 23–29 (2014)
5. Yin, C., Xi, R., Sun, R., Wang, J.: Location privacy protection based on differential privacy strategy for big data in industrial internet of things. IEEE Trans. Consum. Electron. **14**, 3628–3636 (2014)
6. Yao, J., Zhang, K., Yang, Y., Wang, J.: Emergency vehicle route-oriented signal coordinated control: model with two-level programming. Soft Comput. **22**, 4283–4294 (2018)
7. Ren, Y., Liu, Y., Ji, S., Sangaiah, A.K., Wang, J.: Incentive mechanism of data storage based on blockchain for wireless sensor networks. EEE Trans. Ind. Inform. (2018)
8. Wang, J., Yang, X., Li, B., Lee, S., Jeon, S.: A mobile sink based uneven clustering algorithm for wireless sensor networks. IEEE Trans. Consum. Electron. **14**, 895–902 (2014)
9. Khan, A.W., Abdullah, A.H., Anisi, M.H., Bangash, J.I.: A comprehensive study of data collection schemes using mobile sinks in wireless sensor networks. Sens. (Switz.) **14**, 2510–2548 (2014)
10. Sujihelen, L., Senthilsingh, C., Christy, A., Praveena, M.D.A., Roobini, M.S., Mana, S.C.: Energy efficient routing approach for IoT assisted smart devices in WSN. In: 2022 4th International Conference on Smart Systems and Inventive Technology (ICSSIT), pp. 44–48 (2022)
11. Gokula Krishnan, V., Venkateswara Rao, P., Divya, V.: An Energy efficient routing protocol based on SMO optimization in WSN. In: 2021 6th International Conference on Communication and Electronics Systems (ICCES-2021), pp. 1–13 (2021)
12. Fathima Shemim, K.S., Witkowski, U.: Energy efficient clustering protocols for WSN: performance analysis of FL-EE-NC with LEACH, K Means-LEACH, LEACH-FL and FLEE/D using NS-2. In: International Conference on Microelectronics, ICM 2020, pp. 1–5 (2020)
13. Sana, M., Noureddine, L.: Multi-hop energy-efficient routing protocol based on minimum spanning tree for anisotropic wireless sensor networks. In: 2019 International Conference on Advanced Systems and Electric Technologies (IC_ASET), pp. 209–214 (2019)
14. Bajpai, N., Mohapatra, S., Mishra, M.: A novel distributed energy efficient routing algorithm based on clustering mechanism in WSN. In: 2019 International Conference on Intelligent Computing and Remote Sensing (ICICRS), pp. 1–6 (2019)
15. Kumar, V. K., Khunteta, A.: Energy efficient PEGASIS routing protocol for wireless sensor networks. In: 2018 2nd International Conference on Micro-Electronics and Telecommunication Engineering (ICMETE), pp. 91–95 (2018)
16. Haseeb, K., Islam, N., Almogren, A., Ud Din, I., Almajed, H.N., Guizani, N.: Secret sharing-based energy-aware and multi-hop routing protocol for IoT based WSNs. IEEE Access **7**, 79980–79988 (2019)
17. Wang, W., Hempel, M., Peng, D., Wang, H., Sharif, H., Chen, H.H.: On energy efficient encryption for video streaming in wireless sensor networks. EEE Trans. Multimed. **12**, 417–426 (2010)
18. Pantazis, N.A., Nikolidakis, S.A., Vergados, D.D.: Energy-efficient routing protocols in wireless sensor networks: a survey. IEEE Commun. Surv. Tutor. **15**, 551–591 (2013)

19. Aziz, A.A., Şekercioğlu, Y.A., Fitzpatrick, P., Ivanovich, M.: A survey on distributed topology control techniques for extending the lifetime of battery powered wireless sensor networks. IEEE Commun. Surv. Tutor. **15**, 121–144 (2013)

20. Zhao, M., Li, J., Yang, Y.: A framework of joint mobile energy replenishment and data gathering in wireless rechargeable sensor networks. IEEE Trans. Mob. Comput. **13**, 2689–2705 (2014)

21. Liu, Y., Dong, M., Ota, K., Liu, A.: ActiveTrust: secure and trustable routing in wireless sensor networks. IEEE Trans. Inf. Forensics Secur. **11**, 2013–2027 (2016)

22. Tiloca, M., De Guglielmo, D., Dini, G., Anastasi, G., Das, S.K.: JAMMY: a distributed and dynamic solution to selective jamming attack in TDMA WSNs. IEEE Trans. Dependable Secur. Comput. **14**, 392–405 (2017)

23. Choi, J., Bang, J., Kim, L., Ahn, M., Kwon, T.: Location-based key management strong against insider threats in wireless sensor networks. IEEE Syst. J. **11**, 494–502 (2017)

24. Lee, J., Gope, P., Quek, T.Q.S.: Resilience of DoS attacks in designing anonymous user authentication protocol for wireless sensor networks. IEEE Sens. J. **17**, 498–503 (2017)

25. Qin, D., Yang, S., Jia, S., Zhang, Y., Ma, J., Ding, Q.: Research on trust sensing based secure routing mechanism for wireless sensor network. IEEE Access. **5**, 9599–9609 (2017)

26. Hatzivasilis, G., Papaefstathiou, I., Manifavas, C.: SCOTRES: secure routing for IoT and CPS. IEEE Internet Things **4**, 2129–2141 (2017)

27. Alghamdi, T.A.: Secure and energy efficient path optimization technique in wireless sensor networks using DH method. IEEE Access **6**, 53576–53582 (2018)

28. Lee, Y., Choi, J.: Energy-efficient scheme using multiple antennas in secure distributed detection. IET Signal Process. **12**, 652–658 (2018)

29. Luo, X., et al.: CREDND: a novel secure neighbor discovery algorithm for wormhole attack. IEEE Access **7**, 18194–18205 (2019)

30. Wang, J., Gao, Y., Liu, W., Sangaiah, A.K., Kim, H.J.: Energy efficient routing algorithm with mobile sink support for wireless sensor networks. Sens. (Switz.) **19**, 1494 (2019)

31. Yue, Y.G., He, P.: A comprehensive survey on the reliability of mobile wireless sensor networks: taxonomy, challenges, and future directions. Inf. Fusion **44**, 188–204 (2018)

32. Toor, A.S., Jain, A.K.: Energy aware cluster based multi-hop energy efficient routing protocol using multiple mobile nodes (MEACBM) in wireless sensor networks. AEU - Int. J. Electron. Commun. **102**, 41–53 (2019)

33. Alsaafin, A., Khedr, A.M., Al Aghbari, Z.: Distributed trajectory design for data gathering using mobile sink in wireless sensor networks. AEU - Int. J. Electron. Commun. **96**, 1–12 (2018)

34. Wei, D., Jin, Y., Moessner, K., Vural, S., Tafazolli, R.: An energy-efficient clustering solution for wireless sensor networks. IEEE Trans. Wirel. Commun. **10**, 3973–3983 (2011)

35. Chi, Y.P., Chang, H.P.: TARS: an energy-efficient routing scheme for wireless sensor networks with mobile sinks and targets (2012)

36. Nguyen, H.T., Van Nguyen, L., Le, H.X.: Efficient approach for maximizing lifespan in wireless sensor networks by using mobile sinks. ETRI J. **39**, 353–363 (2017)

37. Vijayashree, R., Suresh Ghana Dhas, C.: Energy efficient data collection with multiple mobile sink using artificial bee colony algorithm in large-scale WSN. Automatika **60**, 555–563 (2019)

38. Farzinvash, L., Najjar-Ghabel, S., Javadzadeh, T.: A distributed and energy-efficient approach for collecting emergency data in wireless sensor networks with mobile sinks. AEU - Int. J. Electron. Commun. **108**, 79–86 (2019)

39. Mundada, M.R., Kiran, S., Khobanna, S., Nahusha, R., Varsha, George, S.A.: A study on energy-efficient routing protocols for wireless sensor networks. Adv. Intell. Syst. Comput. **1178**(3), 125–173 (2021)

40. Kaur, P., Kad, S.: Comparative Analysis of PDORP and Modified Trust Value based Technique to Secure Wireless Sensor Network. Int. J. Comput. Appl. (2018)

41. Varun, R.K., Gangwar, R.C.: Hierarchical energy efficient routing in wireless sensor networks and its challenges. Int. J. Eng. Adv. Technol. **975**, 8887 (2019)

42. Singh, M.K., Amin, S.I., Choudhary, A.: Genetic algorithm-based sink mobility for energy efficient data routing in wireless sensor networks. AEU - Int. J. Electron. Commun. **131**, 153605 (2021)

43. Heinzelman, W.R., Chandrakasan, A., Balakrishnan, H.: Energy-efficient communication protocol for wireless microsensor networks (2000)

44. Zagrouba, R., Kardi, A.: Comparative study of energy efficient routing techniques in wireless sensor networks. Information **12**, 42 (2021)

45. Smaragdakis, G., Matta, I., Bestavros, A.: SEP: a stable election protocol for clustered. Bost. Univ. Comput. Sci. Dept. 1–11 (2004)

46. Wang, J., Gao, Y., Yin, X., Li, F., Kim, H.J.: An Enhanced PEGASIS algorithm with mobile sink support for wireless sensor networks. Wirel. Commun. Mob. Comput. **2018**, 1–9 (2018)

47. Moussa, N., Hamidi-Alaoui, Z., El Belrhiti El Alaoui, A.: ECRP: an energy-aware cluster based routing protocol for wireless sensor networks. Wirel. Netw. **26**, 2915–2928 (2020)

Impact of Vehicle Density on Channel Congestion for Vehicular Ad-Hoc Network (VANET)

Bhupendra Dhakad[(⊠)] and Laxmi Shrivastva

Department of Electronics Engineering, Madhav Institute of Technology and Science, Gwalior, Madhya Pradesh, India
bhunesh1992@gmail.com, lselex@mitsgwalior.in

Abstract. Now a day's vehicular communication network (VCN) recognized as a pillar of intelligent transport system. It is a network of communicating vehicles, shares the awareness massage to the neighbouring vehicles which reduces the number of traffics collision and supports safety applications but as the traffics density increases safety applicants required high massages exchange among the vehicles and this causes channel congestion. This paper has been analysed the impact of vehicles density on channel congestion. SUMO NETEDIT 1.12.0 is used for the designing of road map and Network Simulator 2 is used for the simulation by considering IEEE802.11p standard. This paper evaluated network performance metrics include packet loss, end to end delay, instant and average throughput.

Keywords: Vehicular communication network (VCN) · Vehicle-2-vehicle communication (V-TO-V) · Vehicle-2-road side unit communication (V-TO-U) · road side units (RSU) · Dedicated-short-range-communication (DSRC) · IEEE802.11p · Wireless access in the vehicular environment (WAVE) · Federal communication commission (FCC) · Intelligent transport system (ITS)

1 Introduction

Vehicular communication includes V-TO-V communication and V-TO-U communication. The vehicles continuously exchange the awareness messages, includes the information about speed, acceleration, vehicle position, vehicle size, etc. with the neighboring vehicles and road side unit RSU helps to transmit the massages for loge distance. VCN obeys the protocols of DSRC, IEEE802.11p & WAVE (Fig. 1).

In the VCN the massage packets are categories in safety and non safety messages, transmitted in broadcast manner followed by single hop or multi hop routing. The transmission of massage from node to node (V-TO-V) follows both flooding or relaying mechanism and vehicle to RSU communication uses pull-based or push-based approaches. Figure 2 shows the DSRC spectrum decided for the VCN having 75 MHz bandwidth from 5.850 to 5.925 GHz divided in one control channel used for transmission of safety

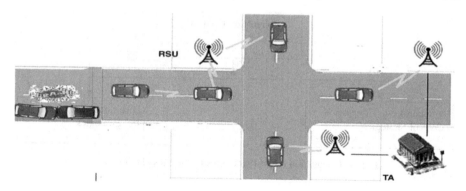

Fig. 1. Realistic architecture of VANET

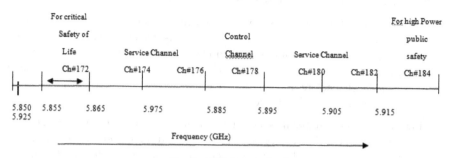

Fig. 2. DSRC spectrum

massages and 6 service channel used for transmission of non safety massages. Each channel having a fixed interval of 100 ms.

ITS-G5 is the first under established VCN in Europe follows IEEE802.11p protocols, CSMA-CA multiple access technique and OFDA multiplexing technique. The vehicle density is increases day by day due to that the transmission of massages also increases causes channel congestion problem, packet loss and collision because the allotted bandwidth is fixed for VCN. 5 to 10% of more energy is required for the retransmission of lost and collide packets [1–3].

In this paper 50 moving vehicles are considered for the analysis of channel congestion in two cases. In the first case only 8 vehicle are actively participated and in second case 16 vehicles are actively participated and communicated to each other and calculated packet loss, end to end delay, instant and average throughput.

2 Related Work

This section includes some of the existing congestion control techniques network are classified in two parts (Fig. 3).

Open-Loop Congestion Control Techniques: These control techniques are applied to reduce the congestion before it happens at the channel. The congestion control techniques

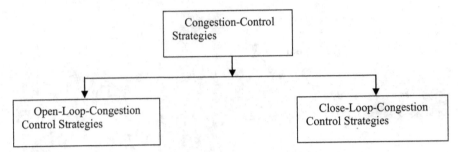

Fig. 3. Congestion control strategies/techniques classification

can be applied either at the source or at the destination. A few of the open loop congestion control techniques/strategies are described below [4-7].

Retransmission Technique: This is based on the re-transmission of the massage packets. If the source/sender node observes that the sent massage packet is off track, it is not reached at the receiver/destination node then the packet requires to be re-transmitted. This re-transmission may increase the level of congestion at the channel so for stopping congestion on the channel, re-transmission timers should be designed in this way so that it can prevent congestion before it occurs.

Window Techniques: Sometimes the window at the sender side can also be responsible for the congestion at the channel because many packets from the Go-back-n window are re-sent, and few massage packets are received without any lose at the receive but this duplication can increase the congestion in the communication channel. That's why; the selective repeat window should be adoptive so that it only sends required packets that may have been lost.

Acknowledgment Policy: The acknowledgment massages can also increase the congestion at the channel. The acknowledgment massages are generally sent by the receiver to the sender. Many approaches can be used to reduce congestion due to acknowledgments for receiving m number of packets receiver can send only one acknowledgment, Receiver sends the acknowledgment only for the retransmission of particular packets which are corrupted or not received at the receiver.

Discarding Techniques: Adoptive discarding techniques at the nodes can prevent congestion. The discarding technique discards the corrupted or less sensitive massage packets without affecting the quality of the message signal.

Admission Technique: In this technique, a mechanism is used to prevent congestion and it is used at nodes. These mechanisms first identify the resource requirement for the transmission of message packets before transmitting through the channel. If it found the chance of congestion then the node deny for the transmission.

Closed-Loop Congestion Control Techniques: These kinds of techniques are used to apply for reducing channel congestion after it happens. A few of the close-loop congestion control techniques are described below.

Backpressure: In this strategy, the congested node (Node 4) stops receiving message packets from an upstream node (Node 3) due to this the upstream node or nodes (Node

3,2,&1) become congested and deny receiving packets from the above upstream nodes or sender. This is a node-2-node congestion-reducing or control technique that propagates in the upstream direction or opposite direction of data flow. The backpressure strategy can only apply in the network where every node knows its above upstream node [8–10]. Figure 4 shows that the 4th node is congested and it blocks receiving message packets from the 3rd node due to this 3rd node will get congested and it stops receiving data from the 2nd up stream node and at last when the 1st node will become congested it notifies the source to slow down messages rate.

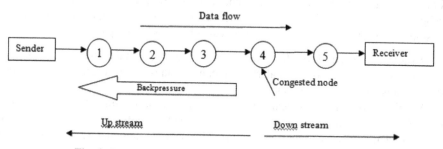

Fig. 4. Backpressure close loop congestion control techniques

Choke Packet Strategy: The choke data packet is nothing but it's an indication packet that is sent by a congested node to the source or sender node to make aware of congestion in the network. Every node in the network monitors its available resources and the utilized resources because of the transmission. When resource utilization is exceeding from threshold value of the available resource then the node directly sends a choke message packet to the source node to make it aware of congestion and give instructions to reduce the rate of sending messages [11, 12]. In this technique the congested node gives instruction only to the sender node by choke packet other intermediate nodes are not alert about congestion (Fig. 5).

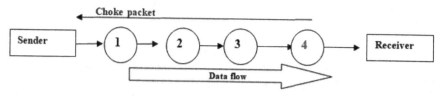

Fig. 5. Choke Packet congestion control technique

Implicit-Signalling Strategy: In this strategy, communication is not stabilized between the source node and the congested nodes. The sender/source node only predicts the congestion in the channel. For this when the source node sends several message packets toward the destination if there is no acknowledgment received by the source node then the source node assumes that the network is congested.

Explicit-Signaling Strategy: In this, if any node experience congestion then it can clearly or explicitly sends a message packet either to the sender/source node or receiver/destination node for the information about the congestion. The only difference between the explicit signaling and choke packet is that the signal is included in the message packets that carry data rather than creating different message packets to stop the transmission like a choke packet technique. Explicit signaling is classified as below on the bases of massage packet flow direction as either in the forward or backward direction.

Forward-Signaling Method: If the signal is transferred in the same direction as the congestion then the destination node is alert about congestion occurrence. In this case to stop/prevent further congestion receiver can adopt any techniques.

Backward-Signaling Method: If the signal is transferred in the opposite direction of the congestion and the source is alert about congestion occurrence and it has to reduce the transmission of the messages.

VANETs give many applications like information about emergency alerts, landmark & destination locations, road safety, prevention from collision, blind crossing, and critical or dangerous situations, many information services, automatic toll payment, and automatic smart cars.

3 Simulation Setup

In this paper work has been done in two phase in first phase sumo netedit is used and in second phase network simulator 2 is used. Netedit is a road network editor. It is used to create road map in natural way and remove the faulty attributes of road map. Netedit provide the facility to work on many more parameters like type of vehicle, Number of vehicle, speed of vehicles, Path for vehicles, length and width of road, Slop on road, Number of lanes, junctions, programmable traffic lights on junctions. Separate path for pedestrian and two vehicles [13–15].

Table 1 shows the simulation parameters and MAC layer parameters are selected as minimum and maximum value of contention window are 15 and 1023, slote time is 0.000013 s, preamble length and header length are 96 and 40 bits, short and long retry limit are 7 and 4, header and symbol duration are .000040 and .000008 s and RTS threshold is 2346. At the PHY layer parameters are selected as gain of transmitter and receiving antenna is one, system loss factor is one, transmission power of antenna is 100mW, CP,CS and Rx threshold are 10,3.162e-12 and 3.652-10 respectively.

The road map is shown in Fig. 6 in which 50 similar vehicles are in moving condition having same dimension. There are four junction with traffic light is taken in road map to avoid traffic collision. Vehicle id zero start its journey at 0 s (simulation start time) after the gap of one second next vehicle start its journey and so on. Up to 200 s all vehicles reached respective destination. Figure 7 shows the simulation view considering the simulation parameter shown in Table 1, MAC and PHY layer parameters.

Table 1. Simulation parameters

S.No	Simulation Parameters	Values
1.	Channel type	Wireless Channel
2.	Radio-propagation model	Two Ray Ground
3.	Network interface type	WirelessPhy
4.	MAC type	Mac/802_11p
5.	Interface queue type	Queue/DropTail/PriQueue
6.	link layer type	LL
7.	Antenna model Type	Omni Antenna
8.	Max packet in IFQ	50
9.	Number of mobile nodes count	50
10.	Routing protocol	AODV
11.	X dimension of topography	3336
12.	Y dimension of topography	642
13.	Time of simulation end	200.0

Fig. 6. Sumo-gui view of road with moving vehicles

4 Results

Channel congestion is analyzed in term of throughput, packet loss and end to end delay under two cases. In the first case 8 vehicles are active out of 50 in second case 16 vehicles are active. All the vehicles transmitted messages in single hope, unicast manner with equal packet generation rate. The network capacity is measure in term of throughput and it is affected by the packet loss, delay, jitter.

Network Bandwidth: It denotes the maximum data transmission capacity of the network. It is shared among the user according to the need.

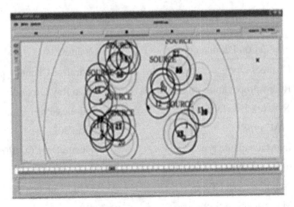

Fig. 7. NS2 simulation view

Total Delay: Total delay is the sum of transmission delay, propagation delay, queuing delay and processing delay. **Propagation Delay:** It is the time taken by the packet to reaches up to the receiver. It depends on distance between transmitter and receiver and propagation speed of the medium. **Queuing delay:** It is denoted as time taken by the data packet in the queue (buffer). It depends on transmission rate and packet size. **Processing delay:** It is time taken by the processor to read & process the data packet (Fig. 8).

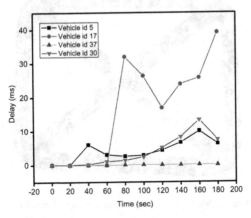

Fig. 8. Delay profile of 4 communication links

Figure 9 shows the delay profile of 4 and 8 communication links. First graph shows the delay of 4 communication links. As the distance between transmitter and receiver vehicle increases the value of propagation delay also increases that is why all the profiles are fluctuated. Propagation delay also change with atmospheric conditions. The maximum delay in case of 4 communication links is 35 ms which is occurred at vehicle id 17. The second profile is for the 8 communication links means 8 vehicles are sender and 8 are receiver. In this profile maximum delay is 250 s occurred at 160 s at vehicle id 31.

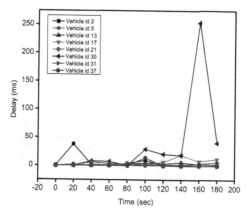

Fig. 9. Delay profile of 8 communication links

Packet Loss: This situation is occur when the data is not reached to the receiver and this is because of poor network connectivity, network congestion, network hardware or software bug. The packet loss affects throughput, communication quality and information loss. It can reduce by TCP protocols because it resend the loss packet towards the receiver with the help of ACK signal but it takes the more time then the UDP protocol to send data packet towards the receiver.

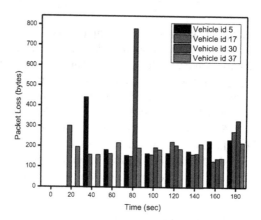

Fig. 10. Packet loss of 4 communication links

Figure10 shows the packet loss profile of 4and 8 communication links. In the first profile 4 vehicle are the sender nodes in this case the maximum value of packet loss is 750 bytes at 80 s for the vehicle id 30. The second profile is for the 8 communication links in this we have record the maximum packet loss is 800 bytes at 100 s time instant for vehicle id 37.

Throughput: It is defined as the amount of data bits flow through the channel in unit of time. It is the actual value of bits transmitted through the sender to receiver. The

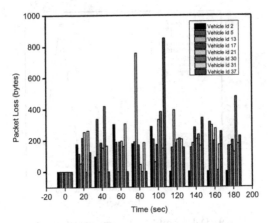

Fig. 11. Packet loss of 8 communication links

maximum value of theoretical throughput is nearly equal to the channel capacity or bandwidth. Average throughput is total number of bits in the network transfer per sec [16].

Instant Throughput of a node (kbps)

$$= \frac{Packet\ Size * Number\ of\ packet\ sent * 8}{Current\ Time * 1000}$$

Figure 11 shows the profiles of instant throughput in 4 cases. The first profile shows the instant throughput of 4 communication links. In this case vehicle id 0, 32, 10 and 20 are considers as sender nodes and vehicles id 37, 5, 17 and 30 are considered as receiving nodes respectively. The profiles show that the vehicle id 17 gives the highest throughput i.e 0.42 mbps at 40 s time instant. Second profile shows the instant throughput of 8 communication links in which vehicle id 0, 32, 10, 20, 1, 6, 12 and 15 are the sender nodes and vehicle id 37, 5, 17, 30, 13, 21, 31 and 2 are the receiving nodes respectively. In this maximum throughput is .25mbps at 100 s time instant gives by vehicle id 37. The above graph shows the fluctuations in instant throughput because all the vehicles are in moving condition and here the considered transmission rage is 250 m (Table 2 and Figs. 12 and 13).

Average throughput (kbps)

$$= \frac{S * Packet\ Size * Total\ number\ of\ packet\ sent * 8}{Total\ transmission\ Time + Total\ dely * 1000}$$

The performance parameters are calculated for same VANET under different conditions. In the first case 4 vehicles are consider as sending node. In the second case 8 vehicles are sending node In the performance table sending packets, receiving packets, packet delivery ratio, end to end delay, normalized routing load and throughput are calculated under 2 different case.

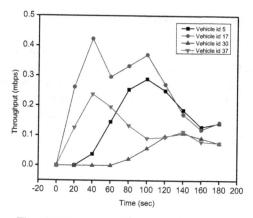

Fig. 12. Throughput of 4 communication links

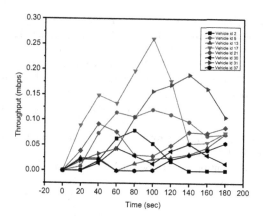

Fig. 13. Throughput of 8 communication links

Table 2. Performance Parameter Matrix.

S.No	No. of sender vehicles	Used Network Capacity%	Sending Packets	Receiving Packets	Packet Delivery Ratio	End to end delay (ms)	Normalized Routing Load	Average throughput (kbps)
1.	4	16	159408	16019	10.049	118.7	0.095	630.43
2.	8	32	319416	13455	4.2123	136.1	0.302	526.39

5 Conclusion and Future Works

This paper analyzed the channel congestion on basis of packet delivery ratio and through-put by considering IEEE802.11p standard. Performance matrix includes packet delivery ratio and throughput for different channel load conditions and results shows that as the number of vehicles are increases packet delivery ratio and average through of the network decreases. Channel Congestion ratio is depends on intermediate distance between vehicles, transmission power, packet size, contention window size, CS Threshold, packet generation rate, RX Threshold etc.

References

1. Sjöberg, K., Andres, P., Buburuzan, T., Brakemeier, A.: Cooperative intelligent transport systems in Europe: current deployment status and outlook. IEEE Veh. Technol. Mag. 12(2), 89–97 (2017)
2. Latif, S., Mahfooz, S., Jan, B., Ahmad, N., Cao, Y., Asif, M.: A comparative study of scenario-driven multi-hop broadcast protocols for VANETs. Veh. Commun. 12, 88–109 (2018)
3. Arena, F., Pau, G., Severino, A.: A review on IEEE 802.11p for intelligent transportation systems. J. Sens. Actuator Netw. 9(2), 22 (2020). https://doi.org/10.3390/jsan9020022
4. Sharma, R., Lamba, C.S., Rathore, V.S.: Congestion control mechanisms to avoid congestion in VANET: a comparative review. Artif. Intell. Speech Technol. 453–462 (2021)
5. Nahar, K., Sharma, S.: Congestion control in VANET at MAC layer: a review (2020). SSRN 3557784
6. Li, W., et al.: Reliable congestion control mechanism for safety applications in urban VANETs. Ad Hoc Netw. 98, 102033 (2020)
7. Jain, R.: A congestion control system based on VANET for small length roads. arXiv preprint arXiv:1801.06448 (2018)
8. Singh, J., Singh, K.: Congestion control in vehicular ad hoc network: a review. Next-Gener. Netw. 489–496 (2018)
9. Rahim, N.F.B.A., et al.: Channel congestion control in VANET for safety and non-safety communication: a review. In: 2021 6th IEEE International Conference on Recent Advances and Innovations in Engineering (ICRAIE), vol. 6. IEEE (2021)
10. Liu, X., Jaekel, A.: Congestion control in V2V safety communication: problem, analysis, approaches. Electronics 8(5), 540 (2019)
11. Elias, S.J., et al.: Congestion control in vehicular ad hoc network: a survey. Indones. J. Electr. Eng. Comput. Sci. 13(3), 1280–1285 (2019)
12. Torrent-Moreno, M., Santi, P., Hartenstein, H.: Distributed fair transmit power adjustment for vehicular ad hoc networks. In: Proceedings of the 3rd Annual IEEE SECON, 2006, pp. 479–488 (2006)
13. Giripunje, L.M., Masand, D., Shandilya, S.K.: Congestion control in vehicular ad-hoc net-works (VANET's): a review. In: Abraham, A., Shandilya, S., Garcia-Hernandez, L., Varela, M. (eds.) Hybrid Intelligent Systems. HIS 2019. AISC, vol. 1179, pp. 258–267. Springer, Cham (2021). https://doi.org/10.1007/978-3-030-49336-3_26
14. Akinlade, O.: Adaptive transmission power with vehicle density for congestion control. Diss. University of Windsor (Canada) (2018)
15. Taherkhani, N., Pierre, S.: Improving dynamic and distributed congestion control in vehicular ad hoc networks. Ad Hoc Netw. 33, 112–125 (2015)

Author Index

Printed in the United States
by Baker & Taylor Publisher Services